A WORLD IN TWO MINDS

A WORLD IN TWO MINDS

Why we must change our thinking
to change our future

K W JAMIESON

SHEPHEARD-WALWYN (PUBLISHERS) LTD

First published in 2018 by
Shepheard-Walwyn (Publishers) Ltd
107 Parkway House, Sheen Lane,
London SW14 8LS
www.shepheard-walwyn.co.uk
www.ethicaleconomics.org.uk

British Library Cataloguing in Publication Data
A catalogue record of this book
is available from the British Library

ISBN: 978 0 85683 521 6

Typeset by Alacrity, Chesterfield, Sandford, Somerset
Printed and bound in the United Kingdom
by Short Run Press

*To my wife Donna and daughters Lauren and Maddie,
for keeping my feet on the ground while
my head is in the clouds*

*To my parents Roy and Jess, for teaching me
to think for myself and to
always love learning*

Contents

Introduction

A FEW YEARS AGO, after yet another news bulletin consisting almost entirely of stories of conflict or catastrophe, I began to wonder if there is a deeper explanation for why our world seems to be in such a mess. When we are such social animals, why does it seem to be so difficult for people to live together in peace? With so much wealth, why are we unable to ensure that everyone at least has the bare essentials of food, water and shelter they need to survive? Why can't we strike the right balance in providing sufficient of life's luxuries today, yet still stop short of damaging the only planet capable of sustaining human life in the future? Why, when almost all of the issues afflicting people worldwide are ultimately man-made, does our species seem to be so intent on inflicting great damage upon itself? Why does global human society seem to be fragmenting as it simultaneously seeks to integrate, and why does it intuitively feel like we are building towards some sort of crescendo which could potentially be catastrophic?

Fuelled (as I would later discover) by a distinctively human degree of delusional self-confidence that I could actually answer these questions, I set off on a long journey which would eventually produce this book. Along the way I have discovered that we are all deeply embedded within what scientists call a 'complex adaptive system' consisting of a whole array of other such systems, including every human-being, every other animal and every single plant on the planet. As if this wasn't complex enough, all of our individual attitudes and behaviours are driven by one of *the* most complex of all such systems – the human brain. So, nested like Russian dolls, these systems all interact with one another, the larger systems exerting downward pressure on their sub-systems, the smaller systems exercising upward influence on the larger systems of which they are part. Through these interactions we effectively co-create the environments we share at every level of our existence. At each level, the inter-penetration of individual minds produces a collective mind we might call culture, which becomes crucial when we discover that over 90% of all our thinking is unconscious to us. Schematic memory and our embodied senses contribute to our unconscious cognition but culture also plays a huge role in bringing forth the conditions we create. Culture colours the lens through which we see the world and therefore shapes what unfolds, either by strengthening a dominant worldview or by swimming upstream to offer an alternative perspective. Much of the chaos we are currently experiencing is the result of worldviews which are changing, clashing and competing for global dominance.

Part One – Seeing – *The Shifting Sands of the Human System* explores how culture is both created by and helps to shape human societies, explaining how it is perfectly possible for the contrary operating modes of the brain hemispheres to create cultures which are cognitively imbalanced, contributing to the poor mental health of individuals within them. It also investigates the source of this sickness, identifying the three competing worldviews at the root of global conflict. Finally it considers the characteristics of all complex adaptive systems, especially the two at the heart of this book – the individual human mind and the collective global mind; the latter arising from the interpenetration of the former. In particular it focusses on how complex adaptive systems change by self-organizing to the '*edge of chaos*', an optimised transition space in which cascading waves of change can evolve such systems to higher levels of coherence and good health. Global human society currently finds itself at the *edge of chaos*, offering great opportunity for a transformative shift towards peaceful integration but just as likely to result in catastrophic breakdown. The future we bring forth will ultimately depend on how we choose to see the world and on our ability to change the way we think. Unfortunately, there are many features inherent to our 200,000-year-old brains which make this a significant challenge.

Part Two – Thinking – *The Modus Operandi of an Ancient Brain* explores how the human brain works, in particular the opposite yet complementary modes of the right and left hemispheres. While we all use both sides of our brain all of the time, we can and often do develop a preference for one mode over the other so it's possible for larger groups to become similarly dominated. Part Two further explains the features of our ancient brains which undermine our ability to cope with the increasing complexity of the 21st century, exposing the many foibles, fallacies and flaws in our cognitive equipment. All outer-world manifestations of human thought originate in the brain and Chapter 7 explores how our liberal impulses are the product of the right mind, while our conservative tendencies are created by the left mind. Our political polarities are direct outputs of the opposing modes of the mind, and our personal persuasions the result of our preference for one mode or the other. Globally the culture of scientific materialism, although still dominant and dangerous, is being progressively undermined by a more liberal outlook, leading to increasingly aggressive militarism as reactionary elites seek to consolidate their power bases. However the increasing democratization of data is weakening their grip, emboldening ordinary people to seek greater levels of self-determination. The political, economic and spiritual structures which have scaffolded scientific materialism and the Abrahamic monotheisms are slowly being dismantled, offering the potential to rebuild them from the bottom up. However, overcoming their influence, the damaging effects of social anomie and our deep resistance to change, all present major challenges.

Part Three – Learning – *Origins and Oscillations of a Global Mind* reviews how scientific materialism came to dominate global society and traces the swings in cultural influence of the left and right mind. For over 95% of our existence we lived in egalitarian societies and worshipped 'earth mother' deities, only inventing 'sky father' gods around 6000 years ago. The advent of patriarchy sent each gender down dual pathways which would lead to differences in the cognitive preferences of men and women. Patriarchal societies ensured the cultural dominance of the left mind, dissociating human-beings from the valuable influence of the right mind, denaturing the human condition and severing the physical, spiritual and social synapses which made people feel whole. Scientific materialism dominated the modern era, reaching its zenith with two World Wars and the dropping of atomic bombs on Japan. Post-modernism has since deconstructed the modern mind, leaving it fragmented with no clear way forward. Yet, within this intellectual maelstrom an Eastern-influenced '*organic*' worldview has been growing, and the wide openness of post-modernism offers a potentially fertile soil from which healthy balance could emerge in the global mind. Only the organic worldview can deliver such a synthesis but is our species smart enough to bring forth this outcome?

Part Four – Growing – *Pitfalls and Possibilities at the Edge of Chaos* considers the critical role of consciousness in achieving the coherence required for global human society to elevate to higher levels of harmonious integration. It explores both scientific and spiritual perspectives of consciousness and the degree to which scientific materialism has suppressed our thinking. Only by reconnecting with the right mind can we regain higher consciousness to reconcile science with spirit in whole-mind synthesis. The widespread adoption of the organic worldview is critical to achieving global coherence, yet it still struggles to gain mainstream acceptance due to the adversarial nature of scientific materialism and the major monotheisms, which can never be reconciled in their current form. Only the organic worldview can achieve reunification by radically reshaping how we perceive both science and spirit. Changes to the global human system require genuine democracy and restructuring can only grow from the bottom up. The most vital changes must be made to economic capitalism, which must be counterbalanced by increased social, moral and human capital to moderate its most pernicious effects. There is no single 'silver bullet' solution for healing human society but increasing the influence of women is the best option we have for accelerating the harmonious integration of our species. The root cause of our crisis is ultimately the dominance of the left mind in global culture, which continues to be exacerbated by the pre-eminence of men amongst societal elites and the outdated 'boy code' to which male children are still raised.

However, the legacy of being inadvertently allocated primacy of by far the more powerful brain hemisphere has better prepared girls for the future. The right mind will provide the core capabilities required in an increasingly integrative culture and will give women a cognitive advantage as computer software progressively replicates our left-mind functions. Women therefore have a big role to play in bringing forth a positive future but the benefits for men are also huge, enabling them to become more whole human-beings. The future we collectively create isn't pre-ordained and we are now reaching a level of global interconnectivity where smart technologies can act as social synapses, sending cascading waves of change across the human system. Each of us is just a tiny node in a gigantic network but we all have a role to play and any one of us could be the catalyst which tips global human society into a new age.

Writing this book has been a long personal journey during which I've learned a lot about how the world works and, in particular, about the species of which we are all members. Understanding the many flaws in the human brain is both fascinating and frightening but if becoming more aware of our own inadequacies can make us all a little more humble and respectful of each other, it will be worthwhile. Individually we are not nearly as clever as we like to think, yet the world we create will inevitably unfold as the result of how we all think and act. What surely gives us hope is that we can actively shape life, mostly in small, local ways yet which, at the right time, could cause seismic shifts across the whole human system. The right time is now. Life at the *edge of chaos* may be uncomfortable but it also offers great opportunity for our species.

Today, people everywhere are sensing that our world is becoming more dangerously disordered yet perhaps without being able to clearly see why. With this book I hope to help readers join the dots between apparently disparate events in the outer world and throughout human history. The simplest way to understand the vast complexity of the global system is the obvious, yet easily overlooked, fact that everything human-beings create ultimately originates in the human brain. By comprehending the contrary cognitive processes which underlie all human behaviours, in particular those which cause conflict, we can better understand different cultures while making their characteristics more relatable through our experience of our own minds. By appreciating the opposing modes of the two hemispheres, their many flaws and the inadequacies of the cultural structures they have created, we realize that such structures don't *have* to be as they are and can be changed, just by thinking differently.

I also hope to encourage readers to become more conscious of their own thinking and more active in changing the world we live in. By making modifications which increase our own inner coherence, while proactively seeking outer coherence, we can all make a contribution towards the greater systemic coherence from which global peace and individual happiness may emerge.

I hope you enjoy it.

PART ONE

SEEING

The Shifting Sands of the Human System

— 1 —

Our Self-Inflicted Sickness

IN THE 5th century BC, Socrates concluded that he was wiser than all of the eminent Greek scholars and philosophers who had gone before him, because he alone recognized his own ignorance. That this observation is simultaneously boastful yet full of humility, illuminates the key characteristic of the human brain which lies at the very heart of this story; its amazing ability to reconcile contradictory concepts. As we will discover, the power of opposites is essential to how we process and experience the world around us every day. While Socrates perhaps possessed one of the sharpest brains ever to produce thought, the 1.5 kilograms of neurons, glial cells and blood vessels which is enabling you to read this sentence still shares this same characteristic, and many more, with the great mind of Socrates and with every other human-being who has ever lived. Those of us alive in the 21st century can now benefit from the accumulated knowledge of all the great scholars who preceded us, from the Western genius of Aristotle, Galileo, Copernicus, Da Vinci, Newton, Darwin and Einstein to the Eastern brilliance of Buddha, Confucius, Lao Tzu, Zarathustra, Al Khwarizmi, Avicenna and Omar Khayyam. If, through the wonders of modern technology, we now have access to most of the philosophical, scientific, economic, mathematical, astronomical, geological, sociological, anthropological, theistic and literary output ever created, the mind of the average modern human must surely be more knowledgeable and infinitely wiser than the famous polymaths of history. Unfortunately, it doesn't seem to work like that! In spite of having the whole history of human development behind us, the intellectual ability of each individual doesn't appear to have snowballed since the time of Socrates. Given everything we now have the capability of knowing, why aren't we all smarter than Da Vinci?

The reason is twofold. First, in the modern world we simply don't need to know everything. Our ancient ancestors, when they shifted from hunter-gathering to farming, had the bright idea of dividing labour so that each individual could specialise and didn't have to master, or even participate in, all the tasks which needed to be performed. It was this social skill – the ability to communicate and work co-operatively with strangers for mutual benefit – which first allowed humans to grow beyond small family groups into the national and international communities we are all part of today. Now, there are billions of us participating in all manner of pastimes and professions, each often requiring very particular cognitive capabilities, and we have not only learned to divide our labour but also to divide our knowledge. Indeed, many of our economies are now primarily knowledge-based and, with so much information available and so many different ways to apply our skills, we have all become accustomed to only learning a very thinly sliced portion of everything there is to know.

However, there is a more fundamental reason why each of us can only retain a few drops of the ocean of data available to us – we are still operating with essentially the same brain as the very first *homo-sapiens*, around 200,000 years ago. While the information available in the outer world has expanded exponentially, our internal ability to process the data we receive has failed to keep up. In this new age of high-speed broadband, digital technology and global connectivity, we still have the same cognitive equipment our ancestors had when they first discovered fire and invented language, so it is perhaps no wonder that each of us can only grasp a microcosm of what we could understand with a more capable brain. We are no smarter than Socrates because our mental tools are no more advanced than his were. Indeed, such is our overconfidence as a species that, even with an additional two and a half millennia of learning, we are often less appreciative of our own ignorance than he was.

Our overconfidence manifests in many ways, one of which is our habit of telling ourselves delusional but comforting tales which reduce any distressing cognitive dissonance we might be experiencing. On this basis, we might be tempted to convince ourselves that only we 'mere mortals' are cognitively challenged. Since large human communities were first created, they have been ruled, not by the ordinary populous, but by a political, academic, religious or commercial elite, which remains the case to this day. Armed with aeons of knowledge, surely our modern societal leaders must be individually smarter than Socrates and collectively wiser than all of the great scholars of antiquity? The state of the world we live in should quickly dispel us of any such notion.

A World in Chaos

These days, global human society seems to be in perpetual turmoil. A review of any 21st century newsreel would feature the terrorist destruction of the World Trade Centre towers in New York on 9/11, the hostile occupation of Iraq and Afghanistan, the re-emergence of a nuclear threat in North Korea and continued tensions between Israel and Palestine. We have seen the Arab Spring uprisings in Egypt, Libya, Tunisia and Yemen and the crushing of demands for democracy in China and Nepal. We've witnessed genocide in Somalia, civil war in Syria and the Ukraine teeters on the brink of implosion, inflamed by Russian interference. The United Kingdom has voted to 'brexit' the most successful customs union ever created and the President of the United States openly condones extreme right-wing, white nationalist groups. A terrorist group has created an Islamic caliphate straddling the border between Iraq and Syria, violating human rights and committing medieval atrocities on a daily basis. People are drowning in the Mediterranean as they try to escape these warzones, and the international humanitarian response to the refugee crisis has largely been lamentable. According to the United Nations almost 60 million people worldwide – one in every 122 humans – have been forcibly displaced from their homes as a result of persecution, conflict or human rights violations.[1] The tragedies reported in our media have become so prevalent that we are almost numb to their meaning. The massacre of school children by the Taliban in Pakistan was quickly followed by the slaughter of thousands by Boko Haram in Nigeria. The Charlie Hebdo murders in Paris, police brutality on black civilians in the US, tourists shot on a Tunisian beach and the bombing of a shrine in Bangkok, all blend into a cacophony of carnage. Every single day new tales of human suffering unfold around the globe. A 2014 study by the Institute for Economics and Peace found the world has been becoming less peaceful every year since 2007, and that only 11 of the 162 countries covered by their research hasn't, in some way, been involved in conflict during this period.[2]

Not only are we killing each other, we are also damaging the only planet in our universe capable of sustaining the human species. There is widespread consensus among the international scientific community that our methods and emissions are having a negative impact on our environment. Global warming, the increase in the average temperature of the earth's air and ocean water, is a proven phenomenon and greenhouse gases, resulting from human activities such as deforestation and the use of fossil fuels, are significant contributors to it. There is broad alignment behind the prediction that temperatures will continue to increase well into this century, with significant implications for food supply, the survival of natural habitats and the availability of fresh water. At the 2009 Sustainable Development Conference, the UK government's chief scientist Professor John Beddington warned of an impending 'perfect storm' of food, energy and water shortages by the year 2030. He predicted that demand for food and energy would increase by 50% and fresh water by 30%, largely as the result of a growing world population which will top 8.3 billion by 2030.[3]

In the developed world we have a surplus of food, yet are eating ourselves to death. Health-care resources are stretched to breaking point as a growth in heart disease, diabetes, cancer and stroke, result from increasingly sedentary and indulgent lifestyles. In developing nations poverty remains endemic, with many governments unable or unwilling to ensure the controls required for sustainable economic development, which could give every person access to their basic human rights of sustenance, safety and shelter.

The citizens of many countries continue to be racked by the after-effects of the 2008 global banking crisis, as governments implement widespread austerity programmes to reduce spending and shrink national debts and deficits. Even in some of the richest economies, inequality of wealth distribution has led to 1 in 4 children being brought up in poverty and, each week, thousands of families rely on charity food banks to survive.[4] Many people face the prospect of unemployment as an increasing number of jobs are off-shored to foreign workers, who are able to replace their labour at a fraction of the wage they would need to maintain their current standard of living. Many others are anxious at the speed of technological development, enabling human muscle power to be replaced by machines which can perform faster, and for longer, than their finite energy resources could ever deliver. Even knowledge workers are increasingly finding that their capabilities can be easily replicated by computer software, against which they cannot compete. Those still in employment are working harder and for longer hours, delivering greater productivity per head for progressively less pay, as businesses down-size to cut costs while increasing profits, enabling directors and shareholders to disproportionately benefit from their collective efforts. As inequality grows in an ever-shrinking world, economic migration is an inevitable outcome, increasing the pressure on societies to assimilate different cultures.

As the pace of social change quickens, most people feel compelled to try to keep up; making more choices, more quickly from a bewildering array of options, all communicated in a technology-enabled deluge of information they don't have time to digest. Many find themselves under pressure to not only make a living, but to generate an income which allows them to compete with peers for the latest gizmo or gadget, as well as meet their children's demands that they must do likewise. Under such social stresses many are driven into debt, some turn to crime, others to substance abuse. Suicide rates are increasing and strains on relationships have driven divorce rates to between 40% and 70% in many developed nations.[5] With weakening family bonds, yet desperate for anchors of stability, many people have no idea who they can trust – the credibility of traditional institutions, like churches and banks, having been shattered by scandal and mismanagement. As politicians cut social safety nets, while feathering their own nests with taxpayer-funded expenses, the elites of society are finally being fully exposed for what they are – ordinary human-beings, with the same flawed brains as the rest of us.

For many ordinary people, life in the 21st century feels like living permanently in the midst of a hurricane, so we are on solid ground to say that the elites who run our world are certainly no smarter than we are. It is equally clear that their strategies aren't facilitating peaceful global integration and that the social pressures produced by their policies, are not conducive to human health or happiness. Socrates believed that all human-beings, by their deepest nature, pursue their own happiness and thought that this could only be achieved through heightened self-awareness. Perhaps if we could understand what actually makes us happy, it might prove to be rather less elusive.

The Source of Our Unhappiness

The 2013 World Happiness Report, conducted across 156 countries by the World Health Organization (WHO), concluded that our average global happiness rating was only 5.2 out of a maximum potential score of 10.[6] These measures vary by region and country. North Americans were happiest at 7.1, followed by Western Europeans at 6.7, while sub-Saharan Africans were least happy with a score of only 4.6. The least happy amongst us, the poor citizens of Togo, returned a despairingly low 2.9 out of 10 but, even for the top ranking Danes, a happiness score of 7.7 still seems like a fairly paltry return for two and a half millennia of post-Socratic self-discovery.

Other studies show that, even in the happiest regions, happiness isn't growing but declining. Not only are we becoming unhappier, we are also very bad at judging what makes us happy. We tend to overestimate the value of work, money and material possessions, while undervaluing relationships. The connection between happiness and money is complex. Overall, people in wealthier countries do tend to be happier than those in poorer countries, but the relationship between the two isn't very strong. In both the USA and UK, over long periods of unprecedented economic growth which brought great increases in personal prosperity, levels of life satisfaction didn't grow but actually declined slightly.[7] Nigerians rate themselves to be just as happy as the Japanese, even though their nation's GDP per capita is only around 1/25th of Japans. Bangladeshis are twice as happy as Russians, although considerably poorer.[8] The picture is the same in Europe. According to Gallup poll data, Britons were happier in the 1950s than they are today[9] and a 2014 poll by the UK Office for National Statistics concluded that people in London, by far the wealthiest city in Great Britain, were more anxious and less happy than those in the rest of the UK.[10] Multiple studies across many countries show either a decrease or no change in wellbeing, despite an increase in prosperity, and that no causal relationship can be found between economic growth and happiness.[11] The consensus across all studies, about the relationship between wealth and happiness, seems to be that a minimum threshold is required for the basic foundations of happiness to be satisfied – such as food, clean water and access to shelter – but that, beyond such rudimentary requirements, there is little or no correlation between increased wealth and increased happiness. Studies by Easterbrook and Layard estimate that happiness levels reach a plateau at a fairly low level of income, between US$10,000 and $20,000 per annum.[12]

So if money doesn't make us happy, what does?

The WHO World Happiness Report found that positive mental health is the single most important determinant of happiness, and that as many as 10% of the world's population suffers from depression or some other form of psychological disorder – over 700 million cases worldwide. Furthermore, mental illness is a common occurrence in all countries and all regions of the world, with no significant difference between rich and poor nations. In August 2014, the death by suicide of the popular American actor and comedian Robin Williams highlighted that fame and wealth are no barriers to mental ill health. The WHO report also discovered that mental illness is massively undertreated everywhere. Even in wealthy countries, less than one-third of those mentally ill were in receipt of any sort of treatment and no government spent more than 15% of their total health budget on mental healthcare, despite mental illness being a considerably greater cause of human suffering than physical illness. In poorer countries these statistics were significantly worse, with lower income nations spending, on average, only 0.5% of their total healthcare budget on mental health. In line with other studies, the WHO report confirmed that economic wealth played no role in creating happiness, beyond the minimum threshold we all need to provide sustenance, safety and shelter.

The World Health Organization places great emphasis on pointing out that positive mental health is not simply the absence of disease or infirmity, but a

> state of well-being in which every individual realizes his or her own potential, can cope with the normal stresses of life, can work productively and fruitfully, and is able to make a contribution to her or his community.

This includes the ability to learn, to feel and express a range of emotions, to form and maintain good relationships and to successfully deal with change and uncertainty. Happiness, therefore, isn't derived from simply not being sick. To be happy we must find the right balance between the intellectual, emotional and social tools we need to successfully interact with the outer world, to meet our goals and to deal with any challenges we encounter. Only these tools, employed in appropriate balance, can enable us to cope with and fulfil our potential in life. What constitutes the right balance will vary from person to person, but we all need to stay within a range of equilibrium to be mentally healthy. So, for example, someone who is too emotionally sensitive is more likely to experience the 'up-and-down' life which may lead to mental illness, while someone who isn't emotional enough, whether through detachment or suppression, is equally unable to access the full benefits of positive mental health.

A chaotic outer world can therefore be extremely damaging to mental health, because it challenges the ability of the human mind to sustain itself within a natural range of healthy equilibrium, and the fact is that almost all of our life stresses are human-made. While natural disasters or viral epidemics do occur, and negatively impact human life, such events are actually very rare. As a species, we can only continue to develop technologies which minimize their effect on us. However, the huge majority of our problems, from wars and environmental damage to unemployment and poverty, are actually inflicted upon ourselves by ourselves. Global human society is ultimately the manifestation of human thoughts and feelings, because all of our actions must first originate in the human cognitive system – our embodied senses, nervous systems and brain structures. While it may be more obvious that our personal behaviour is the output of our own cognition, it is no less true that our collective actions, as a whole species, are ultimately the result of the collective thinking of all of us. While we may not wish to admit it, the communities, cultures and conflicts we experience, are what emerge when we put our minds together.

In short, we are making ourselves sick. The outer world chaos causing our major life stresses is ultimately the product of the same brains which are suffering self-inflicted mental illness, and making us unhappy. How is this even possible, when it runs entirely counter to evolutionary principles for any species to make itself ill? The answer lies in understanding consciousness, culture and complexity.

Our Hidden Driver

We are deeply conditioned to believe that our thoughts and actions are the direct output of our consciousness but, over the last few decades, developments in neuroscience and psychology show that our behaviours are, in fact, predominantly driven by a much more powerful unconscious mind. Indeed, some scientists estimate that as little as 1% of all our cognition may be consciously processed, and most agree that it is likely to be no more than 10%.[13] At least 90% of our thinking may therefore take place beyond our awareness and, far from enjoying total free will, most of our actions are actually driven by automatic processes over which we exercise little or no control.

To grasp how this is possible we must consider the anatomy of the human brain, which consists of three overlapping structures, each of which evolved over millions of years. The oldest of the three, our reptilian brain, contains the brain stem and cerebellum and controls our body's vital functions, such as breathing, heart rate, temperature and balance. The 'thinking' that's required to constantly monitor these functions takes place automatically and unconsciously because we simply don't need to be aware of them, other than when something goes wrong. If there's an emergency, like a significant increase in heart rate or even something less dramatic like feeling too warm, our reptilian brain will alert our conscious mind but, apart from that, it just gets on and does its job without interrupting us. The middle layer, our limbic brain, evolved in the first mammals and its main structures are the hippocampus, amygdala and hypothalamus. It is the seat of our unconscious mind, responsible for our emotions, intuitions and for capturing long-term associative memories. Our limbic brain is therefore the source of most of our thinking. Our neocortex is the newest, outer layer of the human brain and consists of six layers, formed into two distinct hemispheres. These hemispheres have been responsible for the development of language, abstract thought, imagination, spatial reasoning and our self-consciousness. When we think about thinking, it is therefore normally the neocortex we are thinking about. It is the source of everything we are consciously aware of, yet the fact remains that most of what we think isn't the result of our conscious free will, but is automatic and unconscious.

The content of the unconscious mind, the hidden driver of most of our behaviour, is unique to each of us and is formed by a combination of the genetic make-up we inherit from our parents, and the culture in which we live and grow. We are indeed formed by both nature and nurture. We share 99.9% of our DNA with all other human-beings and therefore inherit some traits which are common to all members of our species, such as the fight or flight response to danger and the automatic use of the same facial expressions to convey emotions such as fear, anger or disgust.[14] Other inherited dispositions may be more specific to us, influencing our early development and the type of adults we become in later life. For example, research suggests that high levels of sensitivity to sensory stimulus in babies, may be indicative of more introverted personality traits later in life[15] and that high levels of self-control, demonstrated as a toddler, may be predictive of good academic results as a teenager and career success as an adult.[16] Some of the factors which affect who we become are therefore predetermined through genetic coding.

Yet, while we are all genetically unique, the biological differences between us are actually quite small. Most of our attitudes and behaviours aren't hard-wired into us by genetics, but result from the values and beliefs taught to us by the culture in which we are raised. In *Guns, Germs and Steel*, his extensive review of the development of human societies, Jared Diamond concludes that environmental factors caused mankind to evolve differently, in various parts of the world, rather than any innate differences between *homo-sapiens*. Culture plays a significant role in creating the diversity between us – differences which are primarily ideological rather than biological – and is therefore the key determinant of the content of our unconscious mind.

Culture can be considered to be the aggregate of all the values, attitudes, beliefs, practices, habits and behavioural norms we use to regulate life in human societies. We embed culture in artefacts consisting of all of the systems, structures, processes, laws, symbols, artworks, architectures and institutions we use to define who we are, what we believe in and what we value. Through the constructs and conventions we create, we communicate to ourselves what we collectively consider to be right or wrong, good or bad and true or untrue about the world we live in. Through culture we tell ourselves stories about our past and make predictions about our future, and we use them to determine how we should behave in the present. Our culture tells us how to dress, what to study and what kind of career to pursue if we want to be successful in society. It tells us what to say and not say in different situations, when to laugh or cry, who to listen to and who to ignore, when to suppress our anger or reveal our empathy. It defines for us the boundaries of acceptable norms of thought and deed – such as how to treat animals, how our children should behave and what is acceptable practice in the mating game. Through the heroes our culture idolises, we learn about those human qualities we consider to be admirable and, through gossip, it teaches us about the behaviours we find unacceptable. In short, while it may not provide us with a degree, our culture is a far more effective teacher than any of our universities. Its laws may be largely unwritten but our culture is far more powerful at controlling our actions than any police force.

Cultures provide us with a powerful and reassuring sense of identity. Most human-beings still die within a 50 mile radius of where they were born and most of us will marry someone from the same nationality, ethnic group and social class, with the same values, attitudes and interests as ourselves.[17] So when we open our eyes to the world, we mainly see our own culture reflected back to us, reinforcing our sense of belonging, the pride we feel in our tribe and the validity of our shared values. Culture acts as a social glue which keeps us bonded to those around us, setting common rules, sustaining common attitudes, perpetuating common beliefs and encouraging common behaviour. Our culture surrounds us every day, grounding us in place and time, embracing us with its familiarity and providing us with the knowledge we need to survive and prosper in our environment. By educating us about the collectively agreed norms of social interaction, culture makes our world safer and more predictable, protecting us from the pain of public humiliation and social exclusion.

Yet a strong attachment to any culture can also have downsides. Our culture can easily become so familiar that we believe everything it teaches us is objectively true, rather than merely subjective and learned. Culture creates a narrative we tell to ourselves, about ourselves, so often portrays a rose-coloured interpretation of who we are and leads us to believe that our values have greater value than those of other groups. Such a perspective can fuel inter-group conflicts, cause us to retreat from other groups or reject the inclusion of new members to our group, in order to retain cultural purity. Indeed, we can become so attached to our culture that we even become suspicious of anyone within our own group, who doesn't always conform to its maxims, thus fragmenting the group, creating intra-group conflicts and tempting one sub-group to suppress the other. Culture is therefore the source of much of the conflict in the world yet, rather bizarrely, all culture originates in the mind and all humans share essentially the same brain. Because it is unconscious to us, we often don't appreciate the degree to which culture shapes our mind yet, although it's hard to imagine of those cultures which seem most alien, we would all grow to love cultural characteristics of any group we were born into, if it nurtured and helped to create who we are.

Groups are essential to cultural anthropologists because defining culture simply means identifying and articulating common ways of life – values, attitudes, beliefs and behaviours – which are shared amongst a particular group of people. As individuals, we are all automatically members of many groups based on gender, sexuality, ethnicity, profession, nationality, language, religion or any number of other characteristics. We also often choose to join further groups, based on our hobbies, interests, pastimes, passions or politics. As members of these groups, we invariably come into contact with other members and, as the contents of our minds interpenetrate through conversations and other interactions, a 'collective mind' or culture is formed, as the emergent output.

A useful analogy might be to consider our simplest social group, consisting of just two members such as a married couple. The 'cultural' characteristics of their relationship are inevitably the result of thousands of verbal, physical and emotional interactions between them, in which each partner has negotiated their respective role in their joint social contract, and agreed, often unconsciously, how each will behave within their two person group. Their marriage is therefore a sort of collective mind, which emerges from the interpenetration of their individual minds and lives in the ether around them, enveloping them both within it. Each brings to the marriage their own unique genetic identity plus cultural biases (courtesy of their own parents and the environment in which they themselves were raised), yet together they create a brand new web of values, attitudes, beliefs and behaviours in which they raise their own children. The collective mind or culture they form isn't static but ever evolving, yet there will invariably be dominant values and behaviours they both agree upon, which they consciously or unconsciously embed within the many systems and structures they employ to run their lives. These include hundreds of tiny routines and habits, such as how they manage meal times and how tidy they keep their home, plus more occasional considerations such as where they go on holiday and what type of car they drive.

Although they may appear innocuous, all of these decisions say something specific about the couple's collective mind and, by embedding their values into these decisions, they create and communicate a family culture which fills the unconscious minds of their kids. From the day their children are born, they cannot avoid being shaped by the environment in which they grow; which subliminally soaks their parents culture into them, inculcating their unconscious minds with valuable learning about what's important and how things work, within their family unit. In reality, of course, it's very rare that any child is only ever exposed to his or her parents. Most nuclear families are nested within a wider family group of grandparents, aunts, uncles and cousins, all of whom also co-create and share a common family culture. Like Russian dolls, we are then further nested within layers of successive groups such as villages, towns, regions, countries, continents and ultimately one vast global human society.

Arthur Koestler coined the term '*holon*' to describe such phenomena, which are simultaneously wholes yet also parts of larger wholes. For example, while each of us is a whole, individual human-being, we are all also made of body parts and sub-systems – such as the heart or respiratory system – which can be studied as holons and which themselves consist of holonic parts, such as the aortic valve or lungs. The aortic valve is one small part of our heart and one very small part of our whole body system, yet they are all clearly interconnected and exert mutual influence on one another. A faulty aortic valve can have major consequences for our heart and body, but equally the fuel we feed our bodies can influence the health of our heart and aortic valve. As we will explore in Chapter 3, this notion of nested holons exerting mutual influence is core to understanding complex adaptive systems, of which the human brain and human society are but two of many examples.

The individual and collective minds are thus similarly connected. Culture emerges from the interpenetration of the individual minds in any group, with each person contributing 'upwards' to the collective mind, while the culture they co-create exerts 'downward' influence on each individual, by filling their unconscious mind with content. We don't all contribute equally 'upwards' – elites are more influential than non-elites for example – nor are we equally influenced 'downwards' – we all have a degree of free will – but with more than 90% of our thoughts and actions being unconscious, we are all unavoidably influenced by the cultures we contribute to, and which exert influence on us. Far from being autonomous animals navigating the world with our conscious intellect, how we think and act is largely the product of the values, attitudes, beliefs and behaviours unconsciously imposed upon us by our group memberships. Because most of our groups tend to consist of people pretty much like us – who look the same, have a similar background and already hold many of the same views – the maintenance of culture becomes a somewhat self-fulfilling prophecy.

Our dominant culture therefore acts like a sort of 'brain-cloud' hovering above us. We receive a daily drenching which soaks its values into us, reaffirming the righteousness of what we already believe and directing our thoughts and behaviours for the day. Droplets then condense overnight from the invisible vapour of our attitudes and actions, ready to drench us again the next day in a perpetual and self-sustaining cycle. Culture is so pervasive we are rarely even aware of its existence and we maintain it in millions of tiny ways, from what we gossip about to how we raise our children. From the day we are born an ocean of information fills a deep well within our mind, which we draw upon throughout life. This unconscious well quickly becomes the source of almost everything we know, shapes where we focus in the present and guides our path into the future. From this self-replenishing source, we draw much of the data we need to safely navigate our way in the world and its content – the learning and life-skills taught to us by culture – enables us to fit into our groups, achieve our goals and progress in life. In return, we refill it daily by contributing to a stream of cultural content which subliminally re-soaks the minds of all group members.

Yet, we are clearly not clones of one another – culture forms only part of what drives us. Nor are we automatons – we do have a degree of conscious control over how we think and act. Culture is ultimately rooted in the modus operandi of the brain, in which the interplay of opposites plays an essential role and, as a consequence, culture is never unidirectional but the net effect of contradictory forces, from which dominant values and habits may emerge but which always contains some level of 'counter-culture'. Culture can therefore be changed, because we each have the conscious capability to choose alternative beliefs and behaviours. Groups can create new collective minds and, with enough popular support, a new dominant culture can emerge. As conceptual as this may sound, it is exactly our experienced reality as liberal impulses constantly compete with conservative tendencies to set the agenda for public discourse, and the moral framework for private intercourse. Every day opposing approaches towards all aspects of human society, such as freedom, family, justice, law, war, science, religion, welfare, ecology, human rights and gender roles, vie for pre-eminence. Attitudes certainly don't all point in one direction but compete against each other in a maelstrom of contrary opinions yet, from this interplay of minds, some semblance of order always emerges; the remarkable output of two complex adaptive systems, one nested within the other.

At whichever level of society culture is formed – local, regional, national, international or global – it originates in the human brain and emerges from the interpenetration of group members' minds. Every piece of cultural content we co-create, from a conversation to a company to a common market, is both a product of mind and subliminally shapes the minds of those who encounter it, because it is automatically imbued with our values and beliefs. As such, our creations either sustain the narrative of our dominant culture or push against it by telling a tale from a counter-culture, yet cultures aren't necessarily full of conflict. On the contrary, healthy cultures benefit greatly from the vitality brought by opposing forces which, by pushing against each other, create a 'dynamic stability' which is far better for human societies than the type of order created by high homogeneity and rigid conformity. With too little dynamic diversity a culture can easily become insular, adopting a tendency towards 'groupthink' and thus losing its ability to innovate in order to successfully adapt to external environmental changes; a common cause of societal collapse throughout history.[18] On the other hand, excessive diverse energy can also push a culture too far in the opposite direction, causing healthy competition – that which is conducted within an overarching spirit of co-operation – to escalate into conflict, violence and even genocide. History shows us that when cultures lose control, dynamic stability can escalate into chaos, also resulting in societal breakdown. Extremes of stasis and chaos must therefore be resisted and, to avoid endangering themselves, societies must remain within a healthy range of equilibrium between the two.

Many of us might consider Saudi Arabia, for example, to be an unattractive culture because it appears to be ruled by strictly enforced codes of conduct, with relatively restricted personal freedom. At the other extreme, a country like Somalia perhaps typifies a radically different but equally unattractive culture, in which a lack of governmental control has almost tipped society into chaos. While we may have a more positive perspective, had we been brought up in either state, most of us probably wouldn't choose to emigrate there. Instead, we might reasonably consider that an attractive culture – one which would be conducive to our personal health and happiness – would inhabit the spectrum between the two poles of strict order and uncontrolled freedom. We might be drawn towards Scandinavian egalitarianism or the individualism of North America. We may prefer the familial inclusiveness of Southern Europe, the adventurous spirit of the Antipodeans or the calm spirituality of the East. These stereotypical cultures all vary in the degree to which they are ordered versus free, yet none are as strict as Saudi or as uncontrolled as Somalia. As humans, we understand intuitively that to be healthy requires a balance of opposites, and we would each be attracted towards a blend of cultural characteristics which are consistent with the particular make up of our own mind. The human brain operates by blending opposites to maintain healthy balance and, because all culture begins and ends in the mind, it is no coincidence that both individual and collective minds share this fundamental need. Order and freedom are two opposite, yet essential, characteristics which both minds blend to deliver a healthy level of dynamic stability but which, at either polar extreme, can be unhealthy and even dangerous. Too much order or too much freedom may eventually lead to mental or societal breakdown.

As we'll explore in Chapter 4, a healthy range of equilibrium is maintained in the individual mind by the two hemispheres of the neocortex, which process the information they receive in directly opposite but complementary ways. While both hemispheres play a role in all cognition it wouldn't make evolutionary sense for them to both do the same job, so they take radically different approaches to everything we encounter in life. For example, it is primarily via the right hemisphere through which we are embedded in the outer world of multi-sensory experience; the deluge of data which the right mind passes to the left hemisphere for analysis and categorization. Each hemisphere therefore brings a very different perspective to freedom and order – the right mind revelling in wide-ranging flexibility to which the left mind is compelled to bring essential structure.

Of course, freedom and order are only two of myriad polar consider-ations for the human brain, which basically operates by processing the phenomena we experience as opposites. To see light we must also see dark, to feel cold we must also be able to feel warmth, to grasp the concept of good we must also understand the idea of evil. As those in the East have always recognized, the world is full of opposites and for every yin there must be a yang. Our brains essentially work by blending contradictory concepts but because each hemisphere takes a different approach and because we all have a degree of conscious free will, it is perfectly possible that preferences for the output of either hemisphere, in the individual mind, can become amplified in the collective mind to create cultures which are radically imbalanced. It only takes enough individuals to consistently prioritize the perspective produced by either hemisphere, and to fail to blend it in balance with its counterpart, to shift from healthy dynamic stability towards either stasis or chaos. As we'll discover, the rigid order of Saudi Arabia is strongly suggestive of the cultural dominance of the left mind, while the anarchic freedom of Somalian culture is indicative of an unfettered right mind.

In both cases, failure to blend each impulse with the moderating influ-ence of the opposite perspective, points to a collective mind which is operating at a level of consciousness which is sub-optimal for high quality cognition. We need our consciousness to challenge the validity of dominant cultures and, if they become too imbalanced, to reverse their trajectory to ensure they remain dynamically stable, within a healthy range of equilibrium. If consciousness is suppressed, the collective mind becomes even more ruled by the unconscious than usual, the prevalent culture exerts ever greater downward pressure and individuals become prone to operating on a sort of behavioural 'autopilot', which makes the dominant culture harder to change.

This is why freedom of speech is such a vital characteristic of healthy cultures and why the case of Saudi Arabian Raif Badawi has caused such international outrage. In 2012 Badawi, a 28-year-old liberal writer and activist, was charged with several crimes relating to the content of his online blog and sentenced to 10 years imprisonment plus 1000 lashes. Over a million people worldwide signed Amnesty International's petition calling for his release. Badawi's case highlights why any culture, no matter how dominant, can never be 100% 'pure' because all culture originates in the human brain and our minds will always produce contrary impulses. More significantly, in systems terms, it also illuminates a feature the mind shares with all other living organisms – that they will always attempt to heal themselves. Coherence is the natural state of all complex adaptive systems which, for minds and cultures, means dynamic stability within a range of equilibrium between polar extremes. If they become unhealthy, that is to say imbalanced or incoherent, they will automatically dial up the opposite impulse to try to redress the balance and become 'whole' again. Healing, of course, re-establishes wholeness. Raif Badawi's blog, as insignificant as it may seem, is just one small attempt to regain cultural wholeness in Saudi Arabia by having the liberal voice of the right mind heard.

Culture is therefore very much a double-edged sword for modern humans, operating as we are with ancient brains which aren't fit for the global complexity of the 21st century. Individually we really aren't very smart and there's no indication that we are getting any smarter. However, we became an intelligent species through language and our ability to embed information in cultural artefacts, which convey learning across time and space and enable us to pass knowledge inter-generationally. Most of our actions being unconsciously driven by culture is an evolutionary, energy-saving device which allows us to only use energy-depletive consciousness when we really need it. Our superior consciousness gives us greater free will than any other animal, but it's a mixed blessing because it also gives us greater scope to make collective choices and create cultures which are bad for our health. This is exactly what has happened at the level of our global human holon. Of course, we have damaged ourselves inadvertently – no species would knowingly make itself sick – but an unhealthy global culture is nevertheless the output of all our minds, so if we want to become whole again, we have to change the way we think. In particular we must elevate our consciousness to make better choices.

The Big Picture

On our current trajectory, the future of the human species doesn't look good but dominant cultures can be changed. However, to consistently think in a manner which runs counter to the influence of any powerful culture isn't easy. We must first become aware of the grip it has on us, then consistently guard against its unconscious influence by using our conscious mind to make alternative choices. Other than in the most oppressive regimes, cultural content is rarely homogenous but diverse and multivalent, so if we can elevate our minds to become aware of the possibilities, we can select from an array of options which is only limited by our taste and creativity. The more our culture allows freedom of expression, and the greater openness it has to outside influences, the more we also expose ourselves to people whose minds are different from ours. Culture changes slowly because most of what we choose, consciously or unconsciously, is consistent with those values and structures which are so familiar to us. However, the more often we choose less pervasive, counter-cultural options, and the larger the number of people who make similar choices, the further and faster the culture will shift. If enough people, with sufficient influence, regularly think and act in a manner which promotes values, beliefs, attitudes and behavioural norms which run counter to the dominant culture in any society, its centre of gravity will shift; slowly at first but with increasing momentum until a new prevailing culture can become established. To become sustainable, new values must then be embedded into cultural artefacts, in particular political, economic and civic systems, structures and institutions. In theory at least, a new global culture is therefore possible – one which would be conducive to systemic coherence, global peace and individual health and happiness.

When we look around the world, we could perhaps be forgiven for concluding that there are hundreds of distinctly different cultures, and that any aspiration to find common ground is therefore doomed to failure. Yet all cultures originate in the same human brain so, far from being genuinely different, all cultures must simply be varying blends, and all artefacts different expressions, of the same cognitive impulses. By understanding the human brain, how it works, the nature of its outputs and the many systemic flaws in its modus operandi, we can better understand the global mind we collectively create. By exploring the opposing tendencies of the left and right hemispheres, we can better appreciate how unhealthy cultural imbalance can be created, yet consciously rebalanced.

Given that all humans share 99.9% of our DNA and have the same cognitive equipment, it isn't too much of a stretch to imagine that if we were to consciously create a desirable global culture, most people would select at least some characteristics – such as peace, love, empathy, tolerance and respect – which are rooted in our common humanity. Most of us would accept that a healthy global culture must contain a degree of competition, as long as it takes place within an overarching spirit of mutual co-operation.

A majority might even consider that collaboration between nations, to stop damaging the only planet capable of sustaining human life, is also a good idea. While we are right to protect the uniqueness of our ethnic or national groups, many may see the whole human species as a distinctive group with a long shared history, which also deserves to be protected. Why then, do we seem to be having such great difficulty in creating a global culture which is conducive to peace, health and happiness?

One answer lies in the fact that the global mind can't be controlled but emerges organically from the interplay of over 7 billion individual minds; one of the largest of all complex systems, perhaps exceeded only by the planetary biosphere and the universe for unfathomable complexity. As such, it can't be designed or engineered in any conventional sense and no individual or group, at any level, can manage or even accurately predict its outputs.

A second answer lies in the complex adaptive system between our ears which, in spite of its much smaller scale, is an even greater mystery to us than its larger counterpart. The global mind emerges from the interplay of individual minds but the human brain evolved to help us survive, not to enable us to understand exactly how it works and we certainly can't always control what it produces. All we can try to do, as individuals, is increase our personal consciousness to deliver balanced thoughts and actions which contribute towards the co-creation of healthy cultures.

A third answer lies in the fact that the creation of culture is a joint venture and, although we are innately social animals, we don't always agree with each other. This isn't such a problem in familial groups, where genetic bonds tend to trump inter-kin quarrels, but as soon as social groups expand beyond family and friends, humans have always faced the challenge of how to maintain harmony amongst strangers. Indeed, we rely upon the cultural structures we create – social, legal, religious, political and economic – to promote the common attitudinal and behavioural habits which bind groups together, as well as providing non-violent means of conflict resolution. At every level of human society, therefore, culture is the key to providing peace, stability and co-operation, both within and between groups.

Critically, our minds are increasingly interpenetrating. With globalization the world is rapidly becoming a smaller place and, as groups come into more and more contact with those from other cultural backgrounds, differences of opinion are inevitable. Through politics, the sovereign autonomy of nation states is being eroded, as international and intercontinental institutions exert ever greater influence. Through economics, global markets are connecting consumers and producers from diverse locations, driving new employment opportunities for some but also creating widespread uncertainty. Through technology, we are becoming increasingly connected to multiple networks of individuals, based on all manner of common interests, enabling ideas and unrest to spread like wildfire. Through cheaper travel, we are increasingly being exposed to people and places we have never before experienced. Through transnational migration, cultural assimilation is necessarily taking place but with mixed results, bringing valuable diversity but also conflict. The net effect of these globalizing movements, and many more, is to shrink our planet, bringing people together, making their minds meet and, in doing so, creating cultural tension.

As the sands beneath their feet start to shift, some people inevitably embrace the opportunities presented, while others, feeling increasingly anxious about the uncertainty of change, are doing what humans often do in such circumstances; retrenching into familiar behavioural patterns and building attitudinal walls between their group and those they believe are threatening their lifestyles. Pressures are growing both within and between nation states, as people try to make sense of what is taking place all around us. In particular, at each level of societal holon, friction is being felt between those groups who are deeply attached to the dominant culture, who benefit most from it and therefore wish to preserve its pre-eminence, and those groups who would gain greatest advantage from its transformation. How such tensions are manifesting varies from country to country, shaped by the rich texture of each states unique historical narrative, but none of the 195+ nations of the world are immune from the effects of globalization.

When we are all so busy living our daily lives, it can be difficult to contextualise the chaos taking place in the world as anything other than the 'stuff of life', whipping around us like a whirlwind. Even if we could find the necessary distance to stand back from events, 'joining the dots' across time and space isn't easy. What happens in one location often doesn't appear to be connected to what happens elsewhere, and our time-line only stretches as far back as occurrences we can easily recall. Yet, if we zoom out to see the whole of human society and view historical events through the same wide-angled lens, we are able to discern clear connections between the macro global mind and the micro individual mind, which give us a sharp focus on how our species arrived where we are today. At lower levels of perception, the many tensions and troubles look like wars between nations over natural resources, or political power plays between competing factions within countries. They manifest as fights between religions, or battles between winners and losers in the game of global economics. They appear to be skirmishes based on ethnicity, class and colour, or clear expressions of gender and minority oppression. Indeed, when viewed at lower holonic levels, that is exactly what they are. However, at higher levels clear patterns emerge.

While we may recognize that cultural differences play a role in many such events, it is often difficult to discern a clear connection between, for example, the Arab Spring uprisings, honour killings in India, environmental pollution in China, heightened racial tension in the US and economic austerity in the European Union. It is the contention of this book that they are indeed all connected, not only to each other but to myriad other conflicts in the world today. When viewed at the level of global human society, they are all shockwaves rising from the tectonic plates of culture shifting between dominant worldviews, with three powerful protagonists vying for supremacy. As citizens of the 21st century we are living through an epochal transformation of global culture, as the perspective which has dominated the modern era, bringing many great benefits but ultimately making our species sick, is under attack from two alternative worldviews and their concomitant cultures. The first was formerly pre-eminent for a thousand years and now, sensing the weakening of its ancient adversary, is trying to reassert its authority. The other is a relative newcomer, yet is rooted in our most original cognitive impulses, and is re-emerging as the human system attempts to heal itself. Three distinct cultural perspectives are each struggling for supremacy, are the root source of the global chaos we are currently experiencing and are all connected by their origins in the human brain. The future we bring forth will be co-created by our collective global mind, yet at the moment our destiny is unknown. The human species has a choice to make. It can continue to make itself sick or it can make itself whole again. We are a world in two minds. With our ancient brains, will we be smart enough to make the right decision?

—2—

A War of Worldviews

FOR MILLENNIA, philosophers have understood that the reality we perceive is merely a 'shared illusion' rather than an experience of any external, objective truth. We view the world through a veil, so soaked in the values and beliefs of our culture that we effectively bring forth an interpretation of reality we have co-created with fellow group members. Ever since we developed the self-consciousness to do so, we have invented and shared stories to explain where our world came from, how it works, the significance of our role in it and how it should be navigated. These 'worldviews' form the bedrock upon which all culture is built, providing an outline context within which a great range of tales have been told and distinctive texts have been written. All worldviews originate in the same human brain so, while cultural expressions around the globe and through the ages have been richly coloured and highly diverse, the deeply human impulses upon which they are based are far less disparate.

Over the last 200,000 years we have gradually interpenetrated our minds and integrated our groups, from family-based bands of hunter-gatherers to villages of farmers and towns of diversely employed citizens. We have grown from ethnic tribes into nation states with cities containing millions of strangers, all held together in dynamically stable cultures of their own creation. More recently, we have built international, inter-continental and even global political and economic infrastructures which have made our world smaller, pushing people closer together and ampli-fying the need for a unifying global narrative. In the absence of such cultural glue, globalization has inevitably caused friction and heightened international tensions. As we grow into an increasingly intermixed human society, we must develop the shared stories required to bring forth a healthy global culture – one which retains the rich texture of our differences and encourages vibrant diversity, yet which is sufficiently coherent to create global structures which support peaceful integration, dynamic stability and environmental sustainability.

The conflicts we are currently experiencing are the growing pains of our synthesis as a species into one global human holon, with opposing worldviews fighting to dominate the developing cultural narrative. Going forward, we may co-create an integrated global culture which is conducive to peace and personal happiness, or human society may once again disintegrate into fragmented, warring factions. To have any chance of success we will have to reconcile two powerful perspectives which, between them, have dominated most of humankind for the last 1500 years. However, each is deeply competitive and, in many ways, sees the world from directly opposing viewpoints. As such, they are strongly adversarial and disinclined towards harmonious integration. Our globally dominant culture has been slowly losing power for the past 100 years but not as a result of the re-strengthening of its old enemy. Instead, it has been weakened from within, the once rock-solid foundations of its perspective having been undermined by its own discoveries.

Over the last century a new worldview has therefore emerged, and it may offer the synthesising qualities required to bring together the two belligerent behemoths in dynamic, yet peaceful, stability. It has grown to try to cure the sickness brought upon the human species by both of its conflicting counterparts, but its success is by no means guaranteed. The newcomer remains tentative, still discovering its capabilities, still probing what its perspective can bring. Although its appeal is increasingly widespread its advocates haven't fully found each other, so do not yet form the large, unified constituencies of the two more established perspectives. As human society moves forward, the future we collectively bring forth will largely depend on which of these three worldviews gains global pre-eminence and, while the violent bellicosity of the two older brothers is very real, we are not without hope. Although they behave like arch-enemies, they are really only squabbling siblings as all three worldviews were born in the same human brain. Whether their sister can reconcile them, is ultimately up to us.

The Three Protagonists

To give any culture a name risks diminishing the incredible richness and diverse complexity contained within it but, in the interests of brevity, this is a risk we must take. Over the past 500 years, global human society has become dominated by a culture we will call 'scientific materialism', which is built upon a foundational worldview we will describe as 'mechanistic'. Stretching from the late Renaissance period to the present day, the values, attitudes, beliefs and behavioural norms derived from this particular perspective remain pre-eminent in many of our nation states, but especially those of a Western industrial or colonial heritage. The mechanistic world-view has been the defining lens through which much of the cultural content of the modern age was created and, although its grip on many national cultures has weakened as global human society has drifted into a post-modern '*between ages*' period, it nevertheless remains widely pervasive and extremely powerful.

Scientific materialism takes the ontological perspective that solid, atomistic matter is the fundamental substance in nature, that everything in the universe is made from such matter and that all experienced phenomena are therefore ultimately the result of material interactions. From this viewpoint our cognition and subsequent behaviour is simply the result of biological and chemical reactions between neurons in the brain. Scientific materialism further posits that both the human brain and the outer world we experience, operate to universal laws which are identifiable by the human intellect. The overarching epistemological belief is therefore that everything about the world we live in is ultimately knowable through science and quantifiable through mathematics. The universe and every-thing in it, including us, operates to a set of calculable, physical laws, which we humans can apply our brainpower to decipher. The dominant worldview can therefore be described as 'mechanistic' because, in this narrative, the universe operates like a highly complex machine, full of intricate, moving parts but all in relationships which can ultimately be understood in terms of cause and effect. Once the nature of these relation-ships is comprehended and calculated, the results of their future inter-actions can be accurately predicted, controlled or changed.

In this narrative, the inner world of the human-being is distinctly separate from the outer world of nature, connected only by their common base material. Our interpretation of outer world reality is determined by our mind and informed by our senses and rationality. A definitive,

objective outer world does exist, but it does so purely as material phenomena propelled by physical dynamics. The outer world has no soul or
purpose and is devoid of all spiritual meaning, other than that which the
human mind may choose to invest in it. However, under the ethos of
scientific materialism, the goal of humankind's superior intellect is to
distinguish what is objectively true from what is false and, in order to do
so, we must overcome the pernicious effects of emotion, intuition or faith
– all of which distort our ability to perceive objective reality, which is the
only valid truth. By employing the structured, rational approach of the
scientific method, within an environment of detached objectivity, we are
able to leverage the power of the conscious mind to discern what is true
and untrue about the world we live in. In doing so, we liberate ourselves
from the vagaries of human subjectivity and move beyond prejudice,
faith or mysticism to find pure, objective certainty. Once identified, the
mechanistic universal laws which underpin all experienced phenomena
can be reapplied across time and space, thereby making the future
infinitely foreseeable and malleable.

Scientific materialism came to dominate our planet largely because
of the great influence of Western Europe on the development of human
societies worldwide. The Renaissance and Reformation, along with
the Scientific and Philosophical Revolutions, were largely Eurocentric
movements which led to the Enlightenment and the Industrial Revolution.
Through the interpenetration of a great many minds with a few great
minds, the elites, intellectuals and influencers involved in these movements co-created the political, philosophical, religious, economic and
social climates which came to dominate Western European nations, and
which, due to their colonization of much of the New World, saw scientific
materialism rise to cultural pre-eminence across many parts of the
globe.

The cultural nemesis of scientific materialism is rather harder to define,
as it has always worn radically different clothes in different regions of
the world – a tradition which very much continues to this day. That said,
the military and economic might of Western European nations, which
saw them spread the influence of scientific materialism, also facilitated
the global growth of a particularly Western perspective on what is an
ancient and deeply human impulse. Archaeological records show that
from at least 50,000 years ago human-beings have demonstrated
an intuitive tendency towards what we will call 'spiritual idealism', an
impulse which has since manifested in many different cultural expressions

from animism, paganism and shamanism to the various Eastern belief systems such as Buddhism, Shintoism and Tao'ism. For the last 1500 years or so, the Occidental expression of spiritual idealism has been dominated by the Abrahamic monotheisms of Judaism, Christianity and Islam. Although the origins of all three lie, geographically, in the Middle East, the largest of them – Christianity – very much owes its global reach to the West; initially to the success of the Roman Empire and much later to the empire building of Western European nations, in which Judaism also played an important part. Although Islam emerged then diverged from Judeo-Christianity, and found greatest traction outside of Europe, as a monotheism of the Abrahamic tradition it can still be considered to be Western in origin. Such is the global hegemony of Western culture in the 21st century that almost all of Europe, Oceania, Africa, North and South America plus much of Asia, can be considered to be culturally 'Western'.

All three monotheisms share a common 'creationist' worldview, which posits that the universe, and everything in it, was created by a single, anthropomorphic, transcendent and omnipotent male God, who therefore represents the ultimate reality. The epistemological basis of this worldview is that all knowledge is derived directly from divine revelation, as reported by prophets through the Bible, Tanakh and Koran respectively. God is the embodiment of all that is good and the goal of every human-being is to experience His divine reality and gain His salvation, by living a godly life through unwavering faith, correct thoughts and appropriate actions, as defined by God Himself. In this narrative, nature is hierarchical and, although God has blessed humans with a superior status to all other creatures, we still have the capacity for evil deeds so must resist the temptation to sin. Our reward for living virtuously will be a blissful afterlife with God, but the punishment for straying from righteousness will be an eternity of damnation and suffering.

The Abrahamic monotheisms, and their creationist worldview, dominated most of the known world for around 1000 years during the Medieval period or Dark Ages, between the fall of the Roman Empire about 500 AD and the peak of the Renaissance period circa 1500 AD. This peculiarly Western expression of spiritual idealism enjoyed a millennium of unrivalled cultural dominance, until it was gradually superseded by scientific materialism and its mechanistic worldview, from the Renaissance onwards. All culture changes slowly (unless imposed by military conquest or genocide), with new values and behaviours gradually emerging from a counter-cultural shift in emphasis within the dominant culture it eventually replaces. Thus, the origins of scientific materialism lay in the work of men such as Nicolaus Copernicus, whose advancements in mathematics and astronomy were originally conducted at the behest of the Roman Catholic Church.

Similarly, five centuries later in the early 20th century, a third major worldview would emerge as the result of breakthrough discoveries by men who, far from being antagonistic towards science, were actually some of its most brilliant minds. The 'organic' worldview developed out of the quantum theory of eminent scientists such as Albert Einstein, Niels Bohr and Werner Heisenberg, and has since led to an emerging culture we will call 'integrative monism'. To elaborate further it is necessary to first take a step back, to understand in more detail the roots and fundamental premises of scientific materialism.

From Classic to Quantum Science

In the early 21st century, we may feel a long way removed from the influence of Renaissance era scientists, such as Kepler and Galileo, or the philosophies of Bacon and Descartes, yet their legacy still holds a powerful grip on our unconscious modern minds. In particular the works of Isaac Newton, published in 1687, laid the final foundations for classical mechanics and completed the rise to cultural dominance of scientific materialism. Its primary approach to the development of new knowledge, which still prevails amongst many scientists to this day, was one of 'reductionism' and is perhaps best articulated in Nobel laureate physicist Steven Weinberg's famous saying '*the explanatory arrows always point downward*'.[1] In essence, reductionism is the belief that everything in nature can be explained by breaking any subject of study down into its constituent parts, and that all life is built from the 'bottom up'. In this narrative, societies can be explained in terms of people, people in terms of organs, organs in terms of cells, cells in terms of biology, biology in terms of chemistry and chemistry in terms of physics. At root, therefore, all phenomena are caused by the interaction of atoms and what we experience is simply their ultimate effect.

A central feature of reductionism is a belief in determinism, which has, at its heart, Newton's mechanical laws. To illustrate, imagine a pool table with balls moving on it. The balls are at all times confined in space by boundaries, specifically the table top, cushions and pockets. At any given moment in time, the balls have precise positions and are moving in specific directions at particular velocities. By measuring these initial conditions, we are able to accurately predict the future trajectories of all balls, as they collide with each other or with their boundaries. The initial conditions and the boundaries always determine the evolution of the balls within the 'system'. If we were to repeat the exercise again and again, with exactly the same initial conditions, the balls would always follow precisely the same trajectories. A key feature of these laws are their time-reversibility – if the balls were to be moved in exactly the opposite directions and with exactly the same force, they would all end up back in their original positions. This precisely predictable recurrence is what we mean by determinism, and it underpins a strong cultural belief in direct, linear 'cause and effect', which is prevalent in all Western societies. Through this lens, no phenomenon can happen without being directly caused by another phenomenon. Every effect must have a past cause which is identifiable and every cause must have a future effect which is predictable.

Of course, many aspects of our universe *do* appear to behave in this manner, so Newtonian determinism continues to be successfully applied in many areas of our lives and has proved to be tremendously valuable to humankind. On the basis of his mechanical laws and mathematical calculations, we are able to send rockets into outer space with a high degree of certainty that they will reach their intended destination. Rather more mundanely, we unknowingly apply Newton's laws every time we walk, strike a golf ball or steer a shopping trolley around a supermarket. At our macroscopic level of existence, we experience daily 'proof' of the absolute veracity of solid, material phenomena being propelled by physical dynamics and conforming to deterministic laws, so it is no wonder that the mechanistic worldview continues to provide us with a powerfully compelling narrative, even in the 21st century.

However, the solid foundations of the Newtonian perspective first began to shake around a century ago, when advancements were made in physics which rocked the scientific establishment to its core. Albert Einstein's special theory of relatively laid the groundwork for what would later be developed into quantum theory, by a team of scientists including Einstein, Niels Bohr, Erwin Schrodinger, Max Planck and Werner Heisenberg, and which would fundamentally alter the prevailing worldview within the physical sciences. Established 'truths' such as absolute time and space, elementary solid particles and deterministic relationships between phenomena all had to be rethought, and the discovery that emerging revelations could not be explained by classic physics came as a huge shock to the scientific community. Einstein famously said:

> All of my attempts to adapt the theoretical foundations of physics to this [new type of] knowledge failed completely. It was as if the ground had been pulled out from under one, with no firm foundation to be seen anywhere, upon which one could have built.'[2]

Gradually, the worldview of some scientists shifted from the mechanistic perspective to what could be described as a systemic or organic viewpoint, in which

> the universe is no longer seen as a machine, made up of a multitude of objects, but has to be pictured as one indivisible, dynamic whole whose parts are essentially interrelated and can be understood only as patterns of a cosmic process'.[3]

The most startling discovery of all was that the fundamental matter of the universe wasn't the solid atom of time-honoured theory, but sub-atomic particles – protons, neutrons and electrons – which were made of nothing but pure energy. The revelation was stupefying. Ultimately we, and everything around us, were made of spirit not solid matter. Furthermore, the constituents of the atom had a dual aspect to them, in that they could sometimes appear as particles and sometimes as waves. To physicists in the early 20th century this simply seemed impossible. While behaving as a particle, an electron was capable of converting into a wave and vice versa, confirming that the electron itself had no intrinsic qualities independent of its environmental conditions and the perspective of the observer. The nature of reality was entirely contextual and interpretive.

Although, quite literally, a microscopic discovery, it is almost impossible to overstate the seismic impact this had on the world of science, and on the future direction of our culture. More than anything, it confirmed the ultimate 'oneness' of the whole universe and thus provided a first step towards undermining the foundational principles of scientific materialism. The particle-wave paradox forced scientists to question the very basis of the mechanistic worldview, and Niels Bohr resolved the paradox by demonstrating that the particle and the wave were simply two opposite, yet complementary, descriptions of the same reality. The power of opposites lay at the very heart of all existence. At a sub-atomic level, the matter which formed all sensible phenomena in the outer world did not absolutely exist, but merely showed a tendency to exist. The solids, liquids and gases we experienced were not the sum of building blocks of matter but the result of interactions between immaterial energy, which may or may not manifest in the forms we anticipated. At the very end of the reductionist's journey, there was nothing physical to be found – only relationships between spiritual entities which didn't exist in any objective sense; relationships which had a probability, but no absolute certainty, of resulting in expected phenomena. The world was much less predictable or controllable than the mechanist had believed.

Through this 'new' science, we came to appreciate that there are no static structures in nature and that the appearance of stability is achieved through the dynamic interaction of opposing forces. Einstein's most famous equation – $E=mc^2$ – confirms that mass is nothing but a form of energy and that even apparently solid, static objects have dynamic energy stored within them. Both force and matter have their common origin in the particle-wave energy of the sub-atom. Interacting protons, neutrons and electrons flow in particular patterns, creating the stable molecular structures which build up into matter and which give objects, including us, the appearance of having solid substance. At our macroscopic level, the idea of solid, material form is a highly useful approximation of reality but at a microscopic level we never see any substance as such, just a dynamic dance of energy.

Furthermore, quantum science showed that the observer was actively involved in bringing forth either the particle or wave properties of sub-atomic energy. Logically, therefore, if an electron had no objective qualities independent of the observer's mind, if the mind was ultimately made of the same substance as the electron, and if the observable properties of the electron could only be realized from the interaction between the electron and the mind, they were clearly connected and whatever they created, they must have created in unison. Contrary to the clear separation of mind and matter famously posited by Rene Descartes, we were all, at all times, dynamically involved in bringing forth everything we perceived. If the energy patterns which formed the phenomena we observed in the material world were actually determined by the energy patterns of our mind, then any manifestation of the former must be interdependent with the latter.

As conceptual as this may seem, it is really no different to observing that the nature of how we attend to the world around us, directly influences what we perceive and bring forth as experience. For example, in social interactions how we attend to another person differs depending on who they are – we don't approach a bank manager or police officer in the same way we approach our partner, grandparent or child. We have different expectations from each encounter, so we offer a different aspect of ourselves in each situation and, in doing so, we change the nature of the interaction between us. Every aspect of an encounter with a policeman – our expectations, attitude, tone-of-voice, actions and mannerisms – would all change if we were to attend to him as if he was a child, and would almost certainly create a different set of outcomes. This is not only true of human interaction but also how we attend to inanimate objects. How we attend to a car will vary if we are a driver, a cyclist, a mechanic, a traffic warden or a thief. How we attend to a mountain will be different if we are a climber, a naturalist, a geologist, a photographer or a skier. How we attend to a cathedral will vary if we are a priest, an architect, a window cleaner, an artist or a terrorist. The revealed 'truth' of the car or the mountain or the cathedral varies directly with the attention we pay to it, how we approach it and what we are, consciously or unconsciously, looking for in it.

These breakthroughs presented a real dilemma to the mechanistic scientist who, in spite of using best endeavours to establish pure, objective truth uninfluenced by subjectivity, invariably brought a particular perspective to their topic of study and thereby changed whatever they discovered. Quantum science showed that the experienced universe was ultimately made of nothing but relationships between immaterial 'things' which only came into being through their interaction with other immaterial 'things', including our minds. Thus, the nature of what we experience is co-determined by our nature and the nature of whatever we are interacting with. We directly influence what is revealed to us by bringing forth an experience we have effectively co-created with our environment. There is no single, objective world 'out there' but many potential worlds we can choose from and if all apparently material forms are actually made from immaterial energy, it is entirely illogical to conclude that the same energy cannot also create immaterial forms. Such forms may exist beyond the perception of our empirical senses and be undetectable by the equipment or apparatus employed in the 'scientific method' of study.

In summary, quantum science emerged from developments in classic science but discoveries in the former shattered the foundational premises of the latter, creating an entirely alternative worldview to that which had held sway in the West, since the late Renaissance. Classic science saw the world as a complex, clock-work machine, driven by universal and deterministic mechanical laws which could be deduced by the rational human mind through reductionism. Classic scientists sought to understand our world by reducing everything in nature into ever smaller parts, but when they reached the end of the road they didn't find solid units of matter as expected, but particle-waves of immaterial energy. Contrary to widely accepted Cartesian wisdom – that the inner world of mind and the outer world of matter were entirely separate – quantum science also revealed that, at its sub-atomic source, everything in the entire universe is connected to everything else, or as Werner Heisenberg put it:

> the world thus appears as a complicated tissue of events, in which connections of different kinds alternate or overlap or combine and thereby determine the texture of the whole.[4]

From this new, organic worldview, the universe can no longer be conceived as a machine but as one single living organism; a huge holon in which every part (or lower holon) is connected to every other, in a deeply networked and dynamic relationship which is neither deterministic nor linearly causal as in classic science. The laws of sub-atomic physics are not fixed, mechanical laws but statistical laws based on probability, the likelihood of which is determined by the dynamics of the whole system. While in classic science the behaviour of the whole is driven by the nature of the relationships between parts, in quantum science almost exactly the reverse is the case – the relationships between parts are largely determined by the nature of the whole. While in mechanistic science the world is built entirely 'bottom up', in organic science it is co-created 'top down' and 'bottom up', as is the case with culture. What we experience in the world isn't the sum of building blocks of solid matter but what we bring forth as the result of where and how energy flows.

Of course, the organic worldview which emerged from quantum science isn't actually at all new and is, in fact, possibly our most ancient and original impulse. The idea that everything in the world is connected, and that we human-beings are a deeply embedded part of nature, is found in our oldest known belief system – animism – and still unwinds in the few ancient, indigenous tribes which survive to this day, such as the Native Americans and Indigenous Australians. The core concept of integrative monism – that all worldly phenomena exist as connected opposites which must be blended, rather than as separate, polar entities – has also always been central to many Eastern belief systems. Therefore far from being new, the organic worldview is actually one of our very oldest perspectives, producing an expression of spiritual idealism which was lost in the West through the rise of the monotheisms and which was unacceptable to the precepts of mechanistic science. As such, it offers the potential to reunite science and spirit in a way which neither of its squabbling siblings could ever achieve.

Yet, if it offers such potential, why has it grown so slowly over the last century? The simple answer is that dominant cultures emerge from the interplay of opposing values and both the mechanistic and creationist worldviews are extremely strong and single-minded competitors. As a consequence, integrative monism and the organic perspective have met with much resistance.

The power of the Church is self-evident and, although they have certainly weakened overall, the three monotheisms retain pockets of genuine geographic strength and a powerful grip on the faith of their many followers. Perhaps less obvious has been the resistance to new science from within science itself. The breakthrough in quantum theory came in the field of physics which then, as now, operated mainly as a separate discipline to other areas of scientific study. New science debunked the notion of a deterministic universe but the reductionist approach remained widely pervasive, partly because inertia dictates that it can simply take a very long time for radically new perspectives to be accepted, adopted and reapplied, even within the scientific community. It also remained true, as is still the case, that reductionism often produced acceptably accurate approximations of reality which were very useful in answering many questions about the world around us. However, the reductionist approach was, and still is, insufficient for answering *all* questions about life. To understand some phenomena, particularly living organisms, we needed an entirely different approach.

In no scientific discipline might we expect the organic worldview to be more readily adopted than in the field of biology, but the natural sciences at that time also modelled themselves on the mechanistic model of classic physics. Charles Darwin had provided a strongly reductionist explanation of evolution which was not only ground-breaking but was also highly consistent with the prevailing Cartesian-Newtonian worldview. As such, it was instantly accepted by many people as being unequivocally factual. However, there was possibly a further reason for the haste with which Darwinism was widely embraced, and it lay in the increasing secularization of parts of Victorian society. Prior to Darwin, natural science had largely been explained by the theology-based theories of William Paley, who essentially presented nature as the work of God's hand. Darwin's revolutionary view therefore gave those of a more secular leaning a version of events which could counter the creationist's narrative, as a credible explanation for the origins of life. Darwin had concluded that all biological form was the result of random variation and natural selection and, for a long time, many biologists saw any challenge to Darwin as a step backwards towards Paley. Despite the astonishing revelations of quantum science, mainstream biology therefore continued to follow a largely mechanistic approach and tremendous successes in molecular biology in the 1950s, particularly in understanding DNA, further reinforced the huge value of reductionism in comprehending the micro structure of organisms.

Furthermore, the great challenge for all of the sciences still remained unresolved – to move beyond reductionism and explain how the universe of life was created and sustained. Having spent hundreds of years breaking the world down into parts, reducing everything in nature to biology, chemistry and physics and having ultimately found themselves in a sub-atomic field of nothingness, scientists had yet to explain how the world built back up from particle-waves of immaterial energy to the rivers, mountains, earthquakes, ideas, markets, wars, cultures and societies we experienced all around us. How did the universal energy which was the essence of everything, actually come to form the material and immaterial content of all experienced phenomena? Understandably, many scientists were overwhelmed by the sheer magnitude of the question and continued to cling to the reductionist approach in the hope of a breakthrough, perhaps not because they were entirely convinced that it would yield the answer but because the only alternative appeared to be the teleological argument of the creationists; that there was intrinsic purpose designed into the natural world by an external, omnipotent source.

If such narrow-mindedness had been restricted to science, the damage may have been limited but such was the prestige with which science was held in the West, and such was the dominance of scientific materialism, that it automatically had a huge influence on broader society. Many other professional categories, from psychologists and sociologists to economists and politicians, driven by a desire to make their chosen field more 'scientific', also adopted the mechanistic worldview and turned towards the essential concepts of Cartesian-Newtonian reductionism. Today, this influence remains widely pervasive and still manifests in many of the structures, systems and institutions we take for granted. For example, reductionism can be clearly recognized in how we educate our children in separate subject areas and in how we structure our companies by departmental discipline. An implicit belief in linear determinism drives the many political programmes, such as the 'war on drugs', which impact our lives yet consistently fail to deliver their desired outcomes. For decades it was assumed that human-beings operated as rational, self-interested, utility-maximizing machines, when it came to making economic decisions – a theory which has only recently been demolished by behavioural economists. Cartesian dualism also continues to manifest in the adversarial nature of our legal and political systems, which force us to make binary choices which often lack the flexibility required in an increasingly nuanced world.

Most people aren't scientists and very few of us knowingly see the world through a mechanistic lens, or consciously choose reductionism as our preferred approach to problem solving. Yet our culture is so deeply soaked into us that, like the air we breathe, we are often not even consciously aware of its influence. Nowhere are implicit beliefs in scientific materialism more evident, than in the way our language has evolved to reveal our subconscious biases, preferences and orientations. If we consider something to be significant or important we say that it '*matters*'. If the opposite is true, we may describe it as '*immaterial*'. We sometimes feel we should apologise for being '*too idealistic*' or for an approach which '*isn't very scientific*'. Our unconscious worldview is also revealed through the metaphors and measures we commonly use. We see our economy in mechanistic terms, and concepts such as '*inputs and outputs*', '*efficiency measures*' or '*engines of growth*' all betray a strong orientation towards scientific materialism. The fact that an abstract quantity such as Gross Domestic Product (GDP) – defined by the OECD as '*an aggregate measure of production equal to the sum of the gross values added of all resident institutional units engaged in production*' – is used globally as the defining measure of the success of our societies, suggests we are all deeply entrenched within a mechanistic metaphor.[5] When those 'institutional units' which drive our GDP are functioning well, we may describe them as '*well-oiled machines*' or '*running like clockwork*'. When they aren't performing as planned, we may consider them to have '*broken down*', to '*need fixed*' or perhaps even '*re-engineered*'. Our dominant culture has become so second nature to us that we don't even notice the extent to which we see much of the world we live in, as a machine.

In spite of a widespread awakening to the organic worldview, many humans do still remain gripped by the cultural manifestations of classic science, of which materialism and militarism are perhaps the two most defining characteristics. Since the Industrial Revolution, science has enabled an exponential growth in our ability to produce inanimate objects and killing machines, and these two outputs regularly come together in the institutions which are central to our capitalist economic system – governments and corporations. Once again, we are often unaware of the degree to which military metaphors permeate our minds, but the language used by our political and economic institutions shine a bright light, deep into our cultural unconscious. Political parties still '*launch campaigns*', compete for '*battleground*' states, conduct '*wars*' on social ills and are '*attacked*' by their opponents, often coming '*under fire*' for their policies. Our corporations are known as '*companies*', are structured in '*divisions*' and are run by '*chiefs*' and '*officers*'. They develop '*strategies*', take '*actions*', gather market '*intelligence*', execute marketing '*campaigns*', manage '*logistics*', deploy '*resources*' and utilise sales '*forces*' which focus on achieving '*targets*'. All of the above, and many more such examples, are strongly indicative of the triumvirate scientific-materialistic-militaristic perspective, which dominates the many societies worldwide which remain under the spell of the mechanistic worldview in the 21st century.

The culture of scientific materialism came to define the modern era and has brought many benefits to humankind, from the medical break-throughs which prolong our lives to the economic systems which have empowered millions to increase their personal wealth and improve their living standards. Its rationalism unquestionably freed millions more from the fetters of blind faith in a pre-ordained future, and its technological developments have enhanced all of our lives in lots of ways. Yet, for all the good it has done, it has also wrought great damage. We have leveraged our technologies to subjugate or kill human-beings in great numbers and our voracious appetite for consumerism has over-exploited our natural resources and damaged much of our environment. While generating great wealth, capitalism has failed to share our prosperity equitably and has thereby denied equal access to basic human rights to every person on every continent. Our political institutions have failed to deliver social justice and equality of opportunity for all, while sustaining political and economic hierarchies which remain topped by societal elites, even in democratic nations.

However, for those of us who are deeply soaked in scientific materialism it can still be very difficult to imagine any other culture, because the only lens through which we are able to see is the mechanistic worldview of the West. For many of us, the outlook of our dominant culture is so second nature that it's difficult to imagine viewing the world in any other way. For this reason, it would be valuable to consider what life might look like from the perspective of the organic worldview and, thankfully, some of our original impulses have survived intact in the East.

East Meets West (the Circle and the Line)

Although there are clear differences between all major expressions of spiritual idealism, there is little doubt that the main schism is between Occident and Orient. The three Abrahamic monotheisms certainly have more in common with each other, than with Eastern belief systems such as Hinduism, Buddhism, Shintoism, Taoism and Confucianism – all of which contain some fundamental similarities. Today, the creationist worldview of the West is far more widely pervasive than the Eastern outlook which, although gaining greater global awareness in an increasingly interconnected world, remains culturally significant only in East and South Asia. While descriptions of the respective cultures they have created are necessarily broad-brush, they have nevertheless left distinct and consistent impressions on the Eastern and Western mind. The key differences between East and West can perhaps be symbolised by the circle and the line, signifying the inclusive holism of the right mind versus the linear separation of the left mind.

Central to the Eastern worldview is an overarching belief in monism, in which there is only one reality embracing all opposites, including both the material and immaterial. In the West – culturally dominated by Cartesian dualism – aspects of experience tend to be processed as two distinct realities consisting of polar opposites: heaven and earth, good and evil, day and night, male and female, black and white and so on. While the Eastern mind acknowledges the existence of opposites, it tends to emphasise their similarities, connections and interdependencies, while the Western perspective tends to perceive opposites to be in competition with each other, founded upon their relational differences and the distance between them.

In the East, humans have always been considered to be an integral part of nature without distinction or hierarchy. For example, in Taoism, humanity (ren) and nature (tian) always react to and comply with one another and can never be separated. The enduring oneness of the universe and the unbreakable connection between all opposites is, of course, famously conveyed by the Chinese yin and yang symbol. In the West, humans tend to be seen as distinctly separate from, and superior to, the rest of nature. Hierarchies even exist within humankind, where man is superior to woman and subservient only to a single, omnipotent God, who is always masculine. Deities in the less autocratic and more flexible Eastern belief systems, range from the polytheistic to the atheistic. Hinduism has many deities and avatars, while in Buddhism, Confucianism and Taoism there are no gods, only 'ways'. Where gods do appear, they are neither solely male nor necessarily anthropomorphic. Shintoism worships deities known as *kami* which may be animals, objects or natural phenomena and, according to Shinto, even the smallest ant can have divine powers. While in the Western monotheisms God is clearly separate from His creation and is Himself changeless, in the Eastern worldview all 'gods' are immanent within their creations, and change is therefore as integral to them as it is to nature itself.

Unlike the Western monotheisms, most Eastern philosophies are essentially egalitarian. In Buddhism all humans and animals are equal, and all sentient creatures have value because, as reincarnated souls, their current 'otherness' is merely temporary and illusory. In Western religions, only human-beings can gain entry to God's heaven but in the East all sentient beings are reincarnated, so the principle of karma powerfully underpins Eastern morality. While Westerners may exploit creatures inferior to them, and may or may not be punished in the afterlife by their God, karma dictates that all Easterners will receive back what they give out, in both current and future lives and irrespective of the form in which they are reincarnated. Thus, a wise Oriental is powerfully incentivised to be kind to all other living organisms and to respect and protect their shared environment for future generations. The circle therefore represents the harmonious integration of the whole community, both human and non-human, to which the Eastern individual subsumes part of their autonomy, in the interests of coherence and collective wellbeing. Such a commitment, in ever increasing circles from the immediate family to the global environment, highlights the utmost priority given to the maintenance of positive relationships and the avoidance of destructive behaviour. While the line divides and polarizes, the circle encloses and embraces everything within it, conveying the overarching Eastern perspective that all reality exists as one interconnected whole. The contrast between the organic worldview of the Eastern mind versus the mechanistic lens of the West is self-evident.

Core to the divergence is their differing attitudes towards time. To be perceived, units of time require both reductionism and separation, so only our left mind can conceptualise time and its passing. The line therefore symbolises the dominant Western view of time, as a singular point moving continuously forward from the past through the present and into the future. At the heart of this view lies the creationist narrative of the monotheisms, in which the world was created in the past by an omnipotent God and will, at some point in the future, be destroyed. '*Time waits for no man*' is a popular saying in the West, revealing a strong sense of cultural urgency to optimize the time available during our brief, earth-bound existence and a constant feeling of loss at time elapsed. The Eastern view of time is radically different, in particular its attitude towards past, present and future. The circle symbolises the dominant Eastern outlook that there is no definitive beginning or end of time, just perpetual cycles of birth, death and re-birth, of which our current earthly existence is but one of many. Time is not linear but the cyclical ebb and flow of days and seasons. '*What is lost at sunrise can be regained at sunset*', a saying from *the Biography of Feng Yi,* conveys a very different attitude towards time, to that held in the West.

Our deep-rooted cultural impatience in the West is fuelled by an implicit belief in linear progress, in which each generation must build upon the achievements of the previous generation and the supreme aim in life is to actualize human potential within the limited time available. In this subliminal narrative, the individual takes primacy above all else and, in the spiritual version of the story, forms a one-to-one relationship with God, taking joint responsibility for his or her destiny. In monotheistic mythology, all human-beings are innately sinful and salvation can only be achieved by living a good life as defined by, and under the watchful eye of, an autocratic and omnipresent God. The polar consequences of success or failure are clearly delineated – an eternity in heaven or an afterlife in hell. By considerable contrast, in the Eastern worldview humans are initially ignorant rather than sinful, and personal progress is a journey made through endless cycles of reincarnation, towards ever-increasing levels of enlightenment. In this conception there are many different paths one can take, all based on one's own inner nature, but pursuing a 'middle way', involving healthy balance and the avoidance of polar extremes, is consistently emphasised. In all Eastern belief systems one must look deep inside oneself for answers, rather than slavishly following the word of an external God. A good life is defined by one's ability to find one's own 'true path', while at all times following '*dharma*', our duty to be harmoniously at one with the universe.

Of course, it would be wholly misleading to infer that science has played no part in the development of the Eastern mind. On the contrary, many of the earliest advances in astronomy, mathematics and medicine originated in the East, as did inventions such as papermaking, gunpowder and the compass.[6] However, the East was never seduced by science to the same degree as the West and, within its overarching framework of monism, never came to mistakenly believe that science could provide answers to *all* the mysteries of the universe. While the value of science has always been recognised, it has always been counterbalanced by spiritualism and integrated into Eastern belief systems, as yin is to yang. This approach is still reflected to this day, in how the Eastern mind perceives and practices science. For example, the systematic categorization of the natural world into a taxonomy of animals and plants, with each category sub-divided according to their similarities and differences, is a uniquely Western approach to explaining natural phenomena. By contrast, the Eastern approach to the taxonomy of living organisms and their biospheres, has always been more contextual and has never been subject to such rigid divisions or categories. Similarly, the orientation of an Eastern medical practitioner is to first take a holistic approach to wellbeing, by exploring the patient's background and lifestyle to assess overall health, before considering specific symptoms. By contrast, determinism is deeply implicit in Western medical training, so a doctor will tend to assume a directly linear, causal relationship between symptom, ailment and cure, thereby focussing much more narrowly than an Eastern medic.

Naturally, we must acknowledge the many contradictions to any suggestion that scientific materialism has had little influence on Eastern culture. The Occident and Orient have never been immune to the effects of each other but, much more significantly, every human-being has essentially the same brain, so the cognitive impulses which lead to scientific materialism also occur in the Eastern mind. Broad-brush generalizations, therefore, inevitably yield conflicting examples because all cultures are the net output of the dynamic interplay between opposing forces, so contradictions and counter-cultures must exist within every society. Just as the monotheisms have continued to have a significant influence on a Western culture increasingly dominated by science, both materialism and militarism have always featured in the East. For millennia the Silk Road carried material goods, as well as culture, between China and Mediterranean Europe and today Asia remains pivotal as a global manufacturing hub, producing more material output than any other region. While the famous Mongol Emperor Genghis Khan was an integrationist who, in uniting the nomadic tribes of Northeast Asia, practiced meritocracy and encouraged religious tolerance, he wasn't exactly famed for his pacifism and, today, China has the largest army of any nation on Earth. Similarly, the East has never been immune to the hierarchical categorization of the left brain hemisphere. The Indian caste system is clearly rooted in the four ancient Hindu *varnas* of social stratification (although historians do disagree about the extent to which the present day hierarchy was amplified under the colonial rule of the British Raj). In more modern times it's certainly the case that countries such as Japan, South Korea and, more recently, China have embraced technology and the capitalist economic model of the West. Contradictions are intrinsic to all cultures because all culture originates in the human brain, which is fuelled by the power of opposites.

Nevertheless, it generally remains the case that while Eastern expressions of spiritual idealism remained true to our most original human impulse – an intuitive belief in the essential unity of man and nature – the Western religions, under the early influence of male warrior gods such as Jupiter and Zeus, deviated greatly from this path. While the overarching monism of the East ensured an approach which was largely holistic, synthesising and integrating, the dominant dualism of the West led to polarized perspectives and clear distinctions between perceived opposites. These two overarching cognitive contexts – monism in the East and dualism in the West – couldn't possibly fail to exert downward pressure on the cultural narratives they created; narratives which would, in turn, sustain the pre-eminence of each context by filling unconscious minds in the Orient and Occident respectively.

As we will explore in Part Two, monism is founded in the synthesising approach of the right mind while dualism is rooted in the separating skills of the left mind. The primary function of the latter is to protect us, so it is, amongst many other tendencies, the source of our competitiveness and aggression. Today, there can be little doubt that the Western approach has become more globally dominant than the Eastern way. Furthermore, like brothers brought up in an atmosphere of adversarialism, Western science and religion have squabbled for centuries and continue to do so. In most secular nations, the mechanistic worldview of scientific materialism seems to have 'won', although perhaps only in terms in which it would self-define victory. Worldwide, more than 8 in 10 people still identify with a religion but those who don't are found in higher than average concentration, in the most economically prosperous nations of Europe, North America, Oceania and Asia.[7] Yet irreligion is a peculiarly modern phenomenon, with patterns of distribution which have created a clear chasm between rich and poor. In almost all countries in the Middle East and Africa, irreligion remains practically unknown and belief in God is thought to be essential to morality – a view shared in many poorer nations around the world, including El Salvador, Brazil, Bolivia, Venezuela, Indonesia, Pakistan, Malaysia and the Philippines.[8]

Theories for this divergence are varied. Non-believers are more likely to live in European cities than African villages, so may feel less in need of religion because of the safety nets provided by economic welfare and accessible healthcare. They are also more likely to be college-educated, so may simply have greater faith in their ability to navigate life and determine their own destiny. In poorer, agricultural nations, religions have traditionally promoted large families as a source of free labour and a means of reducing the impact of infant mortality, neither of which are necessary in modern, urban environments where technologies such as contraceptives give people greater control over their lives. Those who live in urban areas may also feel less vulnerable to the hostile forces of nature than those in rural areas, who perhaps feel a greater need for God's protection from life's uncertainties. Other anthropologists point to the availability of psychological and psychiatric interventions as another reason why religion has lost its popularity in wealthier nations, replacing a metaphorical opiate with real-world psychotropic drugs. Further theories even posit that group pastimes, such as sports events, political rallies and music concerts, now provide many of the emotional and spiritual benefits people used to gain from church attendance.

What all theories have in common is a shared faith in scientific materialism and its cultural manifestations. Many anthropologists therefore conclude that science, and the control over nature it has given us, has simply superseded religion in providing reassurance about the predictability of our lives. This is undoubtedly the result of Western cognitive dualism, which sees science and religion as opposites so necessitates an either/or choice to be made, rather than the Eastern monistic framework in which both science and spirit can not only be accommodated but collaboratively integrated. As we will explore in Chapter 4, because both mechanistic and creationist worldviews have been cultivated within a dualistic context, they are both rooted in the left mind within which, with its narrow focus and desire for certainty, there can only ever be one correct answer. These two worldviews are therefore wholly incompatible and incapable of harmonious integration, in their current form. Only the organic worldview, within an overarching culture of integrative monism, offers the potential to reconcile science with spirit, and their successful synthesis is essential to the future of the human species. Western science versus Western religion is central to many of the conflicts global society is currently experiencing, and we cannot afford for either side to win. At the moment science is dominant but spirituality is core to the human condition. Indeed, it was our original impulse for many millennia, long before any concept of science even permeated our consciousness, so consistently suppressing it is deeply damaging, both psychologically and culturally.

In Western culture we persist in seeing science as the opposite of faith yet, as mathematician and philosopher Alfred North Whitehead pointed out, *'the faith in the order of nature which has made possible the growth of science is a particular example of a deeper faith'*.[9] With due acknow-ledgement of the valuable secrets the 'scientific method' has revealed to us about the natural world, our common sense tells us that there is still much of what we experience that science simply cannot explain. Science can't tell us why we love someone. Yes, it can describe the bio-chemical changes in our brain or body when we feel a sensation we call love, but it can't tell us why we are drawn to love one person and not another. Science can't explain why we feel a sense of deep awe in the presence of a water-fall cascading off a Swiss alp, or why we feel uplifted by one particular song yet moved to tears by another. Science can't explain the immense grief we experience at the loss of a loved one and can't prove what happens to them after they die. Science can't tell us why some people find amazing reserves of courage and perseverance in the most appalling of circumstances, while others simply give up. Science can track electrical activity, map blood flow or measure increases in endorphins and other neuropeptides in the human brain, but it can't tell us how to interpret Mona Lisa's smile or predict how we will feel when we first watch a performance of Swan Lake. Science can explain lots of things but we all know intuitively that it can't explain everything. In fact, science can't even demonstrate why science is the best approach for explaining the natural world – the scientific experiment which proves that for all knowledge to be valid, it must be scientifically verifiable, has yet to be conducted.

Classic science and its mechanistic worldview, which still forms the bedrock of scientific materialism, places great faith in the belief that nature is regulated by universal, deterministic rules and in the capability of the human intellect to discern those rules. Quantum science debunked such beliefs a century ago, yet this knowledge is only now beginning to permeate our cultural unconscious. To progress peacefully, humankind must overcome its blind faith in classic science, every bit as much as it must overcome blind faith in the monotheisms. Although our essential spirituality must be rediscovered, to counterbalance science and restore healthy psychological and cultural coherence, the foundational tenets of the three monotheisms make them irreconcilable, not only with science but also with each other. Yet the creationist worldview remains strong and is still the dominant cultural driver in many nations, especially, but not exclusively, in the Islamic world.

Largely due to the growth of the organic worldview, scientific material-ism is weakening and, sensing this, creationism is once again emboldened. Although Christian and Jewish fundamentalism does exist, it is no real surprise that it is followers of Islam who are fighting hardest to re-establish creationism as the lens through which Earth's inhabitants see the world. For centuries Judaism and Christianity have co-existed both alongside each other and with scientific materialism, far more than Islam has ever done, due simply to the Western European and New World nations in which they found most followers. While Islam was relatively marginalised in the Middle East, Judeo-Christianity more closely witnessed the growth of the mechanistic worldview, indeed was in many ways pivotal to it. Renaissance science grew out of Roman Catholicism, and both Protes-tantism and Judaism were central to the development of capitalism. As a consequence, followers of faith in developed nations tend to be Jewish or Christian, rather than Muslim, and are more accustomed to scientific materialism, benefitting more from it. While science and religion therefore continue, at times, to make strange bedfellows, Judeo-Christian funda-mentalists in these countries tend to be less vocal and just as inclined to fight with their rival monotheisms, as to rail against their dominant culture.

We therefore find ourselves in the midst of a complex, and often confusing, culture war but the stakes could not be higher, for the prize is the right to define future reality for humankind. Only an organic world-view offers the potential for the peaceful integration of science and spirit, which is necessary for our individual and collective wellbeing. However, both scientific materialism and the creationist monotheisms can be powerful, dangerous and aggressive adversaries, which will not be over-come by force. They will only be defeated by reducing their power, through the cultivation of integrative monism which is, in its essential nature, pacifistic. Only the emergence of a globally dominant culture of integrative monism can save human-beings from either destroying our planet or killing each other, and only an organic worldview can deliver such a culture. Within each of us lies the power to change the trajectory of our species and to create the cultural conditions required for peaceful co-existence and personal happiness. However, whatever emerges in future as the content of our global mind will do so from the interpenetration of our individual minds – two complex adaptive systems one nested within the other – but neither of them can be controlled, nor their output accurately predicted. No-one, whether scientist, priest or politician, can guarantee a successful outcome and we all, therefore, have to play our part. All we can do, as individuals, is elevate our consciousness in order to proactively make personal choices which are conducive to collective coherence. As an additional benefit, we may also better equip ourselves to deal with the stresses of everyday life, in the process making ourselves whole, healthy and happy. To do so, we must adopt an organic worldview, the development of which benefits from a basic understanding of complex adaptive systems. As we will discover, the chaos we are currently experi-encing may provide very rich soil for the cognitive growth we need.

—3—
The Process of Life

Back in the 1960s, in spite of a powerfully pervasive mechanistic worldview and the on-going influence of classic science, some physicists, biologists and chemists did look beyond reductionism for an alternative explanation of how life is created and sustained. Their approach required the resurrection of a perspective which dated back to ancient Greek times, when the study of substance (what something is made of) and the study of form (the patterns made by substance to create a discernible 'thing') were both extensively explored. Plato had believed that form not only existed in a material object, like a vase, but also in immaterial forms such as 'beauty' and that the two ideas occasionally came together to co-create a beautiful vase. However, with the elevation of scientific materialism in more modern times, the study of substance was prioritized over form and material form was given primacy over immaterial form, the study of which was often dismissed as 'unscientific'. However, quantum science, having identified that all substance was ultimately immaterial, once again turned the priorities of some scientists upside-down, with form taking precedence over substance and study focussing on the patterns of relationships between holons which create form. With this approach, understanding what emerges 'between' parts is just as important as the parts themselves and this perspectival shift is essential to the study of all living organisms. Through this lens, while it is accepted that living organisms are made from atoms, they are not *only* made from atoms but also from the nature of their relationships with all the other organisms in their environment.

Think back to the married couple in Chapter 1. Their marriage does not 'exist' in any material sense, yet it exerts a powerful influence on its two constituents and, in doing so, it shapes them as much as they shape it. Any marriage therefore consists of three elements – two human holons plus the properties of the marriage itself – which make the 'marriage holon' greater than the sum of its two material parts. While the reductionist mind would break the marriage down into two separate individuals, the organic view sees both it and them as a 'live' system, which can only be studied as such. Through this lens, the marriage can only be understood as a whole because its observable properties only emerge at this level, and the behaviour of the couple towards each other can only be understood within the context of their relationship. While their marriage *can* be reduced to two individuals, no meaningful understanding of its nature can be obtained by studying each part in isolation. To comprehend any living system, while it is important to recognise parts, we must focus study at the level at which the properties of the whole system emerge. It is the extra, often immaterial, qualities which make the study of live systems very different from studying inanimate objects, for which reductionism is often perfectly appropriate. Furthermore, only an organic approach can deliver integration of the material and the immaterial, which is required to understand complex adaptive systems such as our minds, marriages and cultures.

Those pioneering scientists who first looked beyond reductionism founded a new stream of systems study now called complexity science, which over the last five decades has greatly enhanced our knowledge of the natural world. Although still in its relative infancy it also shows great potential, with applications across all scientific disciplines including the social sciences. Complexity science focusses on 'emergence' as a complement to reductionism and scientists have identified that complex adaptive systems exist throughout both the natural and man-made worlds, sharing many common characteristics. For example, all such systems are made of multiple parts, or nodes, which are interconnected in a network of non-linear relationships and which, via feedback loops, share information about their environment across the system.[1] What makes them adaptive, and therefore very special, is their ability not only to process environmental data but also to internally encrypt learning from the data-stream, which can enable the system to reshape itself and adapt to future environmental changes.[2] In doing so, such systems are able to generate survival-enhancing change from within. Although we may be unfamiliar with the term, we are actually surrounded by complex adaptive systems and experience them every single day. Our brain is one, as are our immune system, the human embryo, market economies, languages, cultures, social networks, ecosystems, hurricanes, cities and even the universe we live in, to name but a few. While biological systems learn and adapt by encrypting environmental data into the genetic message encoded in DNA, neural systems do so by encoding information into short and long-term memory, and social systems learn and adapt by encrypting data into the cultures they create, the stories they tell and the attitudinal and behavioural norms they promote.

Complex Adaptive Systems

One of the defining, and perhaps most fascinating, features of all complex adaptive systems is their tendency towards self-organization and their apparently magical ability to create order out of disorder.[3] In free markets a web of interactions between companies and customers produces a capitalist economy – seemingly random and uncontrolled but somehow guided by Adam Smith's 'invisible hand' towards dynamic stability, containing powerfully opposing forces yet exhibiting overall order. The self-organizing properties of complex adaptive systems were first discovered by Stuart Kauffman in the mid 1960s. Kauffman, then a second-year medical student at the University of California, wanted to understand how up to 100,000 genes in the human genome yielded only around 250 different cell types. Cells are created from combinations of genes so it seemed counter-intuitive that 100,000 individual genes, giving the potential for $10^{30,000}$ connections, would only produce around 250 distinct results. In the early 1960s molecular biologists Francois Jacob and Jacques Monod had discovered feedback mechanisms, in which genes were effectively switched on and off, and, building on this idea, Kauffman hypothesised that cell types were the naturally ordered output of different types of connections between genes. He set out to explore his idea using Boolean networks, in which each node (representing a gene) is connected in a network with other nodes and becomes either active or inactive in accordance with how they are programmed to react to signals received.[4] It perhaps helps to visualise each node as a light bulb which is either switched on or off by the signals it receives and which, in turn, causes those bulbs to which it is connected to either switch on or off. When activated the network of lights could potentially run through every possible combination or sequence, before eventually settling into any recognisable pattern.

In summer 1965 Kauffman programmed a Boolean network with a relatively modest 100 nodes which could, nevertheless, potentially yield

THE PROCESS OF LIFE   57

10^5 different combinations. Incredibly, the network very quickly settled down into a steady pattern with only 4 different sequences or 'state cycles'. Kauffman had discovered the phenomenon of natural order emerging out of a hugely disordered system, which he called 'order for free' or self-organization. Kauffman went on to experiment with many Boolean networks, with varying numbers of nodes and connections, and firmly established self-organization as a proven phenomenon. He also identified that the critical property of such systems was that the emergent 'global' order, at the level of the whole system, was the result of the 'local' rules – the specific instructions he programmed into each node for responding to information received, and how they behaved as a result. Kauffman concluded that each distinct sequence or state cycle acted as an 'attractor' in the networked system, drawing the random and innumerable possible cycles into a small number of stable, ordered patterns.[6]

Attractors may be considered to be similar to whirlpools in a turbulent sea, where the underlying 'local rules' – the seabed topography and the volume and rate of water flowing across it – cause a current to form which is observable at the 'global' level, and which flows in a particular pattern around and between a number of whirlpools. Although intensely dynamic, this flow pattern will remain remarkably stable over a period of time and will only change if there is a perturbation to its underlying 'rules', such as a change in topography or a sudden increase in flow rate. Simple, local rules causing dynamic, yet stable, order to emerge – in the form of a small number of attractors at the global level – is a remarkable phenomenon but is consistently exhibited by all complex adaptive systems.[7] Again, we are much more familiar with this concept than we might imagine. Consider how dynamic, yet consistent, traffic patterns can be witnessed in any city, as the emergent result of the road network, the specific local rules of the road (such as traffic lights and one-way systems) and the free will of drivers in responding to those rules. No-one is in overall control but order emerges from interactions between human nodes, each adhering to a few simple rules and guided by the layout of the network. The popular routes act like attractors, drawing drivers into steady state cycles of behaviour. Also consider how different neighbourhoods in cities are formed, by attracting people from a similar background or economic status to those who are already there. In doing so, they create distinct suburbs or ghettos which will often remain stable over time but which can nevertheless be changed by a major perturbation, such as the influx of sufficient people with an alternative disposition, lifestyle or outlook. Consider how, in cultures, attitudinal and behavioural norms act as powerful attractors which draw individuals towards them, facilitating group consensus, generating social stability and maintaining public order.

A fascinating paradox of attractors is that it is often very difficult to predict exactly what will emerge at the global level, even with detailed knowledge of the local rules to which nodes within the system are operating. Similarly, but conversely, local rules are often very difficult to deduce, even with clear sight of the global order which has emerged from them. Consider a game of chess which is governed by a few simple rules which anyone can easily learn. However, the free will which each player exerts in deciding which move to make in response to their opponent's last move, means that a large number of potential plays are possible. The exact pattern of how each game will unfold cannot be predicted in advance, even by a grand master, nor could that same expert, upon being shown the end positions of all pieces after a game has concluded, retrospectively reduce the game back down to all of the individual moves made. The global pattern of the game emerges from the local rules but the free will of each participant, even when operating within the rules, coupled with the large number of interactions between players, make the outcome of the game highly unpredictable and make it almost impossible to retrospectively deduce exactly how the final outcome was arrived at.

A chess game, however, is an extremely simple system with only two players and a rigidly fixed set of rules. By comparison, consider the natural ecosystem described in Darwin's famous quote from *On the Origin of Species.*[34]

> it is interesting to contemplate a tangled bank, clothed with many plants of many kinds, with birds singing on the bushes, with various insects flitting about, and with worms crawling through the damp earth and to reflect that these elaborately constructed forms, so different from each other, and dependent upon each other in so complex a manner, have all been produced by laws acting around us.

In such a scene, flora and fauna interact in a complex network of relationships, forming a food web in which predator and prey co-exist, not in harmony but in an environment where opposing forces of competition and co-operation create an ecosystem which is both dynamic and stable. Although we could remove the participants from their habitat and analyse each of them reductively, in doing so we would understand nothing about their role in maintaining the delicate balance of the eco- system. Only by studying the whole system in situ, could we identify the unique characteristics of this particular '*tangled bank*', the nature of relationships between predator and prey and the properties of the food web. The '*laws*' Darwin refers to are the local rules which ultimately generate the emergent global order of the ecosystem. A food web is formed by a small number of inter-related factors, such as the food chain hierarchy (who eats who or what, from top to bottom) and the ratio of predators to prey. In time, a pattern of order emerges between interacting nodes; an order which depends upon the frequency, nature and outcomes of those interactions.

Once again the emergent pattern is neither predictable nor reducible, simply because, unlike in a machine, relationships between nodes aren't predetermined but are subject to flux and a degree of free will. In a chess game there are only two players but in Darwin's tangled bank each creature is not only connected to predator and prey, but also to a multitude of other creatures and organisms in a mutual dance of co-existence. Each living organism, at different times and in different situations, demonstrates opposing tendencies towards competition or co-operation, in order to adapt to prevailing conditions or to modify the behaviour of others. This high degree of inter-connectivity allows information to flow in multiple directions, creating feedback loops which permeate the system in a non-linear way, causing unpredictable knock-on effects and unintended consequences.

This highlights another exciting feature of complex adaptive systems, which is found in how they can change.[8] In such non-linear systems, nodes aren't necessarily connected in sequence or to a fixed number of other nodes, but may be networked via a whole web of multiple and random connections which, as data is processed between them, can produce very different outputs to a linear clockwork mechanism or a deterministic game of pool. In complex adaptive systems a very small change to an initial condition can, as it cycles across the network and through multiple feedback loops, become increasingly amplified and result in a major perturbation, setting state cycles off on a new path and poten- tially establishing new attractors which, if they become established, can ensure that the system never settles back down into old patterns. Any living organism can therefore change itself from within by 'leaping' to a new set of state cycles, creating a new stable pattern for its underlying structure and, thereby, forever changing its form. Unlike pool balls, the non-linear relationship between cause and effect means that a tiny initial cause can amplify greatly, creating a dramatic effect which is not time-reversible and which still has the potential for further, future change. In Darwin's tangled bank, imagine that predator A eats preys C & D while predator B preys upon D & E. A small reduction in the availability of E may cause B to increase consumption of D, which in turn forces A to increase consumption of C, impacting F, G & H all of whom were prey to C but now increase in numbers, negatively effecting I, J & K with whom they are all in direct competition for food and other resources. A small change at a 'local' level can lead to radically different results at the 'global' level, creating new patterns of behaviour in the ecosystem which may never again return to 'normal'.

Perhaps the most well-known example of this phenomenon is found in weather patterns, where small changes, like the famous butterfly wings flapping over central Brazil, can eventually cause a storm to develop over Florida. Scientists studying complexity spend their time trying to identify the local rules within adaptive systems which create their many divergent and unpredictable outcomes. They also focus on trying to identify whether there are common characteristics which are shared by all such systems. The potential for small changes in initial conditions to cause dispropor-tionately large outcomes would appear to be one such property, as would the characteristic that the same initial perturbation won't always lead to the same outcome. A Florida storm may only result one in a million times from the actions of the Brazilian butterfly, and this is another source of the huge unpredictability of such complex, non-linear systems. In linear systems cause and effect are clearly linked, and effect is always directly proportional to cause. The future is therefore predictable and the effect is time-reversible. However, in non-linear systems, due to the amplifying or dampening influence of feedback loops and their impact being guided by probabilities not certainties, the effects can range from non-existent to hugely disproportionate to the scale of the original cause.

In social systems this was brought into sharp focus during what became known as the 'Arab Spring' uprisings when, beginning in December 2010, the Arab world experienced a wave of revolutionary protests and demon-strations which quickly spread throughout the Middle East and North Africa. The self-immolation of just one man, Mohamed Bouazizi, in protest at Tunisian police corruption, sparked unrest in Algeria, Jordan, Egypt and Yemen before spreading more widely. By December 2013 rulers had been ousted from power in Tunisia, Egypt, Yemen and Libya, civilian uprisings had taken place, but been quashed, in Bahrain and Syria, major protests had erupted in Algeria, Iraq, Jordan, Kuwait, Morocco, Israel and Sudan, while minor demonstrations had taken place in Mauritania, Oman, Saudi Arabia, Djibouti, Western Sahara and Palestine.[9] The impact of fruit-seller Bouazizi's suicide could easily have been negligible but one small initial perturbation can lead to a very wide range of outcomes of varying and unpredictable proportions.

To complexity scientists this defining feature, which is exhibited by all complex adaptive systems, is known as 'self-organized criticality' and was first articulated by physicists Per Bak, Chao Tang and Kurt Weisenfeld in 1988.[10] Their idea is simply, yet powerfully, portrayed through the metaphor of a sand pile forming on a table, onto which grains of sand are being added at a slow, steady rate. Each individual grain makes very little difference to the pile, until it reaches a critical point at which just one more grain of sand can set off an avalanche cascading down its slopes. The magnitude of each avalanche may range from very small to very large, so is not at all proportionate to the mass of the single grain which triggered it. Crucially, when the system is in a 'critical' state, the effect of a very small perturbation – adding just one more grain – is entirely unpredictable but could represent the tipping point at which a massive cascade of change occurs. Although there are always more small avalanches and relatively few large avalanches, there is simply no way to know in advance whether each incremental grain will have no effect on the stability of the sand pile, whether it will trigger a small cascade or whether it will prove to be the final catalyst which sparks a revolution.

Perhaps the most incredible, and controversial, discovery in complexity science is that adaptive systems consistently appear to organize themselves towards points of criticality and to 'deliberately' trigger perturbations; most of which cause minor, change-enabling ripples of energy but a few of which create waves of energy which are large enough to enable the whole system to leap to a higher level of complexity. Criticality itself, therefore, appears to act as an attractor towards which the whole system self-organizes over time, enabling incremental adaptive growth but also, more occasionally, presenting the system with windows of opportunity to undergo far more major transitions. By amplifying new patterns of behaviour the system can, if change can be sustained, once again become stable but on a new, higher plateau. In other words it can evolve.

The discovery of the underlying principles of self-organized criticality led, in scientific circles at least, to an epistemological avalanche all of its own, by challenging one of the most powerful manifestations of Newtonian reductionism – Darwin's theory of evolution.

Challenging Charles Darwin

Darwin completed *On the Origin of Species* over half a century before the development of quantum theory, so it is no surprise that it was reductionist in approach and immediately lauded in an environment which was so pro-Newton and increasingly anti-Paley in outlook. In original Darwinism, all biological epiphenomena were explicable by their underlying chemistries which were fundamentally reducible to physical explanations. There was no downward, causal influence from secondary to primary phenomena, the arrow of causality was always and entirely 'bottom up'. The growth of a living organism was the outcome of blind and random mutation in a grasping struggle for survival; survival which would be determined by the 'natural selection' of an external environment which, in deference to Cartesian dualism, was entirely separate from the organism upon which it acted. The organism did not therefore in any way 'adapt' to its environment, but mutated randomly in the hope that it might, serendipitously, create new features which proved to be advantageous in a cold, detached outer world. Neither did selection involve proactive interaction from environment to organism, but rather passive indifference to its fate.

Darwinism cast a long shadow over any lingering creationist claim, that the world had been designed by the hands of an omnipotent and loving God. Instead, the universe came to be seen as an entirely mechanistic system in which more complex organisms randomly evolved from simpler forms. Core to Darwinism was the notion that all living organisms were related by common ancestry and, over billions of years, all life forms diverged from the same common source via genetic mutation. In this conception, the continuous process of evolution produced more variations than could feasibly survive, so natural selection prioritised those which were best adapted to the prevailing environment and some adaptations outgrew, outlasted or out-reproduced others. Darwinian theory was well supported by fossil evidence so was widely accepted for at least a century. Indeed, to this day the fundamental principles of Darwin's ideas aren't disputed but over the past few decades systems biologists have come to challenge, not the underlying premise of Darwinism, but the process via which evolution actually takes place.

In the theory of evolution still taught in schools today, changes result from random genetic variation followed by natural selection, which either reinforces or eliminates the varied gene. So, for example, if a species needs to protect itself from predation in order to survive and will optimize its chances by growing a hard shell, it doesn't knowingly grow a hard shell but instead develops all manner of random mutations. The vast majority of these will prove useless, or at least less valuable than a hard shell, and will eventually die out through natural selection. The hard shell – the variation which does provide greatest protection – will be selected and preserved in the genetic code of the species. However, over the last 50 years this process has been increasingly challenged for two main reasons, evidence for which is found in the fossil records.

Life on earth is estimated to be around 4.5 billion years old but fossil records show that, for the first 3.7 billion years, only single-celled life forms existed. All development towards the multitude of multicellular organisms we now see has, therefore, been compressed into the last 800 million years or so.[11] Today, there are estimated to be around 37 trillion cells in the average 21st century human-being. Mathematical modelling by computer scientists suggests that for us, and all other species, to have arrived at such genetic complexity through a genuinely random process of blind, trial-and-error variation, the timescales involved would have to be exponentially longer than the history of the universe. Even if we assume, as Darwin did, that every useful variation could be gradually added over millions of years, the ancestors of our now hard-shelled little hero would have had to cycle through every possible protective option available via random combinations of genes, to allow natural selection to eventually land upon the hard shell as its favoured option. However, rapid growth in genetic composition also leads to an exponential growth in the potential genetic combinations available, thereby enormously increasing the field of possible future random mutations. Add to this the extremely slow pace with which natural selection preserves or eliminates such modifications and evolution, as a genuinely blind, random and incremental process, looks like a highly implausible explanation. The planet simply isn't old enough for it to have been such a smooth, step-by-step development.

Secondly, the fossil records show that while the first multicellular organisms did appear around 800 million years ago, not much very happened for the next quarter of a billion years. Then, during the Cambrian explosion of 550 million years ago, almost all of the phyla which have ever existed were created, in relative terms, overnight. Within just a few million years the seas were swarming with an incredible array of life.[12] Then suddenly, some 245 million years ago, around 96% of all the species which have ever lived, died out in the Permian extinction.[13] Further mass extinctions, of varying sizes, have since taken place to the effect that over 99% of all species which have ever lived are now extinct.[14] Counter to Darwinian belief, evolution hasn't been a gradual process of natural selection acting on random variation, nor has it travelled along a smooth timeline. On the contrary, the fossil evidence suggests that the pattern of evolution has been more of a rollercoaster ride than a gentle stroll in the park. Throughout evolutionary history, long periods of relative stasis with hardly any genetic mutation have been punctuated by sudden periods of rapid innovation and cataclysmic extinction. Long cycles, sometimes hundreds of thousands of years with nothing to report, followed by dramatic 'sand-slide' transition phases, yielding a flurry of creative activity and the rapid emergence or extinction of a whole variety of species in a comparatively short time. It appears that self-organized criticality is central to the evolution of life itself.

Actually, this isn't all that dissimilar to our real life experience of innovation in the human sphere. Consider the invention of the internet, which has clearly caused a major global transition in how we access information, communicate with each other and perform other daily tasks such as shopping. The history of the internet can be traced all the way back to the 1950s, but not much happened with it for decades and it wasn't until the 1990s that it reached a state of criticality. Then suddenly, not only did it give us e-mails and websites, it also facilitated a wave of inventions which saw the creation of a whole raft of online businesses, many of which quickly succumbed to the bursting of the early dot.com bubble. Since then, the internet has continued to spark countless opportunities for the creation of new companies, some of which, such as eBay, Google, Facebook and Twitter, have fundamentally changed our lives. Yet the internet has also led to the diminishment, if not the extinction, of encyclopaedia, library memberships, letter writing, book shops, travel agents, bank staff, long-distance telephone calls, yellow pages directories, door-to-door selling, insurance brokers, newspaper sales, lonely hearts columns, top-shelf men's magazines and a whole variety of other products and services. Our communications 'ecosystem' has changed forever, creating a new set of powerful attractors, and will never, ever return to previous state cycles.

In the reductionist Darwinian worldview all live organisms, including human societies, evolve randomly by blindly generating alternatives to what currently exists, in the hope that fortunate environmental conditions will favour whatever they have cobbled together. New ideas are thrown against a cultural wall in the hope that something sticks. Progress proceeds incrementally, as natural selection acts to ensure the survival of the fittest ideas and the elimination of those which aren't so strong. While we might be able to point to odd examples of random innovation which have followed the Darwinian model, we may often find it difficult because they are rarely successful. We know intuitively that an organic worldview better reflects the reality of innovation in life. Most successful new ideas are actually formed by challenging current attitudes, assumptions or actions to create new directions of travel for our thinking. As such, they often emerge from within the very concepts they seek to replace. Concepts are generated, not in a void or vacuum, but in response to changing environmental conditions and born of an idealism which focusses us on the changes we wish to bring to our lives – idealism which is rooted in our values, morality and human spirit. New ideas are therefore invented via a combination of top-down *and* bottom-up influences, as we simultaneously reshape and adapt to our environment.

The organic worldview accepts the intrinsic connection between our inner and outer worlds, recognizing that an immanent order is shared by both which yields the flexibility for our co-created reality to unfold in a number of ways, yet restricts the possibilities to within a range of options. Whether biological or ideological, evolution is therefore not a random process but an unfolding of new potentialities which are restricted within finite parameters; parameters which are created by the local rules of living systems and the nature of the attractors encrypted within them. Critically, the idea or organism doesn't evolve in adaptation to a separate, external environment but co-evolves with its environment, in which it is an embedded, nested sub-system. Contrary to blind mutation, evolution is immanent within the structure of the organism itself and creative output – variation – doesn't happen randomly but as the result of self-organization and in the unpredictable patterns caused by criticality. Survival, however, is still not guaranteed because the outcome may or may not result in an environmentally advantageous adaptation for the organism. Although the odds are improved, the idea produced is still only one of several potentialities which could have unfolded, and there are also other organisms evolving and competing for limited resources within a shared environment. Environmental selection still takes place but, in the words of Stuart Kauffman, *'much of the order we see in organisms may be the direct result, not of natural selection but of the natural order selection was privileged to act on'.*[15]

The Reductionist's Dilemma

However, as insightful and intriguing as the challenge to Darwinism may be, it still doesn't resolve the reductionist's dilemma. If the wonders of life cannot be explained in terms of physical mechanics following a bottom-up process, how is growth generated and why do complex adaptive systems self-organize towards points of criticality? Core to answering these two questions is another which continues to baffle the reductionist scientist – how is form actually created? Organisms *can* ultimately be reduced to physics but the creation of concepts, creatures and cultures cannot be explained *only* in terms of physics. Although complexity science still has a way to go to identify a definitive set of shared principles under-pinning all adaptive systems, it is making progress. At the moment no-one can say for sure if form emerges in the same way in every case. All scien-tists can confirm is that there are a large number of such systems, they all have some key characteristics in common and there are some consistent patterns in how form unfolds.

Crucial to all complex adaptive systems are nodes and networks. Nodes could be neurons in a brain, cells in a body, flora in a food-web, ants in a colony or individuals in a community, but every living system needs nodes. Next, nodes need to be connected to other nodes in a non-linear network across which information can flow and feedback loops can amplify or dampen the effect of data transfer. Clearly, a Boolean network of connected light-bulbs isn't a live organism but it is, nevertheless, a useful tool with which to simulate such systems and identify the patterns which emerge at the global level, from the local rules programmed into each individual node. As well as discovering the phenomenon of self-organization, Stuart Kauffman found another fascinating feature of complex adaptive systems – specifically that the number of connections each node has to other nodes, makes a big difference. Too few connections and a system quickly freezes, unable to sustain even a few state cycles. Too many connections and a system behaves chaotically, unable to ever settle down into repeated, recognizable patterns.[16]

All living systems, in order to survive, must maintain a certain level of energy flowing through them to maintain their form. If the energy stops flowing – if the system freezes into stasis – they die. In order to grow, adapt or evolve to a higher level of complexity, an organism must increase the amount of energy it exchanges with its environment but without ever reaching the point where its pattern of organization become chaotic. Without a stable pattern of organization, form can no longer be maintained and, once again, the organism will die. Life, therefore, can only be maintained between the two extremes of stasis and chaos at which death is inevitable. To maintain a level of dynamic stability necessary for survival, all living systems must exhibit opposing tendencies towards orderly and flexible behaviour. In highly ordered systems, growth is restricted by low nodal connectivity, making it difficult for any perturbation to spread significantly and causing the entire system to be relatively insensitive to change. Conversely, in highly flexible systems with high nodal connectivity, small adjustments to initial conditions can lead to the sort of cascading change epitomised by the butterfly effect, enabling incremental growth during small 'sand slides' and the potential for step-change evolution during periods of high energy exchange. Computer simulations also show how systems shift between order and flexibility. Systems change from a flexible to a more ordered state by becoming more internally similar, as data converges onto a smaller number of attractors and feedback loops have a dampening effect on any information which runs counter to the direction of travel. Conversely, systems which move from an ordered to a more flexible state do so by becoming more internally dissimilar, as data diverges and feedback loops amplify novel information, causing the system to increase flexibility by seeking and establishing new attractors.

In living systems, change in either direction is achieved by opposing tendencies towards order, through self-regulation, and towards flexibility via self-creation. Self-regulation is linked to the tendency, inherent within all such systems, to self-organize into stable state cycles and to maintain this order via the dampening effects of negative feedback. This tendency is no more evident than in the phenomenon of homeostasis which, for example, maintains pH balance in blood, regulates the body temperature of mammals and holds the surface of the Earth in conditions conducive to life. Self-creation or '*autopoiesis*' is a theory of living systems, first developed by Chilean neuroscientists Humberto Maturana and Francisco

Varela at the University of Santiago, in which they concluded that the key characteristic of any living system is that it continually reproduces itself.[17]

Maturana and Varela posited that the three key components in the creation of form in a living system are pattern of organization, structure and process. Pattern of organization is the configuration of connections between nodes, such as the atoms in a tree, while its structure is the manifestation of those connections, the tree itself. Categories of things share basic organizational patterns even though each thing manifests as an individual entity. A tree shares an organizational pattern with other trees and, although different from each other in structure and ultimately in form, the similarity in their underlying patterns make them recognizable to us. Our brain is able to detect a 'family resemblance' and to categorize them as trees. Pattern and structure are also characteristic of inanimate objects in creating form, for example tables share underlying patterns of organization and structure which make them identifiable as tables. However, a table isn't a living organism and it is therefore process which distinguishes the living from the non-living. A table is a closed system whose only link to process is that it is in the process of disintegrating back to its constituent energy. By contrast, living systems process a ceaseless flow of energy through them, which they exchange with their environment and which maintains the on-going structured embodiment of their underlying pattern of organization, thereby maintaining life. Process provides the link between pattern of organization and structure and all three are highly interdependent. The process of life is the activity involved in maintaining the structured embodiment of a systems underlying pattern of organization.

In what became known as their Santiago theory, Maturana and Varela concluded that the process of life was ultimately the process of cognition or 'mind', although this represented a radically expanded interpretation of our usual definition of mind. In this conception, a brain is not necessary for cognitive processing and the simplest organisms are capable of perception and therefore of cognition. Lowly bacteria can recognize changes in the chemical composition of their environment and can change accordingly. Plants are able to orient themselves towards alterations in light and dark. All complex adaptive systems are capable of such cognition so, in this sense, have 'mind'.

In the human context, this is also much broader than what we might call thinking or consciousness but extends to the full embodiment of all our cognitive systems. In fact research shows that the nervous, immune and endocrine systems, which have traditionally been considered to be three separate systems in the human body, actually constitute one single cognitive network.[18] In the Santiago theory the relationship between mind and the human brain is clear. Mind is a process, the process of life. The brain is a structure which co-ordinates inputs from our embodied cognitive systems and through which the process of life flows. As physicist Fritjof Capra points out, the Santiago theory provided '*the first coherent, scientific framework that really overcomes the Cartesian split*'.[19] By explaining the role of cognitive process in perpetuating structural form, Maturana and Varela successfully reconciled mind with matter. Furthermore, by explaining the interdependence of underlying organizational patterns and structure, they successfully provided a bottom-up-top-down explanation for *how* form is created. Finally, by identifying the '*autopoietic*' or self-creating nature of living systems, they successfully explained *why* life is maintained. The purpose of life is to perpetuate life itself.

Knowing why life is created and how it is maintained in individual organisms, leaves only the question of how life evolves over time. Through the challenges to original Darwinism we know that life doesn't evolve smoothly over a steady timeline but instead progresses in jerky movements; aeons of relative stability being punctuated by periods of great creativity or catastrophe. As he experimented with Boolean networks, Stuart Kauffman made one further important discovery. As the number of connections in a network grows so too does the data flowing across it but, just prior to the tipping point at which a living system becomes chaotic, he found a 'sweet spot' during which the computational capability of the system is optimized. Although he didn't realise its significance at the time, Kauffman had identified a window of great opportunity for which the evocative term '*the edge of chaos*' would later be coined.[20]

Kauffman would also later confirm that what drives the evolution of complex adaptive systems at the edge of chaos, is their ability to increase their computational ability by increasing the rate at which information flows across their network and the rate at which they extract and encrypt valuable data, in order to better shape and adapt to their environment. This is as true of human systems as it is of plants and ants. Improved information processing is the hallmark of increasingly higher levels of complexity. As Norman Packard, one of the pioneers of complexity science and chaos theory, explains:

Survival has to do with gathering information about the environment and responding appropriately. Bacteria do that by responding to the presence or absence of certain chemicals and by moving. Trees communicate chemically too. Computation is a fundamental property of complex adaptive systems, which you'll remember is optimised at the edge of chaos. Any complex adaptive system can compute; that's the key point. You don't have to have a brain to process information in the way I am talking about.[21]

What Packard means by '*optimised at the edge of chaos*' is that the sweet spot, just before a system tips into chaos, represents a window of opportunity during which the system has maximal computational ability to evolve to a higher level of complexity, meaning an improved level of information processing. Everything in the universe is ultimately made of immaterial energy with the capability to morph into forms, many of which have already come and gone in the evolution of life but some of which have yet to evolve. To maintain their self-organizing capabilities, all living systems must continually exchange energy with their environment and it is this capability which enables such systems to evolve. Time spent at the edge of chaos is a period during which a system is optimized to compute environmental data and therefore achieves maximal evolvability. As such, it is a potential transition phase in which a system can create new patterns of organization, leap to new attractors and evolve new forms which can elevate and sustain the whole system on a higher plateau of computational or cognitive capability. In short, at the edge of chaos a system has the potential to evolve a superior mind. For a plant this could mean the ability to extract a new nutrient from soil, for an ant colony the capability to communicate new messages in the chemical trails they leave. For the individual mind it could mean an enhanced level of consciousness, and for human society the ability to elevate the global mind to a higher plane of integration and unity.

If life in the 21st century feels chaotic it is because we are living at the edge of chaos. We have been born during a period in which our human system has self-organized to a point of criticality, and the conflicts and catastrophes which fill our media channels are simply the sand slides of our age. Evolution requires maximal flexibility so, in order to heal itself, our world has necessarily become more like Somalia than Saudi Arabia. Over the last century, quantum theory and subsequent developments in complexity science have underwritten a gradual societal shift from a mechanistic to an organic worldview, the emergence of which accelerated significantly after World War II. Over the course of history, humans have experienced many major events which caused perspectival shifts but few of the magnitude of those which represented the zenith of scientific materialism. The dropping of atomic bombs on Hiroshima and Nagasaki were perhaps only rivalled by the Nazi death camps for the worldwide revulsion they created, as the epitome of the application of science and technology for the purpose of human cruelty. The Nazis were fuelled by a belief in social Darwinism and applied many of the tenets of the mechanistic worldview in their attempts to engineer an Aryan master race, and in their factory-like efficiency in exterminating anyone they considered to be culturally impure. Never before was the sickness of our species more self-evident.

Largely in reaction to these events, the organic worldview really started to gain traction after WWII. In the immediate post-war period, a large generation of 'Baby Boomers' were born to parents determined to ensure that their children would never have to experience the death and destruction they had just lived through. Although they never used the term, by the 1960s these young adults were the visionaries, poets, artists and authors of what we can now call the organic worldview. Inspired by Beat Generation writers such as Jack Kerouac, they were adventurous, creative and open to exploring new experiences in spirituality, sexuality and drug use. By rejecting materialism and by being staunchly anti-war, they sparked a liberalizing trend in American and Western culture, which would become core to the organic perspective and integrative monism. Although perhaps unaware of the values they had in common, activists were involved in a wide range of social, political and cultural campaigns, including the peace movement, environmentalism, civil rights, gender and sexual equality, the consciousness movement, an array of spiritual expressions from Eastern religions to yoga and meditation, plus the growth of organic food and alternative medicine. Although they didn't seem to be connected, even to activists, these movements were all rooted in a shifting perspective away from scientific materialism and towards a worldview which feels much less revolutionary and more deeply familiar to us, half a century later. When, in 1966, NASA's Lunar Orbiter 1 sent the first pictures of Earth from outer space, the images reputedly caused a sand slide all of their own in confirming the deep beauty of our planet, the essential oneness of its inhabitants and the fragile vulnerability of both. In doing so they reconnected humankind to our original impulse; that we are a part of nature not apart from it.

The organic worldview we have inherited is rooted in our deepest human intuition, yet has come full circle in being validated by modern science. It has once again enabled us to see the universe as a living organism in which everything is connected in ways we don't fully understand. It has allowed us to appreciate that we are essentially the same as other living organisms, sharing spiritual energy as our most fundamental substance. It has opened our minds to the discovery that mind is the process of life itself and that the purpose of all life is to perpetuate life. It has brought us to the dawning realization that the future of our species will be determined by the global mind we collectively create, which will leave a long legacy for generations to come. The organic worldview has necessarily brought our global human system to the edge of chaos in an attempt to heal the sickness endemic in our world, for it is only in this transitional space that we have the potential to evolve a superior mind, balanced in healthy equilibrium. Only at the edge of chaos do we find sufficiently fertile soil for the growth of personal consciousness and the co-creation of a dynamically stable culture, both of which are necessary for the successful integration of our species. What happens next is by no means guaranteed, although the options can certainly be outlined.

Looking Backwards and Forwards

Fear of change is a powerful human emotion designed to protect us, and our instinctive suspicion of cultural synthesis is not without solid foundation. History shows that integration in the past has often been a by-product of military conquest or colonization, rather than the result of any unifying vision for humankind. Painful oppression has too often been the lot of those lucky enough to survive, so we are right to be wary about the effects of globalization. Yet as a species it seems that we are destined to try to elevate our societies towards greater global unity, not simply because elites believe that there's money to be made but because it's inherent within our complex adaptive system to do so. Ultimately our systemic need to co-evolve with our environment to a higher plane of computational complexity, which in human terms means greater integration, has pushed us to the edge of chaos. The exact outcome is unknowable but there are three possibilities which are common to the development of all such systems.[22]

First, we might be successful although we would no doubt have to suffer some more growing pains in the process. Whether such pains are relatively small, in the form of bombs and bullets, or much larger like chemical warfare, is unknown. Nevertheless, breakthrough would necessarily lead to the strengthening of global governance and new unifying institutions in all spheres of global society. National governments would collaborate to harmonize aspects of state systems which currently cause division, and would enable greater freedom of movement across borders. People would become more exposed to other cultures and, although there would still be some friction, increased cultural blending would take place. Individuals would become more interconnected and begin to see other people, first and foremost, as human-beings and therefore part of their group. Nations would take more of an interest in the welfare of all humans rather than only those within their own domain. The world certainly wouldn't become one big utopian commune – there would still be plenty of squabbles, conflicts and even violence – but the overarching ethos would be one of healthy competition within a framework of co-operation, collaboration, respect and tolerance. In systems terms, global society would resettle down into a state of dynamic stability – full of opposing forces balanced within a range of equilibrium between order and flexibility – but on a new, higher plateau of individual consciousness and collective mind.

Alternatively we may instead suffer a breakdown, temporarily giving up on global unification and disintegrating back down into ethnic tribes, nation states or local alliances. Naturally this would cause division and enmity but each country, region or continent would settle back to a position of relative internal stability, albeit with a lower level of international co-operation than at present. Individuals and groups would initially become more insular, defensive and suspicious of each other, leading to inevitable skirmishes, but, over time, the interconnected nature of the modern world would force them back into contact with one another. Tensions and conflicts would certainly continue but, in due course, our global human system would once again self-organize back to a point of criticality at the edge of chaos. In short, while we would initially revert back to a new kind of Cold War which may last for a prolonged period, time would eventually bring us back to where we are today – ready to try again to evolve to a higher level of complexity through greater globalization.

The final option is unthinkable, yet we would be foolish to ignore its very real potential. In this scenario, our global system would tip over the edge into chaos and begin to disintegrate rapidly at every level of society – international, regional and national. Catastrophic warfare would ensue, with the probable use of chemical, biological and nuclear weapons. All unifying institutions and infrastructures would be abandoned and an aggressively defensive form of nationalism would become pervasive.

Indeed, nation states may themselves break down and new groups form, drawn along ethnic, class or religious lines. Individuals would retrench into walled havens of cultural homogeneity, fuelled by suspicion and hatred of the 'other'. In developed nations, ordinary people and minority groups would suffer as elites or majorities grab power, manipulating the remaining political and economic infrastructures to a 'survival of the fittest' ethos and for their own benefit. Those in developing nations would simply be left to die, starved of the international markets and aid support they need to survive. The global human population would be radically reduced and our environment irreparably damaged. Our species wouldn't necessarily disappear but survivors would face a barren future and their descendants a very long journey back to any semblance of civilisation.

The incredibly complex nature of the human system makes our future wholly impossible to predict. Within 15 years we will each be a node in a network of over 8 billion human-beings. The output of this system – our global mind – will therefore result from the interpenetration of 8 billion individual minds, each of which has 100 billion neuronal 'nodes' net-worked by at least 100 trillion synapses. The complexity of these two nested systems is quite literally mind-boggling. While we are all intimately involved, not one individual on Earth can control or accurately predict what will emerge at the global level, irrespective of what some commentators would have us believe. Yet such immense connectivity does present a great opportunity for a system whose ability to evolve to higher levels of integration is enhanced by its ability to rapidly process data across its network. Not only will we soon be 8 billion nodes strong but smart technology is exponentially increasing our ability to interact with each other, potentially providing the social synapses via which our cognitive evolution as a species can occur. Today more than 4 in 10 people worldwide have internet access with almost 9 in 10 in North America and over 7 in 10 in both Europe and Oceania.[23] Around a third of our global population has access to a smart phone and this figure will shortly exceed 2.5 billion people.[24] Facebook alone has more than 2 billion active users and over 500 million tweets are sent every single day. Technology is rapidly connecting us and we are also becoming more capable of being connected. Around 85% of the world's adult population can now read, almost three-quarters of all illiteracy is now found in only 10 countries and English is fast becoming the de facto global language, further enabling worldwide communication.[25] No-one can say for certain with how many degrees of separation we are all connected but when some individuals have over 100 million Twitter followers, it's perhaps already lower than the fabled seven.

As our world becomes smaller and data is increasingly democratised, each of us has an opportunity to shape culture in a way ordinary people have never had before, at any time in human history. Not only do social media increase our access to information, they also enable our voices to be broadcast to audiences unimaginable to even the most international of media outlets, just 20 years ago. In days gone by, only elites had access to mainstream communication channels while the masses remained silent, but now every individual has the potential to directly engage with the world and influence how the future unfolds. Social media undermine the power of the press, increasing transparency and enabling ordinary citizens to become amateur journalists and 'whistle-blowers'; exposing lies, de-bunking myths and unravelling the political spin to which we have become so accustomed. Scandals of all sorts, formerly kept beyond the gaze of public scrutiny by corrupt elites, are progressively being exposed, giving ordinary people greater insight into how our societies are actually run. Despite desperate attempts to control data, such transparency can only continue to increase. Of course, the medium itself is impartial so social media can just as easily be used to spread lies or promote anti-democratic acts such as terrorism. This is a necessary price to pay for freedom of information but it does lead to a deluge of data which requires a higher level of personal consciousness to process. Elevated individual consciousness is essential if the global mind is to successfully extract and encrypt the new learning needed, for us to co-create and adapt to cultural conditions which can bring peace and happiness.

Central to social media's synaptic role is its immediacy. Throughout history events have happened which later proved to be pivotal in shifting social attitudes, from the birth of Jesus to the fall of the Berlin Wall, but the speed at which they can influence culture is driven more by connectivity than by the events themselves. While, over the last couple of centuries, inventions such as the telegraph (1832), telephone (1876), television (1926) and satellite broadcast (1962) have certainly increased global connectivity, they all had limited capability in generating the sort of transformational change which the internet, and particularly social media, now have the potential to create. Social media places real-time information directly into the hands of individuals, rather than content being filtered by media corporations inevitably influenced by elites, so events are now much more likely to send cascading waves of change rippling across the human system than ever before. It's highly unlikely that the Arab Spring would have unfolded as it did without social media and the speed at which the '*Je Suis Charlie*' meme spread around the world, within hours of the Charlie Hebdo shootings in Paris, was simply unprecedented. Systems evolve to the edge of chaos because that's where they are optimized for the maximal data transfer they need to evolve to higher levels of complexity and, for the first time ever in human history, social media may now provide the synaptic connections required for our whole species to undergo just such a transformation.

Indeed, we may be on the cusp of what is perhaps only the fourth truly epochal revolution in human connectivity. The first was undoubtedly the development of language which offered a clear step-change in the ability of human-beings to share environmental information across a wider network. Language enabled us for the first time to co-ordinate group activities such as hunting, which were fundamental to our survival as a species, and to agree the rules and rituals which first bonded non blood-related humans together; a breakthrough essential to the development of all modern societies. Language also allowed us to share concepts such as past, present and future and to develop new cognitive skills like planning, both of which are characteristic of increased consciousness. Archaeological records show that by around 50,000 years ago we were burying our dead, building shelters, producing artworks and hunting large prey, all of which suggest a higher plane of social cohesion than is evidenced by earlier artefacts. The second transformation came around 5000 years ago in ancient Mesopotamia, when the Sumerians invented writing and enabled the conveyance of information in a manner much less restrictive than speech. Knowledge could be disseminated as far as people could travel and learning was only constrained by commonality of language, an issue gradually addressed as empires such as the Akkadian, Babylonian, Hittite and Egyptian dynasties expanded. The three Abrahamic monotheisms would probably have come to nothing without written scriptures and, without writing, the ancient Greeks couldn't have become authors of many of the foundational texts of Western and ultimately global culture. These classic works of Hellenic scholarship would be carried to the far reaches of the Roman Empire, disappearing for a thousand years during the Dark Ages but later resurrected during the third major transformation of the human system.

Beginning with the Renaissance, ending with the Enlightenment and encapsulating the Reformation plus Scientific, Philosophical and

Industrial Revolutions, our third elevation was enabled by another break-through in communication and connectivity – the moveable type printing press. First invented in China around 1000 years ago, it wasn't until it was introduced into mid-15th century Europe, by German publisher Johannes Gutenberg, that it facilitated a cascade of change throughout Europe and the wider world. The Gutenberg press enabled leaflets, pamphlets and books to be produced in mass quantities, thus connecting individual human minds at a pace never before experienced, and their content drove a major transition from one dominant worldview to another. Until the 15th century, creationism had reigned for a thousand years but over the next few centuries society would come to be controlled by the mechanistic perspective of scientific materialism, which remains pre-eminent, though on increasingly shaky ground, to this day. Now, smart technology and social media offer the potential to facilitate a fourth epochal transformation, enabling global culture to change faster than ever before.

Throughout the flux and flow of history, the human species has maintained an inexorable march towards global integration as populations have grown, empires have expanded and technological advancements have made the world ever smaller. During this time the pace of progress towards globalization has increased dramatically, as the duration of each transfor-mational era and the gap between such eras has shortened significantly. For 150,000 years we were hunter-gatherers living in families until, perhaps around 50,000 years ago, language enabled us to move beyond kin-based social units and to peacefully co-exist with strangers. However it wasn't until only 5000 years ago that our civilisations lived in cities and built empires, enabling writing to convey knowledge across time and space. It's only 500 years since the Renaissance began to liberate the rational mind from blind faith and, supported by the printed word, set humankind on the road to Enlightenment. Now, the history of the internet stretches back no more than 50 years, it's 25 years since the World Wide Web was first invented and only 15 years since smartphones became commonplace. Yet we are once again undergoing cultural convulsions which, like contractions in a womb, are becoming more regular and intense as we await another rebirth. At every stage in the long history of human development, not only have we been moving towards global integration but the information which has enabled our growth has necessarily been shifting in the opposite direction, with each transformational phase pro-gressively democratising data by widening its availability to the masses.

It is only the improved processing of environmental information across our network which enables us to evolve to higher levels of complexity, meaning increased computational ability and higher levels of cognitive integration. Critically, there's nothing we can do about it – it's immanent within our nature as a species to try to evolve and, while we haven't undergone any significant genetic shift in 200,000 years, culture enables us to grow far faster than genetics.

During the last century we have created a whole host of organisations to aid global governance, including the United Nations, World Bank, IMF, WTO, WHO, NATO, UNESCO and the International Criminal Court, all of which aim to embody and embed consistent aspects of culture, globally. Indeed, as eminent historian Arnold Toynbee observed:

> Our age is the first generation since the dawn of history in which mankind dares to believe it practical to make the benefits of civilization available to the whole human race'.[26]

Yet, in spite of the positive intentions of such institutions, a global society which is only connected at the level of governments or other elites lacks the cultural glue required to bond ordinary people together. Such a bond is required to overcome the many barriers to cultural integration which still exist.

While the tensions of the 21st century are simply the spasms we are experiencing as we try to evolve into one synthesised human society, it isn't an easy transition because there remains considerable resistance which may yet scupper our success. Resistance comes in the form of scientific materialism and the creationist worldview of the monotheisms, but all resistance is ultimately rooted in individual minds. While no-one can control the whole human system, we do each at least have some ability to influence our own minds. In particular, we can choose how we see the world and by adopting an organic worldview we greatly enhance our ability to contribute towards the creation of a coherent global culture. However, while a change of worldview is necessary, it is, on its own, insufficient. As we will explore in Part Two, the roots of our resistance lie in the opposing modes of the brain hemispheres and, in order to elevate our personal consciousness to the level required, we must overcome the many systemic flaws within our ancient brains.

PART TWO

THINKING

The Modus Operandi of an Ancient Brain

— 4 —

The Power of Opposites

ALBERT EINSTEIN famously proclaimed that he believed only two things to be infinite – the universe and human stupidity – but that he wasn't sure about the universe; a slightly tongue-in-cheek assessment of our cognitive abilities which belies the great advances we have made in explaining the wonders of the world. Yet, ironically, our understanding of the *source* of all our knowledge is the one area of scientific study about which we still know the least. According to Michael Tarr, Professor of Cognitive Neuroscience at Carnegie Mellon University, the basics of how the human brain works are still *'far more unknown than known'* and, despite great progress in the past few decades, the study of the human mind remains *'the last frontier of science'*.[1] We know that mind is the result of sensory data being processed across our neural network but, if a single brain contains one hundred billion neurons connected by one hundred trillion synapses, the potential number of connections is greater than the estimated number of atoms in the entire universe, so it's perhaps no surprise we know so little. In the view of Dr Pyotr Anokhin of Moscow University *'no man yet exists or has ever existed who has even approached using his whole brain'* and that includes this author, so if you are hoping that this chapter will elucidate which specific neurons connected with each other to generate the great idea or the weird dream you had last night, you are about to be very disappointed.[2] In the early 21st century such neuroscientific knowledge lies way beyond our grasp and, although complexity science does give us valuable insight into the underlying principles the brain shares with all other complex adaptive systems, we still know relatively little about how the brain actually operates as a neural network or how it produces what we experience as 'thinking'. Technologies such as functional magnetic resonance imaging (fMRI) and electroencephalography (EEG) do allow scientists to identify which parts of the brain show increased blood flow or electrical activity when a person is performing different types of mental task, but we still don't fully understand how the content of our mind comes to be as it is, or why we think the thoughts we do.

No doubt neuroscience will continue to make advances but such is the complexity of our cognitive system, there may never come a time when we can explain exactly how the hardware of the brain creates the software we experience as mind. Mind is the process of life and evolution gave us a brain to sustain life by creating mind, not necessarily to achieve the ultimate accomplishment of the human brain by fully understanding itself. Science can only take us so far and we certainly can't rely on benefitting anytime soon, from a genetic modification which might provide us with breakthrough insight. Although we may have enjoyed some sort of software upgrade around 50,000 years ago, with the evolution of language and sufficient self-consciousness to develop planning skills, we are still essentially operating with the same cognitive hardware as the very first *homo-sapiens*. However, given our seemingly unquenchable thirst for knowledge we might reasonably assume that an increased ability to encrypt and learn from environmental data forms a core part of our survival strategy, and that it is therefore culture rather than genetics which holds the key to our future. All culture begins and ends in the human brain and we are all capable of becoming a little more conscious than we currently are. If each of us could elevate our awareness and, in doing so, make better decisions, develop more beneficial attitudes and behave in ways which are more conducive to global peace, mutual prosperity and environmental sustainability, we could each help to shape a global mind which might yield a better life for everyone in our human system. Instead of simply adhering to the top-down cultural conditions imposed upon us by elites, we could exert greater bottom-up influence in reshaping the cultural content which so heavily influences the unconscious minds of all of us. A useful place to start is by exploring what we do know about how the human brain works and the mind it produces.

Scans show that the human brain operates at five different wave frequencies. In states of high alertness, such as experiencing adrenaline due to fear, it operates in gamma wave frequencies of 30-42 Hz. The wide-awake state required for conscious thought or concentration requires beta waves between 13 and 30 Hz. Alpha waves between 8 and 13 Hz are experienced when we are in a relaxed state of mind, such as day-dreaming or performing simple tasks like watching television. Theta waves between

4 and 8 Hz are typical of the type of light sleep which produces dreams but can also be accessed during creativity or meditation. Finally, delta waves below 4 Hz characterize both deep, dreamless sleep and the unconscious mind.[3]

As with all neuroscience, investigations into the implications are very much a work-in-progress so there remains much we don't know, but we do know that the boundaries between states are fluid rather than fixed and that different types of cognition may use a blend of various frequencies. It has also been established that while our unconscious mind can process up to 11 million bits of data per second, our conscious mind can only deal with up to 50 bits per second, so it is perhaps no wonder that between 90% and 99% of all our thinking is unconscious to us.[4] Energy efficiency is critical to our survival and the higher the brainwave frequency the more rapidly our finite energy resources become depleted. Conscious thought quickly burns through essential energy our 200,000-year-old brains would prefer to preserve, just in case we need to run away from lions on the African savannah. If we are walking and try to perform mental arithmetic which is in any way challenging, say multiplying 12 x 27, we instinctively stop walking to perform the calculation because both physical and mental exercise draw on the same energy source, so we stop performing one task to divert energy to the other. Evolution designed our brains to enhance our survivability, not to perform calculus while running a marathon, so energy conservation is built deeply into our human system. The concentration required for conscious cognition is effortful and therefore energy depletive, and expending mental energy isn't simply a saying but our reality – when exercising cognitive effort blood glucose levels in our central nervous system are reduced, making us feel tired.[5] Tiring activities are ultimately unpleasant to us so we are all genetically programmed to avoid conscious thinking whenever possible. By automating as many cognitive processes as possible we are able to maximise the energy available for life enhancing physical activities, such as hunting or escaping from predators.

Nowadays, of course, we live less precarious, more sedentary lives, so we do have spare cognitive capacity to increase our consciousness, but to do so we must first overcome the natural tendency of a brain which is still far more suited to chasing gazelles than to creating cultures which can bring peace to a warring world in the 21st century. Unfortunately we can't change our genetics, so the challenge for us all is to overcome the barriers presented by how our brains work, in order to bring about the cultural change we need to bring forth a coherent future for our species.

The Two Hemispheres

It was established by the ancient Greeks that the human brain has two distinct hemispheres connected by the corpus callosum – a bundle of some 300 million nerve fibres – and, ever since, philosophers have speculated about the evolutionary purpose of this intriguing feature. However, it was only in the early 1960s that we first gained any scientific evidence for how the brain actually operates and, in particular, about the differences between the two hemispheres. Roger Sperry and Joseph Bogen surgically separated the corpus callosum of patients with severe epilepsy in an attempt to alleviate their symptoms, and, by introducing stimulus to each hemisphere post-surgery, were able to identify that each attends to the world in a radically different manner.[6] In the years which followed, thousands of books and articles were written on the brain hemispheres – unfortunately many of them speculative and some downright bizarre. The spectrum of nonsense ran from the benefits of 'right-brain' sex to the culinary delights of 'left-brain' cooking, and such literature promoted an urban myth that the two hemispheres operated separately, were each responsible for different functions and that individuals could either be 'right-brained' or 'left-brained'. A backlash against such baloney then led to equally spurious claims that there was no difference at all in how the two hemispheres operated. As is so often the case, the reality lies somewhere between the polar extremes.

More recently, fMRI and EEG scans have provided a clearer picture of what actually goes on inside the brain when we are performing different cognitive functions, and, contrary to urban myth, there is no evidence that the left brain deals exclusively with words and logic or that the right brain is solely responsible for ideas and imagination. Indeed both fMRI and EEG confirm the full involvement of both hemispheres in almost all brain functions. The frontal lobes on both sides serve planning and organizing, the central areas of each impact movement and body sensations, the back parts of both hemispheres control vision, and the lower areas on each side activate and regulate emotions.[7] This shouldn't really come as a surprise as the two hemispheres have a lot in common. Not only are they connected by the corpus callosum but also by all of the lower brain structures including the limbic system, and they share the central nervous system, cerebellum, brain stem and spinal cord. They also share the same energy source in the food we supply them, the same blood and the same hormones. Finally, they share the same experiences and both are aware of those experiences. Each hemisphere of the brain plays a role in almost all of our thoughts and, therefore, in our subsequent behaviour. As psychologist Robert Ornstein confirms *'there is almost nothing that is regulated solely by the left or right hemisphere'*.[8]

However, fMRI and EEG scans also confirm that the two hemispheres do not perform the same functions or operate in the same way and, although neither works alone, different cognitive tasks do not produce symmetrical patterns of electrical activity or blood-flow in each half of the brain. While both hemispheres are always involved, they are definitely involved differently from one another. Unfortunately, neither fMRI nor EEG are sufficiently sophisticated to provide analysis beyond fairly rudimentary maps, so an in-depth explanation of the distinct neuronal activity of each hemisphere is not currently available to us. Nevertheless, evolution gave us two hemispheres for a reason – specifically to optimise our chances of survival – so they necessarily attend to the outer world in different ways, each processing the data they receive in a manner distinct from the other. The two halves of our brain are therefore not interchangeable, nor do they do the same job – that simply wouldn't make evolutionary sense. A divided brain was present in the very first mammals, long pre-dating the arrival of human-beings on our planet, and according to Ornstein *'the division is based on a way of approaching the outside world that evolution worked out long before it thought of us'*.[9]

Although the functional separation of left and right hemispheres can no longer be taken literally, the differences between them are, nevertheless, sufficiently marked and well-established to remain highly useful models of reality. Indeed, a wealth of research does prove conclusively that although neither hemisphere deals exclusively with any single cognitive function, they do generate two very different modes of thinking. I will therefore continue to use the distinction on this basis, and will use the terms 'left mind' and 'right mind' to describe the contrasting cognitive modes which have their roots in the hemispheric differences. Even if both sides are in some way involved in almost everything we process, our mind still emerges from the interaction of these two contradictory yet complementary approaches which, as we will discover, leverage the power of opposites to enable our survival. To accord with scientific logic, dual brain hemispheres must have evolved in mammals to provide an evolutionary advantage to the holder, helping them to survive ahead of other species. According to Ornstein and many others, this advantage lies in the balance between the independence and interdependence of each hemisphere. Both hemispheres collaborate in helping us to make sense of the world, but they do so in opposite ways and our evolutionary advantage lies in the superior ability of our species to leverage these opposing forces, to create the higher levels of thinking required for our species to progress. Our thinking is the net effect of these contrary cognitive impulses, so it should come as no surprise that the global mind – which emerges in the form of culture from our interactions with other human minds – also shares this characteristic.

The source of these impulses lies in the dual structure of the human brain. Ornstein explains that while the right hemisphere provides the *'context'* of our lives by painting the 'big picture' of what we perceive, the left hemisphere creates the *'text'* by breaking our experiences down into their constituent parts. Each hemisphere therefore produces very different interpretations of the same phenomena and widely dissonant explanations for the same events. At the very heart of this strange modus operandi lies a fundamental organizing principle of the two hemispheres, which ultimately has a massive influence on how we interpret the world and how we act as a result. Both perceive holons, but our left mind automatically takes a narrower focus and is therefore oriented towards looking inward or downward, from holon to part (or lower holon). Conversely, our right mind takes a broader focus and is oriented towards looking outward or upward, from part to higher holon. As unremarkable as this may seem, it is impossible to overemphasise the impact this simple operating principle has on everything which follows from it – which is ultimately everything we perceive, everything we think, everything we do and everything we collectively create in our human societies.

This operating model long predates human-beings and is shared by the brains of all mammals. In its most simple expression it is a mechanism designed by evolution to keep us alive. As we encounter the outer world, our right mind is oriented towards 'zooming out' from smaller to larger holons, paying broad vigilant attention and with an emphasis on noticing any changes in our environment which may present a threat to our well-being. Simultaneously, our left mind is oriented towards 'zooming in' from holon to part, focussing more narrowly on the object of our attention and seeking to interpret its identity and meaning. Immediately, we can see the evolutionary benefit in such a dual approach and why this would be useful in helping us, or any other creature, to survive. With a narrow focus we enhance our chances of finding and catching a source of food, while with a simultaneous wide focus we also reduce our likelihood of becoming prey to a larger predator. Similarly, if we are approached by a stranger it is in our evolutionary best interests to accurately distinguish friend from foe, so while our left mind focusses in on the stranger's mouth, ready to receive and interpret the spoken word, our right mind is scanning for non-verbal indicators which may provide an early warning of malicious intent, such as a scowl, the clenching of fists or the narrowing of eyes.

So in all cognitive processing, while both hemispheres are deeply involved they do not perform the same function. That wouldn't make sense because all processing is energy depletive, so any duplication of effort would never be in our best interests. Instead, our brain divides the task and each half plays a clear and distinct role. While both hemispheres always participate, they do so in entirely opposite ways with each approaching and processing the same data in a contrary, yet complementary, manner. As with all complex adaptive systems, the power of opposites is central to the creation of mind and to the conditions of dynamic stability we need to sustain life. We require the talents of both sides of our brain to piece our world together coherently and it is only when they are working in harmony that they function as fully as nature intended. Neither side of the brain works well without the other and to maintain a healthy mental state we need both minds to stay within a range of equilibrium of each other. Indeed, mental illness can be caused by exposure to prolonged or significant conditions of disequilibrium between the brain hemispheres. In the words of Robert Ornstein, *'we need the text of our life to be in context'*.[10]

Nowadays we don't often need to scan the horizon for predators or fight off malevolent strangers, but the basic modus operandi described above still dictates how we process everything we encounter. For example, our dual approach applies to verbal as well as visual stimuli. When we listen to someone speak, our left mind focusses in on the words spoken, concentrating on their syntax to derive literal meaning from what we hear. Meanwhile, the right mind takes a broader focus to decipher the more subtle, non-literal elements of verbal communication which implicitly convey meaning, such as cadence, rhythm, pitch or inflection, as well as interpreting non-verbal cues, like facial expressions and physical gestures, to further enhance our comprehension. It was via split-brain experiments that Sperry and Bogen first discovered that anyone with a non-functioning right hemisphere – so able to use only their left brain – could grasp the literal meaning of words but was left dumbfounded by non-literal communication.[11] They found that while a simple request such as *'please pass me the bottle'* could be fully understood, a very subtle variation such as *'could you pass me the bottle?'* would elicit an affirmative response but no subsequent action, because only the right hemisphere can determine that the latter statement has the same intended meaning as the former. Similarly, a metaphor such as *'conscience is a man's compass'* is entirely unintelligible to the left hemisphere and only the right hemisphere can decode its figurative meaning.

The Holistic Right Mind

Perhaps the most fascinating discovery of all was that the right hemisphere is far more capable of processing left-mind thinking, than is the case in reverse. It is widely known that each side of the brain processes the sensory data and drives the motor skills of the opposite side of the body, but split-brain research also showed that while the left hemisphere can *only* attend to our right side, the right hemisphere can attend to both left *and* right sides.[12] When asked to copy a simple drawing of a clock face, right-hemisphere stroke patients – who were solely dependent on their left hemisphere – only drew the right-hand side of the clock and completely missed out the left-hand side and its numbers. By contrast, patients with comparable left-hemisphere damage, who were solely dependent on a healthy right brain, drew the whole clock face with all of its numbers. Reliance solely on the left hemisphere also resulted in patients failing to read the left-hand side of their newspaper, failing to wash or shave the left side of their face and even failing to dress the whole left side of their body. Reliance solely on the right hemisphere did not produce symmetrical results and patients were still able to maintain a whole perspective. While the left hemisphere is therefore narrowly concerned with only the right side of the body, the right hemisphere remains concerned with the whole body and performs a synthesising role which integrates both left and right. Although it doesn't have the same sharp focus or precision skills as the left mind, the right mind can perform more left mind tasks than vice versa.

In *The Master and his Emissary,* Dr. Iain McGilchrist offers powerful evidence that it is primarily via the right hemisphere through which we are embodied in the outer world, and explains that this may be rooted in the physiology of the brain.[13] Although the two hemispheres are physically similar they are actually asymmetrical, containing different levels and configurations of synaptic connectivity. While neurons in the left hemisphere are relatively more intra-hemispherically connected, neurons in the right hemisphere are more inter-hemispherically connected, plus more strongly linked to the limbic system, the central and peripheral nervous systems, the spinal cord and the brain stem. In other words, while the right hemisphere is more strongly connected to the other parts of the brain structure, the left hemisphere is more strongly connected to itself. The right hemisphere's more powerful connections to our senses, plus greater synaptic links to our unconscious emotions, intuitions and desires, may account for its broader focus and outward-looking, contextual orientation, compared to the more narrow focus and inward-looking, self-referring nature of the left hemisphere.

These differences in synaptic connectivity, along with evidence from the clock face exercise, are also consistent with opposing dualistic and monistic approaches. The left hemisphere is relatively more independent than the right hemisphere, which is more interdependent, and this rather odd configuration enables us to see the world as consisting of polar opposites, while simultaneously understanding that the polarities are actually connected. In simple terms, if we consider any polarity such as hot and cold, the left hemisphere 'sees' two distinct and separate taps – one marked 'hot' and the other marked 'cold' – while the right hemisphere recognizes the polarities but 'sees' only one mixer tap, which can deliver hot or cold at either extreme but also countless temperature blends between poles. The left mind is therefore the seat of our dualism while the right mind perceives one monistic whole and, as a consequence, they don't even 'see' each other in the same manner. While they are each 'aware' of the other in the sense that they are synaptically connected, the relative independence of the left mind causes it to 'see' the right mind as separate and distinct from itself. The left mind processes all experience in terms of polar opposites so, from its 'point-of-view', what it does and what the right mind does are diametrically opposed. Conversely, to the more interdependent right mind, the left mind is simply a complementary part of the same holon to which it belongs – a yang to its yin. While the right mind appreciates dualism and the differences between what each mind does, its orientation is towards leveraging the power of opposites to synthesise both perspectives into one unified and harmonious whole.

In this sense, the left mind's lens – seeing two distinct, opposite entities – is actually nested within the right mind's perspective which, while acknowledging the distinction, sees them as two parts of an integrated whole. This rather strange, lop-sided relationship is difficult to grasp but is fundamental to how our brains function effectively. The left mind focusses narrowly and concerns itself with only the right side of the body but because the right mind focusses more broadly and 'thinks' holistically, it not only operates the left side of the body but also takes overarching responsibility for the whole body. This explains why it is more widely capable than its partner, why it could draw the whole clock face and why, for example, the right mind can interpret both the literal *and* non-literal meaning of words, while the left mind can only interpret literal meaning. Our right mind also operates across a wider range of brain-wave frequencies than the left mind. For example, during all of our waking hours our more broadly-focussed right mind continually scans our environment for danger. Were it to do so consciously, it would rapidly exhaust our energy resources so the right mind performs this duty in the lower alpha or theta states, and thereby acts as the primary conduit to the delta state of the unconscious. Furthermore, while our dualistic left mind is the source of our competitive impulses, our monistic right mind is the source of our desire for co-operation. In any ecosystem, organisms must alternate between competitive and co-operative behaviour to survive, but the two are not equally valuable to either the individual or the collective. At any level of holon, a healthy system requires competition to take place within an overarching spirit of co-operation. In all of the above examples, the right mind takes a wider approach, plays a larger role and is more broadly capable than the left mind, while the narrower left-minded perspective is always nested within the more holistic right-minded worldview. However, it still wouldn't make evolutionary sense for the right mind to be able to do everything the left mind can do, nor to do it as well as the left mind does it. So while the right mind is more powerful overall, the left mind always remains superior in certain areas.

Its broader focus and stronger synaptic links to our embodied senses lead us to first engage the outer world through our right mind, which is constantly vigilant for novelty in our external environment.[14] Consequently, it is a natural explorer which is always open to new experiences and, while part of its role is to protect us, it is less cautious than our more risk-averse left mind. Its outward orientation means it is embedded in the 'real world' which is timeless and constantly changing, making it

comfortable with ambiguity and confident in its ability to interpret whatever it comes across. Experiencing the world 'live' leads it to prioritise
living organisms over inanimate objects, to perceive them as individual
holons and to become highly attuned to the fluid, immaterial nature of
relationships between them. Its orientation from lower to higher holon
makes it keenly aware of the context within which experienced phenomena co-exist, bringing a 'big picture' perspective which is consistent with
its holistic focus and integrative tendencies. Its preference for organisms
over objects lead it to value qualities over quantities and emphasise
aesthetics over utility, plus, strongly connected to the limbic root of
our emotions, it is more reliant on feelings, instincts and intuitions in
interpreting what it experiences. On these many bases our right mind
sends a constant stream of environmental data to our left mind, which, in
order to control and process it, must first 're-present' the information as
an abstraction.[15]

The Ordered Left Mind

It does so by removing information from its real world context and by then
fragmenting, categorizing, prioritizing and memorizing those elements it
considers important. In doing so, the left mind enables us to make sense
of the chaotic outer world by bringing order to the riotous cacophony of
data experienced by the right mind, proving that each hemisphere plays a
distinct role in maintaining dynamic stability within our complex cognitive
system. While the right mind is deeply embedded within the flexible
freedom of the outer world, our left mind brings essential structure by
creating a parallel inner world of mental models, based on associative
memories. This critical operation allows us to build neural pathways which
ensure we don't always have to interpret every new experience from
scratch, but can instead rely on our powers of recall. To enable this
fantastic function, our left mind creates chains of neural connections
and builds them into even larger schematic frameworks, which it commits
to long-term memory for our use again and again over a whole lifetime.
When we pick up a nail, the association our brain automatically
makes with a hammer is extremely useful to us. Life would be incredibly
inefficient if we didn't know instantly that a sock goes on our foot but
instead had to work it out, through trial and error, every morning. By
memorizing associative connections between separate categories, like
hammers and nails or socks and feet, our left mind brings essential order

to our lives by providing a panoply of simple 'rules' we can live by, such as 'socks go on feet'. In the anarchic outer world every single sock is unique but our left mind's ability to group them all together, and to then memorize associations between categories, is very valuable to us whenever we want to get dressed or recall brands of beer, types of bird or countries in Africa.

Categorization is the left mind's energy-efficient tool for simplifying the vast richness of the outer world experienced by the right mind, in which abstract categories such as 'dogs' don't exist, only each individual canine we encounter. It is not in our interests to devote valuable energy to processing the myriad differences which distinguish one dog from another, so our left mind serves us well by decontextualizing each animal and by allocating it to a category it calls 'dogs'. Categories therefore act like neural whirlpools towards which all new experiences are attracted, enabling associative memories to be made at the category level rather than the specific level. Categorization allows us to make simplified but useful generalizations about all category members without having to recall the detail of each individual entity's uniqueness. Dogs can be generically associated with sticks rather than having to associate specific dogs with specific sticks, which would involve far too much energy-depleting effort. Dogs and sticks can also be further connected, in long chains of associative memories and vast schematic frameworks, with leads, parks, walks, barking, food, loyalty, cats, wolves or whichever other associations spring to mind for each of us.

Useful associations such as dogs and 'sharp teeth' also help to keep us safe, although it's worth noting that not all 'memories' are necessarily based on past experience. We don't need to have been bitten to know that dogs can bite. Many of the generalizations which give us useful knowledge or protect us by providing the rules via which we live our lives, are actually taught to us by culture. Cultures create idioms such as 'look before you leap', to inculcate valuable learning which prevents us from having to endure first-hand experience of events which may threaten our wellbeing. We all know fire can burn yet most of us don't have the scars to prove the authenticity of our knowledge. Anthropologists disagree whether our fear of snakes is genetic or cultural but a fear of dogs clearly isn't encrypted in our DNA. Nevertheless, such a phobia is not uncommon. For some people this may be the direct result of painful personal experience, but for many it is just as likely to be the outcome of overzealous parenting and the vicarious transmission of their own fears. Irrespective of the source, if our mind comes to associate dogs with biting, even when there is no experiential basis for such 'memories', they can feel just as real as genuine past experiences. Thus, associative memories and associative feelings become intertwined. The left mind comes to collaborate with the right mind in creating a coherent narrative, where the spontaneous feelings processed via our right mind 'make sense' to the schematic rules-based left mind, irrespective of whether the narrative reflects outer-world reality or authentic experience.

It is our brain's ability to weave such patterns of connectivity across our neural network which creates a powerful relationship between memory and cognition. The storage capacity we would require to remember every word of every conversation, or every contour on the face of every friend, would simply soak up far too much essential energy. Our memory, therefore, doesn't act like a bank vault we visit every time we wish to recall an event, where we extract an exact replica of our past experience from a storage box. Instead, we retain only a small gist of what happened, which acts like a grain of stimulus setting off a cascade of pre-associated connections across our neural network and reweaving the whole memory again from scratch.[16] Each recollection is never a verbatim version of a prior experience but a recreated interpretation of our own perceived reality. This is a valuable energy-saving device which is essential to our survival. Our left mind deconstructs data and converts it into unconscious memory and we are smart animals because we are capable of reweaving unconscious memory back into conscious information, whenever we need to.

Gists and generalizations are therefore essential to how our left mind operates and it is no co-incidence that the left hemisphere is also the seat of our language abilities. We are so familiar with words it is easy to forget they are merely a man-made invention which are abstract referents for real-world phenomena, rather than the phenomena they describe. As such, they play very well to the left mind's preference for decontextualized categorization. The word 'cat' clearly isn't an actual cat but simply a word our left mind recalls whenever our outer-world embedded right mind experiences a real, live feline. While our sensorial right mind processes a cat as a living organism, our left mind processes it as a 'thing' – an abstract referent for a living organism – enabling us to 'make sense' of what we encounter and bring it under our control. It does so by literally re-cognizing the data it receives from the right mind and by spotting 'family resemblances' between the pattern of organization which gives a feline form and a pattern of organization rewoven from associative memory, thus making a connection between the 'thing' and the word it gives to that particular category of 'thing' – cat. So while both left and right minds do experience the real cat, the ways in which they each process the same phenomenon lead to radically different interpretations.

Similarly, mathematical symbols are also abstractions used to explain relationships between real-world phenomena, and are principally manipulated in the left mind. While the right mind does play a role in computation, its broader focus can only provide a sense of whether or not a solution is of the right scale. Only the left mind can brings its sharp focus and fondness for abstract symbols to deduce a definitively correct answer. This difference in approach towards both words and numbers, creates a markedly different level of expectation in each mind with regards to certainty of outcome. The real outer world is ever-changing and because our right mind experiences it anew each day, it accepts a high degree of flux and flexibility. Our left mind, however, largely inhabits an ordered, schematic world of its own making, so much prefers the reassurance of absolute certainty. Such is its narrowness of focus, tests show that the left mind can only interpret one single meaning for each word in a sentence, while the right mind, with its broader lens and ease with ambiguity, is able to simultaneously comprehend multiple meanings for individual words.[17] This desire for singularity of outcome and the need for there to be only one 'right' answer are highly characteristic of the left mind which, unlike the right, is deeply uncomfortable with uncertainty. Once again this difference is rooted in left-mind dualism and its binary logic via which things are either/or. Water is either hot or cold, a mathematical solution is either right or wrong and a 'thing' is either a cat or it's not. Only the right mind can deal with nuance, ambiguity and 'things' which don't fit neatly into clear categories or simultaneously belong to multiple categories.

Never is the left mind more comfortable than when it is manipulating the modern world's favourite abstraction of real-world values – money. Like words and mathematical symbols, money is a man-made invention which allows us to decontextualize outer-world entities by replacing their qualitative values with quantifiable value. Through their conversion into abstract referents, such as $ or £, we extract goods and services from the outer world and bring them into the schematic world of the left mind, where quantities count for more than qualities and where fluid, subjective uncertainty can apparently be replaced by fixed, objective certainty.

This can cause a problem where living organisms are involved and, in particular, when human qualities are replaced by fiscal quantification as the primary assessment of value. When we de-contextualize we automatically de-personalize, which plays well to the abstract categorizing of the left mind but jars with the sentiments of a right mind which, with stronger links to the limbic source of our emotions, is more oriented towards human relationships. Embodied in our senses and embedded in the outer world, the right mind relates to people as unique individuals rather than members of a category, and is therefore more capable of empathy. Indeed, fMRI scans show that the same neurons in the right anterior cortex are activated equally when we hurt ourselves or if we see someone else experiencing the same pain.[18] Left-mind categorization and dualism are therefore protective mechanisms which insulate us from such emotional distress. An abstract category, such as 'refugees', enables us to homogenize individuals within a group and to see them as a faceless collective who are 'other' to ourselves. Our left mind therefore processes their deaths dispassionately as stories and statistics, but as soon as we see the body of a drowned three-year-old child washed up on a Turkish beach, our right mind automatically lights up like Manhattan at Christmas and we cannot stop ourselves from feeling genuine emotions such as sadness and grief. Its enhanced capacity for empathy therefore makes our right mind dominant in forming bonds with other human-beings, where its superior ability to interpret and convey non-verbal communication gives it an advantage in creating emotional connections. Consequently, our right mind attaches higher value to anything which provides emotional meaning, while the left mind prioritises functional and financial value in its assessment of experienced phenomena. Both hemispheres create memory, but while the left mind deals preferentially with the facts, figures and rules which form its schematic frameworks and bring order to our world, the right mind deals primarily with memories which are personal, providing the unconscious mind with a rich network of associative feelings. In fact, several studies suggest that the left hemisphere codes memories for all non-living things, while the right hemisphere may only code memories for living things.[19]

In summary, while all of our thinking always involves both hemispheres, the approach they each take to processing exactly the same phenomena are radically different and diametrically opposed.

Contrary yet Complementary

Greater interhemispheric and limbic connectivity enables our right mind to be more embedded in the outer world and more in touch with our embodied senses, unconscious emotions, passions and intuitions. Its broader focus and outward orientation provide the big picture aspects our lives, appreciating the deep interdependencies of all living organisms in our ecosystem. Anchored in the real world, it is a fearless wanderer in a timeless and ever-changing landscape, necessarily accepting the flux, flow and ambiguity of all experienced phenomena. Our right mind sees every-thing it encounters as a unique, individual entity and leverages its instinc-tive empathy to build relationships through co-operation; valuing qualities and aesthetic form above quantities and utilitarian function, while coding for memories which provide emotional meaning. Its monistic lens and overarching orientation towards integration, allow it to appreciate the full richness of the universe and to blend material with immaterial, explicit with implicit and, ultimately, right mind with left mind.

By great contrast, our left mind processes the same environmental data very differently. More narrowly and inwardly focussed, it decon-textualizes all information in abstract form before deconstructing, cate-gorizing and prioritizing. It uses man-made referents, such as words, numbers and symbols, to homogenize real-world entities, bringing essential order. By building associative schemata, it enables patterns in all new data to be re-cognized against prior knowledge, providing a reassuring sense of certainty and safety. Its relative independence from embodied feelings enables us to exercise a degree of dispassionate detach-ment and to make clear, rational decisions based on binary dualism. Its preference for inanimate objects over living organisms and for creating hierarchies between categories, cause us to prioritise the material over the immaterial, the explicit over the implicit and the verbal over the non-verbal.

None of us could, nor would we ever want to, live solely in the very different worlds created by each hemisphere and our experienced reality is inevitably a blend of the two. On its own, the world of the right mind would feel like a tsunami of sensory data, which would engulf us afresh each day. With weaker links to the essential structures of associative schemata, our right mind would simply be unable to make sense of its many experiences and, like less intelligent creatures, we would be restricted to using only our embodied emotions to inform our responses to sensory stimuli. On its own, the world of the left mind would be a cold, soulless place full of order, categories, objects and rules which may make us feel safe but, detached from the outer world, would be devoid of the emotional warmth, meaning, relationships or risks which constitute much of what it means to be human. To maintain a healthy balance we need to blend the two and, with its holistic approach, broader capabilities and synthesising qualities, only our right mind is able to adequately mix left with right.

For this reason, our cognitive processing follows an imperceptible right-left-right sequence, whereby the right mind interprets sensory data then passes it to the left mind for assessment against pre-existing associative schemata.[20] The left mind then returns processed data to the right mind for the formulation of an integrated, whole-mind response. If we consider a conversation this sequence makes intuitive sense. We process non-verbal and non-literal communication in the right hemisphere, while the left hemisphere interprets the literal meaning of spoken words. The left mind must then formulate the words and syntax of a response but for our answer to be delivered in sync with appropriate intonation and body language, the right mind must be re-engaged to weave the verbal and non-verbal seamlessly together. The left mind, in reductively processing decontextualized and abstracted data necessarily leaves it fragmented and lifeless. It is only via reintegration in the right mind that we are capable of bringing it to life once again, in the synthesised, nuanced and animated manner required for re-engagement with the outer world.

Naturally, much of this blending takes place unconsciously so can be heavily influenced by culture as well as personal predisposition. We may also encounter problems when we consciously try to blend opposing impulses to form coherent and appropriately balanced outputs, not least because our energy-efficient brains are genetically programmed to avoid tiresome cognition unless absolutely necessary. This is but one of a whole host of systemic barriers to high quality thinking which are inherent to our ancient brains, and which we will explore in the next two chapters. For now, we will focus on one specific issue which undermines our individual ability to optimize thinking and the collective ability of our species to build cognitively balanced cultures.

Brain Dominance

We all have two brain hemispheres for good evolutionary reasons and, even if we wanted to, none of us are capable of thinking with only one half – we all automatically use both sides of our brain in everything we do. Each hemisphere takes a different approach, has different skills, performs a different role and our thinking is always the emergent output of their interplay so, in this sense at least, we always employ whole-brain thinking. However, just because both hemispheres are always involved doesn't mean we always optimize our thinking by using each side to their full capability. Like everything involving the brain, the picture is complex. We are all perfectly capable of both right and left-mind processing but different types of task require different styles of thinking, so the cognitive blend we use may vary from day to day, hour to hour, even minute to minute and can constantly oscillate across the spectrum depending on what we are doing. However, tests show that we all have a genetic 'wiring' from birth and that we normally develop an overall preference for taking a particular approach to the cognitive challenges we face. From an early age we habitually use certain neural pathways to solve particular problems and, over time and through repeated use, these pathways – patterns of connections between neurons – become more and more established, just as a real-world path would become more clearly defined as the result of regular traffic. We are attracted towards tasks we enjoy doing and those we are good at, and the more we do them the more capable we become. We are rewarded for our competence in the form of pleasurable chemicals, such as dopamine, being released into our brain, thus reinforcing both practice and preference. Over time, therefore, while we remain capable of balanced cognition, most of us do develop a dominant preference for either our left or right mind.

Ned Herrmann spent over 50 years researching brain dominance, conducting hundreds of thousands of profiling tests all over the world.[21] He found that few adults end up being perfectly balanced in how we think. What often begins as a subtle preference at a young age becomes strengthened as we grow older and develops into a sort of automatic default setting in adulthood. We are all born with an innate capacity for certain cognitive skills, such as analysis or empathy, but small initial biases can stimulate feedback loops in our neural system which get amplified or dampened over time, resulting in core strengths or weaknesses. Our chosen profession can act like an attractor for our strengths, further reinforcing the dominance of our preferred style. For example, if we enjoy the left mind's manipulation of numbers we may pursue a career in accountancy, bolstering both our numeric skills and our left-mind dominance. Similarly, nursing often attracts people with an already well-developed sense of empathy, further boosting their right-mind bias.[22]

However, Herrmann also found that many people do find themselves working in roles which require a dominant cognitive style which isn't aligned with their personal preference. In such situations, although we may still have the ability to do the job to an acceptable standard (because we can all use both hemispheres), our motivation, productivity and the quality of our work may be lower than in a role offering greater alignment. Job satisfaction is almost always highest when our role gives us the opportunity to regularly engage our preferred cognitive mode and, thereby, give full release to our potential. The reverse is also true. On-going exposure to less-preferred thinking styles have been shown to increase anxiety, deliver low job satisfaction, create unhappiness and even lead to long-term mental health issues. Although, overall, Herrmann did find a positive correlation between most people's preference and their profession, he also found thousands of individuals in jobs requiring dominant cognitive modes which were inconsistent with their preferred style. Often, such a discovery comes as a surprise to the person concerned and they experience a 'light bulb' realisation that the gnawing dissatisfaction they have long felt about their career in mechanical engineering, is rooted in having a thinking style which better lends itself to being an art director in a creative agency. Although preference and skill *can* be mutually reinforcing, the two don't always find each other. Indeed, if we find ourselves in a job which requires skills in a non-preferred mode, the on-the-job development of those skills may build our confidence, increase our familiarity and help ease the dissonance we intuitively feel. Conversely, if we never have the opportunity to pursue a path which is aligned with our preference, we may never benefit from mutual reinforcement and may never even become aware of our latent talents.

There are many reasons why we may not find ourselves working in jobs which lend themselves to our natural preference and potential. First of all, our dominant cognitive style is usually unconscious to us; indeed most people have no idea that such preferences even exist, never mind what they might be. Also, to develop sufficient self-awareness may take us well into adulthood, by which time we may feel locked into a particular career path which is difficult to change. Furthermore, no job exists which *only* requires one thinking style, so we will often find at least some aspects of any role which *do* employ our preferred mode and deliver sufficient reward for us to remain in situ. Perhaps most importantly, we are all brought up in cultures which can place greater emphasis on one mode over the other. The approach to data processing taken by the left mind is strongly supportive of scientific materialism, which dominates most cultures globally, so the societal infrastructures we have collectively created are automatically skewed towards the left mind. In school, science and mathematics tend to be prioritised over arts and the humanities, so kids may be pushed in this direction irrespective of their individual preference or innate potential. Influenced by their cultural leanings, societies invest money and create jobs so if our employment market is replete with roles in engineering, science, law or manufacturing but lacking opportunities in counselling, archaeology, advertising or divinity, this will clearly have an impact. In this scenario, mutual reinforcement will manifest between societal demand and educational supply, amplifying and reinforcing our cultural bias rather than redressing any imbalance, thus creating an on-going mismatch between the jobs available and the cognitive profile of the employment pool.

Yet it's important to note that while culture can artificially skew our societal priorities and job supply, it doesn't significantly reshape the personal preferences of people within our societies – as brain dominance profiling shows when we map individual profiles at the collective level. Herrmann's large-scale studies, conducted across many countries and continents, show that nurses tend to have a more similar preference profile to other nurses – all over the world – than they do with people of their own nationality or ethnicity, but who work in other professions. The same is true for airline pilots, engineers, entrepreneurs, chemists, social workers, accountants and many other professions. So, when all nurses are mapped globally they have a very distinct brain dominance profile which is markedly different from the cognitive preferences of dentists, psycho-logists, bankers or homemakers, who also share similar profiles to others in their group. However, it gets really interesting when all pro-fessions are mapped together to create a single overall profile by nation-ality or ethnicity. In doing so, we find that all skews disappear and that large populations of people, when mapped in aggregate, have a balanced overall profile.[23]

At a national level, all Americans, Mexicans, Germans and Indians produce an overall balanced preference profile, although each of these groups accommodate a wide range of individual profiles within them. In all of these nations, people who have a preference for left-mind thinking are counter-balanced by those with a right-mind preference and, in all cases, many individuals are found at every gradient between polarities. Relatively few people tend to have a preference profile which is perfectly balanced between left and right. Exactly the same is true when large groups are plotted by ethnicity; at the collective level there is no difference between Whites, Asians, Hispanics, Blacks or Native Americans and, as the aggregate of individual members, all ethnic groups have a balanced profile. Naturally, it follows that when all individuals from all over the world are plotted onto one single map, our collective 'global mind' also has a balanced preference profile. As a group of between 7 and 8 billion unique individuals we may have a wide and polarizing range of personal preferences, but as a global human community our preferred cognitive state is one of harmonious hemispheric balance. This should really come as no surprise as coherence is the natural state of all complex adaptive systems.

However, it's essential to remind ourselves that while the preferred cognitive state of our global mind is one of hemispheric balance, this does not necessarily guarantee that these are the cultural conditions we collectively create. The cultures we bring forth are the emergent output, not of our preferred cognitive modes but of the *actual* minds we employ every day – minds which are themselves shaped by the very cultures they serve to sustain; cultures which, in the case of scientific materialism, heavily prioritises the left mind. In an ideal world the types of jobs we create would be perfectly matched with the balanced preference profile of our labour pool, but this isn't our experienced reality. Of course all nations need nurses and accountants but the priorities and biases imposed upon our societies, by our cultures, skew the relationship between supply and demand, creating disproportionate employment opportunities in certain fields, pushing people into particular careers which may or may not be right for them, and shaping educational policies which inadvertently ensure the imbalance is maintained.

Consider your personal opinion on the Syrian refugee crisis. We are all capable of feeling empathy with those fleeing war, yet also of being protective of our own nations and those already in them. These are both perfectly natural human responses, each rooted in a different brain hemisphere, yet they are clearly contradictory impulses which can only be reconciled by an integrative right mind. However, one only needs to read public comments about the crisis to appreciate that many individuals are either unwilling or unable to perform the blending required, to arrive at an appropriately balanced perspective. This could be because all commentators are at the polar extremes of brain dominance. Perhaps more likely, it could also be because the overarching Western culture is one in which dualism is pre-eminent; unconsciously conditioning people to take an either/or stance on all major issues. Clearly, European nations have a moral obligation to help refugees but, equally clearly, Europe cannot simply open its borders to all-comers. We don't need to be political geniuses to see that an appropriately balanced solution necessarily pushes each European nation to take a quota of refugees, in keeping with their ability to do so, but also requires identity checks to separate genuine asylum-seekers from opportunistic economic migrants. It also requires a balance between addressing issues in Europe, investing in Middle Eastern refugee camps to reduce the temptation to travel, shaming wealthy nations such as Saudi Arabia and the United Arab Emirates into also playing their part, and seeking a peaceful, political solution to the Syrian war itself. No-one would suggest that these issues are easy to resolve but the failure of EU leaders to come up with a coherent plan, several years after the crisis began, is just as lamentable as it is perhaps understandable. Like us, they only have flawed cognitive equipment to work with, are subject to the same cultural pressures as the rest of us and are ultimately beholden to an electorate who, rather than insisting upon appropriately blended proposals, pull them in opposite directions towards each polarity. Culture is the output of all of our minds and how we think ultimately brings forth what we collectively create.

Unquestionably the most fascinating discovery of all from Ned Herrmann's brain dominance profiling, is that while large groups produce balanced preference profiles when aggregated by nationality or ethnicity, this is not replicated when the same data is aggregated by gender.[24] Large groups of men and women produce different profiles from each other, with the profile of men showing a dominant preference for left-mind cognition, while the aggregate of female preferences shows a clear bias towards the right mind. Clearly, it is critical to emphasise that not *all* men are left-mind dominant and not *all* women display a preference for right-mind thinking. These tendencies are the aggregate of large samples of each gender and there are lots of men and women who show a preference, sometimes a strong preference, for the 'other' mode. However, in aggregate and on average, men skew left and women skew right. This gender distinction is also shown to cut consistently across both nationality and ethnicity but it is difficult to say exactly why this is the case. Brain scans suggest that there is no gender-specific variation in how baby boys and girls are genetically 'wired' and, as far as neuroscientists can tell, both genders think in exactly the same way at a young age. However, scans do show that by around age 15 the neural networks of boys and girls have come to operate quite differently from each other.[25] While boys' brains tend to have developed stronger intra-hemispheric neural connectivity, front to back within each hemisphere, girls' brains tend to have formed greater inter-hemispheric synaptic connections; linking each hemisphere more power-fully to each other, as well as to the limbic system. This would certainly account for a difference in left versus right modal preference but scientists disagree about why this happens. It could be genetic, rooted in the hormonal changes each gender undergoes during puberty, but it could also be influenced by cultural stereotyping and the way in which we nurture each gender.

Extensive tests show that adults do behave differently towards boys and girls from the day they are born, even when we consciously believe we are treating them exactly the same.[26] We speak a little more loudly to boys and set higher expectations of them, in terms of what we think they should be able to achieve at each age of development, pushing them slightly harder to do so. While we may consciously wish to avoid stereo-typing we automatically offer trucks and tool-based toys to baby boys, sparking neural activity in their left minds, while encouraging girls to play with relationship-based toys such as teddy bears and dolls, which stimulate the right mind. Over time, these small initial differences may amplify to form unconscious schematic rules which subliminally suggest that boys should study science or maths and gravitate towards careers involving mechanics or technology, while girls should orient themselves towards the arts or humanities and pursue careers in human resources or caring. It may even be that an ancient cultural convention such as the division of labour, which drove men to greater tool use and women to spend more time look-ing after children, has actually influenced some level of genetic variation in the cognitive preferences of each gender, after millennia upon millennia of practice. The truth is no-one knows for sure why men and women have come to think differently but the modern-day variation in modal preference between genders, is marked and significant.

There is one final, important point which must be made – cognitive preference does not necessarily equate to competence. There is no evidence to suggest that either gender is innately more capable in cognitive tasks which predominantly require a left or right-minded approach. It is, however, highly probable that any cultural influences which give greater prominence to specific subjects, or afford either gender greater practice in performing particular tasks, will build greater competence in those areas. In cultures where opportunities and exposure are not distributed equally between genders, men may well, on average, become better at engineering and women more skilled in managing people, but this is ultimately the output of cultural conditioning rather than intrinsic capability. Similarly Asians, on average, may well become better at mathematics than Hispanics but not because of any inherent superiority, simply because they are raised in cultures which place greater value on the subject and invest more in teaching it.

In principle our minds have the potential to provide fully considered and appropriately balanced cognitive outputs, at all times and in all situations. However, this principle is rarely reflected in practice. Most of us have a preference for either left or right so automatically prioritize our dominant mode in the information we extract from the global mind, thereby also promoting our dominant mode via the data we contribute to it. In doing so we co-create culture which in turn exerts downward influence on a large proportion of our own thinking, as well as that of everyone around us. Cultures too can therefore develop a cognitive preference and to break this self-perpetuating cycle, enough people need to create a counterbalance by consistently prioritizing the opposite mode. However, this requires an elevated degree of individual consciousness in order to overcome the effects of the incumbent culture, which automatically exerts unconscious influence on those same people. This cycle presents a major challenge for human-beings because, as we will explore, our ancient brains are genetically programmed to be overconfident in our unconscious impulses and reluctant to exert the energy required to consciously overcome them. The operating modes of our two hemispheres are essential to our survival and we couldn't function without them, yet, rooted as they are way back in our evolutionary history, they are not perfectly suited to the challenges we face in the 21st century. If we are to create cultures capable of elevating our collective thinking to a higher plateau, we must first raise our individual consciousness to overcome fundamental flaws in how our brains work – each one an unintended consequence of evolutionary design. As we will explore in Chapters 5 and 6, overconfidence and laziness are just two flaws, amongst many, in our ancient brains.

—5—

Leaping to Conclusions

DURING ANY particular era, scientists must necessarily subscribe to fundamental premises about their subject matter – those foundation stones of knowledge which are widely accepted to be true, yet which may later be found to be partially or even totally false. If some aspects of a shared 'reality' believed by great men such as Darwin and Einstein, were later shown to be flawed it's safe to assume that everything we think we know for certain today, may be subject to revision at some point in the future. Ironically, this position is widely accepted within scientific circles and it is only those in wider society who tend to believe that scientific knowledge is forever set in stone. Unbeknown to most of us, over the last few decades the social sciences have undergone a major shift in the fundamental premises upon which their study had been built and to which social scientists had operated for several preceding centuries. Indeed, ever since the Enlightenment it was widely believed, and therefore accepted as 'truth', that the human mind was powerfully rational and that the only factor which stood between humankind and the peak of our intellectual potential – absolute rationality – was an individual's inability to control the destabilising effects of the emotions.

As usual, the origins of our faith in rationalism can be traced to ancient Greece where Plato envisioned that the human soul existed in three parts, which he explained via an allegory of a charioteer trying to control two wild horses.[1] A black, ugly horse represented our base instincts and was rooted in the belly and genitals. It sought to satisfy our primal need for food and sex, was notable for its love of money and physical pleasure, and was strongly aligned to the visceral vices of gluttony, lust and greed. Beside it, a handsome white horse signified our courageous free-spirit and was rooted in the heart. It sought honour and victory yet also had a propensity towards passionate outbursts, fuelled by the dual vices of wrath and envy. To control these two creatures, one base and evil, the other noble but unruly, Plato believed that the soul needed a powerfully rational charioteer who represented the head and was a pillar of wisdom, a lover of truth and the epitome of reason. The correlation between Plato's tripartite soul and the three layers of the brain – our primitive, reptilian layer, our mammalian, limbic system and our much newer neocortex – is clear. Plato strongly believed in the ability of the charioteer – our conscious mind – to control both our base animal instincts and our powerful, if unpredictable, unconscious but he also observed that in the world around him the charioteer appeared to have very little control over his horses. He concluded that this was because the rational charioteer was subject to the final two vices of pride and sloth. Even millennia ago, Plato recognized the lazy and overconfident nature of the conscious mind and its inability to subdue the embodied emotions of the unconscious.

However, buoyed by a belief in classic Newtonian physics, the modern social sciences ignored Platonic wisdom and believed that *homo economicus* could process the outer world with cold dispassion, assessing options using flawless, rational mental models via which we would upgrade our choices to those which delivered '*maximum utility*' – a clearly left-minded worldview. This ironically imaginative fiction was built upon a number of assumptions which were deeply flawed. First, it assumed that reason was a more valuable cognitive tool when employed alone; separated from, rather than connected to, our emotions or intuitions. From its dualistic standpoint it erroneously believed that for reason to be maximised its opposite must be minimised, although we now know that heightened emotion leads to greater empathy upon which more sensitive, nuanced reasoning can be built. We simply think better when we also listen to how we feel and we cannot detach our consciousness from the influence of our unconscious. Second, it falsely assumed that social scientists could peer objectively at human nature, as if from outside the very society in which they themselves were immersed and absent their own genetic dispositions and cultural biases. This notion builds upon the illusion that what we observe gives a reliable, objective view of the outer world, rather than one which is clouded and coloured by who we are and how we approach it. Third, it assumed that human-beings respond to stimulus, in the form of economic incentives, in a manner which corresponded to the mechanical laws of classic physics – linear causality operating to mathematical principles which were identifiable and transferable across contexts. In spite of huge advances in quantum science, the mechanistic worldview still dominated the sciences, including the social sciences, for most of the 20th century.

It was only from the late 1970s that these flawed fundamental premises began to be undermined by behavioural scientists. Research increasingly showed that systemic cognitive errors were commonplace, even amongst highly intelligent, fully-functioning individuals, and that the source of their faulty thinking lay not in their inability to suppress emotions but in the modus operandi of the brain itself. Such research is now so extensive and consistent that it has become widely accepted throughout the social sciences that our minds are susceptible to common, predictable errors in judgement. However, this knowledge has yet to permeate our mainstream cultural narrative. Social scientists have now concluded that our rationality is so heavily bound by our emotionality that the two are inseparable and that, most of the time, our behaviour is driven by unconscious forces over which we exercise neither awareness nor control.[2] Brain imaging shows that we automatically involve our feelings whenever we consider any data which is relevant to a decision, and that it is simply impossible for us to switch this effect off. In particular, our orbitofrontal cortex and anterior cingulate cortex – both parts of the limbic seat of our emotions – light up instantly and there is nothing we can do about it. We may like to think we are in objective control but all of our decisions are highly coloured by what we subjectively feel.[3]

Pride and Sloth

Before reading any further, try to solve the following puzzle:

A bat and ball cost $1.10.
The bat costs one dollar more than the ball.
How much does the ball cost?

If your answer was 10 cents you are certainly not alone but it is the wrong answer. If the ball cost 10 cents the bat would have to cost $1 and the difference between the two would be just 90 cents. To achieve a $1 differential the bat must cost $1.05 and the ball 5 cents. This isn't a particularly difficult puzzle for the numerate left mind to solve yet, before it can do so, our impulsive right mind leaps to an apparently obvious, but incorrect, answer. This simple exercise highlights brilliantly how our brains actually work. Our right mind, which leads our cognitive processing, interprets whatever we encounter and passes its interpretation to our left mind for assessment. However, our right mind lacks the numeric skills of its partner so its interpretation is derived from intuition or '*gut feel*' and the language we use is instructive. We experience a '*sense*' of what feels like the right answer, as it bubbles up from our unconscious mind into our consciousness, and our spontaneous, overconfident right mind quickly leaps to a conclusion which in this case is the wrong one. Just as importantly, our left mind which is responsible for assessing the solution offered by the right, often fails to do its job properly by over-ruling its impulsive partner. In the above 'bat and ball' test, more than 50% of students at Harvard, MIT and Princeton – the cream of American universities – gave the intuitive but incorrect answer. At less elite universities the failure rate was over 80%.[4] Clearly, the tendency of intelligent university students to come up with the wrong answer has little to do with their inability to perform the calculation required but is instead deeply rooted in how the human brain works. An overconfident right mind produces an intuitive but wrong answer, which a lazy left mind fails to correct.

The exercise above highlights that the role of our right mind isn't simply to pay vigilant attention to the outer world and report potentially threatening novelty, to a more intelligent left mind. On the contrary, the right mind not only conveys sensory data but also interprets what it experiences for the left mind. However, the broad attention the right mind pays only allows for a relatively 'fuzzy' assessment of outer-world phenomena, because it lacks the sharp, incisive qualities of the left mind which facilitate detailed analysis. The right mind also experiences a brand new world every day and has weaker synaptic links to the schematic structures of associative memory, against which to interpret environmental data. Instead, it arrives at conclusions by leveraging its greater connectivity to the embodied senses plus limbic and nervous systems – conclusions which blend sensory data with the emotional, instinctive and intuitive impulses it receives from the unconscious mind. Therefore our right mind's preferred approach – indeed the only approach available to it – is to leap to conclusions about what it experiences, based on the limited information available. Nevertheless, it presents its judgements to the left mind with supreme confidence. The role of our left mind is to act as gatekeeper, assessing the outputs of the right mind against associative memories and the many schematic rules it has created to help us live safely, but closing the gate and forcing us to 'stop and think' whenever it is in our best interests to do so. However, self-control requires conscious effort and the conscious mind can only process 1/200,000th as many bits of data per second, as our unconscious. Consciousness also rapidly depletes energy so our left mind is heavily incentivized to be lazy, only employing conscious effort when it deems it to be absolutely necessary. The vast majority of our right mind's interpretations therefore pass without conscious assessment, some of which, as we will discover, would improve the quality of our cognition by being challenged.

Both overconfidence and laziness are core characteristics of the human brain, rooted in the fact that we are still operating with essentially the same cerebral tools that hunter-gatherers had, two hundred millennia ago. Before exploring further, we should perhaps consider how an over-confident and lazy brain could possibly be an evolutionary development designed to enhance our survivability, when such characteristics would surely have the opposite effect? Our brains evolved to help us survive on the African savannah so, in the situation of having to escape from a predator, not only is our ability to rapidly detect danger essential to us, but so too is our willingness to act quickly upon that knowledge without 'thinking' too much. In such a scenario, to consciously consider how genuine or significant the danger actually is, could cause a life-threatening delay as well as wasting valuable energy on cognitive processing which would be better employed in escaping. For the sake of our survival it is the smart move to blindly follow our intuition and conserve all of our energy for running away, even if the perceived threat turns out to be benign and our response unnecessary. In short, it is better to be wrong yet live to tell the tale, than to be correct but dead. Overconfidence also plays a further, somewhat counterintuitive, role in enhancing our survivability by encouraging us to take risks. If our ancient ancestors had spent too long assessing the dangers of hunting large prey, their logical and risk-averse left minds may well have concluded that the better option was to continue to gather berries, instead of pursuing the potential extra calories offered by meat. If racked with fear, our species would never have taken the many risks needed to innovate and elevate our way to where we are today, and our supreme, if sometimes delusional, self-confidence has played an essential role in driving our progress.

Our brain is designed to make fast decisions and just because we have a lazy conscious mind, doesn't mean that those decisions aren't checked at all. Energy efficiency is built deep within our system and is delivered by the associative schematic structures of the left mind, for which recognizing novel stimulus against rewoven memories, isn't its only function. Our left mind also leverages its skills in deconstruction, analysis and linear logic to generate theories about whatever we experience; theories it then uses to invent universal 'rules' which bring order to our lives and keep us safe. It does so by connecting its many associative memories into schematic frameworks, against which we unconsciously assess all future situations and the decisions we make in them. For example, laughter is a spontaneous, visceral reaction we experience whenever we find something amusing. However, if we are told a funny joke at a funeral, we may instinctively want to laugh but are stopped by a simple schematic rule – 'don't laugh at funerals' – which our left mind has derived from many associative memories, including how people tend to react when others do something they deem socially inappropriate. At a fairly young age, our left mind deposits this rule into our unconscious long-term memory for use over our whole lifetime, and it is a valuable, if rather simplistic, rule which helps keep us safe from social censure. We can't say for certain whether our right mind, which leads our cognitive processing, is able to extract this rule directly from the unconscious or whether it instead makes a 'decision' to laugh, which is then overruled by the left mind, but in either event our two minds collaborate unconsciously to ensure we act in an appropriate manner. It is simplistic because the dualistic left mind only deals in certainty – it's either OK to laugh at funerals or it isn't – and, of course, there *are* some occasions when it is acceptable to laugh at a funeral, perhaps in response to an amusing anecdote about the deceased. In those situations, we rely on our right mind to perform the essential third phase of the right-left-right cognitive sequence, by taking context into account and ensuring that we have 'social permission' to join in the laughter.

Critically, this third phase almost always requires conscious processing and we do have to expend a small amount of cognitive energy to ensure the decision we make is the right one. Similarly, if we encounter a canine, our left mind may offer up the useful rule that 'dogs bite', derived from associative memories connecting canines with sharp teeth and aggression. This rule needn't debilitate us, because our holistic right mind can cope with the nuanced reality that some dogs bite and others don't. With a small amount of conscious effort it can blend the left mind's rule with its 'live' contextual assessment of the situation, such as whether the dog is wagging its tail or arching its back, to come to an appropriately balanced conclusion about how we should react. This is a fundamentally brilliant modus operandi, which enables the large bulk of our cognitive processing to be carried out without the involvement of our conscious mind, and we are all unconsciously guided by such rules. Indeed, beyond our awareness we all have access to a vast schematic framework, consisting of all the associations our left mind has ever made plus all the subsequent theories and rules it has ever invented about how the world works and how we should operate to thrive and survive in it. This massive 'mental model' effectively creates an entire parallel, yet abstracted, inner world against which we unconsciously assess all experienced outer-world phenomena. Via this very same operating mode we automatically 'know' not to take off all our clothes in public, even if we are feeling too warm, and we 'know' not to butcher the family's pet rabbit, just because we are hungry. Each of us holds thousands of similar rules in our long-term memory and it doesn't even cost us energy to do so, because we only reweave them whenever we need to avoid the pain of public humiliation, criminal prosecution or being disowned by our children. We only need to engage our consciousness on the very rare occasions when it may be a good idea to laugh at a funeral, get naked in public or kill the family pet. Our mind truly is miraculous.

However, consider this classic experiment in which Deglin and Kinsbourne demonstrated how each brain hemisphere has its own unique way of approaching the following syllogism, with a deliberately false minor premise.[5]

1. Major premise: all monkeys climb trees.
2. Minor premise: a porcupine is a type of monkey.
3. Conclusion: porcupines climb trees.

Participants were asked to assess the 'truth' of the above conclusion. When responding, in the first instance with both brain hemispheres functioning, they naturally deduced that a porcupine isn't a type of monkey and that the conclusion was therefore false. When the same participants were asked the question again, this time with their left hemisphere temporarily disabled and using only the right hemisphere, they again rejected the conclusion on the basis that the minor premise was false. However, when asked the same question for a third time, now with their right hemisphere disabled and using only the left hemisphere, participants willingly accepted that the conclusion was true because it was logically coherent with both the major and minor premises. With repeated similar syllogisms, all with false minor premises, and across many different types of participant, the same results were seen. The implications are clear. The left mind has a strong tendency to follow rules because the ordered nature of its world dictates that rules are meant to be followed. Its assessment of 'truth', therefore, lies only in the logical coherence of new data with pre-existing rules, but not with the validity of the rules themselves. In the above experiment the rules of the syllogism were provided, but the rules which determine our real-life actions are those which the left mind itself has created – the associative schematic rules against which our right-mind conclusions are evaluated.

The effect can therefore be quite debilitating if, for example, our left mind says that 'all dogs bite' and our right mind fails to override this rule. The conclusion our right mind leaps to, in the first phase of cognition, is drawn from sensory data but also from unconscious emotions derived from associated memories. If a feeling of fear is part of this emotional mix, our right mind may well conclude that any dog is dangerous and because this is logically coherent with the left-mind rule that 'all dogs bite', each hemisphere effectively confirms that the other is correct. Coherence is the *only* criteria against which the left mind assesses the right mind's instinctive conclusions and when things 'make sense' (i.e. cohere), we enjoy a feeling of cognitive ease caused by the release of pleasurable chemicals in our brain. As a result, the gate is flung wide open and the instruction to 'stop and think' never arrives. Clearly, the creation of rules by the left mind is a function designed to keep us safe but it can also have unintended consequences in the 21st century, when there is really no need to treat all dogs as if they are dangerous predators. It would be bad enough to be denied a lifetime of canine companionship but, as we will find out later, our left mind is just as likely to create rules such as 'all Muslims are terrorists', 'all black people are criminals' or 'all women are inferior to men', as it is to decide that 'all dogs bite'. What's more, by only checking for coherence with such rules as assessment criteria, the left mind can easily allow sectarian, racist or misogynistic impulses to pass unhindered and without the self-control required to make us 'stop and think'.

To make matters even worse, tests also show that once it has created its schematic rules our left mind is very reluctant to change them; preferring to force-fit unfamiliar information into existing frameworks or dismiss new data as anomalous, rather than reassess or update the frameworks themselves.[6] It will also doggedly defend the veracity of its own creations. That's why, as we get older, we find it harder to challenge long-held beliefs, break habitual behaviours or adapt to significant shifts in our external environment, such as developments in technology. It's also why, at a societal level, the tenets of scientific materialism and the many rules of the mechanistic worldview are so widely pervasive and slow to transform. Once it has built our decontextualized mental model, the left mind has no real interest in the extent to which it accurately reflects outer-world reality, which is actually ever-changing. The schematic structures it creates give the illusion of order, certainty and predictability, providing a comforting sense of cognitive ease from anything which is coherent. However, as a consequence it is overconfident in its own frameworks and lazy in the diligence with which it forces us to 'stop and think'.

Even when it does make us pause for thought, there's still no guarantee that our right mind will perform its third-phase blending function to a high degree of quality, because it is just as motivated as our left mind to avoid exhausting conscious effort. In his best-selling book *Thinking, Fast and Slow*, Nobel prize-winning behavioural economist Daniel Kahneman explains that our decisions are often based on what he calls *heuristics,* which we employ in situations where the topic is complex or we don't have all the information we need, and getting it would require considerable effort.[7] *Heuristics* essentially involve replacing difficult questions with easier questions, which we feel more comfortable answering, and political elections are a good example of when we use them. During election campaigns we know we *should* diligently compare the policies of each party across the broad range of socio-economic topics relevant to our lives. We also know we *should* research the character, personal values and past experiences of each candidate but, frankly, this all involves a lot of hard work. So, in practice, our lazy left mind often neglects to perform due diligence on policy, while our equally lazy right mind fails to fully consider candidates' relational skills. Instead, we select an easier *heuristic* option – do they look competent? Psychologist Alexander Todorov of Princeton University showed students photographs of male faces and asked them to rate the men for attributes such as dominance, likeability and competence. The students were unaware that the men were all candidates for elected office and Todorov later compared their ratings against the actual election results. In around 70% of cases, the election winner was the candidate whose face had been rated highest for competence, based solely on a brief exposure to their photograph and with no context or political content whatsoever. The same study has since been replicated, with similar results, in countries as diverse as Finland, Australia and Mexico.[8] Other heuristic questions we regularly employ in place of more relevant, but more difficult, alternatives include '*do I like it?*', '*does it feel familiar?'*, *'does it make sense?'*, *'what do people normally do?'* and *'what do the experts say?'*

In summary, the way our brain works is quite brilliant but very much offers a double-edged sword in the 21st century, when we are required to deal with complex issues of global integration rather than simply knowing which creatures can kill us or the poisonous berries we should avoid. We are stuck with its original modus operandi yet occasionally it still does work for the purpose nature intended. Psychologist Gary Klein tells the story of a firefighting commander who took the decision to evacuate his men from a burning kitchen, without consciously knowing why, just prior to the floor of the kitchen collapsing into the basement, which had been the original source of the blaze.[9] Only after the event and upon much reflection, was the commander able to rationalize his intuitive 'sixth sense' and explain that the fire was just too quiet for the kitchen to be its locus. When he made the call to evacuate he knew instinctively that something was wrong, he just didn't know what it was. At a critical moment, his right mind was able to leap to an accurate conclusion and, fortunately, the commander had the courage and seniority to evacuate the building based solely on his instinct. Several lives may have been lost, had his left mind forced him to 'stop and think' and to consciously process his 'gut feel' for logical coherence.

Nowadays, few of us have to make life-or-death decisions and the greatest danger we face daily is crossing the road, but our brains evolved to make fast decisions and still operate in the same way, so we simply have to live with the consequences. Laziness and overconfidence are just two such consequences, deeply embedded in the operating modes of our two minds, and both right and left are equally afflicted. However, it comes as no surprise that they are lazy and overconfident in very different ways.

Our right mind is a fearless wanderer in the outer world which uses its strong sensory links and unconscious connections to blend its interpretations, based on a broad but fairly fuzzy understanding of what's 'out there'. Nevertheless, it leaps to conclusions quickly and presents them confidently to our left mind, despite the often flimsy foundations upon which they are built. Occasionally, its intuitive outputs may save our lives, but unfortunately it applies the same approach in all situations and sometimes comes up with the wrong answer. Even when it is charged with blending left-mind data with its own ideas, the conscious effort required can cause it to default to easier *heuristic* options. Our left mind, whose job it is to assess the validity of right-mind interpretations often fails to do so, particularly when it is tired or distracted. Even when it does check, it assesses data against generalized schematic rules based on abstract models of the outer world which are possibly outdated, yet which it defends with dogged overconfidence, determined to preserve the notionally 'life-saving' role of the rules over the degree to which they reflect reality. It also assesses solely for coherence, irrespective of the nature of conclusions presented to it, enabling pernicious, damaging and even potentially dangerous ideas to pass unopposed.

Our two minds therefore have fundamental features which make them both deeply 'flawed' in the 21st century and which make neither perfectly suited for delivering the higher cognitive capability we now need, individually and collectively, to elevate our species to a higher plane of evolutionary adaptation. Our brains haven't changed substantially since the first *homo-sapiens* and haven't undergone any significant genetic modification for at least 50,000 years, so we shouldn't expect an upgrade anytime soon. Ultimately, most of us do want to make life-enhancing decisions for ourselves and others – why wouldn't we? – but to do so requires us to consciously make better judgements, thereby cultivating a global culture which is less dangerous to our species and less damaging to our planet. Few of us willingly make bad decisions or deliberately try to harm other humans but, in our hugely complex system, what emerges as our global mind is ultimately the cognitive output of all of us. Every single day we make lots of little decisions of no obvious importance but which, in aggregate with those made by billions of others, do ultimately influence the world we bring forth. Every few years we also elect political leaders and empower them to make much bigger decisions on our behalf – decisions which most definitely shape the future we collectively create and which could have catastrophic consequences for thousands, millions or even billions of people. No matter the scale or frequency of the calls we make, they all contribute towards changing or sustaining the cultures we live in – cultures which will shape the unconscious minds of future generations and could radically alter the path we, and they, will follow. To change the trajectory of our species, we will have to overcome a whole array of systemic flaws, fallacies and biases which consistently emerge from the complex system in our heads. The roots of these flaws lie in the modus operandi of an ancient brain which isn't fit for purpose in the 21st century but which will, nevertheless, produce the global mind which determines our future.

In Chapter 6 we'll explore the errors inherent within the left mind and the ways in which both minds collaborate to provide a comforting sense of cognitive ease. In the rest of this chapter, we'll focus on the flaws systemic to our right mind.

Fuzzy Feelings and Other Flaws

First, and foremost, is the immense impact our feelings have on our thoughts. We have all been conditioned to believe that thinking takes place exclusively in the head, but this is only the locus of the small proportion of cognition we are consciously aware of. Most of our thinking is actually processed throughout our limbic and central nervous systems, which are deeply connected to our senses and to our whole body. As a consequence, our thinking is powerfully influenced by how we feel and our feelings can change, minute to minute, because they are woven from the sensory and emotional data available to us at any given moment in time. Research now shows that our feelings, plus subsequent thoughts and actions, can be shaped by a whole host of factors including whether the sun is shining, whether we are hungry or whether we have just exercised. Until the 1970s, social scientists believed that our personality had a strong influence on our behaviour and that, because personality traits were genetic and there-fore fixed, we would always respond to the same situation in the same way. However, more recent research has shown this to be totally untrue and that '*our character is not indelibly stamped on us but is dynamic and changing*'.[10] In his book *Subliminal*, Leonard Mlodinow reveals that while our feelings do have a dramatic influence on our thoughts and behaviours, we are usually unaware of these feelings, their source or the impact they have on us.

Research confirms that our judgements are deeply affected by how we feel. Take one of our most distinctive emotions, that of sexual arousal. Studies show that our attitudes and actions vary considerably when we are feeling lustful, whether consciously or unconsciously. For example, women have been shown to wear more revealing clothes and become more sexually competitive with other women, when they are ovulating.[11] It per-haps comes as no surprise that men are even easier to read. Psychologist Dan Ariely conducted experiments with young, male Berkeley University students which explored their attitudes and predicted actions, when pre-sented with a wide array of carnal scenarios.[12] I'll spare you the intimate details but respondents answered each research question twice, once in a cold, calm state and the other when sexually aroused, and the results were perhaps illuminating and disturbing in equal measure. In the 'cold' state these well-bred, intelligent young men were respectful of women, adamant they would always practice safe sex and relatively disinclined towards the odder sexual practices suggested. However, when in a sexually-aroused 'hot' state, 45 percent predicted they would still try to have sex with a date even after she had said 'no', more than 6 in 10 said they would encourage a date to drink more to increase their chances of sex, and more than 1 in 4 even predicted that they would drug a date to get laid – the biggest difference between hot and cold responses to any question in the survey. Participants who could imagine being attracted to a twelve-year-old girl doubled between the two states, a differential exceeded by the ideas of sex with a sixty-year-old woman and sexual contact with an animal. When 'hot', respondents were 22 percent less likely to insist on using a condom if they didn't know the sexual history of their partner, and were even more likely to forego protection if they thought their partner might change her mind while they went to get it. The difference in responses between hot and cold states is hugely insightful. The students were all bright young men whose left minds were generally able, in cold conditions, to exert an appropriate level of self-control over the more visceral impulses of their right minds. When sexually aroused, however, the hot feelings experienced were often sufficient for the right mind to simply overwhelm the left mind, which regularly surrendered its role as gatekeeper or moral guardian.

Sexual arousal may be a particularly powerful example of how our feelings impact our judgement but research also shows that many other emotional states, including hunger, anger, excitement, jealousy or anxiety, can all make a difference to our decision-making. In no profession might we expect judgment to be more sound than that of the law court judge, but a study of eight Israeli judges, conducted over 10 months as they ruled on over 1000 parole applications, suggested otherwise.[13] Each day, hearings ran in three sessions punctuated by two meal breaks and researchers found that at the beginning of the day, judges granted parole to around two-thirds of prisoners – a figure which gradually decreased to almost zero just prior to the first break. Immediately after the judges had eaten, the approval rating shot back up to around two-thirds, falling again as the day progressed towards the second meal break. The same pattern was repeated during the third session and was consistently repeated, day after day, by all eight judges. Other considerations did influence their rulings, of course, such as previous incarcerations, severity of crime and time served, but even when controlling for all other factors, the meal time pattern persisted. The research team came to the simple, but stunning, conclusion that decision-making was mentally tiring and that as each judge became more fatigued it became more and more attractive to default to the easier judgement, which was to maintain the status quo and to deny parole.

While these results should concern us, they shouldn't surprise us. Judges may be highly trained to make robust, balanced decisions based solely on the evidence presented to them, but they are also human-beings whose brains are subject to exactly the same cognitive flaws as the rest of us. Research shows that many experts in their field, including judges but also auditors, pathologists and psychologists, are consistently inconsistent in making judgements, particularly where decisions involve complex data.[14] In other words, they may change their decisions from day to day, even when considering exactly the same information to arrive at their conclusion. This is because our decisions are always influenced by imperceptible messages we receive from our unconscious mind; messages which are highly contextual and may change from minute to minute. A few rays of sunshine, some good news or a minor disagreement can all act like the flapping of butterfly wings in our brain, setting off new cascades of connections, amplifying or dampening feelings and causing a different decision to emerge. Because we are unaware of the tiny differences in initial conditions, we are also unaware of the impact they have on emergent outcomes so we never know whether, on a different day, we might have arrived at an entirely different conclusion.

Our emotions certainly affect how we think which in turn influences how we act but, because feelings are sourced from deep within our unconscious, we are often unaware of them or of their source. Indeed, research shows that even when we *are* consciously aware of bodily sensations, we are often very poor at identifying their cause. Such sensations may, in fact, be unrelated to our experiences yet can exert considerable influence on how we respond to them. Clearly, this can make us extremely unpredictable, even to ourselves. In one experiment, an attractive female researcher asked men to complete a short questionnaire and, at the end of the interview, passed on her contact details ostensibly 'in case the respondent had any further questions'.[15] With one group, the survey was conducted on a solid, wooden bridge around 10 feet above a small stream, while in the other sample the paperwork was completed standing on a narrow, wobbly, 450-foot long suspension bridge over a 230-foot drop onto rocks below. The researcher received a call from only 12% of men in the first group but from 50% of the second sample, who, the team concluded, had wrongly attributed the feeling of exhilaration experienced as a result of their precarious location, to a mutual spark of attraction between interviewer and interviewee. Few of us make decisions while swinging in the wind over a chasm but exactly the same subliminal influence can be experienced if we make an important decision, having just run up a flight of steps or downed a caffeine-laced energy drink. Ditto if we've just watched a happy movie, missed lunch or tripped over the dog.

Of course, brand managers and advertising executives have always understood that our emotions play a far greater role in driving our behaviour, than we ourselves are aware. Central to building strong brands is the creation of associative memories which spark unconscious neural activity whenever we see McDonald's golden arches or the Nike swoosh. Although most brands have physical products connected to them, a brand itself isn't a tangible entity but an immaterial, some might even say spiritual, concept which transcends its material manifestations and exists only in our mind as a series of neural networks. How we feel about a brand ultimately depends on the associations we make to it, how we evaluate those associations and the benefits the brand brings to us. Great brands have spent decades and millions of dollars to ensure that our minds spontaneously associate, for example, Unilever's Dove brand with mois-turising, soft skin and, even more powerfully, with the notion that feminine beauty comes in all shapes and sizes. Such emotional benefits – how brands ultimately make us feel – are always more compelling to us because they meet deep-seated needs we aren't even conscious of having. While other motorcycle manufacturers can make bikes which are cheaper, faster and easier to handle than a Harley Davidson, only one brand can leverage its head-turning engine growl and authentic history with US biker gangs, to help a 50-year-old bank manager feel like a bad-ass outlaw on the weekend. Brand owners would never pour the huge sums they do into marketing if their investment wasn't returned many times over, through the powerfully motivating associative memories their communication creates and the brand loyalty it engenders. Yet, by and large, we are bliss-fully unaware of their manipulation of our malleable minds and genuinely believe that we are in conscious control of our own decision-making.

No profession has borrowed more heavily from the principles of marketing than political campaigners, who now routinely employ focus groups, voter segmentation models and market polling data to shape campaign strategy. Politicians know we are unlikely to read every policy document they produce, so instead seek to seed, in our minds, the sound-bites and snapshots which they believe will attract us to positively judge their credentials as a candidate worth voting for. Whether it's *being tough on crime*, *taking back control of immigration*, *clamping down on benefit cheats* or *helping hard-working families*, we are all subjected to a plethora of platitudes by which we are supposed to differentiate between political parties. Yet, when it comes to voting it seems that we are even more impulsive than the campaigners think, making snap judgements about politicians based on flimsier evidence than their pithy policy reminders. Janine Willis and Alexander Todorov found that voters often assess a politician's trustworthiness within one-tenth of a second of being exposed to their image. They also found that, even after greater exposure, they rarely change their first impression, becoming more confident over time that their initial assessment was accurate.[16]

Our culture may encourage us not to 'judge a book by its cover' but, when it comes to people, it's something we still do all the time and is an impulse deep-rooted in our ancient need to quickly identify friend from foe. Even though we don't really need this mechanism as much these days, it is hard-wired into us so we can't simply turn it off. For example, we are still far more likely to give our support to male leaders who are tall, because in ancient times tall men were usually better fighters and this unconscious association still persists. This isn't an associative memory as such, based on either past experience or cultural learning, but is an embodied associative feeling sourced from the much older parts of our brain structure and accessed via our right mind. One study showed that 58% of Chief Executive Officers of US Fortune 500 companies were six feet or taller, compared to less than 15% of all US men. Almost a third were six feet two or more, compared to less than 4% of all US men.[17] Of course, there are always exceptions. Legendary chairman and CEO of General Electric, Jack Welch stood only 5 feet 7 inches tall, the same height as William McKinley who in 1896 was the last elected US President of below average height and was ridiculed in the media as a 'little boy'. Barack Obama stands 6 feet 1, Donald Trump and Bill Clinton are 6 feet 2 as were George Washington, Thomas Jefferson and Franklin D Roosevelt. Abraham Lincoln and Lyndon B Johnson were both 6 feet 4 inches tall. No-one would suggest that height was the only factor in the elevation of these men to the Oval Office but a wealth of research shows that taller men consistently do better for themselves in business and politics, and that there is no correlation with higher intelligence or performance in office. Four large research studies showed that an extra inch of height can be worth nearly $800 per annum in additional salary.[18] Over a 40 year career, the difference between being six feet 4 versus 5 feet 6 could easily exceed $300,000 in earnings. Next time we complain about our politicians or business leaders, we should perhaps ponder the basis upon which we appointed them.

Like most of our cognitive flaws, our tendency to promote tall men into leadership roles isn't a conscious preference. Our senses gather data which our embodied right mind blends with unconscious associations to leap to a conclusion which makes intuitive, yet subliminal, sense to us – tall men make better leaders. If our left mind fails to exercise the self-control required to challenge this conclusion, the judgement passes without us even becoming aware of the shaky foundations upon which it is built. Our left mind often fails to make us 'stop and think' and sight isn't the only sense which influences us in this way – sound is just as persuasive. While our left mind focusses narrowly to listen to the words being spoken, our right mind works just as hard to interpret all the qualities of voice which have nothing to do with words or their literal meaning. By varying the vocal qualities such as pitch and intonation, of the same voices delivering the same words, researchers are able to isolate their influence on our aural impressions and the results are remarkable. Studies show that we judge people who speak faster, louder, with greater expressive variation and fewer pauses, to be more intelligent, knowledgeable, credible and convincing. Slower talkers, or those with higher-pitched voices, are unconsciously deemed to be weaker, more dishonest and less convincing.[19]

Touch too can make a subtle but significant difference to how persuasive or attractive we find people. In one study, male researchers in France randomly approached young women, politely introduced themselves, explained that they found the woman attractive and invited her for a drink later that evening. During these brief interactions, half of the women received a very short, light touch to their forearm; a tiny gesture yet one which doubled the frequency with which the date propositions were accepted. Similar experiments have shown that just such a light touch can increase the number of signatories to a petition, the value of tips received for restaurant service, the acceptance of menu recommendations, the number of agreements to dance, the willingness to participate in research and the likelihood of purchasing sampled food or agreeing to requests for help. Typically less than one-third of those whose behaviour was influenced, were even aware that they had been touched.[20] Sports teams whose members engage in high-fives and chest bumps have even been found to play more co-operatively as a team, than those who don't.[21] Once again, the root of this strange phenomenon lies deep in our animal ancestry. Touch is one of the most powerful ways in which we form social bonds, signal caring and make connections to one another, and scientists have even discovered nerve fibres in human skin, particularly the arms and face, which are directly connected to those areas of the brain which are associated with emotion.[22] Touch is our most highly developed sense when we are born, plays a vital communications role when we are babies and remains essential to us throughout our lives in building and maintaining social bonds. Indeed, we perhaps see this exhibited even more clearly in our non-human brothers and sisters – many animal species, including those most closely related to *homo-sapiens*, spend hours grooming each other in daily rituals which go way beyond their functional need for hygiene.[23]

Every day we form judgements about people, unaware of the powerful influence their gender, height, posture, face, voice or touch have on the unconscious assumptions we make about them. The strength of their handshake, how long they maintain eye contact, their choice of words and even how they smell, all connect with our emotions and communicate something about them to us. That's why hiring decisions in job interviews are usually made within the first couple of minutes, often before the conversation even gets around to the candidate's qualifications or experience. This phenomenon also makes us highly susceptible to suggestibility or 'priming'. In a famous experiment conducted at New York University, psychologist John Bargh primed unwitting students with a decoy exercise which required them to form sentences using words they would spontaneously associate with old age, such as Florida, wrinkle, bald, bingo, grey and so on.[24] Students were then asked to walk down a long corridor to another room to perform another task, unaware that the real experiment was to measure how long it took them to walk the length of the corridor. Bargh found that these perfectly fit, 18-25 year olds walked significantly slower than other students who hadn't been similarly primed. Another experiment found that those primed with words such as bold, aggressive and rude were much more likely to interrupt people having a conversation, than other participants primed with words like respect, polite and courteous. Our unconscious associations are highly susceptible to priming and can have a significant influence on our actions. Interestingly the same is true in reverse. A German study inverted Bargh's experiment by asking participants to walk around a room for five minutes, at around one-third of their normal pace, and found they were much quicker to recognize words relating to old age than other unrelated words.[25] Not only can our thoughts be primed to manipulate our actions, our actions can be primed to manipulate our thoughts.

Often, when presented with these case studies we find it difficult to accept their veracity. Such is our unwavering belief in our own free will, our conscious mind tells us we couldn't possibly be so easily influenced. Yet the power of unconscious associations is so strong, they can even impact our attitudes and actions when they relate directly to ourselves. Tests show that if black students are reminded of their race before an exam, they will perform worse than if they hadn't been thus primed,[26] and while prompting Asian-American women to think of their ethnicity prior to a maths exam will improve their results, making them think about their gender will have the opposite effect.[27] Such prompts act as stimuli, setting off a cascade of associations across the neural network which influences how individuals feel about themselves during the test, and directly impacts their performance. Yet in every case, the individual is unaware of the influence and, when made aware, understandably finds it very difficult to accept the validity or implications of the findings. This incredible effect has been most comprehensively demonstrated by a research technique known as the Implicit Association Test or IAT. Developed by Anthony Greenwald, Brian Nosek and Mahzarin Banaji at the University of Washington, the IAT identifies the strength of the associations we make by measuring the ease and speed with which we make them.[28] Taken on a computer, so response times can be measured in milliseconds, the test starts by asking respondents to click one button if the word which appears on screen is associated with men (such as John, father or uncle) and another button for female associations (such as Joan, mother or aunt). Similarly, this can be done for career associations (eg capitalist, merchant, entrepreneur) versus home associations (eg kitchen, cooking, family) or science associations (eg velocity, mathematics, microscope) versus art associations (eg painting, dance, theatre) and so on. We would all find this fairly easy and would be able to quickly and accurately make these associations, with the computer measuring just how fast. Next the IAT repeats these exercises but asks participants to distinguish words which are male or scientific from those which are female or artistic, ditto male or career versus female or home. With two criteria on each side this exercise would take us longer than the warm up, but once again we wouldn't find it difficult if we, like most people, associate men with careers or science more readily than we do with the home or the arts, which we more strongly associate with women. However, the power of the IAT really kicks in with the third level of test when the exercise is repeated again, only this time participants are asked to press one button if the word on screen is a male or home word versus a female or career word or, alternatively, male or art versus female or science. At this level, most people find it much harder to quickly categorize words because they may, for example, most strongly associate a word such as kitchen with home but also with female. Clearly, it's perfectly possible to associate kitchen with both career and men (especially for a male chef), but the length of time it takes to decide is a powerful indicator of how strongly we unconsciously associate kitchens with women and the home. While some of our associations are derived from personal experience, the majority are simply soaked into us by our culture.

Since they were first devised in the 1990s, millions of IAT tests have been conducted and the results are fascinating. For example, they reveal a very common implicit association between males and maths and between females and arts. Junior school girls have been found to unconsciously hold this male-maths stereotype, even when there is no difference in ability or performance between genders. However, such early associations are strongly predictive of later attitudes towards maths in high school, self-belief in maths ability and performance in maths exams. What starts as an implicit, yet ill-founded, belief that boys are better at maths can easily become amplified over time and emerge as an explicit, self-fulfilling behavioural manifestation. A study of more than 500,000 respondents across 34 countries, found that more than 70% of people share this subliminal stereotype.[29] What's more, girls who hold strong male-maths associations are more likely to perform badly in a maths test, when primed to think about their gender, than those with a weaker association.[30] Asian-American women do better when primed by ethnicity, rather than gender, because of an equally unfounded, but stereotypical, association that Asians are naturally gifted mathematicians.

Perhaps even more fascinating than gender results, are the findings of Implicit Association Tests which explore race and which commence with a questionnaire on attitudes towards racial differences. As you might expect, most of us say we believe that all people are equal and should be treated as individuals, rather than subjected to racial stereotyping. Most of us also believe that this is how we always treat the people we meet. Respondents are not necessarily being disingenuous – they may well consciously believe this to be the case – but their unconscious minds often tell a very different story. Using the same methodology outlined above, the racial IAT explores the associations we spontaneously and subliminally make between images of black versus white faces, between categories such as European-American versus African-American and between 'good' versus 'bad' values. Speed of association is measured between colour, ethnicity and positive words such as peace, joy, love, wonderful and glorious, versus negative words such as evil, failure, nasty, hurt, awful and so on. The results are consistently enlightening and disturbing. Around 70% of those taking the racial IAT have been found to unconsciously hold pro-white/anti-black attitudes, including many who are appalled to discover that their implicit views run entirely counter to their conscious opinions. Perhaps most surprising is that many black people – around half – also unconsciously hold a pro-white bias on the IAT, meaning it took them longer to associate positive attributes with black faces than with white faces, and they found it easier to link negatives attributes to black people.[31]

The key learning is clearly that we don't consciously choose our unconscious beliefs and biases. Even when we ourselves are part of a minority or socially undervalued group, we find it very difficult to resist the narrative our culture conveys daily through the media and its other artefacts and infrastructures. We are soaked in its story every single day, so it's simply inevitable that some of its attitudes will seep into us irrespective of our gender, race or conscious beliefs. If our cultural narrative implies that women are weaker than men, that black people are more likely to commit crime or that overweight people are lazy, we cannot avoid being influenced by such pervasive perceptions. While we are all born with genetic dispositions which may make us, for example, more extroverted or introverted, we aren't born with any of the cerebral schemata which lead us to unconsciously associate gender, race or any other human characteristics with positive or negative values. The cultural content of our unconscious mind is drip fed to us from the day we are born and is gradually constructed by our left mind into inflexible associative frameworks, providing the rules which guide how we live life. We unconsciously dip into these rules daily to help us negotiate outer-world complexity, using senses, emotions and intuitions to interpret whatever we encounter, and checking conclusions against our own schematic rules to try to keep us safe.

Our right mind, however, is programmed to act very quickly and can only make a fuzzy assessment of experienced phenomena. According to psychologist Daniel Gilbert, the default setting of our right hemisphere is to automatically accept whatever 'comes to mind' because it cannot distinguish whether the conclusion it has leapt to, is the result of genetics, sensory data, emotions, associations based on personal experience or cultural inculcation, heuristics or genuine expertise such as the firefighters intuition. It therefore makes no assessment of the validity of its conclusion but simply presents it to the left hemisphere. Our left mind must either accept or reject whatever our right mind offers, but it has no more idea than its partner about the source of what it receives. Its assessment is not therefore based on 'truth' per se – the degree to which the right mind's conclusion accurately reflects outer-world reality – but on coherence with its own internal, abstract and decontextualized schemata. It will accept anything which coheres and reject anything which doesn't, irrespective of the nature of its content including racist, misogynistic or other undesirable impulses. Of course, much of what it processes *does* legitimately cohere which is why we function so effectively and energy-efficiently. It is the collaboration of our right and left minds to create coherence, which enables us to make sense of the world and avoid the deeply uncomfortable feeling of cognitive dissonance we experience when we struggle to reconcile contradictory perspectives. However, as we will explore in the next chapter, not only are there many further downsides to the way the left mind builds associative schemata but both minds can often collaborate to create coherence where none exists, delivering a comforting, but delusional, sense of cognitive ease.

—6—

Confabulating
Coherence

O UR RIGHT MIND necessarily draws data from many different
sources – genetics, senses, emotions, memories, culture,
heuristics or expertise – because it has primary responsibility for
maintaining the self-creating qualities of our human system, for processing
the unpredictable flux of the outer world and for maintaining our cognitive
flexibility to do so. Conversely, our left mind is responsible for the self-
regulating tendencies of the system, ensuring dynamic stability by bringing
counterbalancing order to the essential freedom of the right mind. In
common with all complex adaptive systems, it does so by maintaining
stable state cycles, by ensuring data becomes more internally similar
through convergence around attractors, and by applying negative feedback
to any data which introduces disorder, thus dampening it. In our cognitive
system this means re-cognizing all novel data against associative memory
structures built around categorization, assessing right-mind interpretations
against schematic rules and rejecting anything which is incoherent and
likely to cause cognitive dissonance. Self-control is therefore an essential
function of our left mind but, although we clearly all possess the ability to
sometimes 'stop and think', experience tells us that this quality is not
evenly distributed. While some people seem to remain calm, cool and
considered in any circumstances, others seem to behave impulsively most
of the time. As we now know, this is rooted in our ancient need to 'act
without thinking' and such is the volume of data we process daily, we just
couldn't consciously consider every decision we need to make. Indeed, to
function effectively most of our decisions have to be made unconsciously,
which is why we are aware of less than 10% of all our thinking. However,
as we saw in the 'bat and ball' exercise in the last chapter, occasionally

we can make poor choices because our right mind leaps to a spontaneous, but wrong, conclusion and our left mind fails to exercise the self-control we need to correct the error. This effect can easily afflict even the brightest and most self-disciplined amongst us.

Sometimes we all need to slow down the cognitive process and challenge the rapid interpretation of an impulsive right mind, yet there's a big difference between employing 1% and 10% of our conscious capabilities. The frequency with which we spot and override right-mind errors is central to this variance but why do some people seem to be full of self-discipline, while others are rather more impetuous? Well, there's good news and bad news. The good news is that we can each train our left mind to exercise greater self-control, to slow us down more often and to become more vigilant for right-mind mistakes. The bad news is that we are all born with a genetic disposition towards self-control, or at least develop it very early in life, which significantly influences our chances of success in later life.

In the 1970s, Walter Mischel of Stanford University conducted an experiment which would become one of the most famous in the history of social sciences.[1] The research participants were all four-year-old children and the test involved Mischel sitting each child down and placing a marshmallow on the desk in front of them. He instructed each child that he was going to leave the room and that they could eat the marshmallow at any time, but if they waited until he returned he would give them two marshmallows instead of just one. About half of the children succumbed to temptation, while the other half were able to resist and were doubly rewarded when Mischel returned 15 minutes later. The children were filmed and the tapes confirm that for a four-year-old, 15 minutes is an inordinately long time to resist their instinctive desire for a sweet treat. Indeed, some of those who resisted had to employ strategies such as looking away or singing, to deliberately distract themselves from thinking about the marshmallow. Significantly, Mischel continued to track and research both sets of children as they grew up and, over time, astonishing results emerged from his work. Those kids who had demonstrated the self-control to delay gratification for just 15 minutes as four-year-olds, later went on to develop better social skills and achieve far better high-school grades than their more impulsive counterparts. Twenty years later they were far more likely to have graduated from college or university and thirty years later they were earning significantly higher salaries.[2] Mischel's famous 'marshmallow test' has since been repeated many times, with similar results, and many researchers now believe that measuring self-control is significantly more valuable than measuring IQ in predicting future performance.[3] We can't do anything to change our genetic wiring but we can all make a conscious effort to 'stop and think' more robustly, particularly about important decisions where a balanced perspective would be beneficial.

We all rely on our left mind for self-control and to remain alert to the possibility that the instinctive impulses proposed by our right mind, may need to be double-checked. However, improved self-control is necessary, but insufficient on its own, for better cognition. When we 'stop and think' our left mind will, in theory, bring its powerful rationality to assess right-mind data for logical coherence against robust schematic structures, enabling it to return rigorously assessed, appropriately amended and officially 'approved' data back to the right mind for 'whole-mind' synthesis. However, as highlighted in the last chapter it will approve any data which is logically coherent with its schematic structures, irrespective of the nature of the content or the degree to which its schemata reflect outer-world reality. Unfortunately, there are several further flaws in the modus operandi of the left mind – in particular the way in which schematic structures are created and maintained – which make the practice rather less robust than the theory.

Consequences of Categorization

If we were to commit to memory, every characteristic of every pheno-menon we ever encounter, we simply wouldn't have the cognitive band-width to cope with the avalanche of data we receive every second of every waking hour. The ability of our left mind to extract only salient elements of experience, categorize them, and commit sufficient stimuli to our unconscious that a reasonable approximation of 'reality' can be rewoven whenever we need it, is a wonderful evolutionary development and vital to how we function. However, there are unavoidable downsides to this operation because when we categorize we automatically homogenize within categories and polarize between categories. Our left mind cate-gorizes by recognizing underlying patterns of organization in new data and, on this basis, allocates new phenomena to existing categories. Its dualistic nature, however, means that the 'walls' between categories are solid rather than porous – things are either/or and can't be both or neither. A road vehicle can therefore be a bicycle, a motorcycle, a car, a bus, a van or a lorry but any vehicle which doesn't neatly fit into one of these rigidly defined categories causes a problem for the left mind, which only deals in certainty. Lacking the nuance of the right mind, which perceives every phenomenon as unique and individual, the left mind must force-fit any entity, even those with characteristics which are resemblant of more than one category, into one category only. In doing so, the left mind automatically homogenizes the entity, ironing out its nuances, ignoring its distinctivities and making it seem more similar to other category members than is actually the case. As a result, it also makes the entity seem more different to members of other categories (which have also undergone the same homogenizing effect) even though they may, in fact, share many common characteristics. This function is essential to our survival because by forcing all phenomena into different neural whirlpools, our left mind is able to maintain stable states cycles and build generic associations at the category level rather than the individual level (dogs with sticks rather than specific dogs with specific sticks), which is hugely beneficial. Compared to the upsides, the unintended downsides are therefore a relatively small price to pay for perhaps wrongly allocating a three-wheeled vehicle to 'motorcycles' and penalizing it via an association we make to that particular category – such as 'dangerous' – rather than categorizing it as a car. This association and subsequent schematic rule – 'motorcycles are dangerous' – keeps us safe and in this particular example nobody suffers, apart from the manufacturer of the three-wheeled vehicle in question, from the overly simplistic categorization of the left mind.

However, this modus operandi can have a hugely detrimental effect when our left mind categorizes living organisms, particularly people, rather than inanimate objects like road vehicles. For example, male and female are clearly delineated in the dualistic left mind, so the solid walls between the two sexes cause it deep difficulty in dealing with transgender or transsexual individuals, who don't fit neatly into either category. In the left mind all individuals *must* be allocated to one of its polarities and, when this happens, everyone within a particular group, whether based on nationality, ethnicity, gender, sexuality, religion, profession, political affiliation or any other categorization, not only become more alike than they truly are but also more different from those within other such groups, than is the case in reality. The unintended consequences of categorizing people can therefore be very dangerous. By forcing unique individuals into homogenized groups and by making associations at the category level rather than the individual level, our left mind automatically creates group stereotypes which don't necessarily reflect the nuanced characteristics of individual members. By exaggerating the differences of one group from another, which has also been similarly stereotyped, the left mind creates unnecessary, untrue and amplified distinctions upon which division, rivalry or even violence can easily feed. When we only see categories and not the individuals within them, we are highly prone to showing disproportionate favour to groups we feel positively about and bias against those to which we are negatively disposed.

Our desire to be part of a group and the great pleasure we derive from group membership is genetically hard-wired into human brains. We are instinctively social animals. In many countries, if we jog or motorcycle or even drive a particular brand of car, we may find that complete strangers who are doing the same thing will routinely nod or wave in acknowledgement of a shared interest. Being part of a group makes us feel valued and helps meet our basic animal need to feel safe and secure. We are all automatically and simultaneously members of many different groups, some which are permanent such as those based on gender or ethnicity, and others which may be more temporary such as those based on our passions or pastimes. Consequently, groups also exist from which we are automatically excluded or which we choose not to join. Scientists call the groups we are part of our 'in-groups' and those of which we are not a member our 'out-groups'. At every level of our existence, the concept of 'us' and 'them' is therefore unavoidable but most of us have been taught to respect all groups and to value fair play in all aspects of social, economic and political discourse. However, by now you may have gathered that our conscious and unconscious minds don't necessarily play by the same rules, and research consistently shows that we unconsciously show bias towards our in-groups and against our out-groups.

Most of the studies in this field build upon the work of Henri Tajfel, a man whose intuitive awareness of the dangers of categorization almost certainly saved his life.[4] Tajfel was a Polish Jew who, at the outbreak of World War II, was studying chemistry at the Sorbonne in Paris. Henri had left Poland because his status as a Jew prohibited him from attending university, so when, a year later and serving in the French army, he was taken prisoner by the Germans, he instinctively claimed to be French rather than admitting his Polish nationality. The Nazis use of categorization was particularly pernicious. To be French was bad enough. To be a French Jew was dangerous but was still preferable to Polish Jewry, which meant almost certain death. Tajfel survived the war but his experiences, in particular his observations and deliberations about the effects of categorization on prejudice, led him to switch his studies from chemistry to psychology. His theories, however, ran counter to the dominant and accepted premises in his new field at that time, which were rooted in a mechanistic belief in the genetic inheritance of fixed personality traits. According to this viewpoint, only those with personalities which predisposed them to prejudice would become sectarian or racist. However, Henri believed the reality was much more contextual and nuanced, having experienced at first-hand how thousands of Germans, who otherwise appeared to be perfectly ordinary people, came to hold extraordinarily extreme views about Jews and other groups. It seemed unlikely to him that such hatred could be attributed to genetic predisposition and he hypothesised that prejudice was, in fact, rooted in ordinary cognitive processes.

It was Tajfel's early work at the universities of Durham and Oxford, which conclusively demonstrated that the homogenizing and polarizing effects described above – where we assume individuals in one group to be more alike than they really are and more different to those in other groups – is a fundamental mechanism of mind.[5] The only situations in which we override automatic homogenization is when we personally know the individuals concerned and know them well, such as family and close friends. However, tests show that we can't know any more than around 150 people in such depth and, on average, actually know far fewer, no matter how many 'friends' we may have on social media.[6] Therefore in many situations and particularly in larger groupings, we don't even have close personal knowledge of all the members of our in-groups, never mind our out-groups. However, we do always have something in common with them – group membership – and research shows that this alone is sufficient grounds for bias. Consider our work profession. In one study researchers asked doctors, waiters and hairdressers to rate the likeability and capability of people who work in a range of professions, on a scale of 1 to 100.[7] The results were highly consistent in that all three groups rated the other categories at around average, 50 out of 100, but rated those in their own profession at around 70. Furthermore, they rated the other professions as being lower in a range of desirable qualities such as flexibility and creativity. We consistently assume both the ability and likeability of people with whom we have something in common, even if we don't know them as individuals. Studies even show that when we do know an individual, but dislike them, their membership of our in-group can be sufficient for us to prioritise them or their work over someone we like, but who is from an out-group.[8] Within a single workplace, we often fall into departmental or functional in-groups or out-groups which are a subset of our overall group membership as employees of the same company. Even in this situation, studies show we still evaluate the work of in-group members more favourably than the work of out-groups, even when we are all members of the same, higher level in-group and when we consciously believe we are being completely fair, objective and treating everyone equally.[9]

In his later and perhaps most famous work, conducted at Bristol University, Henri Tajfel sought to identify the minimum criteria required for one person to feel a common bond with a fellow in-group member and to demonstrate bias as a result.[10] Incredibly, he discovered that the very act of being placed in a group is sufficient for us to demonstrate prejudice and bias. Taking a bunch of complete strangers as test subjects, Tajfel divided them into two groups using an arbitrary method no more meaning-ful than the toss of a coin. Participants were kept apart and didn't know the identity of any other person, only which group they belonged to. Over a series of exercises, participants were asked to allocate variable resources, in the form of points which could later be exchanged for cash, to two players at a time – sometimes two members of their in-group, sometimes two members of their out-group and sometimes one member from each. With no knowledge of the individuals involved and having no common bond with them, other than having been randomly allocated to their group, participants in both groups consistently demonstrated bias towards their own in-group members and against those from their out-group. Even more remarkable was the discovery that, when points were being allocated between one in-group and one out-group member, participants tended to maximise the *difference* between awards allocated, even if their actions delivered a lesser reward for their own group member.[11]

Tajfel's experiment has subsequently been repeated by many resear-chers, across different age groups and nationalities, with remarkably consistent results. While we are clearly biased towards our own groups, we appear to be just as powerfully vested in creating differences between our groups and others – differences which are more important to us overall than individual in-group members. To explain these rather strange results, Tajfel and his student John Turner developed their social identity theory which posits that personal self-esteem lies at the heart of this behaviour.[12] Their theory suggests that our social identity is largely derived from our multiple group memberships, whether based on family, class, geography, race, religion, profession or which sports team we follow, and our participation in these groups is an important source of personal pride and self-esteem. Our unconscious bias is therefore rooted in our desire to enhance the status of any group to which we belong, as our membership automatically confers status upon us. Similarly we are strongly motivated to join any group which we perceive holds high status, which is why £ millions are spent every year on golf, health and country club memberships which are often never used. However, status and self-esteem are relative rather than absolute concepts. For our self-esteem to be maximised and maintained, it must be in comparison to those groups of which we are not a member, fuelling us with a desirable sense of superiority. It is therefore insufficient, on its own, for us to elevate the status of our group but we must simultaneously seek to undermine the status of those groups of which we are not part.

Collaborators in Confabulation

So while categorization and the prejudicial prioritization of in-groups over out-groups are processes carried out by our left mind, the drivers of our discrimination are actually sourced through our right mind. Status, self-esteem and superiority are all feelings rather than thoughts and, as such, initially bubble up from our unconscious via our more embodied right mind. This serves as a timely reminder that neither hemisphere ever works alone. Many other emotions can similarly influence our judgement, including anger, jealousy, fear or excitement, and our inability to accurately identify the source of these feelings can easily cause our right mind to leap to entirely the wrong conclusion at any given moment. What our right mind presents to our left mind is never a verbatim copy of the real world but an interpretive collage, blended from an ever-changing maelstrom of genetic, sensory, emotional or memory data, all of which originates beyond our consciousness. Our right mind is required not only to weave the streams together but also to interpret what the melee means, and much of the time it simply doesn't know for sure. To arrive at its conclusion, it fills in any gaps by 'taking a guess' and scientists call this process of filling in knowledge gaps via guesswork 'confabulation'. Our right mind is a confabulator supreme.

Most of the time this works perfectly well, particularly when we are in familiar surroundings with little novelty or when an approximation of reality is all we really need. Sometimes, however, our right mind gets it wrong and we need our vigilant left mind to ride to our rescue, challenging its counterpart and questioning its conclusions by dissecting them, assessing them for accuracy and only accepting outputs once they have been subjected to full and detailed scrutiny. As we know, our left mind can occasionally fail to perform its duties and, like the kids who couldn't resist the marshmallow, some people just have lower self-control and a higher tendency to accept the impulsive, intuitive answer. Research also shows that there are a number of conditions under which the left mind is even more likely to lower its guard and blindly accept whatever the right mind offers.[13] Being tired or distracted, being in a good mood, being made to feel powerful or being a knowledgeable novice rather than an expert on a specific subject, can all cause our left mind to become less diligent. Yet the story gets even worse. It wouldn't be so bad if our left mind was merely lazy and occasionally negligent but there is also strong evidence that it often collaborates in supporting erroneous right-mind outputs.

When our right mind produces its spontaneous conclusion, the primary role of our left mind is to force us to 'stop and think' in order to check the validity of what it has been offered. However, our left mind doesn't actually *know* why the right mind arrived at its conclusion – it can't do when the right mind itself often can't accurately identify the basis of its interpretation. The left mind will, therefore, accept anything which is coherent with what it already believes because, in its ordered world, coherence is more important than truth per se. However, not only does it check right-mind interpretations for coherence with its schematic rules, research also shows that the left mind may actually use its associative memories to come up with logical, but entirely spurious, supporting evidence for whatever the right mind proposes. In doing so it collaborates with its counterpart in confabulation.

This fascinating phenomenon was first exposed by Michael Gazzaniga and Joseph LeDoux in split-brain experiments.[14] Two separate images were projected simultaneously, one to each brain hemisphere, and partici-pants were asked to pick a relevant, corresponding image from a range of cards. A snow scene was projected into the right hemisphere and with their left hand (controlled by the right hemisphere) patients selected a corres-ponding picture of a shovel. Meanwhile, an image of a chicken claw was projected into the left hemisphere and, with their right hand, patients selected a card showing a picture of a chicken. When patients were then asked to explain why they had picked the card picturing a shovel, their verbal response – delivered via the left hemisphere which is responsible for the formation of words but which had only seen the chicken claw image – was that the shovel was to clean out the chicken shed. Having not seen the snow scene (which was viewed only in the right hemisphere), the left hemisphere was quick to provide a perfectly plausible, yet completely untrue, post-rationalized explanation for a decision made in the right hemisphere.

The tendency to confabulate is therefore not at all exclusive to the right mind but is shared by the left mind, although they do take a very different approach to it. While the right mind confabulates to fill in knowledge gaps while leaping to rapid conclusions, its flexibility and familiarity with uncertainty do allow it to remain open to the possibility of its own inaccurate interpretations. By contrast, the left mind deals only in singular certainty and therefore experiences cognitive dissonance far more acutely than its counterpart. When challenged to provide a supporting rationale for any decision, it is therefore strongly incentivized to create coherence even where none exists. Not only does it often lower its guard, allowing inaccurate right-mind interpretations to pass unchecked, it actually collaborates in creating a coherent story which supports those same erroneous intuitions but delivers desirable cognitive ease. Confabulating a comforting narrative rather than admitting to not knowing, is therefore a common characteristic of a left mind which is responsible for the formulation of words and for which ambiguity is anathema. This effect is also self-reinforcing because the left mind has a powerful tendency to believe whatever it pronounces and can display an inflated sense of its own surety in doing so. Indeed, multiple experiments, with both split-brain and healthy patients, have shown that not only will the left mind tend to make up an answer but it will also invent an elaborate rationale to support and justify its answer. In fact, even when provided with evidence to the contrary, it will doggedly go on to provide ever more embellished explanations of why it is correct.[15] Consequently, even when we are made aware of the source of our decisions, we often have great difficulty in exercising the self-control required to overturn our original judgement, preferring to deny our confabulations and continue to post-rationalize our unconscious judgements to our conscious self.

Both of our hemispheres are therefore arch-confabulators but both are also smart enough to not simply come up with any old nonsense, instead taking 'educated guesses' to find plausible answers.[16] From time to time we are all asked to explain our decisions and much of the time we don't actually know the honest answer, because our actions are the emergent outputs of a complex system rooted deep in our unconscious mind. Research shows that when asked to explain why we voted for a particular political candidate or bought a certain brand of car or chose a particular holiday destination, we undertake a process of introspection in which we genuinely try to answer truthfully, but we can't access our underlying motivations. Instead, we search our associative memory structures for answers which fit a 'cultural norm' model of why people usually do such things, and simply select from the list our left mind produces. In other words, when the question *'why did I do this?'* becomes too difficult to answer, we replace it with a simpler alternative – *'why do people normally do this?'* – and because all the answers satisfy the 'cultural norm' criteria, all are guaranteed to be plausible if not necessarily true.[17] Our left mind thus collaborates in making sense of what we decide and in the delusion that we actually know why we do what we do. This heuristic approach is one of many tools we use to confabulate post-rationalized justifications for judgements which are largely unconscious and emotion-based.

Another method is motivated reasoning.[18] We like to believe we always think like scientists; objectively analysing issues, then building solutions in a logical sequence from the bottom up until arriving at a robust, fully-formed conclusion. However, research shows this isn't at all how we usually think and, actually, our thinking is often much more akin to that of a court-room lawyer. Lawyers think very differently from scientists because they tend to start with a conclusion – either the guilt or innocence of the accused – and work backwards, seeking evidence which supports a decision which has already been made. Our left mind often employs such motivated reasoning to post-rationalize unconsciously-sourced, right-mind conclusions, yet gives us the impression that they are the output of a scientific approach using our free will and linear, conscious cognition. Motivated reasoning uses a number of tactics to find retrospective, rational evidence, including investing more time and effort in searching for supportive rather than contrary data, attaching greater significance to information which supports a decision than that which doesn't, affording greater credibility to 'experts' who support rather than undermine a conclusion, filtering evidence to accept supporting data while removing contrary data, and 'selective testing' which involves rejecting the validity of research which yields contrary results, while accepting only supporting evidence.

In one experiment, participants were asked to review job applications from two candidates for a role as police chief.[19] Two types of profile were created. One portrayed a tough, street-wise cop who was popular and successful, in spite of a poor education and relatively weak administration skills. The other profile was of a well-educated and politically connected individual, who had strong administration skills but relatively little street experience and was known to get along poorly with some fellow officers. Two fictitious characters, Michael and Michelle, were also invented to accompany the two profiles but one set of groups received the 'street-wise' profile for Michelle and the 'well-educated' profile for Michael, while the profiles were switched for the other set of groups. The results showed that groups selected Michael for the job when he had the 'street-wise' profile, explaining that policing experience and street smarts were essential for the role. However, the other groups also recommended Michael for the job when he had the 'well-educated' profile, defining education, connections and administrative skills as the key selection criteria for a police chief. Researchers concluded that all groups were actually making their decisions based on unconscious gender bias, but were also using motivated reasoning to post-rationalize their intuitive decisions by changing the prioritization of their selection criteria.

While motivated reasoning is often a conscious search for rational data to support unconscious decisions we have already made, it is not necessarily a disingenuous act because our conscious mind isn't even aware that it is operating retrospectively. It genuinely believes that it is actively participating in a bottom-up decision making process, rather than post-rationalizing a decision which is already done and dusted. When we try to explain the reasons behind a decision, we are clearly aware of the decision but unaware of the unconscious processing which went into arriving at it. We are, however, highly motivated to believe that our decision was the result of our own free will and the output of our conscious mind, so we can become very dogged in our belief in the veracity of our own thinking. In the above police chief exercise, none of the participants were consciously aware that the gender of candidates had unconsciously influenced their decision, nor had they deliberately reprioritized assessment criteria. In all groups, participants had real difficulty in accepting the findings of the research and this highlights a key ally of motivated reasoning – subjectivity. We value the coherence of the narrative we tell ourselves, far more than any objective truth per se, because a coherent story gives us a highly desirable sense of cognitive ease. In order to ensure cognitive ease, our minds will rarely let an uncomfortable truth spoil a reassuring story. While we actually exercise very little conscious free will in most of our decision making, our subjectivity gives both of our minds a huge degree of freedom to collaborate in confabulating plausible explanations for our actions, which provide us with a reassuring, but delusional, sense that we are in full conscious control.

This powerful desire is a key driver of our motivated reasoning and, like all desires, is more unconscious than conscious to us. In fact, brain scanning shows that motivated reasoning involves several parts of the unconscious limbic system, including the orbitofrontal cortex and the anterior cingulate cortex, as well as the more conscious neocortex. Not only do our right and left hemispheres collaborate with each other but so too do our conscious and unconscious minds. Our whole cognitive system is deeply involved in motivated reasoning and our feelings are always part of the story. In fact, soothing our feelings is often the motivation for such retrospective reasoning. We use it to rationalize why we didn't get the job we wanted, why we are better off single or why the book we wrote was never published. We also use it to reassure ourselves that the loved ones we have lost are now in a better place. Our brain is imbued with this powerful mechanism to automatically ameliorate our suffering and nowhere do we more readily employ motivated reasoning than when it comes to our self-perception. When things go well for us we are inclined to point to our own capabilities and all the good decisions we made, but when things go against us we tend to look to external factors beyond our control for an explanation, overlooking or downplaying any poor judgement. Our self-image is vital to our mental wellbeing and from an early age we become aware of the difference between our idealised image – the person we wish to be and want others to perceive us to be – and the reality we experience every day, through living with ourselves and our intimate knowledge of our own failings, foibles and insecurities. Throughout our lives we continually employ motivated reasoning to convince ourselves that we are actually our imaginary ideal, by overemphasising our strengths and downplaying our weaknesses. If we are naturally introverted we attach greater value to reflective thinking, if we are extroverts we afford greater significance to social skills. We are attracted to and surround ourselves with friends who provide positive feedback which reinforces our desired self-image, and we tend to lose touch with those who don't provide this valuable service. We paint a portrait of ourselves which blends facts, exaggerations, distortions and desires, then actively, if unconsciously, manipulate our external environments so they reflect the illusion back to us. We are thus made to feel good about ourselves and in particular about our competence, attractiveness and the degree to which we are in control of our own lives. Our self-belief and self-esteem become amplified, fuelling a high level of self-confidence which is essential to propelling the self-creating aspects of our complex system.

Studies in Overconfidence

Consider one study of almost a million high-school students, in which, when asked to rate their own ability to get along with others, 100% rated themselves to be average or above, 60% placed themselves in the top 10% and 25% believed themselves to be in the top 1%.[20] For decades, psychologists have consistently observed a widespread human tendency for inflated self-assessment, across all age groups, across a wide range of countries and relating to all aspects of life. In various tests, 99% of business executives overestimated their knowledge of their own industry,[21] 98% of students thought they had average or above average leadership capabilities,[22] 94% of university professors believed they were better than average teachers[23] and 90% of drivers thought they were better than average behind the wheel.[24] Critically, confidence is not connected to competence. In fact, there is considerable evidence that incompetent individuals overestimate their capabilities by an even greater margin than their more capable peers.[25] Ironically, we are pretty good at recognizing overconfidence, but only in others not in ourselves.[26]

Not only do we overestimate what we know, we also overestimate what we *can* know. In complex systems, such as the stock market, it is impossible to consistently and accurately predict how share prices will move, yet traders delude themselves every day that this isn't the case. Stock trading is actually very simple in principle but highly complex in practice. If a share is correctly priced, it accurately incorporates all of the data currently available on the value of the business and the forecasted performance of the stock. Billions of shares are bought and sold every day, with buyers buying because they think the stock is priced too low and sellers selling because they think it is priced too high. We therefore simultaneously have so-called industry 'experts' holding opposing views on the same issue – whether or not the stock is accurately priced – and they clearly can't all be correct. Terry Odean studied 163,000 trades over a seven-year period, tracking the performance of bought and sold stock for a full year after each transaction was made, and concluded that the performance of traders was poor.[27] On average, shares *sold* by traders went on to deliver better returns than those they bought by 3.2 percentage points, even before transaction costs were taken into account. These results were the average so, within them, there were clearly some winners and some losers but other studies have also shown that two out of three investment funds typically underperform the market in any given year, and that the correlation of year-to-year performance is barely higher than zero.[28] In other words, the evidence from a wealth of research data reveals that fund managers fail the basic test of skill – consistent achievement – and that

> for a large majority of fund managers, the selection of stocks is more like rolling dice than playing poker ... the successful funds in any given year are more lucky; they have a good roll of the dice.[29]

Of course, professional investors don't pick stocks by throwing darts while blindfolded. They do, in fact, work very hard in reviewing economic forecasts, market conditions, company accounts, management capabilities and so on. However, the only question which ultimately matters is whether or not this data has already been accurately incorporated into the share price. While the evidence suggests that, over the long-run, throwing darts would be just as successful, brain scans show that when traders have a good day they experience a pleasurable dose of dopamine released into their brain, which boosts their confidence and encourages them to increase the number of trades they make. Further analysis by Barber and Odean found that while those traders who were most confident transacted the most trades, they actually underperformed the market.[30]

The inability of experts to accurately predict the future isn't restricted to stock traders or fund managers, but afflicts experts across many fields. Canadian psychologist Philip Tetlock spent over 20 years studying hundreds of professional advisers, commentators and pundits, across the fields of business, politics and economics.[31] He asked them to make predictions in their areas of expertise but also about other topics, in the above fields, on which they were not so expert. He then analysed around 28,000 predictions for accuracy against actual outcomes, and made some remarkable discoveries. Tetlock synthesised all of the data into three possible future outcomes – the same, more of or less of whatever participants were predicting (eg economic growth) and found that, across all participants and all topics, their predictions were actually poorer than if they had simply allocated a 33.3% chance to each outcome. Even more alarmingly, Tetlock found that experts were not significantly more reliable than non-experts in predicting what was going to happen in their own areas of specialism. Although this may surprise most of us, it is less likely to surprise psychologists as Tetlock's study is just one of many which have assessed the predictive abilities of so-called experts in many fields, and found similar results. Several have even pitted them against statistical formulae and in almost all of these studies, the experts fare no better than predictive algorithms.[32]

It is, however, a little unfair to blame experts for getting their predictions wrong (although we can reasonably reprimand them for believing they could accurately predict the future in the first place). Stock markets and economies are incredibly complex systems, with a very large number of nodes and vast volumes of data being transferred across the network at an astonishing rate, every day. There are so many variables involved – which may lead to feedback loops with amplifying or dampening effects – that consistently and accurately predicting emergent outcomes is simply impossible. And there is no complex system more unfathomable to us than the one located between our ears. If we don't even know how feeling hungry or happy might affect our decisions, how can we possibly be expected to accurately predict the actions of others, the future of market economies or anything else for that matter?

Yet, we are so powerfully wedded to a mechanistic narrative and have become so deeply conditioned to believe in linear cause and effect, that we place great faith in the ability of our scientific mind to understand the past and, in doing so, identify rules we can re-apply to predict the future. When something has happened in the past, we feel a compelling need to explain what caused it so we can gain a sense of control over it occurring again. The reality is, however, that in complex systems emergent outcomes are rarely explicable, because they result from a huge number of small, variable interactions between nodes, the influence of multiple attractors and the unpredictable effects of feedback loops. We also never become aware of what would have emerged had small changes occurred in the initial conditions, which, like in the movie *Sliding Doors*, may have led to very different outcomes. While our right mind engages the outer world 'live' each day and, like the happy wanderer it is, tends to roll with whatever comes its way, the idea that many of our experiences are inexplicable, and could easily have been very different, is deeply unsatisfactory to our left mind with its desire for unambiguous certainty. Without a simple explanation for all experienced phenomena, we would be unable to build the associative schemata we need to create order in our inner world, from the chaotic data-overload of our outer world. Our two minds therefore collaborate to make up a coherent narrative about why things happen, to ease our cognitive dissonance and give us a comforting, but inaccurate, belief that we can understand the past and predict the future. The many 'experts' we are forced to listen to, simply fuel this delusion.

Of course, some things in our world *do* operate to linear, causal laws but as Nassim Nicholas Taleb demonstrates in *The Black Swan*, much of our inability to accurately understand the past stems from our left mind's tendency to weave a causal explanation into *everything* we experience. Taleb shows how '*narrative fallacies*' inevitably arise out of our continual attempts to explain every aspect of the outer world, and posits that this tendency is rooted in our biological need to reduce the dimensions of the information we process, in order that it may be stored, manipulated and retrieved in the most energy-efficient manner possible.[33] Our left mind automatically looks for rules or patterns in data because we then only need to retain the pattern, from which the whole sequence can be recreated, whenever we wish to recall it from memory. Imagine a series of 100 random numbers. We would never be able to memorize, then recall, such a large volume of data but if the sequence began 0-1-1-2-3-5-8-13 we would recognize a pattern and be able to recreate the full 100 numbers, by memorizing only the pattern and not the numbers themselves. Clearly, just like the gists and generalizations from which visual and word-based memories are rewoven, storing numeric patterns is energy-efficient and core to how our left mind works. It has to reduce information into simple rules so it can squeeze vast richness into very small dimensions, which we can easily restore, reweave and reapply whenever we need to – the essential modus operandi of the scientific mind.

However, we are much better at explaining the past than we are at genuinely understanding it. We seek patterns in all events and, if we can't find one, we confabulate something plausible. We create compelling narratives to explain why something happened and, if the stories we invent are logical and infer causality, they make sense to us. The stories don't have to be objectively true, just subjectively coherent. Such tales provide us with simple, clear and credible accounts of people's motivations, subsequent actions and the consequences of those actions. A coherent narrative eases cognitive dissonance and gives us an illusion of comprehension, which is deeply satisfying because we believe that we will recognize the same patterns next time they appear and will be able to predict where they will lead. In doing so, we satisfy our powerful need to feel in control of our future. As Daniel Kahneman explains,

> you build the best possible story from the information available to you and if it's a good story you believe it. Paradoxically it is easier to construct a coherent story when you know little, when there are fewer pieces to fit into the puzzle. Our comforting conviction that the world makes sense rests on a secure foundation: our almost unlimited ability to ignore our ignorance.[34]

A compelling, coherent narrative about past events fuels our illusion that those events were actually predictable before they occurred, which further enhances our belief in our predictive abilities. Studies show that when an occurrence takes us by surprise, rather than revising our assessment of our own predictive abilities – downwards – we are much more likely to adjust the beliefs we claim we held before the event happened, so they fall in line with what actually took place.[35] By employing such *'hindsight bias'*, we under-acknowledge the degree to which we were surprised and over-estimate the degree to which we foresaw what actually occurred. Furthermore, much of our use of future prediction is to help us make decisions in the present. We therefore use our flawed comprehension of the causes of past events to build flawed predictive models and base our decisions on them. Yet, if we make enough guesses we inevitably get some right and when a prediction does come true, we invariably attribute our success to our robust model and good judgement rather than our good fortune, further reinforcing our faith in the flawed model. However, when a prediction fails to come true we simply suppress, forget or even deny that we ever thought it would, automatically increasing our apparent success rate.

A systemic *'outcome bias'* also causes us to evaluate the quality of a decision based on whether a prediction came true, rather than whether the decision was soundly based on the information available at the time it was made.[36] The consequence of this very common bias is often either the *'haloing'* or *'scapegoating'* of those who make decisions – where we erroneously attribute success to genius and failure to incompetence – rather than recognizing the powerful influence of randomness and the great unpredictability of complex systems. For example, major terrorist events like 9/11 are invariably followed by a clamour to find someone to blame for failing to foresee that such attacks were imminent. Conversely, great rewards can be bestowed upon those for whom the cards fall favourably. In *The Halo Effect,* Phil Rosenzweig concludes that stories of business successes or failures consistently overplay the impact of leadership style and management capability on results, yet a whole management consultancy industry has been created on the basis of just such a search-and-reapply model. During the 1980s, Japanese companies were consistently outperforming all others and Western businesses paid handsomely to learn the secret of their success – the 'Kaizen' philosophy of continuous improvement. Unfortunately, in 1990 the Japanese economy crashed, wiping US$2 trillion off the value of Nikkei stock within 12 months, and the unassailable magic of Kaizen has hardly been mentioned ever since. Nevertheless, many business owners still believe they only need to study Apple, Google, Amazon or Facebook to replicate their success. No-one would suggest that the achievements of these companies were solely down to luck but markets are highly unpredictable, complex systems, so the halo effect rarely lasts because no company or individual can enjoy good fortune all of the time. The CEO of UK banking group RBS, Fred Goodwin, was for many years lauded as a business visionary as he presided over his company's rise to global prominence. He was even awarded a knighthood by the British Queen and anointed Sir Fred. However, the banking crash of 2008 and the largest annual loss in UK corporate history of £24.1 billion, put paid to Sir Fred's career. Genius or incompetent fool? In truth, of course, he was neither. Such is the complexity of international finance he was simply lucky for a while until his luck ran out. In 2012 he was even stripped of his knighthood, despite his only crime being to have believed his own narrative fallacy. Fred (as he is now known) discovered to his great cost, that the halo effect of our outcome bias can rapidly flip into scapegoating. While no-one would suggest that CEO's have no impact on the performance of their businesses, there is strong evidence that our assessment of their influence is often as overinflated as their salaries.[37]

Conclusion

Our understanding of the human cognitive system has advanced more in the last 50 years than during any previous period. In particular, we now know that the classic social science story of *homo-sapiens* as rational, utility-maximising machines is a work of pure fiction, and that our emotions play the lead role in most of our thinking. Moreover, our brains are susceptible to an array of systemic flaws, fallacies and biases of which we are largely unaware. The most fundamental flaw of all, is that our impulsive right mind leaps to conclusions based on a blend of sensory, emotional and genetic data about which it only has a fuzzy feeling, yet confidently presents its interpretations to a lazy left mind which is charged with making us stop and think, but which often fails to do so. Even when it does intervene, such is its desire for coherence it is just as likely to confabulate support for an erroneous decision as it is to provide contrary evidence. As a result, the essential third phase in our right-left-right cognitive sequence often takes place without the data we need to form a fully-considered conscious judgement, substituted instead by a simpler heuristic.

More than anything, our cognitive system is designed to help us make sense of the cacophony of information we receive from a data-rich external environment, so we feel in control of our own lives. The principal goal of this operating mode is not to accurately portray outer-world reality but to protect inner-world harmony; its core responsibility being to make us feel subjectively safe rather than to furnish us with objective truth. Our mind therefore provides us with a useful approximation of the outer world but constantly readjusts its interpretation in order to conserve energy, ensure cognitive ease and maintain a reassuring level of self-confidence. It does so by creating the illusion that we genuinely understand past events, identifying causal rules and projecting their effects into the future in the fanciful expectation that events will always unfold in exactly the same way. The truth is that all phenomena are ultimately determined by probability rather than certainty, a principle which makes our left mind deeply uncomfortable. However, much of what we experience does reoccur with great regularity or changes so slowly that it gives the impression of following deterministic, linear laws. This simply serves to reinforce our false belief in the infallibility of our predictive abilities and increase our tendency to assume direct causality in everything we experience. When something takes us by surprise, rather than use our cognitive powers to challenge our own thinking, we simply change the story we tell ourselves to restore cognitive ease and re-establish our sense of control. By inventing a new narrative, the world seems to make sense once again. This illusion is deeply comforting because it shields us from the cognitive dissonance we would feel if we were to be fully exposed to the uncertainty of reality and the reality of uncertainty.

It is to combat such existential anxieties that *homo-sapiens* have been imbued with a great dose of overconfidence and, of all human characteristics, it is probably the most distinctive and double-edged. Psychological studies are full of examples of the huge benefits of holding positive self-perception, along with its consistent corollaries, optimism and good mood.[38] People who hold a happy, confident and upbeat outlook have been shown to be more sociable and popular than those who don't, as well as being healthier and having stronger immune systems.[39] Such people take more risks, so are more likely to be the inventors, entre-preneurs or creatives who drive progressive change in society, their '*optimistic bias*' making them more resilient to setbacks, failures or hardships. They tend to be more co-operative, more highly motivated and more persistent in solving problems and overcoming obstacles.[40] Their approach makes them more likely to succeed, which fuels their self-belief and is further reinforced by the admiration of others. Self-confidence and optimism, even if delusional, can therefore have a very positive effect and can be at least partially self-fulfilling. Almost all of us are overconfident to some degree, although men tend to be more overconfident than women, and an overly positive self-evaluation is both normal and healthy.[41] In fact, studies even show that those people with the most accurate self-perceptions may tend to be moderately depressed or suffer from low self-esteem.[42]

However, the many downsides of overconfidence are self-evident, particularly given the myriad flaws, fallacies and biases to which our cognitive apparatus is susceptible. To date, behavioural scientists have identified more than thirty systemic tendencies to which we are all dis-posed, and no doubt there are still more yet to be discovered. I shall give the final say on the matter to perhaps the most authoritative voice of all, Daniel Kahneman:

> Subjective confidence in a judgement is not a reasoned evaluation of the probability that this judgement is correct. Confidence is a feeling, which reflects the coherence of the information and the cognitive ease of processing it. It is wise to take admissions of uncertainty seriously but declarations of high confidence mainly tell you that an individual has constructed a coherent story in his mind, not necessarily that the story is true.[43]

— 7 —

Blending for Balance

OUR BRAINS work by leveraging the mutual independence, but interdependence, of the two hemispheres to benefit from the contradictions and conflicts they create. Each mind approaches the world from a very different perspective yet, via the integration of opposites, we make sense of what we experience. The right mind, our adventurous wanderer in the outer world, blends what it senses and feels with what it subconsciously 'remembers' and takes an impulsive, but educated, guess at explaining what we encounter. Our left mind, the wary and protective architect of our associative schemata, analyses and validates its output, rationalizing a reassuringly coherent narrative for everything it approves. Finally, our right mind synthesises both right and left outputs to co-ordinate a holistic response which drives integrated, whole-body action. However, as we have discovered, as perfect as our cognitive processes sound in principle, they are deeply flawed in practice. Unable to accurately interpret emotions or their source, our right mind can be over-confident and gullible in its guesswork. Occasionally lazy and always desperate for certainty, our left mind can easily approve false proclamations and may even confabulate evidence to support and dogmatically defend erroneous outputs. Designed to ensure energy efficiency and avoid discomforting cognitive dissonance, our brain prioritizes the coherence of the narrative it creates above all else, including absolute truth. This fuels a valuable, but delusional, degree of self-confidence which affords us the essential, yet illusory, reassurance that we can predict and control the future.

Our ancient brains haven't changed for at least 50,000 years, yet it is only within the last 50 years that we have even become aware of how they work and of the many systemic flaws in our cognitive equipment. Yet, the fact remains that everything humankind has ever created – all of the

149

socio-economic systems, legal frameworks, political infrastructures, religious movements and technological developments – are ultimately both the product of and fuel for the cultures we have created; cultures which are the emergent outputs of deeply defective minds. Individually, few of us hold equal preference for our left and right minds – almost all of us have a dominant and preferred cognitive style. While, in aggregate, our collective preference is one of hemispheric balance, we do not necessarily live within cultures which provide or promote equal opportunities for such balance. Western cultures (and therefore most cultures globally) have a strong tendency to be skewed towards the dominance of the left mind, with its concomitant orientation towards mechanistic, materialistic, 'classic' science. Even a century after quantum science fatally undermined the premises upon which this worldview was built, it still remains strong because cultures change very slowly and it may yet take several more decades for the implications of our 'new' scientific knowledge to fully permeate wider society. Advancements in complexity science, neuro-science and the social sciences, now give us a far greater understanding of how our minds work and the importance of the cultures we create in shaping both the individual mind and our whole human system. As Socrates understood, the path to individual and collective happiness lies in increasing self-awareness, so our species should surely benefit from such knowledge.

The implications of how our minds operate, and in particular the cultural imbalance between the hemispheres we have collectively created, are huge. However, before we expand upon them it is worth reiterating that while we all may have a preference, none of us ever thinks with only one hemisphere. The implications outlined below are therefore descriptive of the extremes of right and left-mode cognition, while our experienced reality is always some fusion of the two. Nevertheless, it is valuable to understand the distinct perspectives of right and left, in order to become more acutely aware of our personal and collective biases. It is also useful to consider the benefits we would enjoy if we were each able to elevate our consciousness to deliberately enhance their integration. In doing so we could create more balanced cultures which would provide an environ-mental context more conducive to the natural harmony of the global mind. With such caveats and considerations expressed, we can now explore the many competitions, contradictions and conflicts which arise from the opposing tendencies of our left and right minds.

Freedom, Order and Justice

Both our minds see human-beings as distinct holons but the outward orientation of our right mind, with its automatic 'zoom out' function, also perceives that we are members of multiple, multi-layered groups which are themselves all ultimately nested within one global human community. Embedded in the real outer world, our right mind makes no hierarchical distinction between individuals, considering them all to be equal in value, but its broader focus ultimately gives primacy of attention to the larger holon – the group – over the individual. Our left mind also perceives individuals and groups but it takes a narrower focus, prioritizing the individual over the group, and its categorizing function always distinguishes between groups. Its automatic homogenization within groups and polarization between groups, artificially exaggerates the similarities of those in the same group and the differences between individuals in different groups. Groups are also automatically prioritized, creating hierarchies in which friends and family are significantly more valuable than strangers. In-groups therefore always take precedence over out-groups and, in its dualistic world, collectives are always divided between 'me and mine' versus 'them and the other'.

The two minds therefore take a radically different approach to concepts such as society, individual freedom, collective order and justice. The former UK Prime Minister Margaret Thatcher once famously claimed *'there is no such thing as society'* because, as she saw it, there were only individual men and women and family groups – a particularly left-minded perspective on the collective.[1] The more holistic right mind, of course, takes a very different view. Both left and right minds place great value on individual freedom but, as always, each has a unique lens through which it sees the world. For the left mind, with its narrower focus, primacy lies with the individual and freedom is therefore the right to be left alone with minimal interference from any outside group. Its strong desire to be in control means it has a natural resistance to *being* controlled, and a resultant preference for small government and maximum personal autonomy. The right mind is also highly interested in personal freedom but, through its wider lens, has a different perspective on it. Embedded in the real world of living organisms, it sees people as unique individuals and its deeper links to our emotions fill it with an instinctive empathy for them. It powerfully perceives the relationships between people, so considers that individual freedom can only be achieved within an ecosystem which offers relative equality for everyone. Our right mind is therefore more instinctively interventionist than the left, and more likely to support initiatives which protect the freedoms of all individuals from being disadvantaged or exploited by some individuals. While individual freedom remains essential, to the right mind it can only be given full expression within a system which actively enables it, so higher taxation and government spending on initiatives such as free education, universal healthcare, social welfare, environmental protection and equal gender pay make complete sense. From its broader perspective, the wellbeing of the individual is interdependent with the health of the whole ecosystem.

The left mind's primary interest is in protecting us and those closest to us, so, with this as its priority, it is automatically more self-centred than the right mind. Its narrower focus and inward orientation at all times prioritises the interests of 'me and mine' over the interests of others. It does perceive individuals but its natural categorization and lower empathy means that people, beyond those it knows personally, exist less as unique entities and more as faceless members of homogenous groups. Its narrow narrative emphasises personal over collective responsibility and its strong belief in its own ability to manipulate life for its own ends, make it self-reliant, competitive and adherent to a 'survival of the fittest' mantra. In its decontextualized world, material objects and symbolic referents such as money are just as important as abstract groups of people it doesn't know, so it is drawn to the corollary of small government – low taxation – believing that individuals should be left to accumulate or spend their wealth as they see fit. Such an orientation makes it instinctively resistant to governments spending our taxes on programmes which attempt to change collective behaviour, thus undermining its core principle of individual responsibility and threatening the fiscal autonomy and financial health of its most valued in-group, 'me and mine'.

In short, while our left mind prioritizes personal freedom for us and those closest to us, our right mind wants freedom for everyone. This is a subtle but crucial distinction. While the right mind wants everyone to have equal freedom to access the full range of benefits offered by society, the left mind wants everyone to be left alone to pursue their own happiness and prosperity, free from external interference. While our right mind suggests we have collective responsibility to build a co-operative society in which everyone can fulfil their potential, our left mind proposes a more competitive model of self-determination. From the above descriptions it may be tempting to simply portray the left mind as selfish and the right mind as benevolent, but this would be misleading. Both of our minds seek to enhance our survival but they do so by balancing equally valuable, but opposite, impulses and it is ultimately the holistic synthesis of their outputs which optimize our wellbeing. Our left mind protects us by focussing narrowly on 'us and ours', while our right mind recognizes that none of us can live successfully if isolated from an ecosystem to which we are, in fact, deeply connected. Contrary tendencies towards selfishness and self-lessness, order and flexibility, competition and co-operation, personal versus shared responsibility and individual versus collective freedom, all therefore vie with one another for our attention. It is their interplay which maintains a healthy, dynamic stability within our embodied system. While our dualistic left mind perceives these to be polar opposites, our monistic right mind sees them as points on a continuum to be blended. Our well-being is optimized when they are harmoniously balanced and while this is our collective preference in large groups, rarely are we individually balanced but tend to hold a dominant preference towards one or the other. Part of our preference is genetic and can't be changed but at least some of it is more malleable; the product of culture and those systemic flaws and biases we can work to overcome.

Observant readers may detect a clear alignment between the respective approaches of our two minds, towards matters such as freedom, govern-ment and taxation, with what are generally considered to be 'conservative' versus 'liberal' lenses on the world. It is certainly no accident that our key political polarities are derived directly from the operating modes of our two minds. Our brain is ultimately the source of all human creations and politics is no exception. Those of us with a dominant right mind may tend towards a more liberal or progressive outlook, while people with a strong left-mind preference are often socially, economically and politically conservative. However, none of us ever thinks exclusively with either brain hemisphere and we are all influenced by the cultures we live in, so we are necessarily subjected to many internal conflicts and contradictions. For example, we may hold a progressive point of view on most matters but lean towards conservativism on others. We may consistently be economically liberal yet socially conservative, or take a liberal stance with our conservative friends but be considered conservative by our liberal friends. Irrespective of how our brain is hard-wired we are also the products of our upbringing, so our natural inclinations may be altered in different social situations by peer group pressure, family tradition or other motivations, such as the desire to fit in with a dominant group or to portray a particular self-image. Our opinions along the conservative to liberal spectrum may even change day-to-day, depending on how we feel at any particular moment in time. We are all unique and our thoughts and actions, while always the emergent output of both brain hemispheres, can be influenced by many intrinsic or extrinsic factors. A natural skew towards small-c conservatism therefore doesn't automatically or always translate into support for a large-C Conservative political party. Likewise liberalism. However, having duly acknowledged all of these caveats, the strong relationship between the left mind and conservatism, and between the right mind and liberalism, are simply too powerful and too consistent to be co-incidental.

As well as a shared passion for individual freedom, both left and right minds also share a strong desire for collective order but, once again, they approach the same objective from very different directions. Ironically, the left mind, which vehemently opposes government interference in economic matters, is more likely than the right mind to advocate government intervention in matters of law and order. Core to this apparent paradox is the left mind's love of rules and the clear, categorized distinction it makes between in-groups and out-groups. Although it places great value on personal freedom, it is also highly motivated to protect the interests of our in-groups and, ultimately, it prioritizes the latter over the former. The natural orientation of the left mind is for maximum individual freedom but the reality is that very few of us live in isolation from the rest of society. In the collective sphere, therefore, the left mind has no problem with prioritizing the rights of our in-groups in order to maximize the personal freedoms of 'me and mine', even if that means restricting the personal freedoms of 'others' i.e. those who belong to our out-groups. Its strong need for rules, hierarchy, control and order, yields a tendency towards power and authoritarianism compared to our relatively egalitarian right mind, so it sees no contradiction in imposing its will on others. Even though it genuinely values individual freedom, its idea of freedom is an abstract and theoretical construct of its own making, rather than the sensory, experienced, real-world freedom enjoyed by the right mind. As such, its priorities are more easily superseded by other constructs it has also created and, in its hierarchical world, 'our' freedoms always trump 'their' freedoms.

It is the politics of the left mind which would induce David Cameron, former UK Prime Minister and leader of the Conservative Party, to pledge to repeal the Human Rights Act which protects the rights of all human-beings equally, and replace it with a British Bill of Rights which would protect the rights of one group and give it the power to deny the same rights to other groups.[2] As long as we are part of the dominant group this actually makes perfect sense to the left mind because, for it, a key role of government is to protect 'me and mine' from all dangerous 'others'. The left mind also offers the verbal skills needed to ensure an appropriately frightening narrative can be constructed to describe any out-group we wish to demonize, whether they are homogenized as 'terrorists', 'immigrants', 'unemployed' or some other undesirable categorization. However, to our right mind, and whether we are part of the dominant group or not, this represents an outrageous, divisive and hypocritical attempt to deny personal freedom in the name of protecting freedom, by prioritizing the rights of one group over another. In the wake of the appalling Charlie Hebdo murders, many an embodied right mind felt a sense of revulsion at the number of political leaders who marched through Paris in support of freedom of expression, yet represented nations in which journalists and others have been prosecuted for claiming the very same rights. For some observers the hypocrisy was almost as sickening as the terrorism itself. In truth, the freedom the left mind desires is neither individual nor collective freedom, but the freedom for some individuals to set schematic rules and impose their view of how society should operate on all individuals. While both left and right minds may therefore claim a belief in democracy, the right mind's version is genuinely democratic while the left mind's preference is actually for an autocratic democracy – the rule of the largest group over the rest – which remains the prevalent model for the creation of political and legislative order in many Western societies today.

In summary, both right and left minds are deeply interested in how we maintain dynamic stability in society by balancing individual freedom with collective order. However, they have almost diametrically opposed views on how best to achieve this:

For the right mind, our flexible representative in the real world of experience, the most important freedom lies in the social sphere and in the freedom of *all* individuals to live life with access to all of the benefits society can offer. Freedom is therefore rooted in freedom of speech and a political democracy in which every individual has an equal right to have his or her voice heard. For the right mind, however, social and political freedom can only be achieved if there is justice in the economic sphere, which necessitates equality of access to education, employment at a fair wage, affordable healthcare, gender equality and a level, meritocratic playing field for all. For the right mind, individual freedom and collective order are optimized when these conditions are met.

For the left mind, which creates the abstract structures that bring order to our lives, the most important freedom lies in the economic sphere and in the self-determination of every individual in pursuing their personal goals, absent unwarranted interference from any other individual or collective. The right to earn money and own property are fundamental rights which can only be protected if there is justice in the social sphere, achieved via the righteous behaviour of all individuals. The role of politics is therefore to ensure law, order and the development of a moral environment in which the needs of the majority can be protected and, if necessary, imposed upon the minority. For the left mind, individual freedom and collective order are optimized when these conditions are met.

The peculiar perspectives of the left and right mind are similarly reflected in their approach to justice. In the left mind, reductionism automatically offers separation as our favoured solution for criminal behaviour, so jail time (which ensures a physical barrier between a 'me and mine' and the undesirable 'other') is the logical solution. Because the left mind doesn't see out-group members as individual people, but as homogenous groups marked 'criminals' or 'drug users' or 'benefit cheats', it has no qualms about denying personal freedom to such faceless collectives. Lacking the empathy of the right mind it genuinely does so without feeling guilty because, from its dualistic perspective, such categories of 'bad people' threaten the rights of 'good people' and it is perfectly legitimate to deny them the freedoms we demand for ourselves, so we can maintain collective order for the majority. Naturally, the 'majority' tends to correlate strongly with our in-groups. The left mind's inward orientation also places great emphasis on personal responsibility, so criminal behaviour is very much the result of aberrant qualities which are inherent to the individual. As such, they deserve punishment and separation from 'decent society', so the left mind favours simple, clear and unambiguous laws against which everyone can be judged, allied to strong sentencing. Automatic minimum jail terms for different categories of crime and even the extraordinarily punitive '3 strikes & you're out' rule, still used by some US states, therefore make perfect sense to the left mind, meeting its powerful need for rules and regulations. To the left mind, bad people are intrinsically bad so repeated offending only confirms that they should be permanently separated from the rest of us. Because responsibility for deviant behaviour sits squarely with the criminal, he or she is also held accountable for their own rehabilitation and must change their ways if they are to be accepted back into community life. Society is absolved from any collective responsibility for non-conforming individuals so, to the left mind, government-funded rehabilitation programmes are an unwarranted use of taxpayer's money which only serve to excuse criminal acts and discharge the criminal of their responsibility for personal redemption.

It is only the broader focus of the right mind which sees the relevance of the context in which criminal behaviour manifests, so it brings a very different perspective to law, order and justice. While our left mind takes the position that we should forcibly intervene when we are threatened, the right mind is instinctively more interventionist but in a much softer way. Engaged daily with an ever-changing outer world, it has an entirely different perspective to that of the mechanistic, rule-bound left mind. While the left mind favours punitive, post-crime intervention, the right mind prefers preventative, pre-crime solutions. It perceives that nothing is fixed, isolated or inevitable and that everything is fluid, organic and connected to everything else. Context is therefore paramount and its outward orientation – seeing holons as part of larger holons – forces it to consider the bigger picture in everything it does. Unlike the left mind it sees the criminal as an individual human-being and, with its enhanced empathy, seeks to understand the environmental conditions in which undesirable behaviours manifest, and to develop interventions which may allow different outcomes to emerge. It is therefore far more likely to seek systemic solutions which address the underlying causes of crime, such as poverty, education and family breakdown, than to simply punish the criminal by separating them from society. Its approach to sentencing is also likely to be one which takes the background circumstances of the accused into account and which makes an appropriately nuanced and tailored judgement. Similarly, it sees the issue of rehabilitation through a very different lens from the left mind; considering that because society has at least been partly culpable for the causes of criminality, we should also take some collective responsibility for the reform of the individual. Rehabilitation programmes are therefore an appropriate use of taxes because the value accrues back to society through the reintegration of reformed citizens. From the holistic worldview of the right mind, this enhances the interdependent wellbeing of the whole human ecosystem and the individuals in it.

The integrative right mind automatically seeks to create harmony through unification, so is instinctively co-operative in comparison with the competitive left mind. The right mind therefore believes that empathy, love and education are more valuable tools than force, separation and punishment, in ordering society. Education takes time but the right mind is time ambivalent, sees the bigger picture and is oriented towards the longer term, while the reductive left mind perceives distinct units of time and experiences time elapsed as time lost. Our left mind is therefore more impatient than the right and wants more immediate, linear and tangible results. Its numbers bias also causes it to place greater value on quantifiable measures, rather than the qualitative measures preferred by the right mind. Years served in jail is therefore the most valid measure of punishment and the threat of imprisonment is always the most obvious, powerful and direct deterrent. By criminalizing and incarcerating those we wish to control, we create a comforting emotional and social buffer between ourselves and the 'other' and, because they refuse to align with our beliefs, a strong sense of self-righteousness allows us to do so with a clear conscience. From this point-of-view, it is not a selfish act but one which is enacted for the greater common good.

War, Morality and Religion

Our outer-world embedded, empathetic and egalitarian right mind is instinctively anti-war and sees tolerance, respect and relationship-building as the paths to peace and harmonious integration. Its timelessness enables it to take a longer-term perspective so, for example, while the left mind may be attracted to tactical military strikes which damage an enemy in the short-term, the bigger picture perceived by the right mind confirms that, in a complex system, small perturbations can easily amplify to yield much larger, unintended consequences. So while left-minded hawks rejoice over airstrikes, right-minded doves recognize that they may merely be strengthening the opposition by rallying more recruits to their cause. Our justifications for war are therefore almost always left-minded narratives. Not only is our left mind more naturally competitive, aggressive and oriented against the 'other', its dualism gives it a tendency to see war as an 'all or nothing' venture which is objectively won or lost, so concepts such as restrained intervention or tactical retreat are anathema. With a very high belief in its own righteousness, once committed it is a determined and dogged adversary.

Our left mind is more warlike because it is inherently more destructive than the right mind, which is naturally constructive. Our left mind is designed to focus narrowly by shifting attention from higher to lower holon, so its toolkit consists of instruments which decontextualize, reduce, divide, separate, analyse, categorize and prioritize. While our right mind spends its time putting together the jigsaw pieces of experience, our left mind is constantly deconstructing the whole to look at the parts. Deconstruction inevitably requires a degree of destruction, so the probing, challenging, questioning nature of the left mind is invariably intrusive, sometimes even aggressive, compared to a right mind which naturally opposes conflict, instead seeking conciliation, compromise and co-operation. For the left mind, competition and a degree of conflict are necessary for ensuring order, and its strong desire to be in control, fuelled by the conviction that it is always correct, make it much more likely to advocate violence. Its clear prioritization of in-groups over out-groups, its weaker connection to the limbic source of our emotions and its ability to see human-beings in abstract terms, all make it much more able and willing to kill an enemy. By decontextualizing conflict, our left mind enables us to distance ourselves from the real-world horrors of war and thus reduces the empathetic pain we automatically feel. In an abstract inner world, detached from the outer world of authentic experience, dead bodies become statistics rather than real human-beings. In fact, research conducted in Rwanda shows that in order to enable moderate Hutus to kill their Tutsi neighbours, Hutu leaders first had to psychologically dehumanize their enemy by portraying them as *inyenzi,* or cockroaches, prior to the genocide taking place.[3] Men are, on average, more likely than women to be left-mind dominant which, when coupled with their greater physical strength, means they are much more likely to use force or violence to impose their will on others. It is no coincidence that the overwhelming majority of the perpetrators of the Rwandan massacres, indeed of all such atrocities, were male.

To further illuminate the contrary attitudes and approaches of the left and right mind, towards war and other matters, we must understand their respective outlooks on morality. In *The Righteous Mind,* social psycho-logist Jonathan Haidt explains the moral foundations of our perspectives, in particular the contrast between liberal and conservative standpoints.[4] Extensive research, conducted by Haidt and colleagues, suggests that there are six innate moral concerns which are shared by all cultures and have their roots deep in the ancient evolution of our species. They are our concerns for Care, Liberty, Fairness, Loyalty, Authority and Sanctity, and they are approached from different directions and with varying levels of priority by the liberal right mind versus the conservative left mind.

Our *Care* concerns are rooted in the ancient evolutionary need to protect the lives of our children and have, in more recent times, expanded to include care for a much wider array of entities including animals, the environment and minority groups. According to Haidt these concerns have expanded much more widely in the liberal mind, with its broader focus and universalistic outlook, than they have in the more narrowly-focussed conservative mind whose priority remains caring for those within our own group.[5] It's not that the conservative left mind doesn't care – it does – but that the liberal right mind simply cares more, cares more widely and is more disturbed by violence or oppression suffered by others.

Our concerns about *Liberty* are connected to care issues, in that they both relate to social justice. Both left and right minds are passionate about liberty but the left mind's conservative perspective is more narrowly focussed and concerned only with our in-groups, rather than all of humanity. Left-minded liberty therefore supports many of the tenets of economic conservatism, prioritizing the freedom of 'me and mine' – my family, my business, my city, my nation and so on – to pursue 'our' goals without restrictions which reduce our autonomy or sovereignty. Once again, right-minded liberals are more universalistic and, allied to their strong care concerns, perhaps more idealistic in wanting freedom from oppression for all individuals and all minority groups.[6]

Our concern for *Fairness* is rooted in our evolutionary need to gain the benefits of social co-operation but to avoid being personally exploited, so contains the instinct to collaborate but also to punish those who take without giving. Fairness is therefore primarily about '*proportionality*' and while both liberal and conservative minds agree on the principle that 'reward out' should be proportionate to 'effort in', they focus their emphasis quite differently. The conservative impulse of the left mind skews strongly towards protecting in-groups from the cheats and free-loaders who want to take more than they give. It's not that such behaviour doesn't annoy liberals – it does – but it annoys conservatives more.[7] The left mind is quick to create pejorative categories into which it can allocate these reprehensible 'others'. Perhaps influenced by stronger care concerns and a more empathetic right mind, liberals tend to be more uncomfortable about singling out such groups and about the harm persecution may cause to individuals within them.

As summarised above, the outputs of our left and right minds cause us to be concerned about *Care, Liberty* and *Fairness* even if they take radically different approaches towards them. While they do share these three moral concerns, the narrow focus, auto-categorization and in-group bias of the left mind delivers a distinctly conservative perspective, compared to the wider focus, empathy and universalism of the liberal right mind. Moreover, Haidt's research also found evidence of three more moral issues which further divide conservative and liberal minds. While the conservative left mind is strongly concerned about the moral aspects of *Loyalty, Authority* and *Sanctity,* they are relatively insignificant to the liberal right mind.

Like fairness, our moral concern for *Loyalty* is rooted in our evolutionary need to form groups which were larger than family-based units. It is therefore no surprise that this concern is felt more acutely in the categorizing left mind, which is responsible for defining our in-groups and out-groups. Like culture, loyalty acts as social glue which binds people together and helps us to trust and be trusted by members of our group. However, misguided loyalty can also lead us to murder people in other groups or to punish, expel and even kill in-group members, who we believe have betrayed us or the group. In one of social psychology's most famous case studies, conducted in the 1950s by Muzafer and Carolyn Sherif of the University of Oklahoma, twenty-two twelve-year-old boys went off to a summer camp with a difference – it was really a social experiment.[8] For the first week, two groups of eleven boys were kept apart, each unaware of the other. Leaders naturally emerged and some low-level 'tribal' behaviour was spontaneously exhibited, including the marking of territory and the creation of group symbols. After a week, the Sherifs ensured that the groups 'accidently' discovered each other and recorded what happened. Very quickly, tribal behaviours increased dramatically and all activities became competitive as both groups contested neutral areas of the camp, each claiming them as their own. Vandalism ensued with each group destroying the other's property, burning each other's flags and even preparing makeshift weapons. Violence was only prevented by adult intervention. The clear conclusion, validated by further such experiments, was that young men in particular enjoy innately tribal activities; activities which create social cohesion but also lead to intergroup competition. In the modern day we engage in this behaviour for fun, through sports and other harmless pastimes, but it is still the same ancient impulse which leads to our unconscious biases towards in-groups and, potentially, to violence and even war. Moreover, animosity for the enemy is often only surpassed by the hatred reserved for those who betray, or are deemed disloyal, to one's own group. While the moral aspects of loyalty are therefore of strong concern to the dualistic left mind, it has little emotional resonance for the integrative, harmony-seeking right mind. To the conservative, however, such dispassionate apathy can be taken as clear evidence that the liberal lacks patriotism, is deeply disloyal and is therefore deserving of their anger and revulsion. Naturally this can lead to conflict, with the left-mind dominant conservative accusing the right-mind dominant liberal of treachery and treason, while the liberal genuinely has no idea why the conservative is getting so worked up.

Closely connected to issues of loyalty are moral concerns around *Authority*, which are borne from our ancient need to form beneficial relationships within social hierarchies. Hierarchies are always the product of the left mind and exist in all societies, although they tend to be more formally structured and strictly respected in cultures which are dominated by the conservative outlook. For a strongly right-minded liberal, who may feel an almost visceral rejection of the concept, social hierarchy often equates directly to the use of power by the strong to control, oppress or persecute the weak, which directly offends their interpretation of liberty, care and fairness. The conservative left mind, however, doesn't see it like that at all. The predilection of the left mind for order, categorization and prioritization, make hierarchy a perfectly logical and valuable mental construct. In its conception, those subordinate in society have a duty to deliver deference and respect to their superiors as well as carrying out clearly delineated roles within the group, while those in dominant positions have a pastoral duty of care for subordinates as well as responsibility for the maintenance of order and the application of justice within the group. Disobedience brings disorder, which is anathema to the left mind, so deviance is often harshly punished. Thus, everyone within a society has a vested interest in supporting the existing order and in maintaining their mutual support for it. Once again the self-referring left mind is internally coherent. Far from being selfish, it has a strong and genuine moral concern for *Care* and takes its responsibilities very seriously. From its perspective, however, care is best achieved alongside an equally strong concern for authority, in the sort of hierarchical structure which the right mind might mock as a '*benevolent dictatorship*'. Indeed, the left mind might happily accept this description but would see no contradiction or irony in it.

Equally bemusing to the liberal right mind is the concern the conservative left mind holds for the moral value of *Sanctity*. Haidt hypothesises that our concern for sanctity is rooted in our ancient need to distinguish contaminated food from that which was safe to eat, and that the emotion of disgust therefore first evolved to protect our physical being.[9] Since then, it has further evolved into being the basis for the moral judgements we make about the behaviour of others. The left mind's powerful penchant for clear rules with binary, 'black and white' measures of value, can compel communities to define and agree the acceptable codes of moral conduct which everyone must adhere to. Within such societies, tendencies towards obedient deference to authority and regular demonstrations of group loyalty both reinforce and reward self-control, but this particular moral impulse goes beyond merely avoiding negative behaviour. Sanctity also involves imbuing certain objects, places, people or principles with a sacredness which sets them apart from the ordinary and which, through them, enables the worship of the communal, revered values which have been vested in them. Thus flags, religious symbols, holy cities and saints can all become soaked in a significance which goes way beyond the comprehension of the real-world embedded, liberal right mind. For example, a national flag may become elevated to a status of spiritual sanctity which far exceeds its material manifestation and, for the left mind, failure to respect such a symbol constitutes a disgraceful display of disloyalty to the group. Similarly, the human body may become seen as a sacred vessel for the soul, rather than a mere biological entity, the purity of which must be maintained physically, emotionally and spiritually. Even a human-made, social construct such as marriage can also become infused with a sanctity which has little resonance for liberals, even those who are religious. This can easily become another sacred symbol over which the conservative left mind wishes to retain control, leading to its opposition, for example, to the extension of marriage rights to homosexual couples.

Although many liberals do hold spiritual beliefs, the strict structures and scriptures of the modern monotheisms may cause the liberal mind to tend away from formal religious practice. For the progressive right mind, moral authority lies squarely with the individual and is a fluid concept which reflects the ever-changing nature of the experienced world in which it is embedded. Moral authority emerges mainly, if not solely, from 'this-world' considerations rather than 'other-world' concerns. Many liberals therefore tend towards secularism and may consider themselves to be more spiritual than religious per se, perhaps drawn towards humanist, univer-salist or naturalist expressions of faith or to the person-centric practices of Eastern belief systems such as Buddhism. Like many during the Enlightenment, they tend to share the conviction that moral imperatives should have the human good as their highest goal and that, as a human construct, morality is perpetually unfolding, conditional and relative. With a real-world orientation and a powerful moral concern for liberty, fairness and care, the liberal mind is both pragmatic and positive, preferring to believe in and adhere to universal ethical principles rather than a single 'right' way. For the synthesising right mind, morality is based on personal experience, moral positions should evolve through rational discourse based on empirical evidence about the human condition, and collective agreements should be based on the quality and coherence of the arguments made in the context of current, real-world issues which need to be addressed. While we all have a collective duty of care towards each other, the fundamental moral principle is that the final decision on what indi-viduals judge to be right, true, good, pleasurable, valuable or worthwhile should lie with themselves, based on their personal experiences and private preferences. Everyone should have the freedom to live life as they choose, as long as they do not harm others in doing so.

Of course, many liberals *do* consider themselves to be religious and follow one of the traditional monotheisms. Comfortable with ambiguity, our liberal right minds are much more likely to take a non-literal, interpretive approach to religious scripture, reading it in the context of the experienced world and reapplying implicit principles rather than didacti-cally following explicit instructions. The 21st century liberal mind tends to subscribe to the modern zeitgeist which emerged from the Enlighten-ment and remains characterised by individual freedom, rationalism and subjectivity, so morality is maintained by flexible guidelines rather than fixed rules and by relativism rather than absolutism. In this interpretation, it is ultimately up to each individual to decide what is appropriate in the many different situations in which they may find themselves. Religious liberals are therefore more likely to see the Bible or Koran as a human document which is already deeply interpretive and which cannot hold binding authority over their moral lives. Instead, it is a valuable reference manual with which to orient their personal choices. They are less likely than conservatives to see religious documents as a literal record of events, but as narrative from which guiding principles can be derived and reapplied to address modern-day issues. Moral truth is therefore not static but ever-changing, and moral authority comes from individual interpretation and collective agreement rather than directly from religious revelation. The religious yet liberal right mind therefore has a very different perspective, even on religion, from the conservative left mind.

Our deeply human impulse towards spiritual idealism, which over time led to formal religion, is actually sourced via our embodied right mind. With its outward orientation and comfort with both the material and immaterial, it first produced our sense that we are part of something much greater than ourselves and the instinctive feeling that there is more to our existence than solely what we can see or physically experience. Our original belief in ghosts or gods is not therefore the product of a logical left mind but of deep intuitions, sourced from our ancient limbic system, as our ancestors tried to understand and explain the bewildering world they encountered. In more recent millennia, the left mind has written narratives to bring structured order to such profound feelings, yet many of the foundational texts remain resolutely progressive. Countless teachings of Abraham, Jesus and Mohammed, such as tolerating diversity, caring for the sick, protecting children and alleviating poverty, are all strongly right-minded values and would clearly be considered to be liberal in today's terms. However, even if its goals are liberal, our left mind can only use the tools at its disposal – specifically schematic structures – to address its wide moral concerns and bring about its desired future. It does so via the creation of clear, unambiguous rules and their universal imposition, irrespective of context or the individual concerned.

To the left-minded religious conservative, therefore, God is a transcendent authority who has defined absolute measures of value, goodness and morality and has used them to set simple, unequivocal rules for living a good life. To the inflexible, hierarchical left mind, these laws are unchanging and unchallengeable because they have been created by a superior power, so there is neither room nor requirement for individual interpretation. Its inability to deal with ambiguity or metaphor negates any scope for nuanced explanation to reflect modern mores. Its dualism dictates that rules are distinctly 'black and white' – our behaviour either meets the absolute moral standard or it doesn't. Once rules are fixed, the left mind's only concern is the coherence of data received with the schemata against which it is assessed and, lacking in empathy, the left mind is a cold, dispassionate judge. In its decontextualized, abstract world, failure to live up to the Divine standard lies solely with the individual and punishment is always the preferred method of correction. It is an extreme version of left-minded religion which is currently being imposed in parts of Syria and Iraq by the Islamic State group, which all moderate Muslims recognize has strayed a very long way from Islam's semi-liberal origins. Indeed, all three monotheisms have travelled far from our original spiritual impulses which were firmly rooted in the right mind. The idea of an omnipotent, male, sky-based God was only invented relatively recently – by the left minds of men – as part of a narrative which elevated our species above the rest of nature and enabled the male human to dominate the female. To this day the unchallengeable word of God is still cited as justification for the subjugation of women by men.

Of course, not all conservatives are religious or even spiritual. While atheists may tend to be skewed towards the liberal outlook of the right mind, there are also plenty of non-believers who are morally conservative. Like all those with a dominant left mind, they still tend to value the clarity of universal laws which can be consistently applied to categories of people, irrespective of context. Clearly, for them, God hasn't written such rules, so guiding principles are more likely to come from the individual's own schematic framework based on their interpretation of the self-evident truths of nature. Through this lens, it is easy to observe that men and women have different physiques and temperaments, so it can logically follow that they should play different roles in human society. Similarly, it is an empirical fact that sexual reproduction is a joint venture between one man and one woman, so it is possible to conclude that homosexuality is a perversion of nature and her universal laws. Thus, a non-religious yet morally conservative individual can logically derive self-defined, universal laws directly from nature and, if living in a similarly conservative community, will support the 'natural laws' against which moral behaviour may be judged in their shared society. Of course, this is merely evidence of the left mind's ability to employ motivated reasoning to retrospectively rationalize emotional impulses arising from moral concerns for authority and sanctity, which are particularly resonant for anyone with a dominant left mind. Nevertheless, it is thus possible for atheist conservatives to arrive at the same conclusions as religious conservatives about how society should be ordered, but by using two different sources for the derivation of moral imperatives.

Dangers of Imbalance

Above are polarized descriptions of the very different approaches our left and right minds take towards major topics such as freedom, order, justice, war, morality and religion. It is clear in every case that the optimal solution is almost certainly a blend of polar extremes – a process which can only be conducted by the synthesising qualities of the right mind. For example, on matters of justice the conservative left mind will ignore the influence of society and simply blame the criminal, while the liberal right mind will blame society, absolving the criminal of personal responsibility. Anyone willing to expend a little cognitive energy on conscious thought can surely see that neither position is entirely right or wrong and that a balanced solution must be blended from both viewpoints. When we understand the modus operandi of our two minds, we come to appreciate that contradiction is essential to how our complex cognitive system works, but also to recognize that external manifestations of our inner thoughts can easily lead to conflict. Our two minds process the same data but, by approaching it from opposite perspectives, each produces a very different interpretation of what they perceive. Our thinking is always the emergent output of their interplay, but the many flaws and biases inherent in our cerebral system plus the narrative fallacies we confabulate to restore cognitive ease, consistently undermine our ability to produce blended cogitation which is both high quality and appropriately balanced.

Yet it would be wrong to simply blame the left mind which can appear to be selfish, aggressive, destructive and even evil, when compared to the more caring, co-operative qualities of the right mind. On the contrary, as the primary conduit to our emotions our right mind is where feelings such as anger, jealousy or hatred first emerge, so we do rely heavily on the left mind for the self-control we need to moderate our more animal impulses. The left mind also brings essential structure which enables us to make sense of our world – comprehending the past, navigating the present and planning for the future – and we couldn't function without this valuable service even if it is occasionally delusional. Furthermore, in sometimes being selfish or aggressive, our left mind is only doing its job which is first and foremost to protect us and those we love, as well as our property and lifestyles. In doing so, denying freedoms to others may be a reasonable and justifiable response even if force is required, because the defence of our life, liberty and values is paramount if we are under threat. This is never a selfish act because it not only benefits us but all members of our in-groups, so is entirely coherent to the self-referring left mind.

However, we'd be foolish not to recognize that the left mind, if insufficiently balanced and integrated by the holistic right mind, can potentially be dangerous to both individual and collective holons. Its decontextualization of data, its adherence to an abstract, unchanging model of the outer world and its emotional desensitization, all result in a cold detachment from reality which would be considered psychotic in an individual. At the collective level, while we would hope that our natural preference for hemispheric balance amongst large groups of people might manifest in dynamically-stable cultures, it is nevertheless perfectly possible for a societal psychosis to develop if excessively dominated by the left mind. Indeed, many may consider that the cultural conditions experienced by those in Saudi Arabia or in areas under the control of Islamic State, come close to exhibiting several symptoms of collective mental illness. As we will explore in Part 3, the global mind, dominated as it is by the West, came very close to swinging seriously out of kilter during the Industrial Revolution and although our human system has since sought to restore its natural balance, the left mind still dominates global culture through scientific materialism. However, for the last century the overarching direction of travel has undoubtedly been from conservative order towards liberal freedom, evidenced by the growth of democracy, secularism, human rights, environmentalism, freedom of speech, the rule of law and more liberal attitudes towards sex, marriage, divorce, drugs and so on. Yet the global development of progressive attitudes and political policies has happened far more slowly than most liberals would like. For example, wealth remains so unevenly distributed that millions of people are still starving and homosexuality remains illegal in around 75 of the world's nations and is punishable by death in at least five of them.[10]

When we are all capable of balanced cognition, why does it seem so difficult to make quicker progress towards a global culture which is conducive to peaceful integration and personal happiness? There are three interconnected reasons which can be summarised as consciousness, change and culture. As we have established, the bulk of our thinking takes place unconsciously and is heavily influenced by the dominant culture we live in, which for most of us is scientific materialism. In any society, the dominant culture is invariably upheld by influential elites who also maintain the political, economic, civic and spiritual structures via which society is run – the outer-world manifestations of our inner-world schematic rules.

Through this cyclical mechanism the effect of the cultural 'brain-cloud' is sustained – informing citizens' unconscious thoughts so their actions are consistent with and contribute to the current culture stream, then re-soaking them daily in the dominant values of their society. This self-sustaining cycle can *only* be broken by conscious effort and by enough people deliberately making decisions which run counter to the controlling culture, in order to undermine its influence and establish a new incumbent. Furthermore, the new culture will only be sustained long enough to seep into the unconscious minds of future generations, if it can create new political, economic, civic and spiritual structures and thereby change how society is run. However, we are naturally resistant to change and society is currently run by schematic rules which maintain the pre-eminence of the left mind and, in particular, the tenets of scientific materialism. This presents a Gordian knot of great proportions and is the subject of the next chapter.

Increasing our personal consciousness is a pre-requisite to achieving any sort of sustainable change and we only have to overcome the inherent laziness of our brains to do so. Indeed, we now live more sedentary lifestyles than at any prior point in human history, so there's no reason why we can't all find the spare energy to think a little more. We all use both sides of our brain all of the time, so even those of us with a strong hemispheric preference are perfectly capable of processing any issue from the alternative perspective, should we consciously choose to do so. Although we may still arrive at exactly the same conclusion, it would benefit any discussion, debate or disagreement if we were to at least explore the topic from the other point of view. If we could come to accept that we all have the same flawed minds, we might acknowledge that differences of opinion are simply the emergent outcome of unpredictable neural patterns, rather than conclusive proof that we are right and the other person is wrong. When we can acknowledge that conflict between humans is caused by minds which disagree, rather than by disagreeable people, we may become more tolerant of one another and learn to differ with mutual respect. Only an increase in our consciousness can give us the awareness we need, of ourselves and others, to recognize the influence of cognitive preference on how we process data, and give us the tools to find appropriately balanced and mutually acceptable solutions.

We must also become more cognisant of culture and the role we play in shaping and sustaining it. By paying attention to how our two minds influence our views, we can become more aware of our personal preference and how to better integrate our thinking by dialling up our less dominant mode. In our daily discourse we rarely discuss lofty topics like freedom, justice or morality; instead our biases are more likely to manifest in conversations about the myriad of minor issues which all add up to create culture. They may seem insignificant but such minor cognitive conflicts ultimately shape culture either towards or away from the one we want to live in and, although we may not be aware of it, our individual voices are becoming louder and more influential. For too long, shaping society was solely the privilege of elites but the last century has seen a significant diffusion of power, through the increased democratization of the data we need to make informed decisions. By elevating our personal consciousness to make different decisions, we can change the direction of the energy flowing across our complex adaptive system. The small perturbations we each make can easily become amplified by our greater connectivity to each other, creating cascades of change which elevate our global mind to a higher level of collective consciousness. To enable this transformation, over the last century we have pushed ourselves to the edge of chaos – our right mind liberalizing society to the point where our human system has sufficient free energy to develop and adapt to new cultural conditions, on a higher plane of complexity. Such a shift has brought forth our current convulsions, which are ultimately the effects of conservative resistance against these liberalizing forces. Our global transition from cultures dominated by scientific materialism to those shaped by an integrative right mind, is therefore by no means guaranteed. Indeed, the threat to our cognitive and cultural elevation goes beyond the fact that the left mind is a powerful and aggressive adversary. There are also several systemic conditions which make us resistant to change and which call into question whether our species will ever evolve to a higher plane of cognitive wisdom. These conditions are the subject of the next chapter.

—8—

Changing Structures

ALBERT EINSTEIN famously defined insanity as *'doing the same thing over and over again and expecting different results'*, highlighting one of the core cognitive tensions we experience from the day we are born until the day we die. We are all creatures of habit who take great comfort from routine, who enjoy the familiarity of faces and places we already know, and feel disturbingly disoriented without the habits, rules and systems we employ to manage our daily lives. Yet life would be unbearably dull if we *only* ever did the same things, went to the same places or talked to the same people. While a degree of structure is essential to our wellbeing, we simultaneously feel an instinctive impulse towards continually refreshing our experiences by trying unusual foods, participating in different pastimes or opening our minds to alternative influences. This necessary tension, caused by opposing pulls towards self-regulating order and self-creating flexibility, is central to how we maintain dynamic stability in our cognitive system, which must continually process energy across our neural network for us to stay alive. However, the type of data we take in is also important and we must regularly process novel phenomena to spark new neural connections, stimulate our senses in unfamiliar ways, blow away mental cobwebs and keep our mind vital. The on-going absence of new stimulus, if processing only the same data over a prolonged period, can lead to the sort of mental breakdown where people go 'stir crazy' while, at the other extreme, the continual intake of unfamiliar information may lead to sensory overload which can be equally disorienting. To remain healthy and coherent our system needs to remain within a range of equilibrium, between the order provided by routine and the flexibility afforded by new experiences.

In its energy-efficient manner, our brain allocates routine activities to our unconscious mind, underpinning them with schematic structures,

171

enjoyable emotions and chemical rewards which incentivise us to perform them without 'thinking'. Consequently, breaking our routines to experience something new or irregular requires us to make a conscious decision to override habitual behaviours and force our actions in a different direction. We all find this easy on one-off occasions but, as anyone who has ever made a New Year's resolution can testify, it is much harder to sustain new behaviours because we usually tend to fall back quickly into our old, automatic habits. This is because, once our unconscious associative structures have been built, our left mind is very reluctant to change them. Replacing unwanted routines with new, preferred behaviours therefore presents a real challenge for us because, no matter how much determination we have, we will eventually return to our old habits if the unconscious scaffolding in our mind continues to support the behaviours we want to change. Strong will is necessary, but often insufficient, to sustain long-term change without also dismantling our unconscious structures and creating new, attractive associations, which spark a different set of neural connections every time we are tempted by the old routines we are trying to replace.

Consider one of the habitual behaviours human-beings find most difficult to break, that of smoking. Over and above the powerfully addictive nature of nicotine, smokers invariably have unconscious associative triggers which encourage them to smoke – perhaps break times at work, drinking alcohol or socializing with friends – and one useful strategy to aid stopping is to consciously remove themselves from these situations, so they are unable to spark the associative memories which make them want to smoke. Other conscious support structures many people use include nicotine patches, gum or e-cigarettes, plus more indirect methods such as keeping the money saved by not smoking in a visible vessel or even using an image of what they will buy with the saved cash, such as an exotic holiday or new car, as a visual incentive to abstain. The options are endless but the point is that in order to dissolve old, unconscious associations we need to consciously create new structures, and keep them top of mind for a sufficient period, so we gradually remove and replace the mental scaffolding which supported our old habits, which do indeed 'die hard'.

The principles for re-programming the collective mind are no different than for the individual mind. Much of our behaviour is unconscious and automatic because our culture provides the many schematic structures which scaffold our collective mind, in the form of the political, economic, educational, social or spiritual systems which regulate how our societies are ordered and operate. Our current capitalist economic system, for example, is so familiar and all-pervasive that we can be forgiven for forgetting that it is actually a human-made structure which doesn't *have* to be as it is. Indeed, many different economic systems have been employed throughout history and in parts of the world less influenced by the West. When we visit countries with radically different cultures to our own, we tend to perceive differences on the surface but perhaps fail to appreciate the alternative underlying structures which create, support and sustain what emerges as a result. It is only by diving more deeply that we see the subliminal scaffolding which supports what we experience so, in order to change any culture, we must consciously alter the underlying structures for the new behaviours we wish to bring forth to successfully and sustainably manifest. However, understanding how change can be created is only half the battle. The other half is overcoming some significant and systemic barriers to change.

Resistance to Change

Core to the essential tension between self-regulating order and self-creating flexibility in our cognitive system, is a corresponding tension between how each mind experiences and deals with change. Our conservative left mind loves order, hates ambiguity and builds fixed, inflexible schematic structures against which to assess all novel phenomena. Meanwhile, our liberal right mind, which lives in an outer world full of flux and fluidity, has no fear of change, indeed embraces and thrives upon it. Our whole mind, the product of the synthesising function performed by the holistic right mind, blends and balances both perspectives to ensure that we can simultaneously develop, yet remain safe. However, it doesn't do so equally. Research shows that we are automatically and consistently more risk-averse than risk-taking and, as always, there is a sound evolutionary reason for this, rooted in the need to prioritize losing a meal over the danger of becoming one.

Consider the following offer which involves gambling on the toss of a coin. If the coin lands on heads you lose £100 but if the coin lands on tails you win £150. Do you accept the gamble? Objectively you should, because you clearly have a 50:50 chance of winning more than you would lose, but most people reject the offer. The reason for this is an emotional response which automatically wells up from our unconscious and overwhelms our rational mind, making us feel much more anxious about the prospect of losses than excited about potential gains. Levels of loss aversion can be measured in individuals by considering how much we would have to gain in order to take the chance of losing any sum. Obviously some people are more risk-taking while others are more risk-averse, but across large groups of people our 'loss aversion ratio' has consistently been found to be in the range of 1.5 to 2.5.[1] In other words, on average we need the prospect of winning £200 to be willing to risk losing £100, so our fear of loss is twice as strong as the attractiveness of winning. In short, our unconscious mind delivers a double dose of emotion when the feeling is negative than it does when the feeling is positive. Loss aversion forms part of a much broader '*negativity bias*' we all experience, in which bad feelings or impressions are faster to form and harder to overcome than good impressions, and bad news is processed more thoroughly than positive data.[2] Our negativity bias is a powerfully protective evolutionary mechanism designed by nature to keeps us safe.

Similarly, research also shows that we attach greater emotional value to things we already own than to the same items, prior to their acquisition. Behavioural economist Richard Thaler first noticed what he called the '*endowment effect*' in the 1970s, in conversations with a colleague who was a wine lover and collector.[3] Thaler observed that his colleague rarely paid more than $35 for a bottle of wine and was equally reluctant to sell a bottle from his collection for less than $100. At prices between $35 and $100 he would neither buy nor sell – behaviour which was inconsistent with standard 'utilitarian' economic theory at the time, which anticipated that he should only place a single value on a bottle. In this rational model, if the single value was $50, the collector should buy at any price up to $50 and sell at any price above $50. However, Thaler hypothesised that the very act of owning a bottle actually increases its value to us, due to the additional emotion we invest in things we own. Subsequent research has shown conclusively that we consistently attach higher value to items we own because the pain of loss experienced, when giving something up, is greater than the pleasure we experience when acquiring the same thing for the first time. Across a diverse range of studies, the ratio of roughly 2:1 appears with amazing consistency as the average weighting we give to losses over gains.[4] It appears that when it comes to change, our conservative left mind has a considerable advantage over our progressive right mind in maintaining the status quo. For example, during the Scottish independence referendum of 2014, in which voters decided whether or not to separate from the United Kingdom, the 'No' campaign supporting the maintenance of political union enjoyed an in-built advantage. For almost two years prior to the referendum, polls consistently showed around a 70:30 split in favour of the status quo, almost exactly the 2:1 loss aversion ratio. The final result of 55:45 suggests that the pro-independence campaign, although it ultimately lost, perhaps did well to shift the dial as far as it did.

A further advantage our left mind holds over our right mind, with regards to change, is that it is naturally more competitive and has a stronger desire to be in control. Our dualistic left mind perceives every-thing in terms of polar opposites, so considers itself to be in competition with the right mind, while its 'adversary' also appreciates left and right but not from a dualistic standpoint. To the right mind they are not separate, but complementary and deeply connected as yin is to yang. Our right mind is therefore instinctively more co-operative, viewing the left mind not as an adversary but as a valued collaborator. Our hierarchical left mind, however, always wants to come out on top and will do whatever it takes to win including lying, cheating and, if necessary, will even resort to violence. Armed with a vast databank of associative memories and strong logic, it can also construct a powerful and plausible justification for its approach, leveraging its superior verbal skills to communicate its ideas in a compelling, coherent narrative. It can further employ its sharp numeric skills to provide quantitative evidence in support of its case. Consider how fluently our politicians and other elites are able to produce statistics to validate their eloquent arguments and how easily we accept their veracity, despite the fact that 77.8% of all statistics are simply made up ☺. If statistics and a silver tongue still prove insufficient, our left mind can further call upon its natural aggression to force its opinion on others, particularly when those others form out-groups and when victory fuels self-esteem, demonstrates loyalty and delivers status to an in-group. Furthermore, the in-groups of left-mind dominant, right-wing conser-vatives tend to be more '*tightly bound*' than those of right-mind dominant liberals, whose tendency towards '*live and let live*' attitudes automatically creates a much wider variety of looser affiliations. Liberal groups wishing to drive change therefore tend to be much more fragmented and diverse, fighting across a broader range of fronts than conservative groups which are normally more narrowly focussed and unified by traditional definers such as religion, colour or nationality. Finally, our societies are never egalitarian but are dominated by influential elites who have a strong incentive, beyond our natural 2:1 loss aversion ratio, to maintain the status quo.

There are therefore many reasons, some genetic and others cultural, why change is so often hard to generate and slow to manifest. Our in-built resistance to change has very long evolutionary roots, so is in itself impossible to amend, although it can clearly be overcome in the right circumstances. Increased consciousness by enough people can enable us to collectively overcome the many tendencies of the left mind outlined above; tendencies which make it so dangerous if allowed unfettered free rein. To do so, however, we must address the single biggest barrier of all to achieving positive, sustainable cultural change. This barrier lies in the greatest advantage of all those currently afforded to the left mind – the right to write the rules of the game we play. Remember, the emergent outcomes of any complex adaptive system are dictated by the local rules by which all constituents play, like the flora and fauna in the food web within Darwin's tangled bank. In human systems these rules are the social, political, economic, legal, civic, religious and other structures we create, which determine '*how things work around here*' and which are, ultimately, outer-world manifestations of the inner schematic structures developed by our collective left mind. It makes absolute sense that this role should fall to the left mind because we all value the clear, unambiguous and consistent order such structures bring, and which only the left mind can deliver. However, this only works well in a healthy, balanced and coherent system, where overarching responsibility lies with the right mind and in which the left mind is a valuable but subsidiary contributor – the author of the rules but not their ultimate arbiter. Systems will only remain healthy as long as the narrowly-focussed left mind remains under the control of the holistic right mind but, if given too much leeway, the left mind can quickly become dangerous, creating rules which amplify the attitudinal and behavioural biases of the left mind itself, rather than promoting a healthy balance. Clearly, if an entire culture gets out of kilter and becomes dominated by the left mind, there's a real danger that the structures we create will reflect this imbalance and serve to sustain, rather than redress, our cognitive and cultural disharmony.

In this context we will soon consider the two key structures of the Western culture of scientific materialism – capitalist economics and adversarial politics – but first we must take a short diversion into game theory. Core to our comprehension are the principles that the left mind is competitive, the right mind is co-operative and, for a system to be healthy, competition must take place within an overarching spirit of co-operation.

The Rules of the Game

One of the most famous experiments in all the social sciences is known as *The Prisoners' Dilemma* and it goes like this.[5] Two men, A and B, have been arrested on suspicion of committing a crime. However, the prosecutor doesn't have enough evidence to convict either of them on a principal charge but is confident they can both be successfully prosecuted on a lesser charge. Keeping them apart, he offers both men the same deal in the hope that one may be persuaded to betray the other and testify that they committed the principal crime. The offer is as follows. If both men remain silent, each of them will serve one year in prison on the lesser charge. If they betray each other, they will both serve two years. Finally, if A betrays B, while B remains silent, A will go free and B will serve 3 years in jail (and vice versa). Logically, there is only one answer to the prisoners' dilemma and that is for both men to compete by betraying each other and to serve two years in jail, even though co-operating by staying silent would result in lesser sentences for both of them. The logic goes like this. B will either stay silent or betray A. If he stays silent, A is better off by betraying B because he will walk free rather than serving 1 year. If B betrays A, A is better off by betraying B because he will serve 2 years rather than 3. The same reasoning applies for B, so if both men are thinking logically each will arrive at the same conclusion – that they should betray the other – and both will serve 2 years rather than taking the mutually beneficial, but illogical, decision to co-operate which would halve their sentences. Thinking on its own (if this were possible), our left mind would always make the logical but damaging decision to compete. *The Prisoners' Dilemma* brilliantly highlights how it is perfectly possible to create rules which produce damaging emergent outcomes, even when the decisions which drive those outcomes are completely logical. In this particular example, the 'system' consists of only two players but the principle nevertheless applies to much larger systems. The healthiest outcome for the whole system would be the one which did most to maintain its overall coherence, with both players serving one year by co-operating. Instead, 'badly written' local rules damaged both the system and the individuals within it, when only the logic of the left mind was employed.

For decades social scientists, soaked in the false belief that all human behaviour was driven by self-interest, were baffled by the co-operative behaviours they witnessed in real human societies. Yet clearly, *only* co-operating would also be a suboptimal strategy, constantly leaving the co-operator vulnerable to the competitive betrayal of other players. Game theory was born in the 1940s in the mind of Hungarian mathematician John von Neumann, who hypothesised that human behaviour was entirely circumstantial and that the best strategy in any compete/co-operate situation should depend on what the other person does. Over the years, many scientists sought to identify the best strategies for long-term success and the conditions in which co-operation might emerge victorious. They found that if players played many repeated games and didn't know when the game would end, co-operation did tend to emerge, but it wasn't until 1980 that a young scientist called Robert Axelrod was able to use computer programming to compare a variety of strategies against each other.[6] He organized a tournament and asked computer scientists to submit programmes to play against each other, over hundreds of games. Of the 14 programmes submitted, each offering different blends of competitive versus co-operative behaviour, the winner was a Russian-American mathematical psychologist named Anatol Rapoport whose programme, tit-for-tat, was as simple as it was brilliant. The strategy behind tit-for-tat was to begin by co-operating then exactly mirror your opponents' moves thereafter. If they co-operate, you continue to co-operate. If they decide to compete, you retaliate by competing until they resort back to co-operation and you do likewise. Amazed yet unconvinced, Axelrod organized another tournament and asked more programmers to try to beat tit-for-tat. A further 62 programmes were submitted but once again tit-for-tat emerged victorious, defeating more competitive strategies which tended to do well in the short-term but fall away longer-term, as they ran out of easy victims in the form of more co-operative programmes.[7]

The implications remain clear to this day. Tit-for-tat is by far the best long-term strategy for the creation of an overarching framework of co-operation, within which healthy competition can still take place, and will only be enabled if societal structures are created by a collective left mind which is appropriately influenced by the holistic right mind. When this is the case, the local rules created will encourage behaviours to emerge which sustain opposing tendencies towards self-assertion and self-control, maintain dynamic stability and ensure systemic coherence over the long-term. Conversely, an imbalanced culture dominated by the left mind will create structures which bring forth excessive competition and discourage co-operation, through, for example, the overprovision of positive feedback for the accumulation of economic capital and a dearth of essential moderating influences, such as social or moral capital, which can have a dampening effect and counter-balancing impact. Under scientific materialism, a culture born of the left mind, our key societal structures have inevitably been designed by a left mind largely unfettered by the moderating influence of everything the right mind has to offer, with its big picture perspective, sensitivity to nature and primacy of human relationships. Ironically, of course, it is these tendencies which make the right mind far more able to understand complexity, empathise with living organisms and create structures which harmoniously balance the needs of individuals and the whole planetary ecosystem. Instead, however, what we currently have are societal structures which were invariably guided by the mechanistic worldview and underwritten by an implicit belief in the survival of the fittest. We will now consider the two structures perhaps most characteristic of the Western world and the modern era – capitalist economics and adversarial politics.

Capitalist Economics

The capitalist economic system remains based on Adam Smith's insight that self-interest is the primary motivator for economic activity, as captured in his famous observation that '*it is not from the benevolence of the butcher, the brewer or the baker, that we expect our dinner, but from their regard to their own interest*'.[8] In Smith's conception, competition, far from being selfish, would actually serve as a regulator of economic activity by keeping self-interest in check. Consider baker A from whom customers buy good quality bread for a reasonable price. If A is the only baker in the village she might be tempted, by self-interest, to increase prices or reduce the quality of her bread to increase profits. However, the presence of baker B in the same village restrains any impulse she may feel to take advantage of her customers, because she knows that they can simply buy their bread elsewhere. Baker B is similarly influenced. Here we see tit-for-tat at work. Customers will 'co-operate' by buying from baker A, as long as she also co-operates by maintaining quality and price. If she 'betrays' (ie competes with) her customers by breaking their tacit agreement, they can retaliate by also acting in their own self-interest and buy their bread from baker B.

Although baker B is in competition with baker A, it is also in their mutual self-interest to demonstrate a degree of co-operation. If either were to compete by reducing the price of bread, the other would have to retaliate, tit-for-tat, to avoid losing business and both bakers would suffer by making less profit. Similarly, it might be in both their interests to increase prices to enhance margins but this would only be the case if higher prices didn't cause villagers to eat less bread, or their profits may actually decline. In short, both have a vested interest in maintaining price and quality at a level which maximises their profits by optimising bread consumption in the village. Although they are rivals, their competition is necessarily conducted within an overarching context of co-operation. This is what Smith meant by '*enlightened self-interest*' – when persons acting to further the interests of a group to which they belong, ultimately also serve their own self-interest and vice versa. Players simultaneously compete and co-operate while the 'invisible hand' of the free market, facilitated by tit-for-tat, keeps narrow selfishness and excessive greed in check. Thus, as in Darwin's tangled bank, the health of the ecosystem is maintained in dynamic balance for the long-term benefit of all in it.

However, Adam Smith lived in a very different era to our post-modern world. Mercantile trade was largely conducted by government-appointed monopolies, while the Enlightenment was in the process of freeing 18th century man from the shackles of religious faith, propelling him towards a self-determining future. The power of reason was emerging as the great beacon of hope with which each man could plan and navigate his own path in life. Yet Smith was not at all unaware of the great influence of emotion on the human condition. In his *Theory of Moral Sentiments* he observed

> how selfish soever man may be supposed, there are evidently some prin-
> ciples in his nature, which interest him in the fortunes of others, and render
> their happiness necessary to him, though he derives nothing from it, except
> the pleasure of seeing it.[9]

Smith understood that trade wasn't a soulless or solely transactional pastime but one which was relationship-based. In Smith's day, local commerce was conducted directly with customers by the individual butcher, brewer or baker, all perhaps located around the village green. In this idyllic scene, the principles of free-market capitalism as a redistributive mechanism, powered by tit-for-tat, are perfectly sound but, writing almost 300 years ago, Smith could never have envisaged that

21st century trade would be conducted on such a global scale or that any company could yield such power. The company or corporation was first created in Smith's 18th century to '*incorporate*' (meaning to form into one body) the rights of several shareholders, as one legal 'person'. In doing so, we effectively created a super-human being with the collective powers of many people but, following the advent of limited liability, very few of their responsibilities. Adam Smith believed that corporate activity would never match private enterprise because individuals in charge of other people's money, would never take as much care of it as they would do if it were their own.[10] Writing in 1776, he clearly could not foresee that today the top 100 global companies would be worth over US$17 trillion,[11] 55% greater than the GDP of China and more than three times the GDP of Japan, respectively the second and third largest economies in the world.[12] The invisible hand has certainly generated incredible wealth but has also distributed it extremely unevenly. In 2017, 55 of the top 100 companies were based in the USA and the 400 wealthiest Americans were worth US$2.4 trillion,[13] around the same as France with a population of 67 million and the sixth highest GDP of any nation. Just 8 billionaires now have as much wealth as half of the earth's inhabitants – some 3.6 billion people – and the richest 1% now own more than the entire combined assets of the remaining 99%.[14] The fundamental reason for such obscene inequality is that tit-for-tat, the optimum strategy for ensuring that healthy competition takes place within a larger co-operative framework, doesn't work as effectively when the game is not played on a level playing field.

Tit-for-tat works extremely well when players have relatively equal resources. As two individuals, each with a small bakery and a single retail outlet, the village bakers A and B had roughly the same power to compete and/or co-operate with each other, by playing tit-for-tat. However, now imagine that baker A is bought over by a big bakery company which has 100 shops and can bake bread in a central bakery with large economies of scale. The new owner closes down bakery A and keeps only the shop open, reducing overall costs by 75%. In their high-tech, industrial bakery, bread can be produced to the same quality as A's old bakery but at 50% of the previous cost. In order to increase their market share in the village, the new owner reduces the retail price of bread by 25%. Baker B naturally plays tit-for-tat by matching the price reduction but, instead of reverting to co-operation, A cuts the price of a loaf by a further 15%. Reluctantly B follows suit but, with her significantly higher cost base, profit margins are becoming perilously thin. Baker A responds by taking a further 10% off the price of bread and B is now faced with an impossible dilemma – if she continues to play tit-for-tat she will be selling bread for less than it costs to bake, and will make a loss on every loaf sold. The more bread she sells the bigger the loss she will incur. She also knows that even if she does reduce her price, the big bakery company may simply cut its price even further as, with a considerably lower cost base, it can still afford to sacrifice more margin. B decides not to reduce her price by another 10% but after a few weeks has lost most of her customers. B has no option but to close her business and A becomes the only baker in the village. In this scenario both players are still making decisions in their rational self-interest, but by significantly shifting the resources available to each of them we create disequilibrium in the competitive power of each player, and the self-regulating influence of tit-for-tat become ineffective. Of course, even between players with similar resources a free market *will* reward superior quality, service or value and penalize inferior players, but the resource differential created will grow gradually and, for a while at least, poorer players will still have comparable resources with which to close the performance gap between them and their competitors. However, no matter how well they perform in the short-term, over a longer timescale small players can rarely compete effectively with much larger companies, because the latter buy and sell on a scale which ratchets their resources to a far greater level, enabling them to leverage superior financial, distribution or marketing muscle to outperform their smaller rivals. A free market, with no restrictions on the size or resources of the businesses in it, is like a boxing tournament with no weight categories – no matter how skilful or fleet of foot the flyweights are, the heavyweights will still knock them into oblivion. By creating 'super-human' corporations, capitalism made the playing field highly uneven, negating the ability of tit-for-tat to moderate the market and dampen its excesses by ensuring the prevalence of enlightened self-interest.

Our left mind loves the concept of companies because they are decontextualized, abstract referents for real world human-beings, but deliver far greater potential for power, status and material wealth than could ever be accrued by a single individual. By incorporating the muscle and brain power of 100, 1000 or even 100,000 people into one 'body', they are able to amplify their ability to compete and in doing so negate the necessity for them to co-operate. Tit-for-tat can only be effective when employed by players with similar resources so, as smaller players are put out of business or bought by larger rivals, categories inevitably consolidate until only a few behemoths are left slugging it out. This has consistently been the emergent global pattern in most industries over the last few decades and the ability of customers to influence market dynamics, by playing tit-for-tat, is significantly compromised. The 18th century villager had real power as one of perhaps only 1000 customers for whom bakers A and B were competing. By acting in their own self-interest, rewarding fair value and punishing any attempts to exploit them, each villager could keep the two bakers honest by directly and materially impacting their profits. However, when baker B went out of business their power became diminished. Once the big bakery company was the only baker left in the village, they not only restored bread prices to their original level but increased them by a further 20% yet, because the increase was less than the cost of travelling to the next village, it still wasn't in the customers' self-interest to buy their bread elsewhere. Some villagers discussed re-opening bakery B but the start-up costs created a considerable entry barrier to the market. Realizing they could never bake bread at a sufficiently low cost to compete with the big bakery company, they abandoned the idea. In protest some did eat less bread and sales in the village fell by 5% but the bakery company hardly noticed. They had already expanded further and now had 120 shops, even higher scale-efficiencies and an even lower unit cost per loaf. They also had 120,000 customers across the whole region so the impact on their business of the tit-for-tat efforts of a handful of upset villagers, was negligible. Once again the greater the gap in resources between the players in a market, the lower the impact tit-for-tat was able to have.

Under such conditions, wealth quickly becomes unevenly distributed as success accrues to the bigger players, with capital and talent flowing to those who already have scale, resources and status, thereby further amplifying their advantage. Customers may derive some benefit, in terms of product range or consistency, but in return they must sacrifice their ability to select from alternative suppliers and the personal warmth of human relationships which previously added emotional value to their choices. In such cases, brands, another left-mind abstraction of real-world values, often replace people as the focus for customers' feelings and our attachment to material objects grows, as our ability to empathise with each other is eroded. Increasingly devoid of human connection, commerce becomes purely transactional and the old 'market' in which genuinely skilled craftspeople served genuinely valued customers, is replaced by one in which faceless companies conduct business at arms-length with equally anonymous consumers. As qualitative human values decline in value, quantitative economic growth becomes the only measure of the health and wellbeing of the ecosystem. As categories consolidate into ever fewer conglomerates, those same consumers become increasingly employed as cogs in gigantic commercial machines. With economic growth as their only goal, they compete against other huge companies, only collaborating in their mutual focus on fuelling overconsumption to satisfy the ceaseless financial demands of their shareholders. As employees individuals are paid to stimulate artificial demand through sales and marketing but, as consumers, those same people must ultimately return their wages to the types of corporations which employ them, by purchasing the products they produce in order to keep those companies competitive and thereby remain in employment. Competition may drive consumer prices down but to increase profits and shareholder returns, costs must always be driven down even faster. One of the major business expenses – staff costs – must therefore be controlled, so wages are suppressed, headcounts curtailed and greater productivity demanded per employee. Chasing the delusional dream of ever-upward growth inflates consumption to the detriment and damage of the only planet which can sustain us, while the fight to capture market share of the bubbles we create – all the while increasing year-on-year profits – keeps jobs and wages growth perpetually behind the earnings curve. Wealth, therefore, isn't distributed evenly but disproportionately allocated to shareholders and to the company directors whom shareholders retain and reward, also disproportionately, for providing them with superior returns.

Chief executives and directors of major global companies have essentially the same brain as the rest of us, with all of its common foibles, flaws and biases, and the markets in which their businesses operate are almost always so complex that outstanding performance depends as much on good fortune as good judgement. Indeed, Richard K Wagner of Florida State University synthesised several pieces of research to assess the correlation between intelligence and performance in business, and con-cluded that IQ predicts only around 4% variance in job performance.[15] In fact, once an individual gets beyond a base IQ level of around 120, there is little relationship between more intelligence and better performance.[16] Of course, CEO's *do* influence company performance but their impact is much smaller than the business press would have us believe. Researchers measure the strength of a relationship by a correlation co-efficient of between 0 and 1, where zero means there is no correlation between two factors and 1 means there is a complete overlap, so the two factors are entirely interdependent. Research suggests that a generous estimate of the correlation between the performance of a company and the quality of its CEO, might be around 0.3 or 30% overlap.[17] Consider pairs of competing companies in which each player has similar resources, except one has a better CEO than the other. If the CEO made all the difference, the better CEO would be found leading the top performing company in 100% of cases while, if they made no difference at all, a random allocation would suggest they should be found in half of the best performing businesses in each pair. A correlation of 0.3 suggests that the highest quality CEO would be found in around 65% of the best businesses – certainly better than no correlation at all but not exactly justification for the vastly inflated salaries currently being paid to many of our corporate leaders. In the US, CEO's of listed companies earn between 300 and 400 times as much as the average worker and over 700 times minimum-wage earners. At the other end of the scale, Japanese CEO's generally earn around 10 times the average salary. No human alive is even 10 times more intelligent than any other fully-functioning adult, never mind being 300 to 700 times as smart.

I certainly don't have the ability to redesign a new global economic system, but I can tell you this much – the capitalist system we have created does not serve the best interests of most humans, nor does it contribute towards a globally coherent ecosystem by encouraging healthy competition within an overarching spirit of co-operation. It does not facilitate tit-for-tat behaviour, which is by far the best strategy we have yet found for ensuring that balanced competition/co-operation emerges from the complex adaptive system in which we live. Yet it's not Adam Smith's fault. There's nothing fundamentally wrong with the free market, indeed Smith's invisible hand will redistribute wealth fairly, if not evenly, by rewarding those who provide better value and penalising those who wish to freeload or exploit others. Tit-for-tat sees to that. But the great power of tit-for-tat is fatally undermined, once an imbalance is created between the strength and resources of the players in the game. With such an imbalance, and with economic growth as their only goal, the big become bigger, their power becomes amplified, wealth is disproportionately distributed to those who are already rich and the ordinary worker becomes tethered to a delusional wheel of progress, enslaved within a system from which there is no rational escape route. Our greatest problem isn't the free market per se, but the structure and strength of super-human corporations within the free market.

Our current economic system has been created by our collective left mind, but a left mind which has been given unfettered free rein because our pre-eminent global culture, scientific materialism, is also dominated by the left mind. As a consequence, our current version of capitalism takes a very narrow focus, prioritizing financial growth above all else yet decontextualized from the wider social, moral and spiritual framework within which it should operate. Its detachment from the outer world has led it to emphasise material goods over human relationships, to replace real-world values with its favourite abstract referent – money – and to an almost psychotic willingness to rapaciously exploit our natural resources. It lauds super-human corporations as an abstraction of real people, rewards competition to the detriment of co-operation, pits groups against each other in a game of 'survival of the fittest' and watches, with dualistic dispassion, as the system it has created inevitably produces polar extremes of winners and losers. However, it doesn't *have* to be as it is. A new economic system could be developed which has a much better chance of delivering behaviours which balance the wellbeing of both the individual and the collective, but it's a difficult thing to do. Such is the immense complexity of our human system, we can only change the local rules and hope that the type of behaviour we wish to see exhibited, eventually emerges at the global level. There's not a single person on our planet with the intellectual capacity to design a fool-proof economic system which would be guaranteed to spread wealth evenly, stop us killing each other over oil or prevent the damage we are doing to our natural environment. What is certain, however, is that such a system could only ever be the product of a collective right mind which is highly conscious of the environmental context in which we live, and which, while valuing the many talents of the left mind, is able to holistically synthesise and therefore moderate the more dangerous aspects of its input.

It is equally certain that the very people who are best placed to change our current version of capitalism – our societal elites – are also the least vested in creating the systemic change we need. Genuinely democratic political systems are therefore pivotal to changing our thinking and changing our future, for only elected governments, authentically representing the best interests of our planet and everyone on it, have the power to enact the new political, economic, social and technological structures we need, if we are to peacefully transition to a higher level of collective consciousness in which the natural balance of our global mind is reflected in the cultures we create.

Unfortunately, because we have been dominated for several centuries by scientific materialism, most of our current political structures are also the product of an unrestricted left mind. While our politicians do try to ameliorate the painful consequences of capitalism by spending taxes on remedial programmes in welfare or education, they too are inevitably operating within a cognitive framework dominated by a linear belief in cause-and-effect. More often than not, therefore, their interventions are unsuccessful or partially successful but have unintended consequences in other parts of our complex system. By failing to appreciate that new structural solutions are required if substantively different outcomes are to emerge, they are simply playing the current 'game', never able to produce alternative results from a system which is structurally stacked in favour of sustaining current outcomes. If our current economic structures incentivise and reward competitive behaviour over co-operation, no short-term political intervention will ever sustain a significant, long-term shift in behaviour, without fundamentally altering the structures themselves. Indeed, if our left mind has defined both the game we play and the rules by which it is played, there is a greater likelihood that left-mind dominant behaviours will not only continue to emerge but will become ever-more amplified over time. None of the structures we have created to run our societies therefore need to change quite as much as the globally-dominant Western political system.

Adversarial Politics

While our economic system is clearly important, the ability of politicians to pass legislation which influences almost every aspect of how we each experience life, makes our political structures the most important of all in our global human system. Our politicians are elected to represent us so they should, in theory, faithfully represent the balanced nature of our collective mind. To do so, they should operate within a political system which is an outer-world manifestation of our optimized inner world, offering opposing tendencies towards conservative order and liberal freedom but ultimately delivering dynamic stability and balanced coherence, arising from an environment in which healthy competition takes place within an overarching spirit of mutual co-operation. Indeed, it is no co-incidence that many Western democracies are principally structured around just two political parties, one primarily representing the perspective of our conservative left mind, the other largely advocating the views of our liberal right mind. However, whether Republican and Democratic or Conservative and Labour, parties actually tend to operate within political structures created by the dualistic left mind, which is adversarial in nature and far more competitive than co-operative. Remember, our left mind automatically sees everything as two separate and polar opposites, while our right mind recognizes polarity but seeks to integrate and synthesise. Only an out-of-control left mind could design a political system in which it is effectively pitted against our right mind, in a winner-takes-all competition. Yet, due to the powerful cultural dominance of scientific materialism, most Western democracies and most member countries of the British Commonwealth still employ just such a system, rather than one which facilitates valuable collaboration between the two parties and our two minds.

The most common reason offered in support of the UK's adversarial, first-past-the-post system, is that it provides the greatest order while alternatives will lead to chaos. We can almost hear the confabulating cogs of the left mind turning to produce such a rationale. While, from the point of view of the winning party, it may well be more stable to have a single party (and single brain hemisphere) dominate for a five-year term of government, it does very little for the quality of cognitive output created. Nor is it beneficial for the health of the whole ecosystem, if we experience periodic cycles in which the pendulum swings from a left-minded, right-wing party to a right-minded, left-wing party. Once we grasp the degree to which our key political polarities and their concomitant parties are a direct manifestation of our two minds, we may realize that an adversarial, winner-takes-all system makes exactly as much sense as asking our heart to run our body, while our lungs take a vacation. Like our vital organs, our two minds must work together to create coherence and so should it be with our politicians, the representative organs and minds of our political system.

Unfortunately, we'd only need to watch most parliaments in action for five minutes to see that the 'game' many politicians are asked to play actually makes collaboration very difficult because, within any adversarial system, competition is strongly incentivised over co-operation. Party lines are clearly drawn and members are often 'whipped' to vote in accordance with the wishes of their party. Tribalism and unquestioning loyalty to one's in-group therefore become paramount. Although it does happen, voting against one's own party is often a career-limiting practice as rebels find themselves shunned or side-lined, even those who maintain the unwavering support of their voters. Irrespective of any natural impulses an individual politician may feel towards co-operation, opportunities for collaborating with the opposition are in short supply as, in many countries, the electoral system is designed to maximise the chances of a single-party majority. For the left mind, a first-past-the-post system is always optimal because it allows the largest party to dominate parliament, even with a minority of popular support. In the 2015 UK General Election the Conservative party achieved a majority government by 12 seats, having received less than 37% of all votes cast and the support of less than 25% of the eligible electorate. This winner-takes-all principle is clearly a mantra of the left mind, enabling a large, yet minority, in-group to dictate to the whole of society. As a consequence all parties, irrespective of their natural inclination, are strongly incentivised to spin, lie, cheat, threaten and manipulate, in order to come out on top. Once elected, decisions which should be made for the good of the whole community are not made via the consensual interplay of opposing minds, but by the imposition of the will of one group on everyone else – exactly the preferred mechanism of the power-hungry left mind. Such structural flaws can easily cause citizens to become disenfranchised from politics to such a degree, that they deliberately disengage, driving voting rates down and creating a serious deficit in democracy.

The right mind is also in danger of becoming disengaged, if continually forced to play against an aggressively adversarial opponent. When the rules of engagement are dictated by the competitive left mind, it becomes almost impossible to work towards collaborative win:win solutions if your counterpart is only willing to play a game of win:lose. It also becomes disadvantageous for any player to be open, honest and to play the game fairly, if an opponent will do whatever it takes to win at any cost. Many instinctive liberals are therefore put off, by the system itself, from participating in politics and research shows that women in particular find the nature of male-dominated, adversarial discourse to be extremely unappealing. The very kind of people who might therefore bring greater hemispheric balance to politics are often under-represented within parliaments, as are those from a working-class background who could provide counterweight to the exclusively middle or upper class upbringing of elites. Consequently, any attempts to radically alter the system, from within the system itself, tend to be resisted by those with most to gain from the preservation of the status quo. Those liberals who are courageous enough to enter the fray, soon encounter obstacles to change which drain their energy or they may simply 'catch the culture', sucked into playing the game as it currently stands and losing sight of the need for structural change to the system itself. In order to perform more effectively within the prevailing system, ideologically-liberal individuals or parties may even become tempted to dial up the influence of the left mind to enhance their ability to compete and, in doing so, lose touch with their core values.

Perhaps this has never been more clearly illustrated than in the advent of New Labour by former UK Prime Minister Tony Blair. Having lost to the Conservatives under Margaret Thatcher in 1979, and then suffered four consecutive General Election defeats, it was only when the Labour Party made a decisive break from its socialist roots and adopted a distinctly neo-liberal approach to capitalism, that it regained power in 1997 via the largest landslide victory in its history. Strategically astute but morally questionable, Blair apparently believed that an authentically liberal mind could never overcome the conservative advantage when playing a political game designed by its adversary, or when trying to appeal to an increasingly materialistic electorate which he believed had shifted to the political right. By embracing the free-market capitalism and overt militarism so beloved of the left mind, he was able to regain power but in doing so had to shift his party to the right of centre, throwing the entire UK political system off its axis.

By contrast the 2015 UK General Election campaign heralded, for the first time ever, the arrival of genuine multi-party politics and for a long time prior to the vote, polls suggested that the long-standing, two-party dominance might finally be broken. It was perhaps poignant that the three parties which brought the most liberal, progressive voices to the 2015 hustings – the Scottish National Party, the Green Party and Plaid Cymru – were all led by women, while the four economically-conservative, socially-authoritarian parties were all run by men. For many observers, the pollsters' predictions of a hung parliament offered the opportunity for a long overdue shake-up of an outmoded and antiquated system which was no longer fit for purpose. Such a shift had the potential to be both significant for the UK and symbolic for the whole world – if the 'Mother of Parliaments' had finally reached the end of its shelf life, perhaps this heralded the end of left-mind dominance. Perhaps the door would open for the potential development of new political structures, created by the right mind, via which collaboration could flourish and healthy competition would be encouraged within a culture of respect, tolerance and co-operation. It's true that several other countries, such as those in

Scandinavia, are already well-ahead of the UK in terms of consensus-based politics and gender balance, but the significance of a structural shift in one of the world's oldest political systems could perhaps have inspired a major cascade of change. In the end, progressive hopes were dashed as the Conservatives were returned to power and the possibility of significant electoral reform disappeared for at least another few years.

All political parties will act in their own self-interest, so it is ultimately up to voters to create the conditions in which their self-interest is aligned with a new, more consensual, less competitive style of politics. The UK's first-past-the-post system is sustained by Labour and the Conservatives because it almost guarantees one of them a majority, yet it is clearly in the self-interest of most citizens that the politicians they elect actively collaborate to develop and execute policies which reflect the balanced wishes of the majority of the electorate, rather than simply imposing the views of the largest minority on everyone else. Some citizens do campaign for a voting mechanism which delivers a more proportional representation of elected MP's to votes cast for each party, but in a referendum in 2011 a proposal to replace first-past-the-post with a more proportional Alternative Vote system was rejected by the UK electorate by 68% to 32%, almost exactly 2:1, on a voter turn-out of only 41%. Research regularly shows that we don't always act in our own best interests, whether due to apathy, media brainwashing or more genetic drivers such as fear. When faced with binary choices between conservative and progressive positions on many issues, we often err towards maintaining the status quo for a whole host of reasons. We are certainly influenced by the 2:1 ratio which makes us naturally resistant to change, as well as a powerful *negativity bias* which enables us to be easily manipulated by scaremongering. We also have left minds which place high value on materialism, demand that we defend the people and property of our in-groups, and are only too willing to denigrate or even attack our out-groups. We live in cultures in which all of our major societal structures have been created by the left mind and in which aggressive competitiveness is therefore revered and rewarded, collaboration is often perceived as disloyalty and co-operation can be considered to be a sign of weakness. Perhaps most significantly, many of us have become so disenfranchised by the self-evident flaws in our political systems that we have simply given up on them and, in doing so, have gifted their dominion to elites who abuse them and therefore abuse us. Our political systems were designed for a bygone era in which the wealthy and influential decided how society should be ordered, but in these post-modern, technology-enabled times with a highly educated and widely connected citizenry, there can be no excuse for anyone being disengaged from politics or failing to have a say in how our world is shaped. Our societies and cultures are changing but our economic and political systems haven't yet caught up with the gradual, global shift away from left-minded dualism and towards the organic worldview of right-minded integrative monism. At some point we may wake up to the fact that our political and economic systems do not *have* to be as they are – dominated by elites working in collaboration with corporations and the mainstream media, to preserve the status quo. They *can* change and ordinary people can change them. New structures, which are both creating and being created by our shifting culture, are providing fertile soil in which tit-for-tat behaviour can once again flourish and in which competition can be nested and nurtured within an overarching spirit of global co-operation. Yet this destination is by no means guaranteed and we each have a small role to play in creating the conditions in which this new culture can grow.

By elevating our personal consciousness to become more aware of the deep flaws in our current political system, and more engaged with politicians and their policies, we can better influence them to develop the economic, social and technological structures we need to build a better future for our planet and everyone on it. Carl Jung's words are possibly even more relevant today than when he wrote them:

A mood of universal destruction and renewal ... has set its mark on our age ... Coming generations will have to take account of this momentous transformation if humanity is not to destroy itself through the might of its own technology and science ... So much is at stake and so much depends on the psychological constitution of modern man ... Does the individual know that he is the makeweight that tips the scales ?[18]

PART THREE

LEARNING

Origins and Oscillations
of a Global Mind

—9—

Source of the Western Psyche

*G*ENUS HOMO first evolved around 2 million years ago, from which *homo-sapiens* are the sole survivors having only emerged some 200,000 years back. In the context of a 4.5-billion-year-old planet, we are a fairly new species and human-beings are still infants in terms of our evolutionary development. For 95% of our existence we were hunter-gatherers, so our transformation into the high-tech urban-dwellers of today has been a recent and rapid ascent. With our modern minds it's difficult to imagine that we were ever much simpler creatures, more like the other animals around us today – sentient but driven almost entirely by unconscious, visceral responses to sensory stimulus. All sentient creatures have some level of consciousness but it's our superior self-consciousness which sets us apart from other animals. We are conscious of our own consciousness to a unique degree and, although we take this skill for granted, our ability to think about our thoughts and to know we have knowledge is actually very rare and something we share with only a handful of species, including apes, elephants and dolphins. Most other mammals don't have this ability and their lives consist of an avalanche of sensory data to which they automatically respond. Like us, they are reliant on two brain hemispheres but with little in the way of associative memories other than learned '*Pavlovian*' responses. Creatures without self-consciousness aren't aware of their own existence, so can't perceive a separate outer world. They experience life as one integrated whole which is lived entirely in the current moment, with no concept of time elapsing or that events may be taking place beyond their immediate sensory aware-ness. For them life just 'is'.

By great contrast, self-consciousness enables humans to '*stand back*' and see ourselves as if from outside our own being, as a separate entity from the outer world. Although we are just as embedded in the real world as a horse or a dog, self-consciousness gives us the impression that we are actually one step removed from it, enabling us to conceptualize time and to reflect upon our past, exercise some free will in our present and plan for our future. The separation required for self-consciousness is a function of the left mind and for it to have evolved over many millennia, the left mind gradually '*detached*' from its original position nested deeply within the holistic right mind. By '*detached*', we do not mean in any physical sense but in the relative independence of its cognitive mode.[1] By doing so, it gave us the '*necessary distance*' for dualism to develop. Creatures which lack self-consciousness never evolved to this extent and their left mind therefore remains more tightly nested than is the case with *homo-sapiens*. It was only through the development of self-consciousness that we were able to progress from living an 'animal' existence, to one we would recognize as uniquely human.

It's impossible to say exactly when our self-consciousness fully evolved, but it may have been much more recently than we might imagine. For example, in some of our oldest extant Western texts, such as Homer's *Iliad* and early sections of the Old Testament, there are no references to concepts we would now associate with consciousness such as intro-spection, self-awareness, mind or free will.[2] What's more certain, is that it was only when we combined self-consciousness with our superior language skills that the exponential progress of our species really took off, by enabling us to embed data in cultural artefacts and thereby convey knowledge over time and space. It is only within the last 5000 years – just 2.5% of our existence – that we invented writing, began to live in settle-ments of any scale and started to rapidly rise as a significantly superior species. Yet, while today we have greater access to information than Homer, Socrates or Aristotle, there's nothing to suggest we are innately smarter than them or than the average Athenian. It is largely the cultural content of the unconscious mind which makes our species super-smart, rather than any personal intellectual progress we have made. Indeed men like Plato, and many others since, effectively created the culture we have inherited, just as we will leave a legacy for future generations. If we are to change the path we are currently on, we must do so consciously through greater awareness of our individual cognitive flaws and the long journey our collective mind has undertaken to arrive in the early 21st century. In particular, we must seek to rediscover the true nature of our species in order that we might consciously seek to rebalance our global mind, thereby addressing the disequilibrium which is causing so much dissonance today.

By understanding our pre-history and especially the influence of the ancient Greeks, we can gain great insight into the development of the human mind, which is essentially the story of the co-evolution of consciousness and culture.

The Prehistoric Perspective

In *Guns, Germs & Steel*, eminent anthropologist Jared Diamond charts the development of human societies and explains that, although few human artefacts remain from prehistoric times, much can be gleaned from what does still exist and from the study of groups whose hunter-gatherer ancestry was most faithfully preserved into the modern age, such as Native Americans, Indigenous Australians and the tribes of the Amazon. According to Diamond, hunter-gatherers lived a nomadic lifestyle which made full use of the abundance of natural resources available to them and, living in small groups consisting of no more than a few dozen individuals, everyone in the group was involved in the daily task of food production. Human populations were small and land was plentiful so hunter-gatherers were largely averse to conflict, which would be detrimental to the whole group, and simply moved on if another band of humans was encountered. Shelter was communal, food was shared equally and skeletal remains show that men and women were more physically similar in size than is the case today, a characteristic still witnessed in the few hunter-gatherer societies which remain, like the indigenous tribes of Papua New Guinea. Grave goods and other artefacts also suggest that hunter-gatherers were politically egalitarian and that women were considered as equals, probably based on their equivalent ability to produce food.[3]

To these early humans, the natural world must have seemed like a truly inexplicable place. Ever since we gained sufficient self-consciousness to discern a separate outer world, our natural curiosity has compelled us to try to explain the environment in which we found ourselves. Driven by the most fundamental of motivations, survival, newly self-aware humans would have first sought to comprehend their experienced reality, in order to bring forth a sense of control over their day-to-day lives. This question could only be answered by the part of their cognitive system through which they were embedded in the outer-world of sensory experience – the right mind. Lacking access to significant schematic structures which would only be built by its counterpart a long way in the future, the right mind could only do what it does best and use senses, feelings and intuitions to leap to a coherent conclusion. The earliest evidence of humankind's oldest cultural narrative dates from around 50,000 years ago. Cave paintings from the Upper Palaeolithic period suggest a deep reverence for nature and that prehistoric 'worship' was closely intertwined with hunting rites, revealing '*animism*' as our most original expression of spiritual idealism. Palaeolithic people intuited that the animals they killed contained an immaterial spirit which equated with their breath and, in return for taking their breath/spirit, hunters developed rituals to offer thanks for their sacrifice. Paintings of thirteen different animal species found in southern France date from over 30,000 years ago and Palaeolithic artworks plus skeletal remains, found in places as far apart as Switzerland and Slovenia, suggest that ceremonial rituals were conducted in worship of bears. Further evidence of animism has been found all over the world including North America, Scandinavia and North Eurasia. The interconnected concepts of animal, breath and spirit are all still etymologically linked in the Latin '*spiritus*' meaning '*breath*', '*anima*' meaning '*vital breath or spirit*' and in the archaic meaning of English words such as animate and inspire, meaning '*to breathe life into*'.

In our earliest spiritual narrative, mankind was neither separate from nature nor superior to it but was very much an integral part of it. Springing from deep within our right mind – instinctive, intuitive and integrative – our existence was defined in contextual, relational terms to the rest of nature and our significance as a species was no greater than any other. In spite of later efforts by Western colonialists to eradicate any trace of them, the threads of our original belief systems still unwind today in Native American and Indigenous Australian cultures, where our importance remains no greater than the mountains, rivers or forests of the environment in which we are deeply embedded. Indeed, for Native Americans some creatures, such as bears and eagles, are still afforded a spiritual status which is equal to or higher than humans, and their role in the creation of the world is still told and retold though the oral tradition of conveying historical narratives in myths and metaphors, which can only be compre-hended by the right mind.

However, as our categorizing left mind gradually became more influential, a hierarchical distinction between humans and animals started to appear in our spiritual ideas but the archaeological evidence suggests that, for many millennia, they remained firmly rooted in nature and were exclusively female. Of particular intrigue are the Venus figurines, a large array of small statuettes of feminine form which appear abundantly in the

Upper Palaeolithic archaeological record.[4] Discovered at multiple sites across Europe and as far away as Siberia, the Venus figurines date mostly from the Gravettian period of 30,000 to 22,000 years ago but are evidenced all the way through to 8000 BC. Scholars agree that they are likely to be depictions of a persona considered to be the *mother of all creatures* or *mother nature* as we might call her today. However, there is nothing to show that such a figure was originally perceived as a supernatural deity. Instead, the prevalence of the figurines suggests that such symbols were largely apotropaic – good luck charms to ward off evil spirits and to bring forth good fortune in hunting and the fertility of the land. As such, the Venus figurines are indicative of an evolution of animism, giving thanks to the source of nature's bounty rather than directly worshipping the animals themselves. As the self-evident birth-giver, such symbols of fertility could only ever be female.

From around 17,000 years ago there is evidence of the emerging 'detachment' of the left mind from the right, with the appearance of zoomorphic images in both grave goods and cave art, suggesting that humans had begun to imagine supernatural beings. Paintings discovered at Lascaux, in southwest France, depict strange hybrid creatures which appear to be half-human and half-bird or half-beast, providing clear evidence of the emerging interplay between left-mind deconstructionism and right-mind constructionism. Once again, the spiritual ideas expressed are an evolution of animism but are also indicative of emerging self-consciousness, separating humans from the outer world and shifting cognitive output from an instinctive sense of what 'is' to a more imaginative expression of what 'could be'.

It was the Neolithic age, from around 12,000 to 4000 years ago, which showed the first evidence of our domestication of plants and animals, and which heralded the widespread transition of human societies from small bands of nomadic hunter-gatherers to larger groups of farmers. This shift also signals a further 'detachment' of the left mind. Farming required the technological skills of the left mind for tool-making, irrigation, deforestation, food storage plus many other such innovations, and the advent of planned agriculture also signalled an emerging separation between humankind and the rest of nature. Thus began the long journey humans would undertake, in their own minds at least, towards becoming a superior category of living organism. With this development we also see clear evidence of how our two minds work together to remove dissonance and restore essential ease in our cognitive system. If, to our collective left mind, humankind was becoming a superior category of being, a spiritual belief system in which we were merely a part of nature and only equal to other animals was clearly incoherent. A new narrative had to be developed, yet there is evidence that for a very long time we remained reverential towards nature in our spiritual idealism. 'Religious' artefacts from 9000 to 6000 years ago show that, by this period, zoomorphic images had indeed been transformed into supernatural, anthropomorphic deities but the focus of our worship, nevertheless, remained female in form and powerfully connected to the natural world. During this early Agrarian era, it made sense that the cycle of growth, withering and regeneration witnessed by new farming communities, would also find expression in their spiritual beliefs. Humankind was as susceptible as every other species to the vagaries of nature, so people intuited that by showing respect for the spirits of their prey and humble gratitude to the source of nature's bounty, they could enhance their chances of survival. Artefacts from a Neolithic settlement in Anatolia, and several other archaeological sites from the Baltic to the Balkans, yield strong evidence of the worship of various 'earth mother' type goddesses including snake goddesses, bee goddesses and bird goddesses as well as universal 'Great Goddess' figures, usually portrayed either as or with majestic creatures such as lions and leopards.

It was with the adoption of farming that we began to produce a surplus of food, over and above that which each individual could consume daily; a radical departure from a principle which had sustained the hunter-gatherer lifestyle for most of our existence. Farmers could no longer be nomadic so settled populations grew from small bands into larger tribes numbering hundreds of individuals. Initially, group membership was still kinship-based and land belonging to the tribe was sub-divided into smaller parcels, each owned by a family group. The opportunity to accumulate wealth, in the form of material goods, was now no longer restricted to what each group could carry but tribal societies nevertheless remained socially and politically egalitarian, with no formal or hereditary leadership roles. Instead, communal decisions were made on behalf of the whole tribe by representatives of each kinship group. As tribes were now static, women were no longer restricted to having only the number of children they could carry at any one time. Food was plentiful and populations grew quickly but as the number of mouths to be fed expanded so did the requirement for further food sources, requiring tribes to extend the foot-print of the land they occupied. The food surplus also allowed people to be fed who weren't directly involved in food production, in particular craft specialists such as tool makers, enabling farmers to trade their produce for other goods which they and their families found useful. Thus began the division of labour and the market society we are so familiar with today. However, as tribes grew and food production struggled to keep up with ever burgeoning populations, sub-groups had to split off from the tribe and travel to find more land to commandeer. Over time, and with increasing regularity, these groups came into contact with other humans and found themselves in competition for available resources. Soon, tribes realised that in order to safeguard existing settlements and acquire more land for food production, a particular types of specialist was required – the soldier.[5]

In the early Agrarian age, man had only sought dominion over plants and animals but conquering occupied land required the subjugation, by force, of those already on it so along with the bounty of land and livestock came a further prize, the human slave. Soldiers proved to be the perfect specialist with which to acquire and defend land as well as control unwilling slaves. In return, they were widely feted and greatly admired. Almost exclusively male and specifically bred for fighting, the soldier received more than his fair share of available calories and so began the divergence in physical size and strength between men and women, which still exists to this day. With the soldier and his warrior ethos also came the emergent dominance of masculine values, such as aggression and competitiveness, thus strengthening the role of the left mind. Because they were less valuable as soldiers, the status of women within the tribe would gradually diminish and, like plants, animals and slaves, the female of the species would progressively become subjugated beneath the heel of the physically superior male.

The advent of the masculine ideal did, however, create one problem for tribal societies – who would control the soldiers? When they weren't required to fight, men who had been trained since birth to be aggressive found it impossible to simply turn off their bellicosity. In the early days, leaders of war-like yet meritocratic societies were always the best warriors, but this proved to be an extremely precarious mechanism for maintaining leadership as there was always a steady stream of new challengers for the title. Collective order had to be maintained, which was relatively easy in kinship groups where everyone knew each other but in larger groups, where individuals were less acquainted, tribal society needed a structure which would formalize authority and maintain control. The dual solutions were hierarchy and bureaucracy, both strongly indicative of a flourishing left mind. The best fighters appointed themselves as permanent chiefs whose leadership was unchallengeable and, in return for on-going support and protection, the new chief bestowed favour upon his key men, offering them hierarchical status within the group. Chiefdoms were made hereditary, ensuring the end of egalitarianism and a privileged future for royal offspring. Initially, brute force and fear were sufficiently powerful for maintaining order but, in time, chiefs appointed bureaucrats – the ancient antecedents of modern-day politicians – to create rules and regulations to further cement their control, including punishments for all those who breached the prescribed code of conduct. Growing civic populations inevitably required further bureaucrats to manage the ever-expanding schematic structures by which society was ordered, so smart politicians elevated their own status by building layers of bureaucracy beneath them.

At this point in our history we once again see clear evidence of our two minds collaborating to ensure essential cognitive ease. If, in our collective left mind, we had moved on from being egalitarian farmers, superior only to domestic animals and crops, to become a society in which men were superior to women plus all those we enslaved, it was no longer coherent for us to worship the 'earth mother' type goddesses of the hunter-gatherers and early farmers. Tribal chiefs needed a new narrative to persuade men, even their most loyal soldiers, to risk their lives in battle again and again, in order to subjugate enemies and commandeer their land. The solution heralded a dramatic shift in the story, from animistic, earth-based and bountiful goddesses to a very different type of deity altogether – male, sky-based, warrior gods. By proclaiming that such gods were on the side of soldiers in battle and would, in the event of their death, guarantee an eternally blissful afterlife, chiefs were able to persuade warriors to look beyond their earthly existence and willingly give up their lives for a greater good. Some chiefs even converted themselves into 'god-kings', as the living embodiment of the greater good, with a divine right to rule and a status equal to the deities themselves. Their credibility was sustained by having their status independently verified by religious figureheads, such as priests, whom chiefs appointed and collaborated with in claiming direct access to the deities. Thus, the hierarchy and schematic structures of social, political, economic and religious elites were first created and provide clear evidence of the increasing power of the left mind.

Male 'sky-gods' are therefore a relatively recent invention in human history, the first evidence of which only dates from around 6000 years ago.

Anthropologists commonly attribute the name 'Dyeus' to the sky-god of the Proto-Indo-Europeans, the loosely-related ancestral tribes which were antecedents of most modern-day Eurasian cultures and languages. However, the evolution of Dyeus and his impact on later civilisations was certainly not uniform and, as his deistic descendants developed, we see a clear and significant divergence between the Orient and the Occident. In the East, Dyeus became Dyaus Pita (literally sky father), the oldest of the Vedic Gods, husband of Prithvi Mata (earth mother) and father to the pantheon of future Hindu deities. In the West, however, Dyeus became Dis Pater in Latin and Deus Pater in Greek and their emergent offspring, Jupiter and Zeus respectively, became very different in character to their Eastern ancestor. While Dyaus Pita retained respect as father of the main deities, he developed into a relatively marginal and benign figure in Hindu mythology. Meanwhile, his Western counterparts became powerful Gods of Gods, famed for their many lovers and violent use of the thunderbolt to smite their enemies. Far from being married to 'earth mother' goddesses who were equal to them in stature, Jupiter and Zeus were married to Juno and Hera respectively. Both women were considered to be goddesses only of marriage and childbirth, and were perhaps most famed for the revenge they exacted on the lovers of their errant husbands. Therein we see the great cultural schism between Western dualism, with the cultural dominance of the masculine left mind, and Eastern monism, with the retention of relative balance between the brain hemispheres and the sexes. Thus cemented, in Western cultures at least, the societal subjugation of the female by the male, a situation she has now suffered for over 6000 years.

Of course, this seismic cultural shift didn't happen at a particular point in time but very slowly over several millennia, and the most detailed, coherent hypothesis of how Neolithic Europe was transformed from egalitarian, peaceful, matrifocal groups into hierarchical, warring, patrifocal tribes, was first offered by Lithuanian archaeologist Marija Gimbutas in the 1950s.[6] Based on a lifetime's study of Old Europe and thousands of findings from many archaeological sites, Gimbutas concluded that prior to around 6000 years ago all ancient Baltic, Balkan, Anatolian, Etruscan, Basque, Celtic, Germanic and Scandinavian cultures had been broadly similar, in the nature of their pastoral, peaceful and even artistic communities. She found commonality in their worship of 'earth mother' type goddesses and in many artefacts which suggested that groups had been matrilinear, matrifocal and egalitarian. Her hypothesis was supported by one of the oldest and best-preserved Neolithic settlements ever found, at Catal Huyuk in modern day Turkey, dating from around 9000 years ago. Artefacts uncovered by Anglo-Dutch archaeologist James Mellaart confirmed Gimbutas' findings, revealing a peaceful, creative civilisation, evidenced by a wide array of pottery, woven fabrics, jewellery and other luxury goods. From wall paintings, sculptures, statues and other remains, Mellaart also demonstrated that the religious mythology of the 7000 inhabitants of Catal Huyuk revolved around the worship of an 'earth mother' type goddess. The burial sites and symbolic grave goods of men and women also strongly suggested that both genders held equal status in society.[7]

Through her work, Marija Gimbutas was also able to provide the first credible answer to a question which had puzzled archaeologists and linguists for almost 200 years. In the late 18th century Sir William Jones, an Anglo-Welsh judge serving in India, had noticed that Sanskrit contained striking linguistic similarities to Greek, Latin and Celtic, and theorized that these languages must have come from a common, ancestral language which was long extinct. In time, the number of languages identified to have sprung from this single linguistic source would rise to over 400 and encompass all major European languages, plus those of the Middle East and Indian sub-continent. Today, they are collectively known as the Indo-European languages and are spoken by almost 3 billion native speakers, yet their original source, the Proto-Indo-European language from which they all evolved, is still fiercely debated. As an archaeologist of some repute who could also read 16 European languages, Gimbutas was perhaps uniquely placed to bring together the archaeological and linguistic strands of Indo-European cultures. In the 1950s, she used carbon dating to accurately identify the age of artefacts found in archaeological digs all over Europe and her research allowed her to develop a detailed chronology of Neolithic events, leading to the formulation of her famous '*Kurgan hypothesis*'.[8] Named after their characteristic burial mounds, or '*kurgans*', Gimbutas identified the people of the Pontic Steppes region, to the north of the Caspian and Black Seas in modern-day Ukraine and southern Russian, as the source of the Proto-Indo-European language. By combining carbon-dated artefacts, such as weaponry from different parts of Europe, along with linguistic evidence Gimbutas was able to build a compelling case that the Kurgans were a warrior race who, over several millennia and in a number of waves, expanded the land under their control by first overwhelming the pastoral farmers of Europe, then by conquering

Central Asia, India, the Balkans and Anatolia. According to the Kurgan hypothesis, between around 6000 and 3000 years ago the Kurgan culture gradually spread, taking with it the source language which would ultimately yield all Indo-European languages. As a result, almost all pre-existing, indigenous languages and cultures were eradicated in just a few thousand years, by an extremely efficient war machine.

According to Gimbutas and other archaeologists such as Gordon Childe, who also studied them extensively, the Kurgans were a highly patriarchal, warrior society who worshipped a violent, male 'sky father' god, practiced human sacrifice and believed in an extra-worldly afterlife. As the first race to domesticate the horse and later to develop the chariot, the Kurgans would have found very little resistance from the peaceful, agrarian communities they encountered and wounds inflicted on skeletal remains confirm that the Kurgan invasion was a violent, military assault. From DNA and dated human remains, there is evidence that older matri-lineal burials, in which people buried in the same grave were related by female lineage (as was common practice in the pre-Kurgan period), rapidly disappeared. Irish-American archaeologist James Mallory also found powerful evidence of a dramatic shift in mortuary practices around the time of the Kurgan invasion, noting that they appeared to become identical to those practiced in the Pontic Steppes region:

> ... these are generally confined to males and are accompanied by weapons – arrows, spears and knives. The rite of suttee, the sacrificial execution of a women on the death of her husband, is indicated in some burials suggesting the patriarchal character of the warrior pastoralists who super-imposed themselves on the local agricultural populations.[9]

British archaeologist Jacquetta Hawkes further confirmed the conclu-sions of Gimbutas, Mellaart, Childe and Mallory, that pre-Kurgan societies were peaceful, egalitarian and matrifocal. Hawkes focussed her attention on the ancient Minoan civilisation of Crete which, due to the remoteness of the Aegean island, had been largely unaffected by any Kurgan influence. Hawkes found compelling evidence that a Neolithic Goddess tradition and gender-egalitarian society had lasted well beyond the timing of the Kurgan waves, and had maintained a peaceful, prosperous and artistic culture well into the Bronze Age.[10]

Like all interpretations of pre-history, Gimbutas' Kurgan hypothesis has received criticism and counter-theory, yet it remains the most compelling and coherent explanation of how over 400 modern languages, covering such a wide geographic span, could all have emerged from a single-source, proto language and culture. Indeed, as American linguistics expert Michael Everson concluded:

> ... the folkloristic and mythological evidence for a pervasive Neolithic goddess cult throughout Europe is in itself so striking that the burden of disproof lies on the critics of this interpretation.[11]

It also explains how peaceful, agricultural, egalitarian societies and their 'earth mother' belief systems could be so decisively displaced in Europe, by a patriarchal culture which would eventually yield warrior races such as the Spartans, Romans, Celts and Vikings.

The overwhelming evidence is therefore that our 'true' nature is to be peaceful and egalitarian, reflecting the overarching orientation of the right mind within which our left mind is a valuable, but subsidiary, partner. This has been the case for over 95% of our existence, during which our intuitive expressions of spiritual idealism have been very much rooted in our oneness with nature and a clear reverence for other creatures. Even when the hierarchy-creating qualities of our left mind first elevated us above other organisms, it was as the mother of nature not as its male subjugator. Indeed, for over half the time since the advent of farming, our symbols of worship remained feminine in form even as they evolved from the natural to the supernatural and anthropomorphic. It is only relatively recently, within the last six millennia or so, that we have seen our left mind come to dominate our thinking and address the cognitive dissonance which necessitated a new spiritual narrative, in the form of war-like, male sky-gods; a legacy we still live with in the West. Yet this path was neither pre-determined nor inevitable and it is only due to Western cultural hegemony that it eventually came to dominate the globe. The modern-day pre-eminence of scientific materialism, and the three Abrahamic monotheisms as our most prevalent expression of spiritual idealism, are not therefore in any way natural or necessary. Although the Occidental worldviews came to dominate, another path was possible and was indeed taken by the near Eastern descendants of Dyaus Pita and those cultures in the Far East which were less influenced by Proto-Indo-Europeans. Core to this divergence was the adoption of an overarching dualism in the West, a distinctly left-minded lens on life, compared to the right-minded monism of the East and such opposing perspectives continue to manifest in the many cultural differences between the Occident and Orient to this day.

The path taken by Western (and largely global) culture ever since, has seen an oscillation in the influence of left and right minds but always within the context of an overarching dominance of dualism during this period. The significant pendulum swing towards the left mind, which began 6000 years ago with the Kurgan invasions, has at various times been partially counterbalanced by the re-emergence of right-mind influence, during Ancient Greek times plus the Renaissance and Romantic period of the late 18th and early 19th centuries, and we are once again experiencing such a rebalancing in the early 21st century. We will now follow this path, beginning in Ancient Greece.

The Influence of Ancient Greece

The long precursor to the creative outpourings of classical Greek antiquity saw the pastoral pre-Hellenes slaughtered by Indo-European hordes, who swept down from the Caucasus via Anatolia around 1800 BC, then again just 200 years later.[12] With their horses, chariots and weapons, they easily defeated the sea-farers of the Aegean peninsula and established brutal patriarchal rule which, according to the poet Hesiod, saw them kill all the men and impregnate all the newly widowed and fatherless women.[13] However, in conquering such a wide area from the Middle East and western China to Scandinavia and the Mediterranean, the Indo-Europeans did establish an intercontinental web of city-states in which trade was able to flourish, based upon sufficiently common elements of language and culture. As has so often been the case throughout history, conquest and commerce were dual drivers of data transfer across the human system, enabling greater integration and collective cognitive development by bringing together and melding new perspectives. Cities sprang up along all the major trade routes, acting as hubs which attracted travellers and facilitated not only the exchange of goods but also the ideas which would ultimately shape the modern global mind.

The roots of our dominant culture, scientific materialism, lie in pre-Socratic Greece where the left mind emerged with a flourish during a period, between c.600BC and 400BC, when there was also a broader blossoming of both brain hemispheres. During this time, the ancient Greeks made great strides forward in the codification of laws, the development of analytical philosophy and the systemic capture of knowledge through advancements in writing. The creation of a consistent alphabet and set of abstract symbols also had a huge impact on the development of the left mind, enabling the recorded history of people and places as well as the development of maps and mathematics. Progress in the left mind was paralleled by developments in the right mind, which brought the democratisation of knowledge, the earliest forms of popular political participation and the increased use of imagination, emotional expression and metaphoric language in art and humour.

According to philosopher and historian Bertrand Russell, what we would today call 'philosophy' first began with Thales of Miletus, a now-ruined city on the western coast of Turkey but, at the time, one of the greatest cities in all of Greece. Son of a Phoenician couple who had settled there around 640BC, Thales became a speculator in olive oil, a trade which saw him travel widely and allowed him to indulge his real passion for politics.[14] Thales was befriended by an influential local tyrant called Thrasybulus and became his trusted counsel, enabling the oil salesman to build a political profile on an intercontinental stage. There, according to Plutarch, he also became friend and adviser to both Solon and Lycurgus, the great lawmakers of Athens and Sparta respectively. Thales was a traveller, connector and thinker extraordinaire, who reputedly learned Egyptian geometry to calculate the height of the pyramids and used Mesopotamian data on the heavens, to accurately predict a solar eclipse in May 585BC. His greatest achievement, however, is to have founded the reason-based mode of thought for which Pythagoras would later coin the term 'philosophia', meaning 'love of wisdom'. Thales was first to throw off the deity-based mythologies and attempt to provide a secular explanation for how the cosmos had come into existence. The world, he declared, had self-assembled from water and what he called 'psyche' which he explained with the statement 'all things are full of gods', an early insight into the immaterial essence of the universe.[15]

We'll never know for sure how much influence Thales had on Lycurgus and Solon, or on the societies they shaped in Sparta and Athens, but we do know that he was a great student of culture and a supreme thinker on how best to mould societies by shaping the behaviours of individuals in them. We'll also never know the degree to which the respective cultures created by the two lawmakers reflected their own personalities, but we can certainly see the powerful influence of brain dominance in the divergent paths that Sparta and Athens chose to take. The key influence of men like Thales was perhaps to shift the creation of social groups from those based on kinship, ethnicity or faith to those founded on reason-based philoso-phies about how ideal societies should be formed and sustained. As a result of the secular, rational philosophy founded by Thales, citizens began, for the first time, to openly debate different visions for the organization and operation of communities. Thus we have the first clear evidence of consciously planned civilisations, with deliberately chosen political, economic and social structures. Both Sparta and Athens were two such societies.

Sparta was largely given shape by Lycurgus, a legendary lawmaker who envisioned a land-based, military society built upon values of deep discipline and authoritarian control. Meanwhile Athens, principally moulded by Solon, developed into a sea-faring, trading culture which was wide open to the import and export of both goods and ideas. While Sparta was resolutely inward-looking, Athens oriented itself outwards towards the rest of the world, each demonstrating a clear difference in left and right mind dominance.[16] While Spartans and Athenians were neighbours and allies within ancient Greek society, they were also fierce rivals for overall pre-eminence on the Aegean peninsula and so the cultural context was set within which their co-operative, yet competitive, relationship would develop.

Sparta

The Spartans were descendants of the warlike Dorian tribes, which had swept down into the southern Peloponnese and crushed the indigenous populations beneath their heel. Highly sectarian, they called themselves the Spartiate or *'those who are alike'* and deemed that only those of their ethnicity could be citizens of Sparta. The Dorians themselves had descended from ancient Kurgan roots and, following the same traditions which had led their distant relatives to establish the caste system of social stratification in India, the Spartans also created hierarchical classes. For example the *perioeci*, like the *vaisya* caste in India, were allowed to call themselves freemen and participate in manufacturing and commerce, while the lowly *helots*, like the *shudra* caste, were made slaves and forced to serve at the feet of their masters.[17] The Spartiate themselves were only a small minority but nevertheless dominated the city-state which bore their name as a ruling elite, allocating resources, creating laws and maintaining order. Lycurgus, guardian of the Spartan king who was too young to rule, had travelled widely to Crete, Egypt and Asia to study different types of government and finally, having consulted the oracle at Delphi, he returned to Sparta with a new constitution.[18] Lycurgus decreed that to prevent being overthrown in revolt by the majority underclasses, the nine thousand

Spartan citizens should permanently militarize and would function best if raised in accordance with ancient tribal traditions. All men were to be housed communally and great emphasis was placed on behavioural conformity and economic austerity. Meals were served in mess halls, with food portions, wine allocation, seating arrangements and even conversation topics all strictly controlled. Anyone who wished to supplement their meagre diet could participate in hunting expeditions to kill their own prey. [19] Eugenics was a passion of Lycurgus, and the breeding of strong, physical specimens was a top priority for his envisioned Spartan society. He believed that sentimental love weakened a man so, even on his wedding night and after spending just a short time with his new bride, a bridegroom was expected to return to barracks and to sleep communally with his colleagues. Indeed, according to Plutarch, a first baby was often born *before the father had seen his wife by the light of the day*.[20]

Producing strong children who could be moulded into military machines was the number one priority in Spartan society. Indeed, if a man encountered another whom he considered superior to himself in mind and body, it was his duty to ask him to impregnate his wife.[21] Each new-born child was inspected and those deemed too weak were abandoned to die. Even for those who made it, life didn't get much less harsh. Boys stayed at home until the age of seven, when they were separated from their family and entered into the *agoge* for military education. There, they would spend the next fourteen years in a brutal environment in which severe punishment was considered to be the path to respect and obedience. Raised in a culture of harsh austerity, boys were kept deliberately under-clothed and under-fed, so were encouraged to develop soldierly skills such as stealth by stealing, even though the punishment for theft was particularly harsh. When they reached adolescence their burgeoning self-will was constrained by the imposition of heavy labour and the threat of life as a second-class citizen for anyone who rebelled. Their self-control was also consciously moulded by a litany of rules which dictated, for example, that they could only speak when spoken to and, when in public, must walk with their heads bowed and their gaze fixed only on the ground straight ahead. The powerful influence of the left mind is clear for all to see.

Competition was core to Spartan culture, with the three best young leaders each allowed to select one hundred of their peers to form elite in-groups, while the unworthy rejects banded into bitter out-groups; resentful, watchful and eager to catch out elevated rivals who failed to live up to the prescribed code of conduct. According the Xenophon, children were perpetually '*at war*' and had to be prepared at all times for the fights which would inevitably break out. Although they did not attend the *agoge,* female Spartan children were also expected to take physical exercise and compete in tests of speed and strength. Girls even ran and wrestled against boys, rode horses and chariots and competed in sports such as discus and javelin, while more sedate pastimes such as weaving and cooking were left to slaves. The result was a powerful, yet deeply disciplined, societal elite who were subservient to the Spartan ideal like bees to a hive. While Lycurgus' planned society created an awesome military machine, it also produced an automaton citizenry who had been bred for obedience and uniformity which made them easier to control. Under the Spartan constitution, deference to authority was paramount and Lycurgus created the *Gerousia,* a body of thirty male aristocrats, to run the country. This council of elders were elected for life, notionally via democratic means but in practice simply drawn from the two royal houses, the *Agiad* and the *Eurypontid.* The *Gerousia* prepared motions for a wider citizens' assembly known as the *Apella* to vote upon, but in practice had the power to close down discussions and veto anything approved by this group. Via this structure, just thirty men effectively formed the Supreme Court in Spartan society and could overrule any decision made by any other body in the political system.

Thanks to Plutarch, Sparta is one of the earliest documented examples of a consciously planned culture in which the subject of his biography, the legendary figure of Lycurgus, envisioned the type of society he wished to create and deliberately designed the political, educational, legal and social structures he believed would best deliver his vision. It is true to say that the Spartan society which emerged had all the hallmarks of a left-mind dominant design. Hierarchy, order, control, separation, categorization, patriarchy, uniformity, competition, militarism, authoritarianism and a lack of emotion or empathy are all characteristic of extreme left-mind dominance.

Perhaps Thales was conducting the most brilliant social experiment ever invented or, perhaps much more likely, we are retrospectively creating a compellingly coherent narrative about the influence he may have had on Lycurgus and Solon, but the chief lawmaker and cultural architect of Athens could not have thought more differently from the Spartan.

Athens

Athens had been inhabited since the Neolithic age and later became the focal point of the Mycenaean civilisation. Unlike Sparta, the heavily buttressed hill-fort on the Acropolis was never breached by Dorian invaders and many Athenians would later claim to be ethnically 'pure' Ionians, with no Dorian influence. By 900BC Athens was a leading centre for trade and the most prosperous city in the region, ruled by a land-owning aristocracy known as the *Eupatridae,* or 'well-born', which consisted mainly of four tribes whose members held an array of rights and privileges. Over the next two centuries, Athens successfully brought the other cities of Attica under its patronage through the process of *synoikismos,* or 'bringing together into one house', and collectively they formed the largest and wealthiest state on the Greek mainland. However, this synthesis also brought together a large body of people, many of whom remained outside the political classes which were still exclusively populated by the 'well-born' nobility. By the 7th century BC, social unrest was widespread and Draco was appointed to draft strict new laws to restore order. However after his 'draconian' efforts had failed, Solon was appointed around 600BC to create a new Athenian constitution.

The reforms instigated by Solon significantly impacted political, social and economic structures in Athens and would shape Athenian culture for centuries to follow.[22] The large estates of the *Eupatridae* were broken up, making commerce more widely accessible and enabling the emergence of a wealthy, urban trading class. Solon also undermined the economic power of the aristocracy by forbidding the enslavement of Athenian citizens who fell into their debt, and even the poorest underclass, the *Thetai* (who made up the majority of the population), were given political rights for the first time and could vote in the citizens assembly, the *Ecclesia.*[23] In doing so, Solon laid the groundwork for Athenian democracy upon which all demo-cratic societies are still essentially modelled to this day. As Athens grew as an accessible, commercial city built upon diversity and democratic debate, it opened its doors to all-comers and attracted a wide array of people and perspectives. Philosophers such as Protagoras from the Balkan city of Abdera, Anaximenes from Miletus in Anatolia, Parmenides from Italy's Elea and Georgias from Leontini on the island of Sicily, were all magnetically drawn to Athens. There, their insights could be shared and blended with those of contemporary thinkers from much further afield, such as the Persian Zoroaster and the Chinese Lao Tzu, whose ideas were carried as cargo along international trade routes. It was from such an abundance of rich stimulus that arch-blenders Socrates, Plato and Aristotle would later come to create the philosophies upon which the Western world, in particular the culture of scientific materialism, is built today.

Most inhabitants of Athens, of course, weren't philosophers but the influx of such a diverse range of intellectual options left no less a mark on the wider Athenian populous, than it did on ancient Greek philosophy. While Spartan citizens had very little social stimulus to choose from, ordinary Athenians were bathed in an embarrassment of riches from trade groups, religious societies and debating clubs to sports gymnasia, drinking dens and high-class whore houses.[24] Sub-cultures of every hue were not only tolerated but encouraged within a highly liberal, pluralistic cultural outlook. Philosophers even started their own schools and won many followers, eager to subscribe to one blend or another of cognitive chemistry. Far from killing off their weak, introverted or oversensitive children because they might make poor warriors, Athenians encouraged them to express their individuality, to seek out others who shared their passions and to follow their own path in life. While Spartans willed self-control and controlled self-will, Athenians liberated the consciousness of their young to venture forth, explore and experiment. While Sparta sought to mould citizens into a single cultural straitjacket, bringing the order, structure and certainty so beloved of the left mind, Athenians sought to engage the rich ambiguity and sensory experience of the real world, via a deeply-embodied, outer-embedded right mind. While Sparta exercised ideologies in authoritarianism, nationalism and militarism, Athens practiced libertarianism, internationalism and democracy. Which won? The Peloponnesian Wars between 431BC and 404BC concluded when Sparta, supported by the Persians plus rebels within some of Athens' subject states, destroyed 168 Athenian ships at the battle of Aegospotami and effectively won the war. Rather more metaphorically, of course, their battle remains unresolved to this day and is still going on, both in our minds and all around us.

Yet the Spartan victory was critical to what later unfolded, for the cognitive blend inherited by the modern Western world and which forms the foundation stone of scientific materialism, was principally Platonic. Plato was 23 when his home city of Athens fell to the Spartans and was a handsome, athletic young man, as well as a gifted mathematician, musician and playwright.[25] Unsure whether to follow a career in politics or poetry he discovered philosophy through a family friend who would soon become his mentor, Socrates. When Athens fell, its democracy was replaced by a pro-Spartan oligarchy which soon became known as the Thirty Tyrants; so-called for its brutal oppression which caused the death of some five percent of the Athenian population, including at least 1500 prominent democrats, during its brief, thirteen-month reign. The Tyrants leader Critias was a cruel, inhumane man yet was a friend and relative of Plato. He was also a former pupil of Socrates, who stood up to the oligarchy and was only saved by their sudden demise. Critias was killed in the coup which overthrew the Thirty, but the citizens of Athens struggled to recover and to reconcile with those who had supported the tyrannical reign. A few years later, and still in a state of turmoil due to political infighting, the newly restored democratic government turned on Socrates, accusing him of corrupting the youth of Athens and of impiety – not believing in the gods recognized by the state. Finding him guilty, Socrates was sentenced to death by drinking poisonous hemlock.

Disturbed by the death of his mentor and deeply disillusioned with the Athenian state, Plato fled to Egypt and Cyrene, in modern-day Libya, where he came into contact with other philosophers, particularly eminent Pythagoreans such as Philolaus and Eurytus.[26] Pythagoras had been a 6th century BC philosopher who, after thirty-seven years of gathering knowledge on travels throughout Gaul, Phoenicia, Anatolia, India, Persia and Arabia, eventually founded his own school and religious sect in the Croton region, a Greek colony now in Italy. There, he attracted a following of several thousand acolytes. Naturally introverted and deeply disciplined, Pythagoras created a cult-like community in which disciples took oaths of loyalty, eschewed all luxuries, wore identical clothes, adopted common behaviours and were prohibited from consuming all manner of foodstuffs. Temperance and abstinence were the watchwords of the almost-monastic Pythagorean system, and only after five years of extensive study and unquestioning obedience to every command, were adherents allowed direct access to the wisdom of the master himself. Although not much detail is known about the religious beliefs of this secretive society, many scholars concur that it was highly esoteric, doctrinaire and occultist. What's more clear, is that Pythagoras was a great admirer of Spartan methods for the formation of strictly regimented minds, and greatly valued mathematics, geometry and science in explaining nature and the cosmos. So popular was Pythagoreanism that his exclusive clubs were opened in other cities across *Magna Graecia*, and his totalitarian societal structures soon permeated the entire Croton state. Unfortunately for him, many non-members objected to the imposition of his type of austere, exclusive autocracy on wider society and his headquarters and many of his schools were burned down by angry mobs, scattering his followers and destroying Pythagoras himself.[27] However, his influence lived on and, still dedicated to the teachings of their master, his brotherhoods were resurrected first in Southern Italy and then in several Greek states, where they continued for another 300 years. His successors continued to advance the mathematical and scientific principles first established by Pythagoras, including prime numbers, early algebra and the geometric theorem for which he is still famous, as well as hypothesising a round Earth which revolved around the Sun. Indeed a thousand years later, both Copernicus and Galileo would be recognized as followers of the Pythagorean tradition.

More immediately, however, the teachings of Pythagoras would greatly influence Plato. Indeed, in *A History of Western Philosophy* Bertrand Russell contends that Pythagoras should be considered to be the most influential of all Western philosophers.[28] Upon returning to Athens, Plato founded his own *Akademia* around 385BC and the Platonic Academy had all the hallmarks of heavy Pythagorean influence, from its exclusivity to the motto inscribed above its main entrance – *Medeis ageometretos eisito* – 'Let no-one without geometry enter here'. Plato's greatest legacy was his famous *Dialogues* in which he laid out his views on many subjects and also related the perspectives of predecessors and peers, none more so than Socrates. Plato's overarching belief was that the cosmos offered deeply ordered, transcendent and universal principles, which belied the apparent chaos of life and which were only accessible to the human intellect via the medium of reason.[29] According to Plato, these principles existed beyond sensory perception as absolute, eternal truths, in *Forms, Ideas* or *Archetypes* such as Beauty, Goodness or Wisdom, which were separate and superior to the earth-bound entity in which they manifested. Thus, a beautiful vase which was perceptible to the senses, was but a mere imperfect shadow of true Beauty which would eternally transcend all such tangible expressions of beauty, long after the vase had lost its lustre. Authentic reality therefore lay somewhere deep, beyond temporal and transient appearance. If a woman looked beautiful to the eyes, it was only because she was temporarily participating in the absolute, pure and eternal Form of Beauty, and her earthly attraction would soon fade.

In his broader conception, all aspects of experienced reality were underpinned by polar pairs of timeless essences, including Light & Dark, Love & Hate, Male & Female and Night & Day, and every aspect of existence given perceptible form was thus imperceptibly patterned by the *'veiled essence of things'*.[30] Plato's comprehensive theory of reality also extended to the moral sphere where universal values such as Goodness or Justice were deemed imperative for the avoidance of amoral relativism. Similarly, in natural philosophy, he believed that in spite of the constant flux and flow of the experienced world, all natural phenomena could be comprehended by the intellect through the identification of the mathematical and geometric principles to which they operated – a fundamental foundation stone of what would later become known as science. Plato's perspective is clear evidence of a fully-formed left mind in its de-contextualization and abstract categorization of real-world phenomena.

For Plato, it was self-evident that all individuals who appeared to be wise or brave merely drew from a universal Wisdom and Bravery, which existed, in pure and absolute form, somewhere in the ether; transcending earth-bound mortals but uniquely perceptible to the human intellect. Thus, all individual trees shared an essence of 'treeness' and all individual red objects participated in a common 'redness'. A critic of Plato once observed that he saw only particular horses but not 'horseness', to which Plato replied *'that is because you have eyes but no intelligence'*.[31] To Plato, the archetypal Horse, which gave form to all other horses, was a more fundamental reality than individual, real-world horses, which would come and go while the archetypal Horse was immortal. Plato therefore directed the philosophers gaze inwards – from the particular to the universal – in classic left-mind abstraction and, in a deft twist, also turned ancient Greek reality on its head. Plato held a strong distrust of knowledge derived from the senses because such knowledge, embedded in the outer world, was constantly changing and highly subjective to the individual. He believed that sensory knowledge was therefore based on ever-altering opinion and was unsound, while true knowledge was only achievable through direct comprehension of the universal *Forms, Ideas or Archetypes*. These were pure, eternal and unchanging, uninfluenced by the chaos and imperfections of the physical world.

In this, the Platonic perspective can be traced back to Parmenides, who preceded Plato by about a century and was the first philosopher to mark a distinct shift away from the holistic, right-mind orientation of Thales and Anaximander, which had been continued by Plato's contemporary, Heraclitus. Parmenides key work, a poem titled *On Nature*, described two views of reality: what he considered to be *'the way of truth'*, in which existence was timeless and uniform and change was impossible, and '*the way of opinion*' in which the sensory faculties misled the perceiver to subjective and false conclusions. Parmenides work appears to have had a strong influence on Plato (and much later on Descartes) because it was the first to posit a clear, dualistic, either/or view of the world with a distinctive left-mind intolerance of ambiguity and a strong suggestion that whatever was logical must be true, no matter how much it was contradicted by sensory experience. In one of his dialogues *Theaetetus*, Plato recalls Socrates pointing out that Parmenides was the only respected ancient scholar to deny that all reality existed in change and motion yet, despite this Socratic warning, Parmenides still persuaded Plato and through him shaped most Western thinking.[32] Plato's belief that all true knowledge must be universal and unchanging, inevitably leads to the conclusion that all outer-world data which is particular and changing, must be unreliable. Only the knowledge created by the left mind is therefore objectively true and, to Plato, this was the only reality, while the subjective knowledge accessed via the right mind was transient, illusory and false. Only the decontextualized abstractions intelligible to the left mind offered the universal truths upon which all reality was based. In a brilliantly audacious cognitive coup, the powerful left mind of Plato had convinced us that what was purely conceptual was actually real, and that what was experienced as real by the senses was actually an inauthentic shadow of the only true reality; that created by the left mind itself. Thus, in *The Republic* Plato writes:

> The stars that decorate the sky, though we rightly regard them as the finest and most perfect of visible things, are far inferior, just because they are visible, to the true realities ... we shall therefore treat astronomy, like geometry, as setting us problems for solution, and ignore the visible heavens, if we want to make a genuine study of the subject.[33]

By prioritizing rationalism over empiricism, and by separating the static and eternal from the fluid and transitory, Plato would leave an indelible mark on the Western psyche which is still with us to this day. By emphasising the qualities of the left mind over those of the right, he inadvertently laid the groundwork for the elevation of the scientific and materialistic over the artistic and humanistic, which would last for over two thousand years. Pre-Socratic Greece had been built on a tradition of myth, metaphor and empirical observation but with Plato '*the Heraclitean respect for the testimony of our senses had been lost*' and through his *Dialogues* he displayed his deep admiration for Spartan order and austerity, in the portrayal of his utopian vision.[34] In *The Republic* he suggests that the work of all painters is '*far removed from reality*', that art is a '*poor child born of poor parents*' and that all poets should be banished from the city. All metaphor is dismissed as fiction, dramatists are chastised for corrupting the minds of their audiences and literature is deemed full of dangers to the young, so must be strictly censored. His proscriptions on music are equally totalitarian, concluding that there is no requirement for a wide harmonic range and that many musical instruments should therefore be banned.[35] In *The Laws* he further portrays his ideal nation as one which is perpetually ready for war and which, even in times of peace, retains the hierarchies, regulations and disciplines of a militarised state.[36]

By his later life Plato had clearly travelled a long way, both literally and metaphorically, from the youthful musician, playwright and poet he was when Athens fell to Sparta. That he admired the culture of his conquerors, more than that of his birth, was but one of many contradictions evident in Plato's perspective, for he not only possessed a sharp mind but also a whole one. He himself occasionally used myth and metaphor in his writings to explain concepts which were difficult to articulate, such as his *Allegory of the Cave* in *The Republic.* He also hinted in *The Symposium* that he recognized that his *Forms, Ideas and Archetypes* first had to be intuited before they could be rationalized, and that the way in which they drew people towards them was instinctive rather than logical. He also lived in a very different time to us and Plato's use of the word Idea had a very different meaning to the modern day. In Plato's time an Idea wasn't solely a mental construct, privately experienced by the individual, but an objective, spiritual entity which existed independent of the form in which it manifested, which could be either material or imaginary. As such, Plato's Ideas transcended inner and outer worlds, connecting rather than separating them. A cat was a cat because it participated in the Idea of the Cat and the human mind could recognize a cat by virtue of its own participation in the same archetypal Idea. For Plato, therefore, in spite of his strong left-minded dualism, the human mind and the natural world were still deeply connected because they were both ordered according to the same universal Ideas, in which they both participated. Similarly, abstract mathematical symbols or geometric shapes were not simply quantitative structures, created by the human mind and imposed on the outer world, but perfect, transcendent and eternal entities which existed independent of both the natural phenomena they ordered and the human mind which could perceive them. However, although he did undoubtedly seek to reconcile our inner and outer worlds, there can be no question that it was primarily a left-minded version of the world Plato put forward.

Plato's greatest pupil, Aristotle, did however do a great deal to rebalance the classical Greek mind, by reasserting the value of the senses in scientific study. After 20 years of studying under Plato, he founded his own philosophical school, the Lyceum, and developed his own unique point of view which partly built upon and partly disagreed with that of his teacher. Aristotle could not concur with his mentor's conclusion that true reality could only be found in transcendent, immaterial Ideas and, in particular, he criticised Plato for the way in which he afforded equal status in his theories to qualities such a 'beauty', 'tallness', 'blackness' or 'fastness', with substance such as 'horseness'.[37] Through his *doctrine of categories*, Aristotle asserted that substance took priority over all else as the primary reality because without the substantial existence of the horse itself, all other values which described the horse such as beautiful, tall, black or fast, couldn't exist. Furthermore, 'horseness' couldn't exist as a general or universal concept without being substantially embodied in the physicality of a particular horse. In this, Aristotle reversed the premise of Platonic logic by concluding that if substance did not exist, nothing else could exist. Substance was therefore the basis of all reality and could only be perceived by the human senses in the individual objects or organisms they experienced in the phenomenal world. Thus, Aristotle inadvertently laid the foundation stone for materialism – the primacy of substance over form – which would become the principle ontological premise for scientists until the development of quantum and complexity theories in the 20th century. Yet ironically, perhaps even tragically, Aristotle was actually a remarkable whole-mind thinker and brilliant polymath, who had a deeply insightful, intuitive knowledge of quantum science and complex systems at least two millennia before these terms were even coined.

Aristotle believed that substance was not purely a unit of lifeless matter but contained intelligible form within it.[38] While Plato thought the essence of reality transcended phenomena and existed independent of form, Aristotle concluded that the essence of reality was immanent within matter and ultimately gave it form. Rather than participating in an external, archetypal Idea of 'dogness' or 'humanness', the qualities which created the individual dog or particular human were encoded within the substance – in modern terms the DNA – from which they derived their unique form. What's more, for Aristotle form was not static but dynamic, with each organism striving to grow from a state of potentiality to a state of actualization by realizing its fully-formed capability.[39] While Plato considered all phenomena to be imperfect, mere shadows of pure Ideas, Aristotle proposed that all living organisms were in the process of moving from imperfection towards perfection, drawn by imperceptible attractors towards becoming that which they were inherently meant to become – the acorn to the oak, the embryo to the child, the child to the adult and so on.

For Aristotle form and substance were relational terms, each nested within the other, whereby the form created by matter could also become the matter from which a higher form could grow – a very early explanation of holons. The '*being-becoming*' dilemma, which had first been developed by Plato in response to the very different worldviews of Parmenides and Heraclitus, was thereby resolved by Aristotle as actuality and potentiality and was widely evidenced in the natural world. While Plato perceived ultimate reality as static and prioritized 'being' as objective truth, relegating 'becoming' to subjective opinion, Aristotle balanced the brain hemispheres by providing the process of 'becoming' with its own reality, asserting that substance and form were perpetually and dynamically engaged in striving for their mutual potentiality. While Plato distrusted knowledge derived from sensory perception, preferring to directly deduce universal principles, Aristotle considered that knowledge of the natural world must first be apprehended by the senses and from the particular, before underlying patterns or universal principles could be identified. In doing so he re-established as a valid source of knowledge, the empiricism which would much later be resurrected by Francis Bacon and others during the Philosophical Revolution, as a key cornerstone of the 'scientific method'. Rather more immediately, his legacy would largely be lost until the Renaissance and even then it would primarily be his lessons in logic and rationalism (along with Plato's abstract mathematics) which would resonate, rather more than his brilliant, intuitive grasp of quantum science and organic biology.

In summary, from the Pre-Socratic scholars there is strong evidence of the pre-eminence of the right mind, running from Thales and other eminent Milesians, such as Anaximander and Anaximenes, through to Heraclitus. They and many others concurred that the opposites they observed in life and the mental dichotomies they experienced, did not compete or cancel each other but instead '*define one another and bring one another into existence*'.[40] Heraclitus famously observed that '*all things flow*' and is perhaps most well-known for stating that '*one cannot step into the same river twice*', a powerfully right-minded position compared to the stasis required for left-minded analysis.[41] Possibly more than any other early Greek philosopher, Heraclitus grasped the essential balance between the two hemispheres and believed that contradiction was a necessary aspect of their character. He recognized that opposites, far from negating one another, instead gave life to each other through their interdependency and mutual struggle. He understood the value of the hidden, implicit aspects of nature as a complement to the obvious and explicit, and noted that dynamic flow was a necessary condition for sustaining life via their mutual interplay. Heraclitus valued the empirical evidence of the senses, recognized the importance of relationships and believed that experienced phenomena could be altered by the context in which they manifested. A very long time before split-brain experiments, Heraclitus demonstrated an incredibly insightful understanding of the independent, yet interdependent, operating modes of the two minds.

However, first with Pythagoras then Parmenides and particularly with Plato, we see clear evidence of the emergent left mind and a self-conscious '*standing back*' from experienced reality. This enabled us to look, as if from the outside, at how things around us worked. Standing back allowed the ancient Greeks to rationally consider all aspects of the cosmos and natural world, as well as to review their social, political, economic and spiritual structures, providing the earliest concrete evidence of the distinct separation of left and right minds. By delivering heightened awareness of the contradictory pulls between intellect and intuition, the emerging left mind caused right-minded emotions – which previously would have been acted upon instinctively – to instead be reflected upon and called into question; clear evidence of a blossoming self-control which enabled the left-mind intellect to 'stop and think' by challenging the intuitive, right-minded response. Without such self-consciousness there could be no consideration of whether our thoughts were right or wrong, because there could be no distinction between the inner mind and the outer world it experienced. At the '*necessary distance*' this distinction was created and we started to realize, perhaps for the first time, that the voices in our heads did not belong to the gods.

In the final analysis, pre-Socratic Greece brought forth a powerful flowering of both the left and right minds, which would have a hugely beneficial influence on Western philosophy and society. From the right mind, supreme advancements in art, poetry, sculpture, drama, literature and architecture enabled the full expression of human qualities such as empathy, passion and humour. From the left mind, great progress in writing and mathematics enabled the systematic capture of transferable knowledge, the creation of a legal system, the study of philosophy and history, the development of maps in geography and drawings in architecture, plus real advancements in geometry and physics. However post-Socrates, from Plato onwards and despite the best efforts of Aristotle, the phenomenal world of the senses would come to be considered unreliable, with only the abstract 'ideas of things', rather than 'things' themselves, believed to represent true reality. Gradually, experiential knowledge gained from the right mind would become increasingly downgraded in favour of the conceptual knowledge of the left mind and the corresponding diminishment of the value of implicit, intuitive knowledge would leave an indelible mark on the Western psyche for the next 2500 years.

—10—
Emergence of the Left Mind

I N THE SECOND HALF of the 4th century BC when Alexander 'the Great' of Macedon conquered lands from Greece to Egypt and India, he created one of the largest empires ever known in the ancient world. As a youth Alexander had been tutored by Aristotle and held a passion for classic Greek culture, which he widely disseminated throughout his kingdom. Although a powerful military leader, Alexander was inspired by a unifying vision of humankind's inherent kinship which saw him grant clemency and political rights to those he conquered. His life was short – he died at just 32 – but his great legacy was to create a Hellenistic culture in the East, aspects of which would last into the Byzantine era of the mid-15th century.[1] Nevertheless, Alexander's premature death led to dynastic struggles which tore his empire apart in the West, and paved the way for the rise of the Romans around the first century BC. Like the Greeks and the Alexandrians, the Romans were militaristic yet largely libertarian and rapidly absorbed the Hellenistic culture; their scientists and philosophers continuing to work within the intellectual frameworks created by Socrates, Plato and Aristotle. The Romans successfully extended their empire to cover the entire Mediterranean basin and stretched their sphere of influence from North Africa to Northern Britain. In doing so, during the 1st and 2nd centuries AD they established the '*Pax Romana*' or Roman Peace across most of Europe, under which Greco-Roman culture continued to flourish.

If considered as a single entity, the classic Greco-Roman civilisation lasted for roughly one thousand years, from 500BC to 500 AD. At the mid-point on this timeline, out on the eastern edge of the empire, a young Jew lived and died who would perhaps have a greater impact on human culture than any other person, before or since. Jesus of Nazareth was born into a Judaic religious tradition which had already been established for over 1500 years and which prophesied that a messiah would come to establish their one true God's kingdom on earth. Having waited for so long, the Judaic soil was perhaps particularly fertile for the proclamations of Jesus' followers, that he was the son of God and that his death and resurrection would bring divine redemption for all of mankind. Yet we know nothing of what Jesus himself thought. Like Socrates he left no writing, so everything we know about the figurehead of what came to be called Christianity was scribed by his followers, one of whom – Paul of Tarsus – was his main missionary and theologian.

Paul was actually travelling to Damascus intent on suppressing what he thought was a dangerous threat to Judaism, when he was transformed by his vision of a resurrected Christ. Although he never met Jesus 'in the flesh', under his tutelage the disciples of Christianity would create an impressive narrative in which the human world was reconciled with God, but not yet redeemed by Him for the original sin of Adam and the subsequent fall of man. Followers of Jesus soon became entranced by their belief in the potential salvation of man, and evangelical in their commitment to propagate the faith. Their small religious movement spread out from the Middle East towards Anatolia, Egypt, Greece and Rome, yet actually had relatively little success in converting Jews to Christianity. In fact, in their story Jesus' followers had created an intellectual and spiritual synthesis which was of much greater appeal to the pagan, Greco-Roman temperament. Indeed, Paul was a Roman citizen who spoke Greek as well as Hebrew and was the product of a Hellenistic cultural upbringing. Core to Christianity, and consistent with Greco-Roman philosophy, was a belief in universality and the spiritual ideal that all of mankind could ultimately be united under one God. In spite of its strong-arm militarism, the Roman Empire had been remarkably non-sectarian, transcending nationalities and offering equal citizenship to those under its dominion. Furthermore, the Hellenistic culture it promoted was trade-based, cosmopolitan and inclusive, joining far-flung communities together under the Roman banner. In spite of the opposition of many early Christians towards their rulers, the spread of Christianity therefore benefitted greatly from the freedom of movement enabled by the *Pax Romana* and from the fact that, first Alexander and then the Romans had already united a multitude of people, languages and cultures.

By comparison, the Judaic character was of a more autocratic and sectarian temperament. Perhaps the Jews hadn't expected, as their long-awaited messiah, such an apolitical, deeply humanistic pacifist but they rejected Paul's assertion that the opportunity for salvation should be open to non-Jews as well as Jews. This led to the focus of recruitment for the new religion being outside of Palestine and on the wider Hellenic world. Christians saw many commonalities between the teachings of Jesus and Platonic philosophy, in particular the ideas of transcendence, absolute perfection, eternal wisdom and the primacy of spirit over matter. Indeed Socrates and Plato were hailed, by some, as divinely-inspired, pre-Christian visionaries. In return, many Greeks saw Jesus as the singular embodiment of Platonism. However, no matter the similarities with Hellenistic philosophy, the foundations of Christianity were still most strongly derived from its Judaic roots. Hellenism had generally been open to the exploration of all perspectives and tolerant of ambiguity and contradiction. To the Greeks progress remained largely cyclical, characterised by the dialectic ebb and flow of intellectual discourse. The Jews, however, were rather more linear in outlook. Able to trace their heritage directly from Abraham and to project it forward to a time when God would dramatically renew His sovereignty on Earth, they were impatient to restore themselves to their rightful place as His *'chosen people'*. While the Hellenistic approach was therefore about balancing alternatives, the Judaic perspective was more singular, narrowly-focussed and time-bound; a clear orientation towards the left mind.

Under the Judaic influence, the religious pluralism of the Greco-Romans was therefore gradually replaced by a single Christian worldview.[2] Their pantheon of polytheistic and pagan deities was discarded, with all of their valuable characteristics being subsumed within a new cast of characters including God, Jesus, Virgin Mary and the Holy Spirit. Satan became the singular embodiment of all undesirable traits. All remaining traces of ancient animism were dispensed with – only men, not animals, trees or rivers were the prophets of God and worthy of His salvation. Any remnants of 'earth mother' goddess belief systems were no longer required in light of an omnipotent, male sky-god. The naturalistic 'death-rebirth' mythologies of pagan belief systems were now manifest in Jesus Christ himself. The wide-ranging, intellectual exploration of reality, from the naturalism of Thales and Heraclitus to the rationalism of Parmenides and Plato, could now all be forgotten as only the supreme God and His divine revelations via the Bible, offered absolute truth. The phenomenal world had become insignificant in comparison with revealed spiritual reality. Although Christianity placed high priority on personal responsibility, self-control and moral behaviour, the individual intellect and the self-development of knowledge about the experienced world were discouraged. Faith was now the primary source of all learning, as conveyed by the teachings of Jesus Christ. Both rationalism and empiricism were therefore relegated to inferior functions – '*In the context of the new order the simple faith of a child was superior to the abstruse reasonings of a worldly intellectual*'.[3] With the truth of reality now so clearly articulated and firmly fixed, there was no longer any need for the individual to think for himself; mere obedience to the scriptures was all that was required. And so, the panoply of philosophies, the variety of belief systems, the wide-ranging intellectual debate and the sheer richness and diversity of Hellenistic culture were all replaced by one God, one church, one truth and one worldview. The open, ambiguous and tolerant religious multiplicity of the right mind was substituted for a version of spiritual idealism which, while originating from a right-minded impulse, was now firmly in the powerful, controlling grip of a singular, intolerant and narrowly-focussed left mind. Thus, brought into sharp relief we see the two contradictory faces of the Abrahamic monotheisms – on the one hand committed to the loving, all-embracing, all-forgiving salvation of their flock, yet on the other hand exclusive, authoritarian and judgemental; ever remindful of human failings and the unworthiness of the mortal soul for God's redemption. On the one side emphasising the primacy of the individual and the need to take personal responsibility, while on the other discouraging independent thought and intolerant of dissent or deviation from scripture.

Despite such unreconciled paradoxes, Christianity continued to flourish but it was not until it was adopted by Emperor Constantine, in the early 4th century, that it really took off and became firmly established as the official religion of the Roman Empire. By the end of the 5th century, Rome and its western colonies would be conquered by various Germanic tribes and the focal point of the Empire would move east to Constantinople. With it were transferred many of the great works of the Hellenic philosophers; works which would help the Byzantine and Islamic empires to prosper for the next 1000 years and wouldn't be returned to Europe until the Renaissance. In the meantime, the West would enter the Middle or 'Dark' Ages which would last for the same millennium. Science and philosophy, already decaying towards the end of the Roman Empire, would receive little nourishment, only briefly illuminated by individuals such as Albertus Magnus, Thomas Aquinas and William Ockham. Instead, the reign of the Christian Roman Catholic 'empire' of the Middle Ages would become most notable for its increasing militarism. Challenged by the dynamic growth of Islam, Pope Urban II launched the first Crusade in 1095 to reclaim the Holy Land around Jerusalem and other sacred sites. There then followed a 200-year struggle, with six more major Crusades and many minor campaigns, ending in 1291 and beyond which the Catholic empire made no further military incursions into the East. The major schism between all three Abrahamic monotheisms over the lands of the Middle East, remains unresolved to this day and still lies at the heart of much of the religious warfare we experience in the 21st century. When Moses descended from Mount Sinai with the Ten Commandments he could hardly have foreseen that, with Judaism and its two errant offspring, the direct word of God '*thou shalt not kill*', would come to be so widely ignored and regularly abused in His name.

The Early Renaissance

The evolution towards the global dominance of the modern Western worldview really begins with the European Renaissance of the 14th to 17th centuries, although its roots remain in classical Greece. The Renaissance was a cultural movement which began in 14th century Italy but was later accelerated by the fall of Constantinople in 1453. In escaping from the Ottoman Empire, many of the finest Byzantine scholars – artists, philosophers, architects, poets, scientists, politicians and theologians – brought classical Greek texts back to Europe for the first time in 1000 years. The impact was to spark a 're-birth' of interest in the teachings of the ancient Greeks and to inspire, in polymaths such as Da Vinci, Michelangelo and many others, the greatest 'leap forward' in intellectual, creative and scientific pursuits since the Hellenic era.

Throughout the millennium of the Middle Ages, the Roman Catholic Church had strictly controlled the thoughts of the ordinary person, focussing their lives on the need to behave in accordance with the doctrines of the Church in order to access spiritual redemption in the afterlife. During this period, the voices of art, philosophy and science, although never completely silent, were but a whisper compared to the booming tone of the Church. The Renaissance, however, pulled the West out of these dark times and brought an unprecedented explosion of intellectual, cultural, artistic and scientific development, the like of which the world had never seen. With it also came the flowering of the human spirit and a rebalancing of the brain hemispheres, via the re-emergence of the right mind to counter the powerful, controlling grip of Roman Catholicism. Indeed,

> with the Renaissance, human life in this world seemed to hold an imme-
> diate inherent value, an excitement and existential significance, that
> balanced or even displaced the medieval focus on an afterwordly spiritual
> destiny.[4]

Yet, far from being a revolution directed against Roman Catholicism many aspects of the Renaissance were in fact supported or even sponsored by the Church, which had become so omnipotent that it was perhaps unable to conceive of any possible threat to its dominion. Saint Peter's Basilica and the Sistine Chapel in Rome, plus many other great works of art, stand testimony to this day to the power and glory of the Catholic Church and to the role it played in the Renaissance.

Like all major cultural movements, the Renaissance wasn't one thing but a multitude of many different and sometimes contradictory dynamics, all of which flourished due to the energy and mutually reinforcing powers of paradox. Indeed, the Renaissance holds a unique position in history for its simultaneous melding of many opposites into one synthesis – science with religion, philosophy with art, modern with classical, individual man with collective church, and left mind with right mind. The ancient Greeks, both pre- and post-Socrates, firmly believed that the human brain and the natural world were intrinsically connected and patterned in the same way. The pre-Socratics mainly perceived a universal order in which everything was fluid, dynamic and uncertain, and in which the empirical evidence of the senses was therefore the most reliable source of knowledge – a primarily right-minded perspective. The post-Socratics, however, mainly believed that the cosmos conformed to natural, universal laws which could be understood via mathematics and science, and that concep-tual, intellectual rigour was therefore the path to truth – a predominantly left-minded worldview. The early Renaissance period embraced both pre- and post-Socratic perspectives and briefly re-established a balancing of the brain hemispheres. It did so via a radical insistence on placing no strict divisions between different aspects of human knowledge or experience.

Its greatest exemplar was undoubtedly Leonardo Da Vinci, possibly the greatest polymath ever to have lived. Born in 1452, Da Vinci would become famous not only as a painter and scientist, but also as a sculptor, architect, mathematician, engineer, inventor, anatomist, geologist, botanist and writer.[5] More than anyone, Da Vinci epitomised the humanist ideal

'Renaissance man'. Propelled by a wide array of interests and unparalleled whole-brain ability, it was Da Vinci's combination of unquenchable curiosity and powerful creativity which allowed him to transcend genres, making intuitive right-minded leaps yet grounding his insights in granular left-minded rigour. For the same person to have produced some of the world's greatest and most enduring works of art, to have established some of the foundational principles of modern science and to have 'invented' the bicycle, airplane, helicopter and parachute, some 500 years ahead of their time, remains the greatest single body of work ever synthesised by one human brain.

Among the myriad of other inventions which also sprang forth during this period, the mechanical printing press developed by Johannes Gutenberg around 1440, possibly had a greater impact than any other in facilitating the spread of the Renaissance movement. By enabling the Europe-wide dissemination of ideas emanating from countless strands of intellectual, artistic, scientific and philosophical development, the Gutenberg Press effectively democratized information, transforming the digestion of knowledge from a private to a public pastime.[6] In doing so, it freed the ordinary individual from the tightly controlled, authoritarian voice of the Church and exposed them to alternative perspectives, growing their sense of personal empowerment and individual intelligence. When Christopher Columbus reached the new world of the Americas in 1492, he not only began a period of expansion, conquest and colonization which would last for several centuries, he also opened up trade routes which would establish cities such as Venice, Florence and Milan as the most advanced commercial hubs in all of Europe. Geographic expansion also brought forth further expanded horizons in the Western mind, exposing Europeans to new ideas, belief systems and ways of life. In doing so, it gradually led to increasing scepticism about the definitive absoluteness of the Roman Catholic worldview, and an increasing relativism towards many aspects of Western culture.

According to Richard Tarnas in *The Passion of the Western Mind*, while the constituent factors contributing to the Renaissance can be easily identified in the rediscovery of classical antiquities, it was parallel developments such as geographic expansion, burgeoning commerce, the development of city-states and various technological inventions, including the printing press, which made the impact of the Renaissance much greater than the sum of its parts. Tarnas attributes the influence of the Renaissance on so many fronts to an emphatic emergence of a new consciousness – expansive, rebellious, energetic and creative, individualistic, ambitious and often unscrupulous, curious, self-confident, committed to this life and this world, open-eyed and skeptical, inspired and inspirited.[7]

In short, what actually happened in tangible terms during the early Renaissance, was perhaps less significant than the shifts in the human psyche which underpinned new behaviours. Medieval man, who had been subordinated for a thousand years by the authoritarian collectivism of the Church, emerged as a bright-eyed, individual, intelligent, adventurous and courageous Renaissance man, intent on making his own way in life and understanding the world on his own terms.

However, what followed in the later Renaissance period would ensure that the rebalancing of the collective mind which had taken place in the earlier era, wouldn't be sustained in the longer term. Three further developments would ultimately be critical to the creation of the modern Western worldview and would swing the cultural pendulum back strongly in favour of the left mind:

- The Reformation, led by Luther, which created a schism in Christianity between the Roman Catholic Church and Protestant reformers.

- The Scientific Revolution, in particular the development of the heliocentric model of the universe by Copernicus plus Newtonian physics.

- The Philosophical Revolution, pioneered by Bacon and personified by Descartes.

Religious Reformation

The seeds of the Protestant Reformation, which would erupt throughout most of Europe, were sown when the German monk Martin Luther visited Rome in 1511. Luther was disturbed to discover that the city he considered to be holy was actually, in his view, full of moral and spiritual corruption. Of particular shock to Luther were the priests he discovered, who were privately mocking the very rites and rituals they publicly celebrated and which he held so dear. He was also horrified to find that many priests and papal courtiers were living hypocritical lives of luxury, lewdness and

shameless impiety, concluding '*if there be a hell, Rome is built upon it*'.[8]
Luther wanted to purify the Church from what he perceived to be the drift
of its hierarchy towards social and economic privilege, and to return it
to its pious roots and austere foundations. In 1517, incensed by what
he considered to be the theologically-dubious practice of selling spiritual
indulgences to fund architectural and artistic masterpieces, he nailed his
Ninety-Five Theses to the door of Wittenberg Schlosskirche; an act which
would ultimately cause religious revolution across Europe. Ironically, it
was Luther's desire for a return to greater ecclesiastical authenticity – a
right-minded sentiment – which would ultimately undermine the powerful
Roman Catholic Church and unwittingly spark the revival of the dominance of the left mind throughout Western Europe. Luther's desire for
fidelity was supported by his followers but manifested in their rejection
of the mythical, ceremonial and mystery-laden approach of the Catholic
Church. Rich in metaphor and ritual, the Catholic liturgy was torn asunder
in favour of literal and unambiguous certainty.

Perhaps fuelled by the emerging Renaissance spirit of intellectual freedom and self-determination, in addition to his powerful faith, Luther
refused to submit to pressure from the authorities to recant his criticisms
and was eventually excommunicated from the Church and outlawed as a
heretic. However, supported by a rebellious German monarchy, Luther's
'local' dispute fanned the flames of a revolution which cascaded across
Europe and irrevocably split the Christian Church in two.[9] The great
paradox of the Reformation was that it was simultaneously deeply
conservative yet radically libertarian, emphatically demanding a return to
Bible-based Christianity yet asserting the right of each individual to have
a direct relationship with God, rather than via the Church. In challenging
the supreme authority of such a powerful institution, and in asserting the
primacy of the individual over the rights of the collective, the Protestant
Reformation was an unprecedented revolutionary act in human history.
Yet in creating such a schism with Catholicism, the two contrary characteristics which would come to define Protestantism – the omnipotent,
omnipresent God and the independent, autonomous human-being – were
synthesized.

Herein lies the enduring yet unintended consequence of the Reformation. While its intent was unambiguously religious, its long-term effect
was deeply secularizing.[10] By overthrowing the all-powerful autocracy
of the Catholic Church, the Reformation opened the door to religious freedom of thought, which gradually led to religious plurality, religious

scepticism and ultimately to a world containing the full range of religious perspectives from the devout to the atheistic. In shifting the locus of power to the individual, the Reformation also shifted the final assessment of truth.[11] This had a momentous effect on the Western worldview which whole-heartedly retains a lens of personal autonomy to this day. Each individual is ultimately the arbiter of his or her own perspective, free to choose what to believe, who to believe in and how to behave. Yet, while partially liberating, at the time of the Reformation the choice remained resolutely one of either/or. Citizens could either be Catholic or Protestant but must nevertheless follow the rules such strict categorizations entailed, retaining the strong left-minded doctrine of all the monotheisms. The relative tolerance of Catholicism, which had enabled the Renaissance and Luther's challenge to its authority, was replaced by harsher, hard-line Protestant dogma. In response, the eventual Catholic counter-reformation brought the revival of a much stricter, less tolerant form of Catholicism, further dividing the two strands of Christian faith and driving the dualistic dichotomy even deeper into the Western psyche.

The Protestant Reformation also had two further significant influences on the Western mind, the legacy of which we still experience today – the shifting of collective authority from the Church to the State and the creation of capitalist economics.

Post Reformation, the unifying power of the Roman Catholic Church was fatally undermined. From this grew an increasingly fractious tribalism along with the creation of nation states out of the disparate array of kingdoms, principalities, fiefdoms and cities, all of which had previously been held together by their allegiance to the Church. Now, with no higher authority to govern them either spiritually or geographically, formerly separate units formed alliances in an intense competition to solidify power and strengthen themselves against attack from each other. Each individual 'nation' gradually became the defining unit of political and cultural authority and the key signifier of self-identity for the people within them. The 30 Years War, from 1618 to 1648, saw the culmination of the disinte-gration of the formerly unifying Roman Catholic Empire into a distinctly fragmented European society, divided along lines of nationality and reli-gion. With each government or ruler now free to determine the religious outlook of their territories, power had shifted irreversibly from the Church to the State. Many of the principal monarchs chose to remain Catholic, particularly those in Southern Europe, so Protestantism, which by the mid-17th century had become strongly associated with the cause of personal, political and economic freedom, became pre-eminent across Northern Europe.

In turn, this had important consequences for the economic development of both Northern and Southern Europe. The Protestant ethos, with its focus on moral discipline and the holy dignity of hard-work – the famous 'Protestant work-ethic' – led to greater material productivity which, in combination with their affirmed austerity and renunciation of selfish pleasures, inevitably led to capital accumulation. Having thrown off the pre-determined fatalism of the Catholic outlook, they now saw wealth as their reward for behaving in the manner demanded of them by their God. Within just a few generations, this perspective had played a major role in driving the growth of an economically-flourishing middle class, tied to the rise of capitalism and the market economy. Eventually, via the Industrial Revolution, the nation states of Northern Europe would come to financially prosper, well ahead of their Southern European counterparts. As the sociologist Max Weber pointed out, Protestantism and capitalism are strongly linked by their shared desire for power.[12] The Lutheran Church monitored the behaviour of its followers much more closely, and was far more punitive for straying from its prescribed moral code, than the Roman Catholic Church had ever been. The structure of Protestant churches, with towering pulpits and orderly rows of hierarchically-tiered pews, also symbolized the strong desire of Protestantism for control over worshippers and for the maintenance of strict social order. The power which capitalism holds over the lives of most of the Earth's inhabitants, with its endless production of inanimate consumer goods, needs no explanation for anyone alive in the 21st century. Power and control are, of course, both strongly grounded in the left mind.

Scientific Revolution

Nicolaus Copernicus was born in 1473, ten years before Martin Luther, in Royal Prussia in the Kingdom of Poland. A gifted mathematician and astronomer, it wasn't until just prior to his death in 1543 that the publication of his work *De revolutionibus orbium coelestium* (On the Revolutions of Celestial Spheres), started what would later become known as the Scientific Revolution. Copernicus proved by way of astonishing mathematical calculations that the Sun did not revolve around the Earth, as had been accepted 'truth' for over a thousand years, but that the Earth and all other planets in the universe actually revolved around the Sun. Many historians believe that Copernicus deliberately delayed publication of his findings until close to his death, because he was aware and fearful of the implications of his revelations. Up until that point the Roman Catholic Church had resolutely believed that, as God had created the Earth specifically for mankind, anything other than a geo-centric view of the universe was inconceivable. Ironically, one of the driving forces for the development of Copernicus' heliocentric model was that Renaissance Europe badly needed a better calendar, and the Catholic Church undertook its reform. As an eminent astronomer, Copernicus was asked to advise the papacy. Fuelled by his Pythagoras-inspired belief that the workings of the universe were infinitely knowable and could be defined in mathematical terms, Copernicus diligently reviewed all of the ancient scientific manuscripts and spotted numerous irregularities in their validations for a geo-centric universe. He instead hypothesized a Sun-centred universe with Earth as one of its many planets and worked out the mathematical implications for such a scenario, which supported his heliocentric model. In 1514 he shared his findings with some close friends but it wasn't until the last days of his life, almost 30 years later, that Copernicus finally held a published copy of his work.

Initially his fears appeared unfounded and opposition did not come from the Catholic Church. Copernicus was held in high esteem as a papal advisor and the Church was, at that time, open to intellectual speculation, still feeling secure in the enduring power of its doctrine. Indeed, such tolerance and latitude was the source of much of the criticism it received from Luther and the Protestant reformers. Luther felt that by allowing the exploration of revitalised Hellenistic philosophical, scientific and secular thinking, the Church was enabling faith in the literal truth of the Bible to become undermined. Thus, criticism initially came from the Protestants and Luther called Copernicus an *'upstart astrologer'*.[13] However, later, in Prague in 1609, when Kepler mathematically proved the elliptical journey of all planets around the Sun, and, at the same time in Padua, when Galileo turned his newly invented telescope to the heavens, support for the Copernican heliocentric theory was secured. At this point, the Catholic Church felt compelled to take a firm stand against the findings of its former adviser. From being originally open and permissive, it now reacted violently to what it pronounced was a fundamental challenge to its authority and the veracity of its teachings. Using all of its powers to suppress and condemn the heliocentric theory, Galileo was arrested, interrogated at length by the Church's inquisitors and forced to publicly recant his views. All written materials upholding the idea that the Earth revolved around the Sun were destroyed and their teaching prohibited, although Galileo's manuscripts were smuggled to the safety of Northern Europe. Major Catholic Copernicans were dismissed from their roles, as the Church's long-held ambivalence towards the tension between science and faith, finally snapped. Years after his death, Copernicus had temporarily healed the rift between Catholics and Protestants, who were now united in condemning him and his theory. The Christian Church, of both shades, would stick dogmatically to its belief in a static Earth and a geo-centric universe, even in the face of overwhelming evidence to the contrary; a characteristic which powerfully illuminates the dominance of the left mind. However, in doing so they lost their authority over the fully-independent intellect of humankind and created a schism between religion and science which has yet to be resolved.

It finally fell to the Englishman Isaac Newton, born in the year of Galileo's death in 1642, to complete the Scientific Revolution by firmly establishing gravity as the mathematically-explicable force which held the universe together. Through his theory of gravitation and three laws of motion, Newton was able to brilliantly explain the moving Earth as it journeyed around the Sun and to connect the findings of Copernicus, Kepler and Galileo into one set of universal, physical laws.[14] In doing so he removed any final doubts about the validity of the heliocentric model of the universe, and laid the foundations of the mechanistic worldview which would dominate scientific thinking for the next 300 years and remains at the heart of scientific materialism to this day. Such became the widespread belief in the Newtonian perspective, Voltaire would later refer to Newton as *the greatest man who ever lived*.[15]

The work of Copernicus, Kepler, Galileo and Newton seemed to vindicate the view of post-Socratic scholars such as Plato, that the universe operated solely to scientific principles which could be understood by the human intellect and explained through mathematics. Their efforts unquestionably advanced our knowledge of the cosmos and laid the groundwork for further scientific discoveries which would greatly benefit humankind in the future. Yet they also fundamentally changed the nature of our relationship with God and with the Earth. If the Sun and other planets didn't revolve around the Earth, as had been believed for centuries, our planet was no longer at the centre of the universe and neither, therefore, were we. God may still have created the universe in which our planet existed, but Earth was now less essential to His creation and operated mechanically, rather than being guided by His divine hand. God no longer intervened in our day-to-day experience of the natural world and while we could still have a direct relationship with Him, for many that relationship felt somewhat colder and more detached. We were now somehow less significant in the grand scheme of things. Renaissance man was on the road to becoming an independent, autonomous individual, responsible for making his own way in life, but in an ever more uncaring and impersonal world.

Philosophical Revolution

Francis Bacon was born in London in 1561, three years before Galileo was born in Pisa, so the scientific and philosophical revolutions evolved in tandem, each stimulating and providing a foundation for the other. No-one would do more than Bacon to promote the transfer of the allegiance of philosophy from religion to science. Bacon believed that the new world of science deserved the corresponding discovery of a new method of thinking, which could move beyond the prejudice, mysticism, subjective distortion and blind faith of the prevailing religious mind-set. Of course his 'new' way of acquiring and validating knowledge – empiricism – actually dated back to pre-Socratic Greece and Bacon flipped the medieval supremacy of the spiritual over the material on its head, by championing the physical world, as experienced by the human senses, as the most valid source of reality and truth.[16]

Yet Bacon was also a deeply religious man who believed that God had created man to interpret and dominate nature, so he saw his study of natural science for the benefit of humankind as his religious duty. To Bacon, progress could only be made if man were able to subdue the distorting effects of the emotionally-tainted intellect, in favour of pure, cold, hard facts derived from uncontaminated empirical evidence. Bacon's approach was forensic yet in no way jarred with his religiosity. Only by separating God's mind from man's mind could we hope to truly understand God's intentions. Only by separating man from nature could we gain power over nature as God intended. Kept separate, both theology and science could better flourish and man could better serve God by controlling His creation. Bacon believed that through the skilled development of abstract experiments to decontextualize and 'replicate' nature in a scientific environment, man could force nature to give up her secrets. Bacon always referred to nature as female and much has been made by scholars of the language he used and the misogynistic attitudes it perhaps reveals. What Bacon actually said was that we learn more by constraining the conditions under which we observe nature, that is to say via focussed and controlled experiments rather than by simply observing nature *au naturel*. Bacon was respectful of nature and also wrote '*nature to be commanded must be obeyed*'.[17] Whatever his attitudes, there can be little doubt that Bacon saw nature as distinctly separate from mankind and essentially passive. She was in possession of secrets but, through decontextualization and the detached, impersonal application of his '*scientific method*', mankind could establish control over her and use the knowledge she revealed for his own benefit. While Socrates equated knowledge with virtue, Bacon equated knowledge with power.[18] Although his religiosity and preferential use of the senses perhaps hint at the right mind, every other aspect of Bacon's attitude and approach suggest a strong left-mind orientation.

There can be little doubt that Bacon influenced another key philosopher in the creation of the modern worldview, Rene Descartes. Descartes was born in France in 1596, spent much of his life in the Dutch Republic and died in Sweden in 1650. He was a gifted mathematician as well as a philosopher and it was perhaps this background which led him to reject both the imagination and Bacon's empiricism as foundations for absolute knowledge. Descartes found inspiration in Pythagorean Platonism and in the rigorous methodologies of geometry and algebra which, when applied to philosophy, led to his acceptance of only those ideas which could be deduced via clear, logical reasoning, free from contradiction. Descartes thereby established a method in which critical rationality could always overcome the inherently untrustworthy and subjective information provided by the imagination or senses. In this, Descartes revitalised yet another philosophical perspective from ancient Greece, that of scepticism, which, when combined with a mathematical approach using reason, came to define the powerfully left-minded Cartesian method.

By questioning everything that had gone before him, Descartes reduced all human knowledge to perhaps his best known statement – '*cogito ergo sum*' – 'I think therefore I am'.[19] To Descartes, the only thing of which the human mind could be 100% certain was the thinker's own self-consciousness. Everything else – all of the imagery, perception and sensory experience of human existence – could in theory be merely an illusion, a construct of the human mind and that alone. Logically, if a rational person knows only their own awareness to be certain then it must be entirely different from, and separate to, the external world of material substance, which is less certain and can only be perceived as an object by the thinker as the subject. This rationale came to be known as Descartes' dualism and still forms the bedrock of the Western mind. In this conception, knowledge resides solely in the human mind and can only be determined rationally, as the senses are prone to error and the imagination to flux and distortion. By contrast, all objects in the outer world lack subjective awareness. They are purely material objects, physical phenomena and soulless entities whose existence is without purpose, spirit or meaning. As such the outside world could be considered to be a machine, operating to consistent, physical laws but entirely devoid of human characteristics or qualities. After all, Descartes observed *'it is not less natural for a clock, made of the requisite number of wheels, to indicate the hours, than for a tree which has sprung from this or that seed, to produce a particular fruit'*.[20]

For Descartes, the universe was not a living organism as Heraclitus, Aristotle and others had believed. Instead it was composed of non-vital, atomistic matter which was constructed by God, operated to mechanical principles of cause and effect, and could be deconstructed by reductively analysing it into its smallest parts. With measurable mechanics operating the universe and human reason firmly established as the supreme authority in all matters of knowledge, Descartes had created a highly practical world. By directly understanding the forces of nature, man could turn those forces to his own purposes. According to Descartes, and in accordance with Bacon, science could make us *'the lords and masters of nature'*.[21] In concluding that *'I could take it as a general rule that the things we conceive very clearly and very distinctly are all true'* he reveals the error which would undermine Western thought for the following 350 years.[22]

Once Newton had made his discoveries about gravity and the laws of motion, the 'Newtonian-Cartesian' schematic structure became firmly established as the basis for the Western worldview. Between them, Newton and Descartes had defined both the reality of nature and the nature of reality. The natural world was a perfectly ordered machine, comprehensible by science and governed by mathematical laws. Religion hadn't disappeared, far from it, but by the beginning of the 18th century all educated men and women *'knew'* that the Divine creator was master architect, artist and mathematician all rolled into one – a *'clock-maker'* of supreme talent. God had created the perfect machine then stood back from it, allowing it to run to the immutable laws He had defined. Man's reward for having the intellect to penetrate nature's essential order, was dominion over it. Fully separated from an unfeeling outer world, mankind could now use his superior knowledge to exploit nature for his own benefit.

Together, the Renaissance, Reformation plus the Scientific and Philosophical Revolutions served to fatally undermine the authority of the Roman Catholic Church, not just in matters of religion but in all aspects of life. In doing so they transformed the medieval mind and transitioned Western society into one which we would today recognize as 'modern'. Medieval man had been largely unable to think for himself, so dominated was he by the Church whose left-minded iron will imposed a right-minded blind faith upon all of its followers. Modern man, however, emerged as a more autonomous, free-thinking individual, still tentative but less dependent on an omnipotent God, more certain of his distinctiveness from nature and more confident in his ability to control her for his own ends. Yet God and the Church certainly weren't rejected altogether; they were far too powerful and had dominated the human psyche for too long for that to be the case. The shifts were gradual and subtle but nevertheless clear and impactful. In the medieval mind, God had not only created the universe but was actively and continuously involved in its daily unfolding. Each man's fate was literally in God's hands. Religion was the ultimate authority on all matters of knowledge, the purpose of which was to enable man to better serve God's will. The universal order was supernatural and each individual did not have the capacity to comprehend it, other than through Divine revelation or Biblical scripture. The spiritual and transcendent took primacy over the material and sensible, with an overarching focus on the eternal afterlife rather than the earthbound current life. In the modern worldview, God had still created the universe but had stood back from it, allowing it to operate to the mechanistic laws He had created – laws which could now be comprehended by the human intellect and explained through mathematics. Man's fate would no longer be determined by an interventionist God. Knowledge was God's gift to man, the purpose of which was to bend nature to man's will. Man stood apart from nature, superior to it and with the capacity to control it for his own ends. Thus, the Christian dualism of God and universe was replaced by a scientific dualism of man and nature – a subjective inner world versus an objective outer world which, thanks to Descartes, could be further reduced to mind versus matter.

Although the original impulse of the Renaissance had been to resurrect the knowledge of classical antiquity, what followed on from it actually cut the ancient Greeks adrift. Although they differed in their preferred path to truth, both pre- and post-Socratics shared the view that the universe had an intelligence in which the human brain could directly participate, because they both had the same intrinsic order and operating principles. While early Renaissance man had briefly unified the brain hemispheres in seeking cosmic coherence through science, the late Renaissance split them apart again. The world outside the human mind was now a cold, impersonal place, operating mechanistically and devoid of any consciousness, intelligence, meaning or purpose. There was no order, neither transcendent nor immanent, which unified inner and outer realms and they operated to very different principles. Man was not a part of nature, but apart from it. Nature's only intrinsic value lay in its utility to man, whose duty to God was to use his rational abilities to exert control over it and to harness mechanical forces to manufacture material objects, for the glory of God and mankind.

The culmination of the Scientific Revolution came on the back of almost 200 years of internecine religious warfare, waged across Europe, which provided very fertile soil for an entirely new belief system. Just as ancient Jewish society had been ripe for the arrival of a new messiah, European society in the late 17th century was crying out for a different perspective. That this new worldview was less controversially subjective and followed rational and empirically-verifiable principles, made it a very attractive proposition for the educated classes. When Newton's *Principia* was published in 1687 it completed the groundwork, started by the Renaissance, for building a completely new type of society – one which would replace the authoritarian, aristocratic, absolutism of the Medieval Age with new societal structures built upon the '*self-evident*' principles of personal liberty, individual rights, empirical science and the rational intellect. The construction of such a society, which would finally drag the West out of the Dark Ages and into the full light of the modern era, would be conducted during a period which became known as the Enlightenment.

The Enlightenment

One significant effect of the Roman Catholic Church's demonization of Galileo, and other erstwhile Copernicans, was to push radical thinking from its Renaissance heartland in the Mediterranean out towards safer, more secular territory in North-West Europe. Beginning in the late 17th century and building on Newton's breakthroughs, the modern worldview continued to evolve during the Enlightenment with a wide range of writers and philosophers, such as Locke, Shaftesbury, Leibniz, Spinoza, Voltaire, Rousseau, Berkeley, Hutcheson, Hume, Smith and Kant, to the fore. While they varied in their religiosity and disagreed on a multitude of specifics, they coherently added to the foundations of the Newtonian-Cartesian schema.[23] David Hume, for example, was a deeply sceptical and secular thinker who considered that any argument for the existence of an immaterial, omnipotent God was philosophically preposterous. Immanuel Kant, on the other hand, was a religious man who concluded that neither rationalism nor empiricism could provide unequivocal evidence for God, but that people should nevertheless have faith in Him without ascertaining that their inner beliefs were verifiable in the outer world. Jean Jacques Rousseau took a more nuanced approach, placing high value on critical rationalism yet reasoning that spiritual belief was intrinsic to human nature. Rousseau, however, placed no faith in any of the monotheisms or their splintered offshoots, considering any claim to be the one true religion to be an absurdity. Rousseau also demonstrated an understanding of the need to balance the brain hemispheres, when he warned that an over-reliance on reason might take a man too far away from his inherent nature and his unconscious desire to act upon his feelings, emotions and intuitions. Rousseau's conception of 'religion' was therefore one which was universal and based on the magnificence of nature, in which everyone could comprehend

> reverent awe before the cosmos, the joy of meditative solitude, the direct intuitions of the moral conscience, the natural spontaneity of human compassion, a 'theism' of the heart – these constituted the true nature of religion.[24]

Whatever their individual approach to religion, the collective effect of Enlightenment philosophers was to diminish the regard in which traditional Christianity was held and to bring a secular humanism to the forefront of the societal mind. The Judeo-Christian God was a figment of the notoriously unreliable human imagination. Mind and matter were the only empirically-verifiable realities. Equipped with science and the rational intellect, humankind could shine a light into the darkness of medieval Christian dogma, illuminating its mysteries and showing its greatest fears to be nothing more than superstition. In doing so they could bring human society up to date in the newly modern world. And so, from the Enlightenment emerged a positive and inspirational narrative of humans as free-thinking, independent and self-determining beings, with the intellectual capacity to comprehend and control nature for their own ends. They no longer needed to be told what was true because they possessed all the faculties required, in their rational intellect and empirical senses, to determine the truth for themselves. God hadn't necessarily disappeared but each person now had a direct relationship with Him, and no higher authority could impose a dogmatic theology or ethical code on an unwilling individual. Each human-being now possessed everything they needed to be the architect of their own future, the master of their own morality and the ultimate arbiter of their own reality. God could exist but only if the individual decided so.

Principles of individual liberty inevitably led to demands for political and economic freedom too. If the natural sciences had exposed ancient and almighty authorities as arbitrary, then this must also apply to their earthly counterparts. If the traditional hierarchies of the Church could be toppled so too could the ranks of the privileged in all walks of life, from absolute monarchs and aristocrats to wealthy landowners and mercantilists. Locke argued that God had endowed all humans with certain natural, inalienable rights, while Rousseau claimed that individual power and equal opportunity demanded a new social contract based on democracy and a market economy in which all could participate. The post-Reformation principle of the primacy of the individual flowed seamlessly into the Enlightenment and was further extended in the concept of equality, which very much came to the fore during this period, playing a major role in both the French and American Revolutions. Such revolt brought forth the political, social, economic and technological fruits of a new, 'enlightened' worldview. Yet, like the content of all complex systems which serve to shape culture, the Enlightenment wasn't one thing but the dynamic confluence of many, sometimes contradictory impulses. In this regard, the French, British and American Enlightenments shared many common themes, but were also quite different in their emergent focus and emphasis. The movements in France and the new world were, quite literally, revolutionary while the changes which permeated Britain took more of an evolutionary path. While the French became vehemently anti-clerical and deified reason instead, the British had no intention of overthrowing the Church and took a more nuanced approach to balancing the brain hemispheres. Many of the leading French thinkers were materialists and militant atheists, whose elitist rationalism only thinly veiled their deep contempt for the ignorance of ordinary people and their blind faith. In its pursuit of *liberte, egalite* and *fraternite,* republican France duly sent its key aristocrats and clerics to the guillotine along with thousands of other 'enemies of the revolution', while the British showed no real inclination towards revolt or deposing their monarchy.

The British Enlightenment perhaps differed from its continental counterpart because many of the leading British thinkers were first and foremost 'moral philosophers', who believed that sentiments such as empathy were deeply entrenched in the human soul. Shaftesbury thought that all humans had an innate moral sense and that virtues like compassion were rooted in nature and instinct, rather than derived from reason, religion, sensory perception or self-interest. Adam Smith also believed that feelings of sympathy and benevolence were core to the human condition and would consistently manifest in a laissez-faire economy. Both men concurred that moral conscience was a universal human attribute which complemented reason and self-interest in the cognitive process, and which preceded both but could easily be corrupted by either. Unlike the French, British philosophers never gave absolute priority to reason and recognized its limitations. David Hume famously concluded that *'reason is, and ought only to be the slave of passions, and can never pretend to any other office than to serve and obey them'*.[25] Of course, the distinction between France and Britain wasn't clear cut and the reality was more complex and contradictory. Several French philosophers such as Rousseau and Montesquieu were more aligned with the British perspective, while the likes of Locke and Paine were more oriented towards the French viewpoint. Although born in England the latter was an influential activist in the American Revolution, which borrowed and blended elements of both European Enlightenments into its own constitution and culture. Melding the potential paradox of freedom and morality, the American movement built the most capitalist economy on the planet yet, unlike the French, retained religiosity as its primary source of moral inspiration – the clear legacy of the Protestant roots of many of the Founding Fathers.

And so the Enlightenment manifested in several different blends but whichever recipe one tasted, and in spite of all having high optimism as a common ingredient, it did not ultimately lead to unparalleled progress in human development. What it did do, however, was to create the belief that each individual could be anything they wanted to be, and the expectation that success or failure was entirely down to themselves and their own endeavours. In the Enlightenment narrative each person became an island; intelligent, self-sufficient and responsible but ultimately alone in a cold, soulless world with no higher authority to protect them or meaningful purpose to provide guidance. In the overarching Enlightenment analysis, science replaced religion as the primary intellectual authority, while human reason and empirical evidence replaced theology and mythology as the primary sources of knowledge. Critically, Cartesian dualism prevailed. There was no common nature between the human mind and the outer world, as the Greeks had believed. The two were utterly separate and different – one mind, the other matter – and the two worlds of inner subjectivity and outer objectivity continued to operate on very different principles. Our inner world processed our conscious interpretation of the outer world but, apart from that, they had nothing in common. The outer world was mechanical and unconscious, operating to fixed rules but devoid of any 'intelligence'. Only humans possessed intelligence and this, coupled with their capacity for reason, gave them the right to manipulate nature for their own ends. However, while science liberated human-beings from theological dogma it also alienated them from many of the experiences which seemed to constitute being human. Intellect relegated qualities and values such as emotion, ethics, morality, altruism, wisdom, imagination, intuition and love to pointless and unnecessary adornments. Utility, the core left-mind value, was all that remained and all that mattered.

Thus the ancient Greeks, who had believed that true knowledge required the synthesis of all types of thinking, including the emotional and imaginative, were further cut adrift. Their goal of unifying man and the cosmos through their common consciousness was abandoned, as was the Christian objective to reunify fallen man with his God in a blissful, eternal afterlife. The sole goal of newly modern humans was not to unify but to separate themselves from God, from nature and from other people, by exercising their freedom and intelligence in pursuit of personal desires. Science became their new faith, conceivable to the intellect, comprehensible to the senses and thereby offering epistemological certainty. For many, religious beliefs were downgraded to nothing more than '*useful palliatives for man's emotional nature*.[26] The left mind's triumph over the right was almost complete. In the post-Enlightenment world the source of received wisdom could no longer be spiritual or supernatural, only rational or empirical, and it wasn't long before both would create their own concomitant belief systems. Empiricism, born of the right mind, confirmed that the tangible, physical, material world was the only outer-world reality. Rationalism, born of the left mind, confirmed that only mankind possessed intelligence and was the ultimate arbiter of truth and knowledge. All faith in a consciousness beyond that discernible by human senses or intellect – whether in nature or God – was simply a reassuring fantasy created by an overly emotional imagination. Thus, scientific materialism became firmly established as the rock-solid foundation of Western thought while impulses towards spiritual idealism underwent yet another soothing transformation, embracing an expression perhaps best described as secular humanism. With this, in the collective mind, a balance of sorts was achieved and cognitive ease was once again restored. A new *'religion'* had been created in which individual humans were elevated to God-like status, without the need for higher authority or purpose other than that which they deemed appropriate for themselves. And so, any remaining notion of universal ideals was finally laid to rest. All moral, ethical or aesthetic judgements were subjective, relational and solely in the gift of each individual. Even Plato, the arch-architect of the scientific mind, was to be finally and fully left behind. Beauty now existed nowhere but in the eye of the beholder.

Industrial Revolution

The Enlightenment and the Industrial Revolution are inextricably linked, with the latter bringing about the physical manifestations of the changes to social, philosophical, political, scientific and religious thinking, created by the former. The Industrial Revolution also provided the perfect outlet for everything that was powerful and dangerous about the prevailing Protestant mind-set in post-Reformation, North-West Europe. Theistically-prescriptive, socially-ascetic, hierarchically-controlling, economically-voracious and politically-ambitious, Protestantism was perfectly suited to industrialisation and the mechanistic worldview. From around the mid-18th century onwards, these elements came together in a perfect storm which would create the capitalist economic system from which we still experience the down-drafts to this day.

Prior to the Industrial Revolution, North-West Europe was still a largely agrarian society albeit an advanced one, featuring complex divisions of labour, an extensive trading network and an emerging manufacturing sector. However, the main energy sources propelling 'industry' were still human and animal muscle supplemented by wind and water power, all of which were relatively inefficient. Elemental sources were seasonal and therefore notoriously unreliable, while animal muscle required food and shelter as well as, in the case of humans, clothes and fuel for warmth. Ultimately all these energy sources required land, so as land became more expensive so too did the power required to work it. A truly trans-formational breakthrough arrived in 1776, when a Scot named James Watt perfected the ability of the steam engine to convert heat into motion. When Watt and his backer, Matthew Boulton, demonstrated that their new engine could pump sixty feet of water from a mineshaft in just sixty minutes, while burning one quarter of the coal used in older machines, they also revealed its potential to transform society by increasing produc-tivity to unprecedented levels.[27] At the time Britain was ruled by wealthy, land-owning elites to whom the common man remained little more than a feudal vassal, so Watt's invention also liberated working men and women from agricultural servitude. They flocked from the countryside to the burgeoning towns where, as newly enlightened, autonomous and self-determining individuals, they could pursue their own path to personal prosperity.

One of the first manufacturing sectors to seize upon the value of steam power was the cotton industry, fuelling the creation of textile heartlands such as Manchester which, by the mid-19th century, would become home to over a hundred cotton mills. Cotton wouldn't grow in Northern Europe and until the 17th century Britons had worn warm, itchy wool, so when traders began importing light, cotton cloth from India there was a strong demand for garments made from the new material. Spinning cotton was highly labour intensive, taking a spinster using a pedal-powered wheel around 200 hours to produce a single pound of yarn.[28] Mechanization increased efficiency exponentially, as inventively-named devices like *Hargreaves' Jenny*, *Arkwright's Throstle* and *Crompton's Mule* produced the same pound of yarn in three hours or less. Their repetitive movements made them perfect for steam power and the first industrial spinning mill, powered entirely by Watt's engines, opened in 1785. Although the United States had declared independence from Britain in 1776, they were still open to trading with their former colonial masters and the cotton business boomed. The States turned millions of acres into cotton plantations, put hundreds of thousands of slaves to work on them and production soared, from just 3,000 bales in 1790, to 178,000 in 1810 and 4,500,000 in 1860.[29]

Back in Britain, the application of steam technology leapt from industry to industry and a revolution was truly sparked, driving the largest and fastest societal transformation in the whole history of the world. By 1870 Britain's steam engines would generate 4 million horsepower, the equivalent of 40 million men using traditional muscle power; men who, (had they even existed – Britain's total population at the time was only around 27 million), would have had to consume more than three times Britain's entire wheat crop to generate such output. Thus *'fossil fuel made the impossible possible'* and Britain's social development – a measure of the technological, economic, political, infrastructural and cultural accomplishments via which a nation feeds, clothes, houses, organizes and defends itself – took off, on a steep upward trajectory.[30] Great factories churned out inanimate objects with ever-increasing efficiency and at ever-decreasing prices, making many goods available to the common man which previously could only have been afforded by the wealthy elite. Fuelled by market liberalization, capitalism and the Protestant work ethic, industry rapidly grew the British economy and the personal prosperity of many of its citizens. A burgeoning middle-class of doctors, lawyers and managers emerged and, from 1775 onwards, the wages of British workers rose and consistently grew ahead of those in continental Europe. However, while the machines supplemented by human labour certainly drove economic growth, the invisible hand of the market failed to evenly redistribute the wealth they jointly created. Those with capital to invest in raw materials and machinery expanded their riches, while those without capital often worked in dangerous conditions and, in spite of increasing wages, still lived in relative poverty. While output per labourer between 1780 and 1830 grew by more than 25%, wages increased by only 5%, the difference skimmed off in profits and into the pockets of factory owners, who bought grand country homes and other lavish expressions of their success.[31]

Inevitably the gap between rich and poor grew and former class distinctions quickly reappeared as social hierarchies. Many workers found they had simply swapped one kind of servitude for another, replacing the land-owning elites of the agrarian era with the factory-owning elites of the industrial age. Anger mounted as workers formed unions and demanded improved conditions but, more often than not, found that their complaints fell on deaf ears as demonstrations were crushed and union activists were jailed. Even those who stayed in the countryside weren't immune to the impact of mechanization, with farm workers attacking threshing machinery which threatened to replace them and destroy their livelihoods. In 1845 Friedrich Engels wrote *The Condition of the Working Class in England,* in which he described in great detail the appalling conditions he witnessed during a stay in Manchester and Salford. The experience shocked Engels and would greatly influence *The Communist Manifesto* he co-authored with Karl Marx just three years later. To Marx and Engels the issues with industrialisation seemed clear; it was driving social development at breakneck speed but was doing so at a great cost, driving human-beings into wage slavery and urban squalor as cogs in industrial machines, while destroying nature and emptying the countryside of future generations.

In 1860 Britain was still the only thoroughly industrial economy, producing half of the world's iron and textiles, but first with Belgium and the Netherlands, then France through Germany, Austria, Poland and the US, the industrial era spread. Sustaining it required unprecedented urbanization and the mass migration of labour from the countryside into towns and cities. Not only was there mass movement from rural to urban environments but, between 1850 and 1880, more than 5 million Britons also emigrated taking their new skills with them, mostly to North America. In 1800 the population of New York had been less than 80,000 but by 1890 there were 2.5 million inhabitants in the Big Apple. Chicago also exploded from just 30,000 occupants to over 1 million by 1890, making it the sixth largest city in the world and leaving one observer horrified by what he found there:

> sawmills screamed; factories, their smoke blackening the sky, clashed and flamed; wheels turned, pistons leaped in their cylinders; cog gripped cog; beltings clasped the drums of mammoth wheels; and converters of forges belched into the clouded air their tempest breath of molten steel.[32]

The Industrial Revolution unquestionably represented the left mind's most audacious attempt to cement its superiority over the right mind, and delivered the most significant shift in our collective cognition ever experienced to that time. It was the ultimate expression of humankind's unchallenged dominion over nature and resulted in the rapacious exploitation of our natural resources for the purpose of making ourselves economically rich, through the production of inanimate objects. Imbuing such goods with great value inevitably narrowed the focus of human societies from people and other living organisms to '*things*' which, for a left mind which deals in decontextualized manipulation, is infinitely preferable because things are much more controllable than '*beings*'. The right mind deals with aspects of experience which are ambiguous, unpredictable and difficult to manage, subject to the everyday flux and flow of the real world. An abstract world full of machines, production lines and physical objects is therefore utopian to the left mind; controllable, foreseeable and replete with absolute certainty.

To the ambitious, Protestant capitalists of the 18th and 19th centuries, steam power must have seemed like a gift from their God and confirmation of their righteousness in His eyes. Until then, their main source of power had an annoying habit of answering back, following irrational desires and getting sick, none of which were characteristic of machines. Perhaps even more importantly, the lessons of industry could be just as effectively applied to the social sphere. A planned, mechanistic future could be much more predictable than our organic, human past, so the erratic, meandering path of social history was replaced by a new vision of linear determinism. Progress would be the principle against which all proposals were to be judged and people would benefit from being subordinate parts of a social machine, moving in an efficient and orderly manner towards clear political, economic and social goals. These goals, naturally, would be defined by those who would benefit disproportionately from their achievement – the societal elites.

The impact of the Industrial Revolution on the mind of the ordinary worker was radically different. As country folk gravitated towards cities to become enriched by an industrial machine with a voracious appetite for raw materials, they also became more and more detached from the very nature under assault by their new employers. Rural areas not only lost their labour force but came under the increasing control of countryside management methods which saw genuine wildlife and wilderness gradually disappear. Towns and cities too became unnatural places, the planned product of the left mind's abstract intelligence. Architects replaced the imperfect forms of the countryside, carved by nature or human hands, with invariant shapes such as perfect circles, squares and linear grids, which are found nowhere in nature but are loved by the left mind. As towns and cities grew, the innately social animals now living in urban squalor became ever more isolated; physically closer yet never more emotionally distant from each other, unable to recreate the natural pace and social support structures of rural life, in an alien environment.

Social disintegration is unquestionably one of the lasting legacies of the Industrial Revolution and has left a painful and permanent scar on the Western psyche. The shift from rural to urban life by notionally self-determining individuals, all in pursuit of the Enlightenment dream, created 'societies' which were actually aggregates of atomistic automatons, each chained to a wheel of social progress from which there was little chance of escape. Many people even ended up as paupers, separated from their own flesh and blood and ignominiously placed in the poor houses, their dreams shattered by the harsh realities of social breakdown and the loss of any sense of belonging. The word '*belonging*' shares the same etymological root as '*longing*' and they are connected by the powerful sense of emotional attachment, to people or place, which is so essential to human happiness and which is destroyed by social disintegration. Such attachments to our roots run very deep into our animal past and when we are wrenched from these attachments, whether by migration or the rapid pace of change around us, we easily become disoriented and dislocated from place or time, a major source of cognitive dissonance and emotional trauma. It is ultimately these attachments, our web of relationships with people and places, which give our life meaning and without which we feel anchorless and adrift. Physical dislocation disrupts our sense of self-identity and its derivation from our forebears, while fast change, particularly that which radically alters tradition or erases prior ways of thinking, dislocates our sense of connection to our past. So while many people did improve their standard of living and set their descendants on a path towards greater economic prosperity, there was also a huge price to pay. Rapid industrialisation and urbanization destroyed the social fabric of real-world, rural life, the rolling hills and meadows of the right mind, and replaced it with the mechanistic factories and rectilinear landscapes of the left mind, which are every bit as alien to our instincts as living on Mars. In doing so, their wheels and cogs crushed our intuitive sense of connection to the natural world, deeply denaturing us and shattering our sense of belonging to place and time. Moreover, they cut our deep social bonds with each other, fragmenting our 'societies' into the aggregates of separate individuals they remain to this day.

Through the Industrial Revolution the left mind finally revealed the full extent of its ambition, brazen audacity and delusional self-confidence. For the first time in history it stepped beyond its role in decontextualizing the richness of the real world, and instead attempted to manufacture an outer world of its own design. Full of impressively durable, inanimate objects which could be categorized and quantified, all conforming to schematic blueprints which were infinitely repeatable, the mechanistic world was utopian to the left mind because it was devoid of the frustrating foibles and frailties of the human alternative. If the left mind could create an external world in its own image, it would no longer be limited to analysing an abstract version of real life but could instead operate directly in the inanimate outer world it had created. The right mind would no longer be required to interpret ambiguous or unpredictable phenomena, because the outer world would now be automated, consistent and certain; full of lifeless objects manufactured and controlled by the left mind. At last, its cognitive superiority would be secured. The right mind may continue to provide its emotional and imaginative interpretation of what was 'out there' but it would no longer be subject to flux. The real world would be fixed and fool-proof, no longer the subjective narrative of a flawed right mind but the objectively perfect product of an imperious left. And thus, the left mind exposed its own biggest weakness – its inability to see the bigger picture.

Naturally, the right mind would refuse to accept the hegemony of its junior partner.

— 11 —
Rise and Fall of Modernism

I N AROUND 1800 the Romantic era emerged, largely in reaction to the secularism of some Enlightenment scholars and the dehumanizing effects of the Industrial Revolution. The roots of Romanticism were in Germany, where intellectuals such as Fichte, Schiller, Goethe and Hegel had begun to question the validity of the scientific perspective which was gripping Western Europe.[1] The Romantics brought the deep value of emotion to the fore once again, countering the cold rationalism which had taken hold of the political, philosophical and economic discourse of the time. Their movement also reignited a powerful passion for the arts and, in doing so, fought to re-establish right-mind parity in the collective consciousness of polite society. Contrary to the Enlightenment view of the cosmos as a material machine driven by universal laws, discernible by reason and evidenced by empirical experiment, Romantics saw the world as a unitary organism, deeply mysterious and full of unpredictable complexity. To them life was an inexhaustible drama, passionate and emotional with endless twists and turns, rather than the calm unfolding of observable events which were predictable by the scientist. They placed the greatest value not on utility but on imagination, creativity and self-expression and, just as the Renaissance had drawn inspiration from the ancient Greeks, the Romantics returned to the early Renaissance for lost treasures. Thus, their cultural outputs were characterised by subjective involvement over objective indifference plus a preference for the particular over the generic, the natural over the conceptual.

While the Enlightenment sought truth which was concrete, fixed and permanent, Romanticism saw truth as multivalent, layered and ever-shifting. The Romantics were equally motivated to search for a unifying order within the universe but they perceived the scientific approach to be far too restrictive. In their view, a much wider range of human faculties was required for complete cognition; imagination and feeling must accompany sense and reason if humankind was to have any hope of fully comprehending the mysteries of life. In the Enlightenment view, nature was an object for observation, experimentation and manipulation while, for the Romantics, it was full of vital energy and mystery, something which would only reveal its secrets through dynamic engagement and not via the cold, analytical stare of science. The Romantic heroes were Goethe and Beethoven rather than Descartes and Newton. Goethe rejected Newton's mechanistic view of nature, writing that nature was animated by spiritual forces:

> We all walk in mysteries. We are surrounded by an atmosphere about which we still know nothing at all. We do not know what stirs in it and how it is connected with our intelligence. This much is certain, under particular conditions the antennae of our souls are able to reach out beyond their physical limitations.[2]

Equally insightful was how the Romantics understood human consciousness. While the Enlightenment focussed on sensory perception and the intellect, Romanticism explored the deep complexity of human nature, diving to the darkest recesses of the psyche to illuminate every aspect of humanity from the pure and innocent to the evil and disturbed. While the Enlightenment stood detached, outside of the human condition looking in, Romanticism was powerfully introspective, exploring the mysteries of our inner world in a profound attempt to bring the dark unconscious into the daylight of consciousness. For example, only the Romantic era could have produced Mary Shelley's Frankenstein and other such classics.

Each movement also differed in how they viewed history and time. Through the Enlightenment lens, the modern age was unequivocally superior to ancient civilisations and each intervening society was an improvement on the previous. While history provided a valuable record of prior thinking, in comparison to modern methods its knowledge was outdated and deficient. Once anything useful had been captured, the past could provide very little of value going forward. Time was linear and progress inevitable, so only the present and future mattered. By great contrast, the Romantics saw the past as a hugely rich source of learning and inspiration. To them, time was cyclical and they were far more ambivalent about the acclaimed 'brilliance' of the modern era. Their deepest desire was to revivify history in order to unfold all of its mysteries and wisdom. From the ancient Greeks onwards, they perceived the past to be pregnant with potential, full of imagination, ideas and insights just awaiting rediscovery. The respective influence of the left and right mind in each movement is self-evident.

Attitudes towards religion found common ground yet also fundamental differences. Both streams of thought were rooted in the Reformation so individual freedom and personal responsibility were valued equally. Enlightenment thinking, however, diverged towards the secular, rejecting the stricture of theological dogma and belief in the supernatural, in preference for empirical evidence and rational knowledge. Where faith was sustained it was not in the form of an interventionist, theistic God but as the deistic creator of the machine who had long-since stood back from His masterpiece. The Romantics' attitude towards religion was more complex. They too rebelled against the hierarchy and authority of mono-theistic religion but were less willing to reject the sacred, mysterious or unknown from their belief systems. Spiritual idealism remained part of their make-up but manifested in myriad ways, most of which held a common belief in the limitations of human learning, an acceptance of the existence, beyond those limits, of as-yet unknown knowledge and a strong sense, shared with the ancient Greeks, of *'a numinous creative force within nature and within the human spirit'*.[3]

Instead of subjecting experience to detached scientific study, the Romantics emphasised the need to actually live life in order to fully understand it. They sought to explore the human condition as it was authentically experienced, through the holistic right mind rather than conceptually contemplated in the abstract world of the left. Therein lay the rich provision of meaning which, in their view, was lost to the cold, rational mind of the scientist. Yet, in keeping with their desire for whole-mind synthesis, the Romantics weren't anti-reason but simply believed that it must be combined with imagination to yield superior outputs. Through living life fully, by focussing on 'being' with all of its spontaneity, passion, complexity and ambiguity, and by retaining an open mind to what life could become, they unleashed a creative force which inspired an impressive body of artistic, literary and dramatic work which has stood the test of time and remains highly valued to this day.

However, the Romantics' radically broad conceptions of human reality could not easily be accommodated within the ever-more narrowly focussed vision of the Enlightenment. In particular, their willingness to continue to countenance the spiritual was antithetical to the material temperament of science and an increasingly secular society. Similarly, the unwavering faith of scientists in rational reductionism, and their pretensions to absolute knowledge, remained untenable to some Romantics. Nevertheless, over the centuries many had tried to heal the rift by synthesising both positions into a coherent, sustainable narrative and none made greater efforts than the Romantics. Goethe, for example, believed passionately that humankind could not grasp nature's deepest truths by standing apart from it and employing impassionate abstraction. He believed we had to stand inside nature and comprehend it from within, via a combination of empirical observation and imaginative intuition. In Goethe's vision nature permeated everything, including the human mind, so could not exist as something independent and objective but would only be revealed in the very act of cognition.

The Romantics' many attempts to resolve this dichotomy culminated in Hegel's famous dialectic, where he envisioned that all things unfold in a dynamic, evolutionary process in which every state of being automatically brings forth its opposite.[4] In the third stage, thesis and antithesis are reconciled but at a higher, more harmonious level of integration. Thereby, both are elevated into a richer synthesis which forms the new base upon which the dialectic process can once again begin. In common with the pre-Socratics, Hegel understood that all human thought is permeated by contradiction and recognised the power of opposites in bringing forth higher levels of comprehension. For Hegel, it was the on-going desire to resolve such conflicts which drove humankind in a never-ending quest for elevated levels of consciousness. Through the continued dynamic interplay of thesis, antithesis and synthesis, human society could progress. Hegel's genius was to recognize that at any given moment in time humankind would believe that what it held to be true was fixed and certain, when it was actually in the process of being overcome by the emergence of its opposite or being synthesised into a deeper level of truth: '*every era's world view was both a valid truth unto itself and also an imperfect stage in the larger process of absolute truth's self-unfolding*'.[5] When first made public, his philosophy was widely regarded as the most satisfying in the history of the Western mind and as the ultimate and perfect integration of spirit and science. Hegel had temporarily healed the age-old schism.

However, with great irony and as predicted by his dialectic, his views were also widely criticised and his concepts countered by inevitably antithetical positions. Around the middle of the 19th century there arose, also in Germany, another intellectual movement with its roots firmly in the Reformation and Cartesian philosophy.[6] Rather fittingly this group became known as the Left Hegelians, although the name referred to their political leaning rather than their mode of thinking. While Hegel had fought hard to preserve the role of the right mind in balancing reason, the scientific bent of his successors led to their rejection of intuition and imagination as fundamentally flawed approaches to knowledge and, for the first time, the word 'materialism' was used to describe their perspective. In 1848 revolutions swept across much of Europe and part of what changed was the re-establishment of the authority of the scientific mindset. In 1853 a prominent British politician and scientist, Lyon Playfair, declared that '*science is a religion and its philosophers are priests of nature*'.[7] The Romantic ideal was apparently dead and

> with Hegel's decline there passed from the modern intellectual arena the last culturally powerful metaphysical system claiming the existence of a universal order accessible to human awareness.[8]

Modernism

When, in 1859, Charles Darwin published his seminal theory of evolution in *On the Origin of Species,* it perhaps seemed that the triumph of science over spirit was finally complete. Not only was nature mechanistic and distinctly separate from the inner world of mind, it was also soulless and blind. Human existence was not part of any grand master plan, imbued with significance, purpose or meaning, but merely the product of biological happenchance. The history and future of our species was a game of genetic dice over which we could have no control. Although the Judeo-Christian perspective continued to have influence, it was relegated to a significantly marginalized role; the individual life was neither pre-ordained nor subject to Divine intervention. Science was the new voice of authority, its methods the new theology and its voice the only source of knowledge, truth and power. Like religion, the metaphysical discourse of the philosopher was categorized as subjective, theoretical and speculative, unworthy of serious consideration in understanding the objective world.

With Darwin, the ancient Greeks were left even further behind. Having provided the original impetus for rationalism, a tradition revived during the Renaissance and brought to fruition during the Enlightenment, the Greeks had nevertheless sought to reconcile the intellectual with the transcendent, the empirical with the spiritual. Now, their desire to integrate rationalism with emotional, aesthetic, ethical, idealistic, imaginative and relational modes of thinking was deemed distortional to the supreme objectivity of the preferred left mind. Darwin also fatally undermined science's final compromise with Judeo-Christianity which had portrayed God as the maker of the mechanistic world. It was no longer at all certain that man even came from God but from prehistoric primates. Nature no longer seemed to be the product of His divine design but the result of a random, amoral struggle for survival by competing species. While Greek philosophy had, as its ultimate goal, the unification of human intellectual and spiritual activity, and while the Judeo-Christian goal had been the unification of man with God in the perfect afterlife, the ultimate goal of modernism was confirmed as the optimization of the freedom of the individual to explore and exploit the natural world. There was no viable unification. The two realms of humankind and nature were pushed even further apart, distinctly separate and operating to different principles. Only our subjective mind and its ability to perceive the objective outer world connected us. With Copernicus and Newton, the Earth had become just another planet driven by inertia and gravity. With Darwin, the human had become just another animal sustained by random variation and natural selection. Success, in the form of survival, would not go to the virtuous but to the fittest. Our knowledge of the universe had expanded exponentially through the efforts of explorers, cosmologists, astronomers, anthropologists, biologists, physicists, chemists, sociologists, geographers and philosophers, and the more we learned the more insignificant we had become. Through the increasing advancement of science, human-beings had been irreversibly diminished, our self-image irrevocably damaged. Not only had the spatial and temporal significance of our universal dominion been shrunk, we had ourselves been downgraded to mere atomistic matter, our consciousness reduced to physical and chemical phenomena serving biological imperatives.

Thankfully, in true Hegelian style, the human brain would rescue the Romantic ideal from the brink of oblivion by piquing the interest of those intellectuals still hungry for a source of meaning in the world, still reeling from the inability of religion, history or philosophy to provide it and still sceptical about the infallibility of science. It did so by turning in upon itself. The psychoanalysis of Sigmund Freud was heavily influenced by German Romanticism and examined, in particular, the deeper, darker realms of the human mind. Freud revealed many insights which laid bare the structure and nature of the human psyche, opening the door to the mind beyond consciousness.[9] In doing so he undermined the Enlightenment as the ultimate triumph of the left mind. Freud discovered that beyond our awareness lay a vastly greater, yet murkier, unconscious mind which didn't easily open itself to rational analysis or conscious manipulation. In demonstrating that our unconscious desires were powerful and primeval, he even called into question the extent to which we exercised genuine free will. With Freud our species took on a new challenge, destined not only to toil in the outer world but to also endure a life of internal conflict, struggling to suppress our essential, animal nature. Following on from Darwin, Freud further cast humankind out of the privileged position given to us by Judeo-Christianity as God's chosen species. According to Freud, our core instincts were irrational and primal and our only goal in civil society could be to suppress the worldly manifestations of those desires. The highest humans could aspire was to be less beastly than other animals. Suddenly our history of wars, atrocities and inhumanities made sense. Humans destroyed other humans, not for the glory of God but because it was in our nature as beasts. The civilised, rational and intelligent individual of the Enlightenment was exposed as a myth.

Freud had a significant influence on fellow psychologist Carl Jung, who found that all humans appeared to have a common approach to processing certain phenomena, unconsciously structuring it according to powerful archetypes or attractors. Jung concluded that although human experience was vastly diverse and influenced by a wide array of cultural, environmental and biological factors, at a deeper level there were certain universal patterns and modes of cognition.[10] His exposure of our '*collective unconscious*' ignited great interest in psychology and in its range of applications. Central to this was the search for meaning in human life; meaning which could no longer be found in religion or in the science of the impersonal, outer world. Thus, psychology became a valid middle ground between science and spirit, exploring our inner world and sensitive to the subjectivity of human experience yet also striving for solid scientific knowledge, grounded in objective observation. And so the two worlds continued to co-exist but not on equal terms. The secular, modern mind of the scientist dominated the cultural '*centre of gravity*' as well as the outer world of objective reality, while the romantic mind of the idealist was allowed to permeate the inner world and, in particular, the socially and intellectually marginalized arts and humanities. Spiritual, emotional and aesthetic values still had their place but their place was very much on the periphery of human experience. Scientific rationalism was at its heart and in the grand scheme of things, only matter really mattered. Although the role of the right mind was rescued, the triumph of the left mind, the dominance of the mechanistic worldview and the cultural hegemony of scientific materialism were complete.

Yet for all scientific man controlled and manipulated nature to his own ends, his empirical observations of the natural world and his deep-rooted sense of spirituality continually led him back to an intuitive awareness of his own intrinsic unity with nature. The more humankind strove to understand mother nature, to stand apart from her and with dominion over her, the more we discovered which subsumed our species directly back into the very nature from which we wished to escape. Quantum science opened the door to this new knowledge but was wholly at odds with what we already 'knew' to be true about our world, and such a powerful cognitive dichotomy would remain unresolved during the 20th century. Throughout this period, human-beings would experience an almost imperceptible, yet nevertheless irreconcilable, conflict between the on-going spiritual impulses arising in our inner mind and the apparently soulless indifference of the outer world in which we found ourselves. A sort of societal schizophrenia inevitably ensued.

Human-beings had become more personally empowered than ever before but the mass societies in which we now lived necessarily brought political, economic and social bureaucracy, which smothered the Enlightenment dream of the autonomous, self-determining individual. We were economically free but commerce yoked us to a colourless, repetitive life on a treadmill of social progress. Knowledge of the mechanistic movements of the natural world was available to all, but such learning held little value when the world had no meaning and our place in it had no significance or purpose. Secularism liberated us from the shackles of monotheistic scripture but, in the absence of a blissful afterlife with God, our earthly endeavours were to be rewarded with nothing but eternal isolation in a void of darkness. Technology had delivered great advances in improving the human condition yet our advent of killing machines made us feel more vulnerable than ever before. Humans held powerful influence over the natural world of living organisms yet it was a cold, competitive place in which only the strongest could survive the struggle for life. The optimistic goal of the Enlightenment – that humankind could leverage the power of science to transform society to a new visionary ideal, based on rational principles and delivered with machine-like efficiency for the benefit of all – was then perversely twisted into nightmare reality with two World Wars, the Holocaust and the dropping of atomic bombs on

Hiroshima and Nagasaki. And with this perhaps the penny also finally dropped. Modernism had spectacularly failed to deliver self-determining individuals progressively improving their own lot, as well as society at large, via rational discourse based on empirical evidence. An overwhelming volume of information had become widely available from every sphere of study; knowledge about the macroscopic universe and the subatomic world, about other cultures, their beliefs and behaviours, about history and contemporary society, about the natural world and the human psyche. Yet much of it was contradictory, conflicting and confusing. It seemed that the more we learned, the less we actually knew.

Meanwhile, continued urbanization further increased our feeling of dislocation, undermining our sense of identity and fragmenting our social bonds. Capitalism and consumerism became the new bases for human relationships, delivering interactions based on competition, greed and utility rather than connection and community. Alienation from our natural environment led to the decontextualization of life and a loss of meaning in the experienced world.[11] Life became characterized by disorder, uncertainty, ambiguity, and incoherence. The prevailing mind-set soon became one of emotional detachment, depersonalisation and cold objectivity, full of cynicism and a mistrust of authority and each other. The result was the loss of our sense of belonging and purpose – '*thus our attachments, the web of relations which give life meaning, all come to be disrupted*'.[12] According to the sociologist Max Weber, the key change to the modern mind was that man became disenchanted with the world. Modernism had dissolved traditional, spiritual worldviews and placed great faith in reason to replace them. Reason alone, however, could not justify the creation of universal principles with which to guide human life without fatally undermining its own foundational logic. What it left was a void which would come to be filled by relativism, the defining characteristic of the post-modern age.

Post Modernism

Relativism may provide the pivotal insight into the post-modern mind yet, as with all Western thought, its roots can be traced back to ancient Greece where the pre-Socratic sophist Protagoras controversially claimed that '*man is the measure of all things*'. Much later, Enlightenment philosopher Immanuel Kant further elucidated this notion by pushing Descartes' '*cogito*' to its logical conclusion – if the human mind and the outer world were distinctly separate, then the mind's comprehension of the world was entirely interpretive and could in no way guarantee its objective accuracy. All reality must therefore be relative because no mind could claim a mirror-like understanding of what actually existed in the outer world. Furthermore, as all interpretation was structured according to the nature and predispositions of the observer, there could be no guarantee that any two individuals would perceive exactly the same '*truth*'. All knowledge must therefore also be radically uncertain because there was no perspective-independent reality. All perceptions were soaked in pre-existing theories and biases, shaped by pre-existing desires and emotions and processed in accordance with pre-existing structures and associations, in the mind of the perceiver. There could be no universal ideals so, like truth, morality was contextual, subjective and relative. Each individual was indeed the measure of all things.

With this, Kant completed the diminution of humankind began by Copernicus and progressed by Darwin. With Copernicus we moved from being the epicentre of God's creation to being an insignificant dot in an infinite cosmos. With Darwin we were relegated from God's supreme design to the product of random, biological serendipity. With Kant we even became alienated from nature's processes, unable to ever comprehend our shared essence. And so, post-modern people find themselves trapped within a logical absurdity of their own making. Sub-atomic science has demonstrated that we are made of the same essential substance as the rest of the universe yet, wedded to Cartesian-Kantian philosophy, we are unable to participate directly in understanding nature and therefore in understanding ourselves. Our inherent sense of soul and instinctive quest for spiritual connection with the outer world can only be rendered meaningless, for there can be no guarantee that whatever we find is anything other than a delusional self-construct. Our destiny is to be one of total estrangement between our experience and our consciousness, a fundamental schism between how we feel and how we have been culturally conditioned to think.

The overarching cognitive approach of post-modernism has been to push left-mind reductionism to its limits, while rejecting all attempts to propose synthesising theories. To their critics, in a world of only relative, subjective '*truths*' in which all reality lies solely in the mind of the beholder and is therefore empirically unverifiable, any claims to the identification of universal laws, principles or archetypes must inevitably be underpinned by intellectual authoritarianism and therefore automatically dismissed. In a chaotic and objectively unknowable universe all accepted '*truths*' must be considered to be merely temporary beliefs, which are always subject to further challenge, revision and rejection. The defining characteristic of post-modernism has consequently become its vast diversity of perspectives yet very few common or agreed under-pinning principles. The post-modern ethos has been to relentlessly and fundamentally challenge the fixed certainty of modernism, but its foun-dational relativism has inhibited the formulation of a coherent perspective with which to replace its predecessor. In the post-modern world we have copious grains of intellectual sand but such dunes form poor bedrock upon which to build our future.

Indeed, throughout the post-modern era the focus of many commen-tators has been to continually criticise our past, rather than to envision a new future. Modernism has been widely attacked as a futile project, undertaken by ego-driven scientists and historians seeking to comprehend and explain an illusory reality, when there is no single, objective narrative which could ever be written. To the perspectival post-modern critic, deep-rooted in relativism, perceived truth is merely a conceptual construct created through social discourse, so those same scientists and historians have no greater authority than anyone else with an alternative point of view. The Western obsession with applying reason to every aspect of life and presenting history as a linear sequence of events, which are retro-spectively explicable and prospectively predictable, is therefore considered to be an exercise in self-delusion. Furthermore, the dominant discourse in any society invariably reflects only the interests and values of elite groups, and is therefore exclusive, undemocratic and unrepresentative. Finally, the language through which knowledge is conveyed is also inherently flawed as it is automatically influenced by the linguistic preferences and personal biases of the narrator, who also tends to be part of the societal elite. So to the cynical, sceptical post-modern mind, we can never absolutely trust anything we learn.

As well as attacking the foundational principles of the modern mind, the post-modern view has been highly critical of modernism's track record in using science and technology to deliver the Enlightenment goal of progressing human societies for the betterment of all. Modernism has been widely condemned for its history of conquest and colonialism, its extermination or enslavement of indigenous populations and for the unwarranted theft of their land. It has been reproached for the iniquitous inequalities it has created; greatly enriching some while others have suffered and starved. For many of its critics, modernism has been characterised by repulsive materialism and war-mongering militarism, by the ruthless destruction of nature to the detriment of future generations, and by the personal avarice of elites and their marginalization of women, minority groups and political dissenters from the mainstream of civil society. Most damningly it has been criticised for facilitating the politically-enabled exploitation of ordinary people and the technology-enabled exploitation of our planet, both purely for profit.

Indeed as early as the 1920s German philosopher Walter Benjamin recognized the dangers of capitalism, with its elevation of economic progress and personal wealth to God-like status. Benjamin called capitalism a '*religion of destruction*'; untested and unproven but built upon the unwavering faith of its acolytes in science, materialism and rationalism.[13] Benjamin said capitalism in the West had developed parasitically, particularly on Protestantism and that '*Christianity in the time of the Reformation did not encourage the emergence of capitalism, but rather changed itself into capitalism.*'[14] Benjamin believed that the real goal of global capitalism – '*its systemic hope and transcendent ideal*' – was the destruction of nature because it was only through spreading despair that the world could eventually be saved. Having been abandoned by God to a life in which the only guarantee was an eternal after-death in a dark void, humankind was now punishing God's beautiful creation through ever more violent attempts to subjugate and destroy her. By increasing the voracious appetite of consumptive capitalism and through the expansion of human despair this would inescapably bring forth, humankind hoped that the burden of guilt must surely move God to return and with Him bring their salvation. For Benjamin, this was the only possible metaphysical explanation for the unconscious drivers of the modern mind. Almost a century later and with the goals of capitalism, as defined, coming ever closer to being realized, do we yet have a more lucid rationale for the religion of modern capitalism and its contribution to the cultural and existential crisis of the post-modern era?

Modern and Post-Modern Maladies

In the early 21st century we find ourselves feeling lost, as if adrift mid-ocean between changing worldviews, with no land in sight and no solid ground beneath us to which we might anchor. Modern and post-modern perspectives still co-exist, compete and clash. Within this cultural maelstrom two thoroughly modern hydra – Western capitalism and Islamic fundamentalism – fight a vicious, titanic battle for supremacy. One seeks to perpetuate the primacy of scientific materialism, the other promotes a faux medieval version of spiritual idealism. Meanwhile, those of a post-modern persuasion find themselves in a state of abject flux, unable to focus, connect, align or agree a clear way forward. Still bewitched by a pervasive sense of Kantian relativism, or perhaps even imbued with a dose of Nietzschean nihilism, the post-modern mind continues to find life devoid of certainty, meaning, direction or purpose. The social fragmentation and alienation from nature, so characteristic of the modern mind, have been exacerbated by post-modern relativism in which there are no universal values or moral imperatives which bind all humans together.

According to Louis Sass, Professor of Clinical Psychology at Rutgers University, modern and post-modern minds share many characteristics not only with each other but also with schizophrenia.[15] Core to the connection is hyper self-consciousness in which, rather than simply engaging with and experiencing life, we become prone to standing back and analysing our social interactions from a position of detached observation. It seems that the necessary distance which first enabled the left mind to detach its perspective from that of the right, enabling our development of self-consciousness, may have gone too far and for some unfortunate souls is in danger of detaching them from everyday reality. In fact, Sass offers the opinion that madness may be

> the end-point of the trajectory consciousness follows when it separates from the body and the passions, and from the social and practical world, and turns in upon itself.[16]

According to Sass, hyper-consciousness can cause people to 'stare' at the outside world as if it were an inanimate object, rather than simply engaging with it as a living entity. This effect may be connected to another core characteristic of schizophrenia in which automatic processes, which are normally conducted by the unconscious, are pulled into the full glare of consciousness and make thoughts which are usually implicit become explicit, disrupting the coherence of our experience. In short, we move beyond a healthy range of equilibrium between thinking and just 'being' and start to overthink every encounter, becoming more self-conscious than is good for us. Sass sees this as the result of an 'unworlding' of the outer world, which seems very similar to Weber's 'disenchantment' as a common feature of modern and post-modern minds. The more we retreat from the outer world, the more we become alienated from our embodied right mind and from the feelings which make us human and give us a sense of wholeness. In doing so, we lose touch with our intuitive sense of context and connection, both of which give meaning to our experiences; experiences which feel fragmented and incoherent as a result, causing us to retreat a little more. However, the further we withdraw into the self-referring world of the left mind, the more we become alienated from our own body, leading to a sense of devitalization, listlessness and inner numbness in which everything physical and emotional is cut off from us. This *'anaesthetised state of modernism'* can easily lead to social alienation and extreme loneliness in the outer world, but also to paranoia and other mental health issues which appear to be peculiarly pervasive in modern and post-modern times.[17] In fact, instances of schizophrenia appear to be very rare before the 18th century but grew with industrialisation throughout the 19th century and increased dramatically in the 20th century – a pattern which can be consistently traced across Europe and North America. Today, the condition is more widespread and more severe in first-world and Western nations, and the risk of developing schizophrenia is almost doubled in urban versus rural environments.[18]

There is evidence that a number of very common, modern-day mental illnesses may all find their root cause in an overly dominant left mind and a correspondingly deficient right mind.[19] Indeed the word schizophrenia is derived from the Greek *skhizein* meaning to split and *phren* meaning mind. For example, multiple personality disorder shares many symptoms with schizophrenia and hemispheric imbalance may also be central to eating disorders such as anorexia nervosa. Overreliance on the left mind can lead to a sense of alienation from the body and a self-image which becomes psychotically distorted, leading to self-loathing and self-harm. Research, including brain imaging scans from anorexia sufferers, indeed suggests that the condition may be associated with an overactive left hemisphere and an underactive right. Then there are conditions such as autism and Asperger's syndrome which are both thoroughly modern maladies, first described in 1943 and 1944 respectively. Many of their defining characteristics such as a lack of social intelligence, difficulty in interpreting non-verbal or implicit meaning, low levels of empathy or imagination, obsession with detail and feelings of alienation from the body or self, are all strongly suggestive of left-mind dominance and an underperforming right hemisphere. What all of these conditions have in common is a sense of 'dissociation'; either feeling or craving to be cut off from the outer world and from one's own embodied existence, resulting in a lack of emotion, a lack of connection with other living organisms and a fragmented sense of the unitary self. While no medical professional would suggest that the causes of such complex conditions can be simply defined, or that the patterns of dominance and deficiency manifest in the same way in each case, they do all appear to have some degree of hemispheric imbalance, in favour of the left mind, as a core component. What's more, they have all become much more prevalent in the modern era. While accounts of ailments such as melancholia and manic depression are easily recognizable in texts from ancient Greece, Rome and Egypt, no such descriptions of schizophrenia or similar conditions appear from those times.

Dr Iain McGilchrist attributes this to an increasingly '*unplugged*' left hemisphere which, without the grounding effects of the right, can find nothing except what it already knows. While the real-world embedded right mind could yield the excitement of genuinely new experiences, sensations or relationships, the left mind can only deliver rehashed and repetitious novelty; briefly stimulating yet ultimately transient and meaningless:

> Crude sensationalism is its stock in trade. The left hemisphere, with its orientation towards what is lifeless and mechanical, appears desperate to shock us back to life, as if animating Frankenstein's corpse.[20]

Here we see a strong connection between devitalisation and the desire for artificial stimulation. We come to feel detached, restless, bored and lifeless so, in order to counteract such ennui, seek out the overstimulation, sensationalism or hyper-consumption we need to enable us to feel anything at all. Too easily, this can result in unhealthy levels of hedonism, promiscuity, alcohol consumption, drug-taking or comfort-eating which have all become particularly prevalent in modern times.

Of greatest concern is when such attitudes, feelings and actions move from being random, individual afflictions to become culturally conditioned and endemic within our societies. The more we individually rely on the left mind, the more we collectively empower it to define what is culturally 'normal' and to influence the unconscious minds of everyone around us. It is therefore perfectly possible that entire societies have slowly dissociated their collective left mind from an increasingly deficient right, not only causing mental illness to become more widespread but also allowing its behavioural symptoms to become culturally normalized. As psychiatrist R D Laing pointed out back in the 1960s, culture plays a dual role in the development of mental illness by creating the pressures, stresses and strains which increase psychotic behaviour but also by setting the norms against which sanity is judged.

In Western culture the defining characteristics of positive mental health – a clear sense of self, positive self-image, temporal awareness plus skills in self-organization and logico-deductive reasoning – all require that an individual's outlook is consistent with the Newtonian-Cartesian framework. Often this is not only regarded as the principal frame of reference but also as the only accurate description of reality, so anyone able to access non-ordinary levels of consciousness is automatically incentivised to suppress such experiences, or force fit them into the prevailing framework, for fear of being labelled insane. Conversely, anyone operating solely in the Newtonian-Cartesian mode is considered to be 'normal', as defined by scientific materialism, but cannot truly be considered to be mentally healthy.[21] Such individuals may typically lead a goal-oriented life and be driven, competitive and ego-centric, focussing narrowly on manipulating the outer world and measuring success solely in terms of material wealth. Psychiatry shows that for such people, no level of wealth, status or power can bring sustained satisfaction or lasting happiness, so their inner world becomes infused with a sense of pointlessness which no amount of external success can alleviate. A life dominated by the left mind is '*the madness of our dominant culture*' and extends right throughout Western society, from the ordinary person to the academic, corporate and political elite.[22] How else might we explain a culture in which political leaders who proclaim their willingness to commit genocide using nuclear weapons are lauded, while any leader who makes it clear they would never push the nuclear button under any circumstances, is considered to be weak and lacking patriotic loyalty?

The Fertile Soil of Flux

So in just 300 years since the start of the Enlightenment, the global mind has undergone a dynamic dialectic of great magnitude. In that time our collective cognitive pendulum has swung from great belief in our own intellect, certainty of our God-given dominion over nature and boundless confidence in our planned future, to a debilitating sense of insignificance, loss of spiritual faith, radical moral relativism, uncertainty of all knowledge, guilt over our destruction of nature and widespread symptoms of societal schizophrenia. Yet the swing has been anything but uniformly experienced or universally accepted. Scientific materialism and the mechanistic worldview remain widely pervasive and, through capitalism, the modern mind continues to express its lust for power and money, still raping nature to feed rampant consumerism. Simultaneously our most modern expression of spiritual idealism, the creationist worldview of the three monotheisms, continues to exert its desire for control over the lives and minds of millions across every continent. Meanwhile the post-modern mind wanders lost, rejecting everything and believing in nothing other than that it must use its own intellect and moral compass to navigate life alone. One thing modern and post-modern minds do have in common is their unwavering belief in the superiority of their own perspective. While the modernists' confidence is based on their absolute conviction that they know more than their predecessors and on their blind faith in God or classic science to continue to deliver linear progress, the post-modernists' self-belief is built upon the rock-solid assurance that they haven't fallen into the modernists' delusionary trap and that they therefore know nothing at all with any certainty. Yet, in the final analysis, the post-modern perspective is simply a different kind of metanarrative which, by its own logic, is also subject to challenge, revision and ultimately rejection. As such it must be deemed subjective, relative, culturally and linguistically-bound and coloured by the prejudices and preferences of its proponents who, even if communications are now more democratized than ever before, still remain part of the societal and intellectual elite. Thus, the foundational arguments of post-modernism automatically undermine themselves.

With post-modernism our species has found itself in a state of epistemological and existential flux. Over the last century, as technology and travel have expanded, we have all become more connected and increasingly cognisant of the different perspectives, values and moral codes of other cultures. We have also increased our awareness of the paradigmatic nature of the human mind and our appreciation of both rationalism and empiricism has grown, although we still have no real consensus around how to balance or synthesise them. Furthermore, we have become increasingly open to the existence of sources of knowledge beyond reason or sensory experience, more tolerant of unorthodox, minority or repressed views and more self-critical of our own structures and cultural biases. A great many realities are therefore available to us, although none are necessarily superior to the other and we have no agreed criteria for the assessment of the relative merits of each. Such is the fluidity and flexibility of the post-modern mind that, as yet, there may be no firm ground for any single, coherent worldview to emerge globally.

However, on the flip-side of such flux we find the very conditions which could make post-modernism a fertile soil, replete with the potential to pull us out of our existential crisis and yield a new Hegelian synthesis. The core characteristics of post-modernism – openness to challenge, willingness to revise assumptions, tolerance of diversity, comfort with ambiguity, appreciation of complexity, acceptance of science, spirit and a multiplicity of possible realities – have created a rich environment in which the cross-pollination of ideas and opinions can easily take place. Such a context is highly conducive to creativity from which a new worldview could emerge; not one which simply reverses current flexibility back towards ordered, dogmatic dualism, but one which embraces and builds upon the benefits of post-modernism to provide a more unifying and coherent synthesis at a higher level of cognitive wisdom.

Due to the wide connectedness and deep inclusiveness of the post-modern perspective, practically every intellectual or emotional standpoint ever posited, can currently be found somewhere in the world. At present we stand in a whirlwind of almost all of the philosophical views, religious outlooks, scientific theories and social conventions ever conceived. Modern religions continue to exert strong influence on society but now exist, cheek-by-jowl, with ancient belief systems such as animism, paganism, shamanism, polytheism, pantheism and all forms of Eastern mysticism, as well as widespread humanism, agnosticism and atheism. The diminished provision of scriptural guidance, formerly delivered more widely by the monotheisms, appears to have transformed our sense of personal responsibility for the self-creation of direction, meaning and purpose in life. We are therefore witness to a burgeoning spirituality, way beyond formal religious practice, as more and more people find alternative avenues for sacred self-expression, perhaps the result of a re-awoken desire to unite brain, body and soul. Science too is being gradually transformed to become more self-aware, self-critical and perhaps even more humble in its proclamations. There is certainly greater recognition that the reductionist approach, which remains valuable in some areas of science, is limited or even seriously flawed in others. In some disciplines a more holistic, polymathic approach is blurring categories, offering greater flexibility, broader applicability and enhanced integration. There is now a new appreciation of the power of the unconscious mind within our cognitive system and, in particular, of the role played by archetypal attractors in structuring and shaping all human cognition. Although subject to large cultural variation and individual interpretation, archetypes share common and unwavering universal characteristics so perhaps offer threads from which a tapestry of global cognitive synthesis could be woven.

The unravelling of the mechanistic worldview and the growth of the organic alternative also bring forth a powerful implication, in an increased recognition of the inherent malleability of the experienced world and the degree to which it is influenced by the observer. Post-modernists subscribe to a belief in the relative nature of all reality, the subjective nature of all truth and the transient nature of all knowledge. From the organic world-view, underpinned by quantum and complexity science, reality is a fluid, unfolding process in which truth is always fallible, knowledge is never fixed and prediction is always based on probability. Reality also emerges in accordance with the approach of the observer, so the outer world can never be considered as an objective entity in its own right, independent of interpretation, but rather it comes into being through the act of engage-ment, sensory experience and human cognition. Inner and outer worlds are therefore intrinsically connected by their shared universal essence, underlying patterns of organisation, immanent evolutionary options, archetypal attractors and many other features of complex adaptive sys-tems. The organic worldview can therefore accommodate the post-modern perspective, not through the imposition of intellectual authoritarianism but by demonstrating the existence of universal premises and principles via which synthesis is a viable goal.

Through the organic lens our minds are not passive receivers of data but active creators of our perceptual reality. We can never consider ourselves to be impartial spectators observing an objective outer world, because we are always actively engaged in the transformation of whatever we bring forth. The unconscious structures of our mind, along with our personal desires, are intrinsically involved in everything we create, even if we can never fully recognize their role or enjoy a '*pure*' real-world experience, independent of their influence. Descartes was wrong. We are never truly apart from the outer world but always an embedded part of it, continually engaged with and connected to it, even if only subliminally. However, the more conscious we can become, the more we can bring our wilful choices to bear on the realities we create for ourselves and others. As our knowledge of alternative intellectual frameworks and cultural options becomes greater, we are able to choose from a much wider array of schemata and thus bring forth a far broader range of possible realities.

Such a position offers immense potential for the human condition. With a wealth of worlds available to us, the more intellectually conscious and ideologically free we can be, the more we can proactively produce the hemispheric blend which best suits our temperament and best enables us to pursue our personal and collective goals. Perhaps even more importantly, we could all become increasingly tolerant of others and begin to see their views, not as a confrontational challenge to our intellect or integrity but simply as a different blend of cognitive outputs, seeking to bring forth an alternative reality. Some degree of competition, or even conflict, is always inevitable because the human mind is capable of countless opinions, sometimes incoherent and often contradictory. However, discourse based on an appreciation that we all share the same deeply-flawed minds and conducted within a context of respectful co-operation, could surely yield mutual compromise. From such conditions our species should be able to create a global culture in which we can at least co-exist in peace and relative harmony. By building awareness of all perspectives and by constructively collaborating we can bring forth any world we choose. However, as Richard Tarnas points out *'the human challenge is to engage that worldview or set of perspectives which brings forth the most valuable, life-enhancing consequences'*.[23] There can be little doubt that the organic worldview offers our best hope. Whether we can collectively engage with it, for the benefit of all of humankind, remains to be seen.

And so, having cut ourselves loose from all that was fixed and certain, our unprecedented criticism of modernism inadvertently set our species on a path from which we might yet find solid ground and synthesis on a higher plane. The impact of the incredible revisions we have made to conventional knowledge, across all disciplines, has been to shatter the schism between science and faith, between the two brain hemispheres and between all other apparently irreconcilable opposites in the human experience. In doing so, we have shifted our entire human system to the edge of chaos and prepared the groundwork for the potential reintegration of our global mind. Long-established dichotomies such as male or female, mind or matter, body or spirit, have all been reduced to their essences and found to be intrinsically connected, merely poles on a continuum. The door has therefore been opened to the holistic approaches which were inconceivable to the dualistic, modern mind. Today, post-modern society is blessed with a wealth of perspectives but without a consensus on how best to engage the issues it seeks to resolve. The potential benefits of such broad pluralism could easily become overwhelmed by contradictions and counter-arguments. Although there are surely some universal human values, and in some areas even common goals, there is no agreed approach, no approved process and no consensus around the criteria which should be used to judge alternative options. While such a wide-open conversation is certainly more conducive to creative output than monolithic dogma, it is not without significant challenges. Within such a fluid landscape it can easily feel that no solution is possible. In the absence of a common vision or agreed framework, old prejudices can easily come to the fore, inhibiting the potential for new ideas. The major challenge is to create and agree upon a flexible set of premises, of universal applicability, which do not constrain the complexity and multiplicity of potential realities, but which instead serve to mediate, clarify and synthesise. The overarching objective must be to bring coherence from the current fragmentation, ensuring quality while creating the environmental conditions in which as yet undiscovered ideas may flourish.

In the Hegelian dialectic, if modernism was the thesis, post-modernism is certainly its antithesis. Yet the great challenge for what comes post post-modernism is to proactively stand for something positive, inspiring and visionary, towards which enough people are motivated to strive. In an ever more interconnected world in which no cultural, religious, social or political standpoint is definitively sovereign, we find ourselves in unfamiliar, open territory which offers the intellectual and moral freedom for a greater global cross-pollination of ideas, than has ever been achieved in human history. Unfortunately, both modernism and post-modernism remain locked in the debilitating grip of the left mind yet, in its rejection of the fixed certainty of the modern outlook, post-modernism has at least opened the door to the ambiguity and tolerance of diversity required for the reintegration of the right mind. The great unknown is how long we can remain within our current state of imbalance and whether or not it will become even more disorienting, possibly as a prelude to catastrophe. Or are we merely experiencing life at the edge of chaos as a temporary transition phase, from which a new global civilization will emerge with universal human values and a widely shared worldview? Today, we may be standing at the edge of an epochal evolution of the global mind to a new synthesis at an elevated level of cognitive wisdom. Alternatively, our global human society might fail to evolve, disintegrating once again into more division, death and destruction. What is certain is that the path we choose should not be left to the influential elites who have led us to the brink of the abyss.

PART FOUR

GROWING

Pitfalls and Possibilities at the Edge of Chaos

— 12 —

Cultivating Coherence

I N THE EARLY 20th century a small group of eminent, European scientists found themselves in intellectual, emotional and existential crisis, as they discovered that the universe wasn't made of solid matter but of pure, immaterial spirit. Little did they know that their breakthrough research would catalyse a global cultural shift which, one hundred years later, would lead to the whole of humanity experiencing a similar crisis. Even less could they have foreseen that their ground-breaking work would also lead to discoveries which may yet save human-beings from destroying each other and stop them from damaging the only known planet conducive to human life. By beginning to gradually shift the focus of science from a static, mechanistic worldview to a fluid, organic perspective, Planck, Einstein, Schrodinger, Heisenberg, Bohr *et al* slowly reopened the mind of the West to the ancient wisdom of the East, laying the groundwork for the potential reunification of the brain hemispheres and of science with spirit. These two essential, yet opposite, orientations of the human mind were never subjected to the same level of separation in the monistic East as they have been in the dualistic West, and are still perceived in the Orient as yin and yang rather than as polar opposites. As a consequence the Chinese have always understood the connection between crisis and change, their word for crisis – '*wei-ji*' – combining the opposing characters for danger and opportunity. In the early 21st century we face a global crisis in which deeply interconnected issues, such as widespread poverty, endemic inequality, human-rights abuses, international terrorism, employment migration, excessive militarism and environmental damage, are all symptomatic of our human system having self-organized to the edge of chaos. Our post-modern problems present a great danger to our health, wellbeing and happiness yet also offer us great opportunity. Having subjected the modern mind of scientific materialism to its own analytical approach, reducing it to fragments and finding many of its underlying premises to be fundamentally flawed, post-modernism now provides a fertile soil in which positive, lasting change can potentially be cultivated. Yet the post-modern mind is incapable of taking our species forward because it lacks the creative qualities required to generate new solutions, it refuses to countenance synthesising, universal values and it operates at a level of consciousness too low to elevate our thinking beyond its narrow focus, short time horizons and shallow moral relativism.

Today, although more and more people are undoubtedly waking up to the organic worldview, collectively we are still seeing the world primarily through a prism of scientific materialism. Despite Einstein's warning that '*we cannot solve our problems with the same thinking we used when we created them*', our appreciation that everything in the universe is intrinsically connected and that we humans are deeply embedded within an interdependent, complex adaptive system is still insufficiently widespread. Yet the inescapable fact remains that the cultures we create and the societal structures we put in place which sustain them, are always the product of the human brain. With the exception of natural events, everything we experience in the outer world we have effectively co-created with others and brought forth in conjunction with the environment in which we find ourselves. Our existential global crisis is ultimately of our own making and we will not solve it by continuing to employ the same cognitive mode which led us to this point in human history. To change our future we must change our thinking and our knowledge of quantum science and complex adaptive systems, our awareness that our brains and societies *are* such systems and our appreciation of the way in which change can rapidly cascade across neural and cultural networks, all give us hope. We might be able to make the cognitive alterations we need to avoid the many pitfalls ahead, to leverage our full potential and bring forth a better future for all of us.

The good news is that the cognitive tools we have at our disposal, as flawed as they may be, aren't inherently damaging to us. How could they be? They evolved to enable our survival so their output does not naturally threaten the wellbeing of our species, quite the contrary. However, by choosing for so long to prioritise and pay particular attention to one part of our mind – the left mode – while marginalising its counterpart, we have inadvertently undermined the viability of our own species via our collective thinking. Although many people, from the religious to the romantic, have loudly objected over the centuries, their voices have largely fallen on the deaf ears of a modern age mesmerized by classic science, and magnetized by the material prosperity promised by capitalism. Nevertheless we do have sufficient free will to fundamentally change our global human system, by consciously choosing to rebalance our individual minds and thereby elevating the contextual, relational and synthesising capabilities of our right mind to greater prominence in how we think collectively. To be successful, however, we must somehow break the spell under which scientific materialism holds us and be willing to forego at least some of the attachments we hold to the fruits of such a culture.

Only the widespread adoption of an organic worldview can achieve this because it provides the only holistic lens through which the world appears as a single living system, enabling us to overcome and reconcile the polarizing dualisms of the left mind, in particular the debilitating schism between science and spirit. Only a culture of integrative monism can mediate these apparently irreconcilable adversaries, by increasing our awareness that they are both essential to the human condition and to the evolution of our global system to a higher plane of harmonious integration. Only the right mind is capable of synthesising both left and right modes, enabling healthy dynamic stability to emerge at the global level, yet no individual is capable of designing or controlling such a system. Our success will therefore owe as much to shared serendipity as individual genius but, nevertheless, each of us can still play a small part by managing our own minds. We are each just a tiny node in a vast neural network, yet the decisions we make and the actions we take *do* make a difference to how our collective future unfolds. We all shape our system in small but significant ways so if we want a future in which peace and personal happiness are prevalent, we can all make a contribution. However it's simply impossible for our human system to positively evolve at the low level of consciousness at which we currently think. We must all therefore up our game by becoming much more aware of our personal consciousness and why it is so essential to the future wellbeing of our human system. A good place to start is to understand the key characteristics of all healthy complex systems.

Inner and Outer Coherence

We humans all exist as individual holons, each containing parts such as
our organs, but also as parts of external or outer holons such as families,
communities, regions, nations and continents; each nested within the next
in increasing scale and complexity. In all such living systems and at any
nested level, the health of the organism is always determined by its inner
coherence – the degree to which the parts are harmoniously integrated
within the overall structure of the larger holon.[1] When we are internally
coherent we are physically healthy, that is to say our organs and body
functions are working efficiently and in an appropriately co-ordinated
manner, thus maintaining the integrity of the whole body. However when
inner coherence is low our immune system becomes weakened and we are
more susceptible to infection, disease or malfunction. If individual cells
become sufficiently incoherent and begin to self-reproduce they become
cancerous, causing the organ itself to become incoherent with our whole
body system and potentially threatening its ability to maintain life. In
systems terms, therefore, good health equals high coherence. We must also
consider outer coherence because we are all embedded in holons larger
than ourselves. Our outer coherence relates to the way in which we
contribute towards the health or ill-health of the holons we are part of, and
is determined by how we interact with friends and family, wider society
or our natural environment. Through such interactions each of us helps
to make the holons we are part of either more coherent or less coherent.
Naturally the health of our outer holons also has a reciprocal impact on
our inner health.

As abstract as holons and coherence may sound, they are not simply
cerebral concepts but our experienced, everyday reality and a necessary
condition for optimal functioning. We must feed our body healthy foods
and engage our brain in healthy pastimes to keep them both coherent and
they are mutually reinforcing; a healthy mind sustains a healthy body
and a healthy body supports positive mental health. This is equally true
of the relationship between our inner and outer worlds. Research shows
that people who are psychologically secure within a network of family
or friends are less likely to become physically sick, and that those who
are in good physical and mental shape are less likely to engage in
emotionally-damaging relationships or antisocial behaviour.[2] We all have
a vested interest in maintaining our own inner health but also in contributing towards the coherence of our external holons, because the degree

to which our inner and outer worlds are coherent with each other also impacts our overall health. Health here, of course, isn't a purely physical notion but relates to our mental and even spiritual sense of wholeness – the words health, whole and holy all share the same etymological root and are thus connected. Our integrated sense of *'being'* consists of these three spheres – mental, physical and spiritual – and our health or wholeness is derived from the degree to which we are internally and externally coherent, both within and between each sphere. Furthermore, research shows that our happiness and sense of meaning in life, both of which are essential to our health, also emerge in accordance with the degree to which we feel coherent and whole.[3]

Critically, all living systems are naturally coherent and demonstrate opposing tendencies towards self-regulation and self-creation in order to maintain dynamic balance and remain healthy. Any living organism which is sick will automatically try to heal itself and, as far as scientists can tell, there is no living system within our entire biosphere which would deliberately or continually hinder its own coherence. Why would any organism do so when coherence equals good health and could make the difference between life and death? It runs entirely counter to evolutionary principles for any species to make itself sick and it's certainly not in the nature of *homo-sapiens* to do so. Yet this is exactly what we humans have done, albeit inadvertently, and central to understanding how this is even possible is our evolution of self-consciousness. Our species is uniquely blessed with a greater degree of self-consciousness than any other creature, which is derived from our superior ability to process environmental data across our neural network, affording our left mind the *'distance'* it needs to perceive ourselves as if from outside our own being. Consciousness naturally correlates with free will, giving us more flexibility than any other organism to pick and prioritise the data we extract from the flow and how we respond as a result. Consequently, we have far greater influence in co-creating the environmental conditions in which we grow. While a plant also processes environmental 'information' in order to grow – for example its coherence will be damaged if it is denied access to water or sunshine – the plant actually exercises very little influence over these essentials. In contrast, our environmental conditions – the cultures we create and the impact they have on our own cognitive development – are to a large extent the output of our own minds so if we choose, inadvertently or otherwise, to create conditions of intellectual drought or moral darkness which damage our own coherence, we are ultimately free to do so. Superior self-consciousness and higher free will can therefore be a double-edged sword, when the choices we make cause us to become internally incoherent and unhealthy. They also place greater responsibility on our shoulders to contribute positively to the wellbeing of the larger holons in which we are embedded. A particular plant species will play a part in maintaining the homeostasis of our whole planet but its impact is marginal. However, if the human species builds a global society which causes cancerous growth, such as the economic outputs of an unfettered free market, the impact on our ecosystem is exponentially greater and may last for a very long time into the future. For many millennia our free will has enabled us to extract some information from the environmental data stream, while choosing to suppress or ignore other information. By collectively and consistently prioritising left-mind data over that produced by the right mind, we have created cultural conditions which have made our species sick and now threaten our future on the only planet which is conducive to sustaining our lives.

We have done so neither consciously nor deliberately but the cultures we have created are, nevertheless, the aggregated outputs of all our minds. This fact, however, also gives us hope. Our free will created the global crisis we find ourselves facing today, so it can also resolve it by changing our current trajectory. All living organisms automatically try to heal themselves when they are sick and the shift in our human system, over the last century, can be seen as just such an attempt. To heal means to 'make whole' and adaptive systems self-organize to the edge of chaos so that they might evolve to a higher plane of complexity, yielding greater coherence and better adaptation to new environmental conditions. Our crisis therefore presents us with an opportunity for greater integration of the global mind, but this will never be achieved with the level of thinking which caused the crisis in the first place, which is more likely to lead to catastrophe than cognitive synthesis. The great challenge for our species is therefore to elevate our consciousness in order to create those cultural conditions which are conducive to inner and outer coherence, thus making us whole and healthy both individually and as a global human society. The good news is that coherence is our most natural state and it is only our imbalanced cognitive output which sustains the incoherence which is damaging us so badly. However, scientific materialism has become deeply ingrained in us over several centuries and, despite the many benefits it has brought, has served to shatter human health, severing us from our true nature and severely restricting our ability to fully actualize our potential as whole human-beings. To do so, we must expand our consciousness and become more coherent but what does this really mean and what can we do to achieve it?

Consciousness and Non-Local Coherence

We are exposed to two primary views of consciousness. First, there's the perspective of classic science, that the phenomenon we experience as consciousness is the result of bio-chemical reactions in the brain, sparked by the processing of data from our senses and mingled with information provided by our unique genetic predispositions and preferences. Most neuroscientists today would still subscribe to this model. Alternatively there's the ancient, rather more mystical, view that there are levels of consciousness which exist beyond those accessible to the senses and which can only be reached in non-ordinary states of awareness, if necessary via techniques such as meditation, religious incantation, hypnotic trance or the ingestion of hallucinogens. Through the ages, countless testimonies have been recorded describing the experiences of those who believe they have gained access to deeper knowledge by directly connecting their own mind to a collective, global, planetary or even cosmic level of consciousness. Because such accounts transcend the individual concerned, they are usually described as '*transcendental*' or '*transpersonal*' and often report strong feelings of elevated awareness which are inexplicable within any framework of classic Newtonian science. So just as the organic worldview goes beyond the mechanistic view of science but embraces it, so too does the mystic's view of consciousness exceed yet encompass that of the scientist. However by many scientists, emboldened by the dualism and dominance of scientific materialism, the mystical mind has been disregarded as a harmless delusion at best or a dangerous heresy at worst.

Yet while quantum theory led to complexity science and thereby offered the opportunity to reconcile classic with new physics, so too did it produce evidence which has unified the scientific and mystical outlooks on consciousness. We now know and accept that all forms are fundamentally made from the same immaterial, universal energy. We now know and accept that all living organisms are complex adaptive systems which share underlying patterns of self-organization. We now know and accept that life is maintained via the ability of such systems to process energy across nodal networks. We now know and accept that evolution occurs by organisms extracting data which provides the potential to co-create and adapt to environmental changes through evolutionary '*leaps*' to higher levels of complexity. We now know and accept that all living organisms are capable of such energy-processing and adaptive leaps, so therefore have 'mind' which is the process of life itself. Just as individual humans have mind so too do our collective human systems, all other living organisms and all of our shared higher holons. The mystical view of the existence of a global mind, planetary mind and cosmic mind are all, therefore, scientifically-validated concepts. The only outstanding debate is whether or not these higher levels of consciousness can be directly accessed by the individual human mind.

Yet this question has also been affirmatively answered and accepted by the scientific community, in principle if not yet fully in practice, for over half a century. Back in the 1920s Albert Einstein was troubled by some of the implications of quantum science, in particular the theory of non-local coherence. Posited by Niels Bohr and others, the theory was that hidden variables in quantum science might possibly be '*non-local*', that is to say instantaneously connected to other parts of the universe or even to the universe itself. While the variables in classic science were always local and deterministic, connected like the parts of a machine, the probability-based, immaterial nature of quantum science meant that, at the atomic level, it was much harder to separate distinct parts from the holons in which they were embedded. Although he had instigated the revolution in 20th century science and had gone way beyond Newton with his theory of relativity, Einstein's worldview was still fundamentally mechanistic.[4] While he accepted that quantum theory, as interpreted by Bohr, was logically consistent he never believed in the existence of non-local coherence and remained convinced that a deterministic interpretation, explained in terms of local variables, would be found in the future.

However in 1964, less than ten years after Einstein's death, John Bell disproved his position by showing that the sole existence of local hidden variables was inconsistent with quantum science.[5] The simplest explanation of Bell's discovery is to imagine two fast-spinning electrons in which the direction of spin is highly variable, driven by probability, but in which their net spin is always zero. In other words, although the axes around which the two electrons spin are constantly changing, both electrons are at all times spinning around exactly the same axis but in opposite directions. Now imagine that the two electrons drift apart and, even though they become separated by some distance, their combined spin will still be zero. Central to the experiment is the fact that the distance between electrons could be huge – one could be in London and the other in Los Angeles – but they would at all times remain directly connected in their complementarity to one another. At any moment in time the scientist can choose to measure the spin of one electron, at which point it will acquire a definitive axis of rotation in the process of being measured, and if the spin of electron 1 is found to be *'right'*, the spin of electron 2 will always automatically be *'left'*. Yet if electron 1 is in London along with the scientist and electron 2 is in Los Angeles, how can electron 2 *'know'* to spin, oppositely, along the same axis as electron 1 for the duration of the measurement? There is no time for it to receive such a signal by any conventional mode of information transfer. No known method of communication can travel faster than the speed of light yet the connection between the two electrons is instantaneous and clearly non-local. Bohr had theorized and Bell had proved that the two electrons were part of an indivisible whole and, even though they were far apart in space, they were nevertheless always and instantly linked via non-local coherence. [6]

Quantum science had shown that the world cannot be accurately analysed into independently-existing parts, the idea of which is but a useful approximation of reality at the macroscopic level at which we live. However our macroscopic world is ultimately constructed of microscopic energy particles which are connected to each other in ways we don't yet fully understand, but which go far beyond our common interpretation of connectivity which is still based on local adjacency, mechanistic causality and linear determinism. In quantum science, experienced phenomena do not necessarily have a clearly identifiable cause because they may be the result of immaterial connections – potentially cosmic connections – which are non-local to the phenomenon itself. We can therefore never accurately predict when or if an event will happen, only its probability. If the behaviour of any part of any system can be determined by its non-local connections to any of its higher holons, and because we cannot accurately identify these connections, we have to replace mechanistic, causal laws with statistical laws of probability in which the likelihood of an event is determined by the dynamics of the whole system. While in classic science the properties and behaviours of the parts determine those of the whole, in quantum science the exact reverse is the case. It is the nature of the whole which determines the behaviour of the parts because everything in the universe may be deeply, and non-locally, connected to everything else in ways we simply don't yet understand. Because the individual human mind is nested within the global, planetary, universal and cosmic minds they are connected by non-local coherence, proving the mystics' perspective that knowledge derived directly from non-ordinary sources is perfectly possible. Furthermore, this also helps us to understand how systems stay healthy by using their self-regulating properties to maintain coherence; even in highly complex, deeply-nested systems with great '*distance*' between parts and whole, the entangled nature of particles can enable non-local coherence to occur.

In *Quantum Shift in the Global Brain*, Dr Ervin Laszlo provides many examples of how non-local coherence – instantaneous connections between apparently unconnected phenomena – has now been discovered, not only at the level of quanta but also at the level of the cosmos, the biosphere and even the human mind. At the leading edge of neuroscience there is a growing file of research results which show that the minds of separate individuals can achieve coherence, even at great distance and when there is no ordinary method of contact between them. Of course, accounts of this phenomenon occurring between identical twins have been recorded for centuries, but it is only much more recently that the telepathic coherence of consciousness has been measured and validated by science. In particular, non-local coherence seems to occur when one twin is experiencing pain, about which the other twin reports an intuitive sense or even feels the same pain. In tests, around 25% of identical twins seem to be able to tap into this ability but electroencephalographic (EEG) brain wave recordings also show that such coherence can occur between non-identical twins, non-twin siblings and even between individuals who are not related.[7]

Italian neuro-researcher Nitamo Montecucco found that during deep meditation both the left and right hemispheres of different individuals can become synchronized with each other. In one EEG test, 11 out of 12 meditating pairs achieved 98% synchronicity across the full spectrum of their brain waves and further studies with groups of simultaneous meditators in Tuscany and Milan – separated by over 300 kilometres – showed wave correlations way beyond the level of chance.[8] At the National University of Mexico, Jacobo Grinberg-Zylerbaum paired unrelated subjects and asked them to meditate together for 20 minutes, synchronizing their brain waves. He then separated them into sound-proof booths with no visual contact, administering stimulus such as light or sound flashes and small electric shocks to one of the pair, while using EEG to measure the brain waves of both. He found evidence of the effective '*transfer*' of stimulus between remote partners, measured by simultaneous changes in brain-wave patterns, in around 25% of cases.[9] The synchronization of brain waves has also been shown to be central to healing. In England, Maxwell Cade found that the brains of healers operate in a very distinctive blend of states – specifically wide alpha waves, moderate beta and theta waves, with no delta waves – and that during healing this characteristic wave pattern was transferred from healer to patient. Once again it has even been shown that this effect can happen when the healer and patient are separated by distance, with no form of ordinary contact.[10]

While such extraordinary, non-local coherence may sound mystical, it's perhaps no more than we regularly experience when we feel relaxed in the company of family or friends. Although we don't strap EEG equipment to our heads every time we have a conversation, we certainly do find that we get along best with those with whom we feel '*in tune*' and make friends more readily with people who are '*on our wavelength*'. Perhaps there's more to this intuitive sense than a mere turn of phrase. It's perfectly possible that the increased feeling of comfort we experience when we are with friends, is the result of the gradual synchronisation of our mind with those around us. What's more, it is well established in science that natural phenomena and even static objects contain stored, resonating energy. Who's to say that the sense of elevation we feel in the presence of an awe-inspiring mountain or the instinctive empathy we feel for an ancient tree aren't, at least in part, due to the unconscious coherence of our respective 'minds' connecting on the same wave frequency.

Through our haze of scientific materialism and post-modern cynicism, it's easy to mock or dismiss such notions as mystical mumbo-jumbo but the natives of Australia and the indigenous tribes of North and South America have long believed that mountains and trees are every bit as alive as we are. Perhaps science is only now catching up with what our ancient ancestors knew all along but which we have long-since forgotten. It's also perhaps worth reminding ourselves of the deep flaws in our 200,000-year-old brains and the fact that every human generation has always assumed that it knew pretty much everything there was to know. As recently as 1000 years ago most people still thought the Earth was flat and only 500 years ago few would have even contemplated that our planet might actually revolve around the Sun, rather than vice versa. The truth is we don't know how much we still don't know and our species, in evolutionary terms, is still in its infancy. Even based on what we *do* know today, it's entirely possible that our descendants will laugh at old footage of us sitting inside metal tubes powered by decomposed dinosaurs to fly across the Atlantic, while they teleport from place to place. They may well point to mobile phones in museums and explain that we needed them in the days before telepathic communication was commonplace. Quantum science makes both these scenarios possible, in principle if not yet in practice, and that's not even including all the discoveries we haven't yet made! While we may be the smartest animal on the planet, we don't yet truly know whether that is simply the intellectual equivalent of being the tallest pygmy in the village. Only time will tell.

Levels of Consciousness

It is indisputable that quantum science brought the mystic spiritualist and the classic scientist within touching distance of one another, in terms of their respective interpretations of consciousness. However, the latter would never accept the former while operating within the narrow confines of the Newtonian-Cartesian framework. Several notable individuals have since closed the gap even further by developing unifying theories of consciousness, the most well known of which are perhaps Ken Wilber's *Spectrum Psychology* and Stanislav Grof's *Transpersonal Psychology*. Although various models posit different layers of human consciousness most are essentially built around three core levels, based upon the mental, physical and spiritual aspects of our being and the degree to which we are coherent across and between them.

Level 1 is our psychological level, which develops largely as the result of the daily interplay between our inner and outer worlds. At this, our lowest level of consciousness, we are heavily influenced by the unconscious mind so much of our behaviour is automatic and impulsive. Ken Wilber called this the '*ego-level*' at which our behaviours are primarily driven by inner wants, needs and desires and by searching for ways to deliver their fulfilment in the outer world. At this level, somewhat overwhelmed by the visceral impulses flowing from our right mind and with relatively little self-control being applied by the left mind, we are often rather selfish with little concern for the needs of others or for the consequences of our actions. While we are highly '*me-centric*' our ego also has a strong need for the acceptance and approval of others, so we do look to family, friends and societal norms for guidance on how we should behave, thus increasing the influence our culture has over us. Over time we learn to share and consider others in order to function in society, but our *'me-centrism'* never really leaves us and satisfying the needs of the ego always comes first. We therefore tend to be rather reactionary, responding to events as they occur without considering the long-term implications of our actions. In reactionary mode, we often don't feel fully in control of our own lives and can consequently be less calm and more fearful of what may befall us in the future. On occasion this may lead to defensive, angry or aggressive impulses.

We see ourselves at all times as individuals co-existing in a world of other individuals and not only do we have a fragmented view of society, we also have a fragmented sense of self. At Level 1 we don't identify with our whole being but only with a self-imagined representation of ourselves in which we consider *'me'* to be separate from *'my body'*. We will therefore conclude *'I have a body'* rather than *'I am a body'*. We see our happiness as being derived from externalities so may seek it in meaningless relationships, material goods or many forms of hedonism, readily blaming any feelings of unhappiness on circumstances beyond our control and without ever appreciating the need to cultivate greater coherence. At the psychological level, inner coherence can only be achieved by synchronizing the brain hemispheres but the counterbalancing cognition we require is often inaccessible at this low level of consciousness, particularly when under the influence of a strong, imbalanced culture. The only options available are therefore to confabulate false narratives which reduce our cognitive dissonance, to seek short-term doses of hedonistic pleasure through alcohol, drugs or food and to dull the pain by pursuing mind-numbing pastimes involving excessive use of television or technology. Level 1 should feel very familiar to anyone brought up in modern and post-modern times under the tutelage of Cartesian dualism and the influence of scientific materialism. This is pretty much everyone in the Western world and because many of us are so completely soaked in our dominant culture, we may even find it difficult to believe that higher levels of consciousness exist and are accessible.

Level 2 is our psychological-physiological (or neurophysiological) level, where our inner coherence is enhanced by perceiving our mind and body to be one integrated whole system. At this level, hemispheric balance is regularly achieved and any mind/body dualism is consistently overcome so we appreciate that the whole of our mental and physical being is deeply connected from top to toe. We maintain a healthy, dynamic balance by feeding ourselves good food and positive thoughts, all the while keeping both mind and body suitably exercised. We consequently feel centred, at peace and in harmony with ourselves and this elevated sense of our unified self automatically drives the retreat of the more debilitating aspects of self-consciousness. We no longer feel alienated from our own body but instead are deeply comfortable in our own skin, confident in our own integrity and content to just be as we truly are. We no longer have a tendency to hold back in social situations or to 'stare' at life as if from the outside, instead spontaneously and naturally engaging with it. At this level we have probably experienced love beyond that of parents and family and have developed the ability to put the needs of others before our own egotistical desires, for no reason other than feelings of care or compassion. We have probably also experienced intense neuro-physiological harmony through sex. We have likely come to appreciate the value of higher feelings such as love, empathy and altruism, and the role they play in delivering lasting personal happiness beyond the reaches of shallow sensory gratification or hedonistic pleasure.

Morality is more likely to permeate our decision-making as we increasingly seek to balance our own personal needs, wants and desires, with the needs of others and perhaps of society as a whole. While level 1 is '*me-centric*', level 2 is very much more '*us-centric*' in attitude and outlook. We understand intuitively that the more energy we invest in building relationships the more our commitment will be reciprocated by others, but we are also ever-mindful that we can easily drop back to level 1 if we allow negative thoughts or emotions to permeate our conscious-ness. For example, fear of a partner's infidelity or anger at a friend's perceived lack of commitment to a relationship can easily manifest in negative behaviour which, when duly reciprocated, results in a downward spiral. '*If I give now I may not have enough later*' is another sentiment, borne from feelings of fear or greed, which is common at level 1 but which is always overcome at level 2. Levels aren't fixed but fluid and we can easily move between them but it is especially easy to slip back downwards, if we allow impulsiveness or raw emotion to overwhelm us and tempo-rarily imbalance our mind.

Level 3 is the level of spirit at which our whole neurophysiological self – our integrated mind and body – further synthesises itself with that part of us which is greater and deeper than the merely cognitive and biological aspects of our being. At this level we connect with a higher, nobler sense of self – which for centuries saints and sages have called our '*soul*' – and experience feelings of complete inner coherence across each level of our existence, mentally, physically and spiritually. What's more, we may even experience uplifting feelings of universal oneness through the sudden realization that we are part of and connected to everything else, bringing a strong sense of outer coherence. Such feelings may even fill us with unconditional love for all other living creatures and for the planet, universe and cosmos which nurture and sustain us. So while level 1 is '*me-centric*' and level 2 is '*us-centric*', level 3 is very much '*all-of-us*' or '*world-centric*'. At level 3 the superficial façades created by our ego are stripped away, we acknowledge that we are ultimately made of spirit and accept that our physical body is no more our identity than a turtle is its shell. By accessing our spiritual essence we come to understand our true self, providing deep insight into our purpose and the meaning of our existence. It is only with such knowledge that we can seek to actualize our full potential and become what we are inherently meant to become. Such knowledge brings a level of complete coherence many of us have never experienced, along with feelings of joy, harmony, peace and happiness, as we embrace our authentic self as the very highest expression of our whole being.

With this level of inner coherence we automatically want to cultivate the same level of coherence in the outer world, so our behaviour becomes governed by how we translate strong feelings of cognitive elevation and inner virtue into meaningful actions which are beneficial to others and our environment. From this we derive no direct benefit other than inner nourishment. Stanislav Grof called this our '*transpersonal*' level of consciousness because it resolves the remaining dualisms between the whole individual and the collectives beyond his or her personal social sphere, specifically the global human system and the planetary biosphere.[11] At this level, not only are our psychological, physiological and spiritual selves united but we are also connected, beyond the narrow confines of the senses or intellect, to the consciousness of the collective mind; of all people, of all living organisms and even of *Gaia* herself. At the end of Ken Wilber's spectrum of psychology, the very pinnacle of transpersonal consciousness, is a level at which one personally identifies with the whole universe.[12] This has been the goal of Eastern mystics for millennia and is the ultimate state in which all individualities are dissolved and all boundaries are transcended in undifferentiated, universal oneness. According to Wilber, while we can directly *perceive* reality at the transpersonal level, we only *become* part of this reality at the very highest level of consciousness. Wilber called this the level of Mind.

In such an elevated state of consciousness we can tap directly into the stream of universal spirit and, through non-local coherence, can access knowledge which exceeds sensory perception, logical reasoning or scientific analysis and, as such, often defies conventional description. Our ancient ancestors traditionally used the language of mythology to describe such experiences, but in the modern world we have become culturally conditioned to equate myth with fantasy and falsehood, rather than to see it as a richer lexicon with which to describe non-ordinary experiences of reality. Yet as Indian scholar Ananda Coomaraswamy observes, '*myth embodies the nearest approach to absolute truth that can be stated in words*'.[13] In recent times we have found it particularly difficult to accommodate paranormal or psychic phenomena within our preferred framework of rational thinking and empirical evidence, yet quantum science shows that all living organisms process mind and EEG experiments prove the potential for non-local coherence between minds. Thus science and spirit have effectively been reconciled, although in witnessing the great many tensions in the modern world between the mechanistic acolytes of scientific materialism and the creationist followers of the monotheisms, we could perhaps be forgiven for being entirely unaware of this development. While the humble holism of the organic worldview very much incorporates all science and all faith as natural outputs of the human mind, the Newtonian-Cartesian paradigm continues to prohibit the acceptance of spirit by classic, mechanistic science. Meanwhile, the dogmatically divisive monotheisms refuse to countenance any and all expressions of spiritual idealism which aren't their own, especially those of each other. Finally, traditional science and the three monotheisms, all dominated by the left mind and all singing from the same Cartesian hymn sheet, certainly can't accept each other without undermining the foundational principle of dualism – that if one of them is right, the other must be wrong.

Quantum science shows that the limits of human consciousness go way beyond the sensory empiricism, intellectual rationalism, mathematical models and non-mythical words of classic science. Conceptual models, such as those proposed by Wilber and Grof, at least offer a method of understanding and explaining non-ordinary conscious experience, yet continue to be dismissed by some as unacceptably unscientific. However as physicist Fritjof Capra points out, it simply depends on how one defines science. Capra is happy to broaden the definition:

Science, in my view, need not be restricted to measurements and quantitative analyses. I am prepared to call any approach to knowledge scientific
that satisfies two conditions: all knowledge must be based on systematic
observation and it must be expressed in terms of self-consistent but limited
and approximate models ... A true science of consciousness will deal with
qualities rather than quantities and be based on shared experience rather
than verifiable measurements. The patterns of experience constituting the
data of such a science cannot be quantified or analysed into fundamental
elements, and they will always be subjective to varying degrees. On
the other hand, the conceptual models interconnecting the data must be
logically consistent, like all scientific models ... Grof's and Wilber's maps
of consciousness are excellent examples of this new kind of scientific
approach.[14]

This broader conception of science offered by some physicists, chemists, biologists, psychologists and psychiatrists (who have almost "always
been classically trained but have stepped beyond the restrictions of the
Newtonian-Cartesian framework to embrace the new organic worldview)
has opened the door to a synthesis of science with our essential human
spirituality. Critically, men like Bohr, Laszlo, Wilber, Grof and Capra
aren't tree-hugging New Age hippies or robe-wearing spiritual swamis,
but serious scientists whose credentials deliver the credibility "required
to convince those on the periphery of both mechanistic and "creationist
worldviews to adopt a new perspective. Their hard-nosed yet open-minded
approach to science provides a platform from which we can all potentially
create the cultural conditions required, to evolve our whole human system
and broader planetary ecosystem to a higher level of mutual coherence.
However, to do so we must first understand and overcome "the degree to
which scientific materialism has suppressed our collective consciousness
and widely restricted our thinking to its lowest, psychological level.

Overcoming Cultural Suppression

When we are all born, live and die within a short window of 75 years
or so, it is understandably difficult to see just how fragmented and
narrow the modern mind actually is. However, the influence of scientific
materialism has been to significantly shrink our consciousness, to shatter
many of our most natural, multi-level coherences and to detach us from
higher levels of reality to an almost psychotic degree. Core to this, of
course, has been the influence of the left mind with its reductionist

approach and separating tendencies, from which cognitive myopia and social fragmentation are self-fulfilling outcomes. Our dominant culture has separated our scientific mind from our embodied sense of spirit, instantly cleaving our experienced reality in two by splitting the material from the immaterial and prioritizing the intellectual over the intuitive. Our natural spirituality was thereby marginalized and pushed to the outer reaches of our consciousness, fit only for the intellectually feeble and emotionally incontinent rather than the wisest and most cognitively-balanced amongst our species. Our planet too was demystified and desacralized, no longer our womb or even a living organism but an unfeeling entity to be despoiled and exploited. The huge diminishment of both religion and nature damaged our coherence at the highest, spiritual level of consciousness, undermining our ability to connect to sources of knowledge, meaning and purpose much greater than ourselves.

In compensation, the rationalism of the Enlightenment elevated each of us to God-like status in which we were masters of our own destiny and the measure of all things, but only in a much shallower world where virtue was a personal choice, morality was relative and we were without any universal values to guide us. Our ability to achieve and sustain level 3 consciousness was thus fatally undermined. The Industrial Revolution then contributed more to the denaturing of humankind than any event before or since. Not only did it physically wrench human-beings from their natural habitats, breaking long-rooted bonds to past and place, the mechanization of labour also snapped the sinews which connected people to the soil and to their own embodied physicality in working the land. Our ability to maintain level 2 neurophysiological coherence was therefore also undermined, as was the powerful connection – long understood by mystics and monks – between repetitive physical toil and the nurturance of spiritual purpose in doing '*God's work*'. Replacing manpower with mechanization further served to separate body from mind by splitting the physical from the cerebral, thereby locating our '*sense-of-self*' solely in the head and relegating the rest of the body to machine-like status. This also suppressed our consciousness to level 1 by undermining any notion of a unified mind-body which could be home to a spiritual soul. Further-more, the urbanization of the Industrial Revolution severed the social bonds which sustained our outer coherence and supported our psycho-logical and physiological wellbeing. By shrinking these essential social synapses and by locating the existential identity of the individual firmly in the psychological sphere, scientific materialism radically reduced what it meant to be human, a condition further contracted by the pre-eminence of the left mind over the right mind, through which we are connected to our physicality, emotions and spirituality.

As a result, our modern-day experienced reality has become one which is far smaller than our true potential, a shrivelled '*knowledge economy*' based on an extremely narrow, shallow and short-sighted definition of human capability. By restricting us to the intellect and empirical senses as the only doors to new knowledge, scientific materialism has made us blind even to the existence of other doors, never mind the alternative realities which may lie behind them. It laid a trap into which we have fallen, believing that all we can perceive is all that actually exists and, in doing so, it has denied and continues to deny us the opportunity to become fully whole human-beings. As a result, we have lost touch with our right minds and therefore with our bodies, intuitions, instincts and emotions. We have lost touch with the land beneath our feet, with our embodied skills and with the communities which once rooted us in time and place. We have lost touch with our spirituality and with the sense of meaning we found in connecting with entities and essences much larger than ourselves. We have lost touch with divinity and with the elevating sense of awe we got from the beauty and power of nature. We have lost touch with our inner virtue and those ennobling values, such as love, goodness and empathy, which gave us our soul. Perhaps more than anything we have lost touch with each other and with our inherent sense of our species' shared humanity. In the final analysis, scientific materialism along with its many concomitant contributors – the late Renaissance, Reformation, Enlightenment plus Philosophical, Scientific and Industrial Revolutions – for all the benefits they undoubtedly brought, also drastically diminished humankind by shrinking our existential landscape, by narrowing the horizons of our minds, by shallowing the scope of our potential and by driving our consciousness down to level 1 and solely into the psychological sphere – the only level at which the left mind is able to dominate.

Yet even in such constrained circumstances our inherent need to be wholly coherent human-beings hasn't simply disappeared. Deep in our unconscious, the gnawing intuition that our potential was much greater than our experienced reality never really left us, which is why the flames of our spiritual idealism have been dampened but never fully extinguished by the logic of the left mind. Nevertheless, the voices of romantic and religious rebels have been but a whisper compared to the grinding cogs and chiming tills of science and capitalism. Post-modernism has since smashed their pinched perspectives into a thousand pieces and also allowed many alternatives to re-emerge, including ways to access higher levels of consciousness which were second nature to our ancient ancestors, but which those of us in the West have long-since lost. And so we find ourselves deeply dissociated from our right mind; the right mind we need to rebalance our coherence at the psychological level and to rediscover higher levels of consciousness which modernity has pushed beyond our current cognitive capability. It is imperative that we relearn these skills, for it is only via a revolution in our consciousness that we can hope to rebuild the fragments offered by post-modernism, into a future which is conducive to our health and happiness. Through scientific materialism we have brought forth an experienced reality which is coherent only through the myopic lens of the left mind. Now, instead, we need to co-create a global culture which nurtures the needs of whole human-beings – mentally, physically and spiritually – and which cultivates both inner and outer coherence. Can we consciously create conditions which would be conducive to the emergence of global peace, social harmony, positive health and personal happiness for over 7 billion people and for the sustainable wellbeing of our planet? There are no guarantees in such a complex system but there are certainly a number of things we can do, individually and collectively, to give us the best possible chance of avoiding disaster and of unifying us with our own sense of self, with each other and with our biosphere.

First of all, we can choose to adopt an organic worldview and play our part in creating and promoting a culture of integrative monism. When we change our view of what's real in the world, pretty much everything else changes too. While most of the daily thoughts driving us are delivered unconsciously, how we choose to see the world is one thing we can consciously control and it automatically shapes whatever emerges from it, influencing the world we bring forth for ourselves and others. A seismic shift in the world we co-create certainly cannot happen without enough individuals adopting an organic worldview and developing a higher level of personal consciousness. To do so, they must each overcome the many cultural barriers to cognitive elevation presented by prevailing modern and post-modern perspectives. In particular, they must expand their minds beyond the narrow confines of scientific materialism to access and incorporate non-ordinary sources of knowledge into their everyday thinking. While this transformation will be personal, the journey cannot be made alone but only with the encouragement, love and support of others. As individual nodes, each deeply embedded in wide, entangled networks of human relationships, personal growth and collective coherence can only emerge from our interactions with those in our environments and at each level of our being; psychologically, physiologically and spiritually. We must therefore find and mutually support one another, exerting enough influence on sufficient others to cause catalytic change to cascade throughout the whole human system, providing it with the energy flow it requires to be sustained and to organically evolve. Only then do we have the possibility of reinventing the economic, political, social and spiritual structures which are currently making us incoherent with ourselves, with each other and with our planet. Only by changing such structures can we achieve and maintain our coherence as a unified global species and align our collective consciousness with that of our planetary ecosystem, bringing forth the environmental conditions conducive to our long-term life and sustainable peace, health and happiness. Such transformative change can only begin with the transformation of individual minds which must tap into both science *and* spirit to achieve higher consciousness.

—13—

Elevating Consciousness

THE PRACTICE of repetitive, rhythmic chanting in spiritualism is believed to date from pre-historic times and the oldest record of what we might now call meditation can be found in the Hindu tradition of *Vedantism*, from around 3500 years ago. Perhaps the most well-known, modern-day method of accessing higher consciousness is '*transcendental meditation*' which was first made famous by Maharishi Mahesh Yogi approximately 50 years ago. Since then over 500 scientific studies have been conducted into the effects of meditation, which have found that the practice can have profound effects on our consciousness and psychological, physiological and spiritual coherence.[1] The Maharishi's method involves the silent repetition of a mantra containing meaningless sounds, specifically chosen to resonate with the natural rhythm and spiritual energy of each individual. According to its principles, regular experience of transcendental consciousness should enable the practitioner to incorporate its elevated state, alongside the normal waking state, into everyday experience and thereby leverage its numerous benefits in the daily discourse of life. Indeed, research confirms that such meditation does develop the entire human nervous system in a manner which is consistent with descriptions of Eastern spiritual enlightenment and which delivers considerable cognitive benefits to the meditator.

EEG experiments confirm that in an elevated state of consciousness accessed by meditation, brain waves show higher levels of coherence and wave peaks become synchronized across different parts of the brain in patterns which are very different to normal. Tests also confirm that this unique state of consciousness is characterized by a feeling of deep, inner calm and by highly-integrated neurophysiological function, leading to optimized performance and on-going health benefits. Critically, with regular practice of around 20 minutes twice daily, neurological patterns established during meditation *do* become more and more established outside of meditation and are therefore increasingly incorporated into everyday cognitive states. Neuroscientist Dr Frederick Travis used EEG to compare regular practitioners of transcendental meditation with two control groups and found that the minds of meditators functioned very differently from non-meditators, even when performing the same simple, everyday tasks.[2] He found that the strong coherence patterns associated with transcendence during meditation, had been successfully integrated into the daily functioning of practitioners and that their reported feelings of higher consciousness were supported by markedly different EEG patterns when compared to the control groups. More importantly, Travis discovered that those who meditated were able to function more effectively and efficiently at the tasks, keeping their brains at the minimum level of activity required yet performing at higher levels of capability in a calm, precise manner and without the anxieties or frustrations commonly witnessed amongst control groups. Travis' research confirmed the clear functional benefits of elevated consciousness – a higher level of integrated thinking delivering better cognitive performance with lower expended energy – as well as providing quantitative support for the many qualitative descriptions of transcendence provided by practitioners. Such experiences have been variously described as '*a permanent state of bliss*', '*deep inner peace*', '*silent unbounded awareness*', '*oneness with the universe*', '*immovable serenity*', '*all-encompassing love*', '*total nothingness*', '*deeply intense aliveness*' and in many other ways.[3] Thus, EEG research once again brings together the scientific and the mystical, confirming that transcendental meditation works by synchronising our psychological, physiological and spiritual levels of consciousness, optimising our inner coherence and giving rise to the wide awareness, deep intuition, high creativity and sharp focus we need for peak performance in the outer world.

The transcendental technique is only one of many methods of meditation, which include the Buddhist tradition of '*mindfulness*'. Buddhism is often erroneously considered to be a religion but is really just a way to access our spiritual level of elevated consciousness, as Robert Thurman, professor of Indo-Tibetan studies at Columbia University, explains:

> the Buddha founded an educational movement rather than a religion ...
> He understood the most important factor in the quality of life for a human
> being is how the person's mind is managed ... the Buddha therefore

focused on human beings, on the transformation of human consciousness, rather than on God.[4]

Studies across various methods of meditation, including mindfulness, have shown the practice to be extremely valuable in improving physical and mental health by producing results which are characterised by a high degree of synthesis of the whole nervous system. It works through focussed attention and regular repetition, which gradually ingrains increasingly integrated patterns of neural connectivity, enabling healing as well as the improved co-ordination and higher cognition such coherence brings. It is well established that many dysfunctional behaviours in society are the result of an individual's traumatic associative memories, which can result in consistently aberrant behavioural responses to such recollections. For example, this is a powerfully established pattern in child abuse where those who have been abused are much more likely to become abusers as adults. Meditation has been used, with positive results, in the rehabilitation of abusers and other criminals and in overcoming post-traumatic stress disorder (PTSD) in war veterans.[5] It has also been successfully used in psychotherapy where it is able to dissociate traumatic memories from their corresponding emotional and behavioural responses. In this field, meditation perhaps has even more potential than traditional psychotherapeutic methods which, although they can achieve the same dissociation, don't actually rewire the neural network, causing the patient to remain unstable and sensitive to relapse even after successful treatment. Meditation works by not only addressing dissociation but by also establishing new, coherent patterns of connectivity. This creates neural pathways which strengthen healthy functioning and provide an increasingly strong, sustainable base for maintaining a positive outlook, high tolerance to stress and good cognitive function. In this manner, elevated consciousness can heal psychological scars and result in renewed, healthy and harmonious functioning, quite literally healing or making the patient feel whole again.

Over the last few decades hundreds of scientific studies into the benefits of meditation have been conducted, and while some have approached the subject from different angles their results all tend to point in the same direction – that the technique can help individuals access higher, non-ordinary states of consciousness, thereby increasing mind-body coherence and delivering higher functional performance plus enhanced neurophysiological wellbeing. Its many health benefits include reduced anxiety or depression, increased emotional control, improved memory, decreased feelings of loneliness, improved sleep patterns and enhanced support for weight loss.[6] Moreover, it has even been shown to make us more virtuous towards other people. Perhaps, as Paramahansa Yogananda suggests, *'peace in the world starts with peace in individual hearts'*.[7]

Beyond Meditation

Another, rather more controversial, approach to the study of elevated consciousness was pioneered by psychiatrist Stanislav Grof who, for seventeen years, included the use of LSD and other psychedelic substances in his research. Before public outcry led to legal restriction, Grof and several colleagues conducted over 5000 psychotherapeutic sessions using psychedelics, in both the US and Europe.[8] They convincingly concluded that their research wasn't the study of special effects induced in the mind by psychoactive substances, but rather the study of the natural human mind beyond ordinary levels of consciousness, facilitated by chemical catalysts. Someone taking LSD didn't therefore experience a toxic psychosis, as many of its critics claimed, but instead was able to undertake a deep journey into those areas of the mind which were not normally accessible. So convinced was Grof about the power of psychedelics to unlock the door to higher levels of consciousness, he wrote:

> It does not seem inappropriate and exaggerated to compare their potential significance for psychiatry and psychology to that of the microscope for medicine or the telescope for astronomy.[9]

Another scientist who experimented with psychedelics in consciousness research was Walter Pahnke of Boston University, who wanted to test if naturally-occurring psilocybin would act as a reliable entheogen in subjects who were already positively predisposed towards religion.[10] He recruited twenty theology students from Harvard's Divinity School and gave ten of them psilocybin while administering niacin, also known as vitamin B3, as a placebo to the other ten. B3 creates real physiological changes, such as face flushing and skin tingling, so some placebo students initially believed they had received the psychedelic drug, but the results showed that those in the psilocybin group actually experienced far more powerful spiritual feelings. Pahnke found that most subjects in the psilocybin sample reported almost all of the nine characteristics of spiritual experience he had set out to measure, including transcendence of time and space, a sense of oneness with the universe, difficulty in expressing experiences in words, feelings of great joy, ecstasy and awe and the belief that they had been changed for the better as a result of their experience. Indeed, most of the psilocybin group described the experience as one of the most important of their lives and one participant, Huston Smith, who later became a religious scholar called it *'the most powerful cosmic homecoming I have ever experienced'*.[11]

Of course, ancient mystics have always used natural psychedelics to invoke similar states of non-ordinary awareness. Psilocybin occurs naturally in 'magic' mushrooms and the Aztec word for psilocybin mushrooms – *'teonanacatl'* – literally means *'God's flesh'*. Descriptions of elevated consciousness have been highly consistent through the ages and reports of transpersonal experiences offer deep insight into the highest dimension of human consciousness, explaining our ancient impulse towards spiritual idealism which long predates any conception of science. Humans were practising *'religion'* at least 50,000 years before the ancient Greeks even *'invented'* natural philosophy and our original belief systems almost certainly evolved as the result of our ancestors elevating their minds to the transpersonal level of consciousness, a capability which came much more easily to them than it does to us. It's just another example of the pernicious power of the left mind, and the way in which scientific materialism has narrowed the scope of our existence, that we should arbitrarily categorize psychedelics as Class A narcotics alongside genuinely dangerous substances such as heroin and crack-cocaine, including them in our militaristic *'war on drugs'* when they could offer humankind great potential for exploring the heights of our own consciousness and cognitive capabilities.

As a consequence of their unwarranted prohibition most people have never experienced psychedelic *'drugs'* and, while there are millions of practitioners worldwide, most people don't regularly meditate either. The majority of us, therefore, have never experienced the positive effects of either method so it is perhaps understandable that many people still remain cynical about their efficacy, or even about the existence of non-ordinary, elevated levels of consciousness. Yet many of us have, at some point in our lives, probably had fleeting exposure to higher consciousness, perhaps without even realizing what we were experiencing. As a teenager I played a lot of football (soccer) and can still vividly recall a few brief periods, in perhaps just a handful of matches, which felt very different from the thousands of other minutes I played the sport. The experiences are difficult to explain in words (which is always a tell-tale sign) but during these short sequences it felt as if the whole game had slowed down and every other player was moving in slow motion. I felt like I was in a trance during which my every movement was fluid, my mastery of the ball was effortless and my every touch was perfect. I didn't feel like I was running but rather gliding across the pitch, full of boundless energy yet completely relaxed and calm, breathing effortlessly and in complete control of my situation, performing on a plane above every other player yet in total synchronicity with my team mates. I was certainly 'playing well' but to describe those few brief periods in such terms simply doesn't do them justice – they were completely different to the many times I played the game to a competent standard. In those moments I simply didn't have to think about what I was doing, indeed if I had thought about it I probably wouldn't have been able to do it. It was as if my mind and body had a telepathic understanding which would have been broken by the intrusion of conscious thought – something I could only recognize in hindsight because at the time I was aware of nothing other than playing the game. Those experiences were a long time ago but to this day I remain convinced that I was either briefly blessed by the hand of Diego Maradona or, rather more realistically, I was afforded a small taste of what the world's top sportsmen and women regularly feel when they are '*in the zone*' and performing at the very peak of their abilities.

It wasn't until many years later that I found a word to describe my few youthful experiences on the football field – '*flow*' – a term coined by Hungarian psychologist Mihaly Csikszentmihalyi to describe the deep enjoyment his research subjects reported, when they were in a state of total immersion in a challenging but pleasurable task which exercised maximum use of their capabilities.[12] People variously described experiencing flow while driving fast, skiing, playing sport, painting, dancing, singing, writing and even taking photographs, and Csikszentmihalyi called the state '*flow*' because all of the descriptions had a common sense of effortless, fluid movement. Characteristic conditions for finding flow were a clear challenge with which the individual was fully engaged, having the skills to complete the task but only when they were fully stretched, and gaining instant feedback on progress towards the end goal for the duration of the event. With each chicane negotiated, ball kicked, brushstroke laid or word written, the feedback received served to amplify the intensely pleasurable feeling of flow to the point that participants reported '*losing themselves'* in the activity and a subsequent sense of total detachment from time and space. During periods of flow our conscious and unconscious minds become synchronised but in a way which is very different to the *'autopilot'* mode we have perhaps experienced when driving on a motorway, when our unconscious mind seems to take over and our consciousness seems to switch off. In flow states the task is much more challenging so our conscious mind must be highly alert and fully engaged in the exercise, yet such is our need for focussed concentration that with heightened consciousness we lose all sense of self-consciousness. During flow, we are so exercised by needing to draw on all of our neurophysiological capability that we don't have the spare cognitive capacity to 'think' about the task in hand. We must simply immerse ourselves in it and literally go with the flow, staying alert and adapting to feedback as we progress. In these special moments we achieve complete coherence of mind and body, the neurophysiological level 2 of consciousness in which we are no longer divided by Descartes, but are totally at one with ourselves.

We don't therefore have to practice transcendental meditation or take psychedelic drugs to experience elevated consciousness. In adulthood I have often experienced flow again, sometimes when working but particularly while running – indeed some of the insights and ideas in this book have come to me while jogging at a comfortable pace and listening to music with a steady beat. Common to both meditation and flow are the underlying principles of repetition and rhythm, which serve to synchronize the brain hemispheres as well as mind and body, providing the conditions in which high functional performance can take place. Not content with just finding flow Csikszentmihalyi also wanted to understand the role it played in people's lives, particularly those who were creatively productive in the arts and sciences. With his student Jeanne Nakamura, he interviewed hundreds of successful dancers, musicians, painters, poets, writers, photographers, biologists, physicists and psychologists to explore just how their lives had come to be so extraordinarily inventive. The interviews showed that, although everyone's story was unique in its specifics, they had all essentially followed the same path from initial interest in their chosen topic and enjoying occasional moments of flow, to becoming fully engaged in a whole web of relationships which gave a far greater sense of meaningful purpose to their work and lives.[13] Csikszentmihalyi and Nakamura called this *'vital engagement'* and defined it as *'a relationship to the world that is characterized both by experiences of flow (enjoyed absorption) and by meaning (subjective significance)'*.[14] Critical to vital engagement is the duration over which elevated consciousness, in the form of flow, can be maintained due to the experience being part of a larger project which extends beyond the purely pleasurable to something of higher purpose or significance. While each purpose was personal to the individual, in all cases the maintenance of vital engagement required a connection beyond the individual to something larger and more meaningful; something which was embedded in neither their inner nor outer worlds but in the dynamic coherence between the two. The stronger the subjective significance of the activity, the higher the level of vital engagement and the more frequent the feeling of flow. We are all therefore capable of finding flow in whatever we do, but particularly through our work or leisure pursuits which are often where we spend most of our time. By employing the *'zoom-out'* facility of the right mind we can all better understand the context in which we contribute to the coherence of our larger holons. Through this lens, the school cleaner sees that he is part of a team helping to educate the leaders of the future, the garbage collector realizes the vital role she plays in maintaining the health of the nation and the bricklayer understands that every house built will become a home for someone. We all have an inherent need to find meaning in life and one of the ways we do so is by feeling that what we produce has a higher purpose.

Eminent psychologist Abraham Maslow extensively studied the deeply human need to feel connected to something greater than ourselves, along the way collecting many reports of what he called *'peak experiences'*. Maslow is perhaps most famous for his *'hierarchy of needs'* model which proposes that self-actualization is the ultimate human goal and, like Aristotle, he believed that the purpose of life and the route to personal happiness was to actualize our potential by fully becoming what is inherent in our nature to become. He described peak experiences as *'moments of high happiness and fulfilment'* which, as well as delivering superior functional performance, were also

> exciting, oceanic, deeply moving, exhilarating, elevating experiences that generate an advanced form of perceiving reality, and are even mystic and magical in their effect upon the experimenter.[15]

In this he is clearly describing experiences of elevated consciousness and, like flow and vital engagement, triggers for Maslow's peak experiences could include sport, art, music, poetry and scientific experimentation but also sex, deep introspection, interaction with nature and religious practice. Maslow considered the pursuit of peak experiences to be the most important pastime in life because it is only from the feeling of being wholly coherent with one's own true nature, that we can actualize our full potential, find meaning in life and serve our true purpose – to become all that we are meant to become.

In *Religion, Values and Peak Experiences*, Maslow lists many features of peak experiences all of which are very similar to those described in transcendental meditation, psychedelic research, flow and vital engagement. For example, the feeling of *'being one whole, harmonious self'*, being *'free of dissociation or inner conflict'*, perceiving the universe *'as a unified whole where everything is accepted and nothing is judged'* and feeling *'personally unified with something much larger than oneself, such as the universe or God'* are all clearly suggestive of multi-level coherence. Being *'filled with feelings such as love, awe, joy and gratitude'* suggests the same ecstatic sense of elevation described in other descriptions of higher consciousness. Functioning *'effortlessly and easily without strain or struggle'*, the feeling of *'using all capacities and capabilities at their highest potential'*, having a *'free mind that is flexible and open to creative thoughts and ideas'*, while enjoying *'naturally flowing behaviour that is not constrained by conformity'* all point to the heightened capability and creativity experienced during flow and other such states. Finally a *'loss of judgement of time and space'*, the *'loss of egocentrism and goal-striving'*, being *'without inhibition, fear, doubt or self-criticism'* and enjoying *'complete mindfulness of the present moment, without influence of past or expected future experiences'* all strongly suggest the suppression of self-consciousness in favour of heightened and holistic levels of consciousness.

Maslow's objective was to show that peak experiences, especially religious experiences, were an essential aspect of human nature and that spirituality has deep intrinsic meaning to human-beings. Since the beginning of recorded history and across all geographies and cultures, humans have reported *'religious'* experiences and Maslow's view was that all recognized spiritual practices probably began with the peak experiences of individuals, who then shared their stories with others who in turn recognized something familiar, aspirational and ennobling in them. Spiritual narrative was therefore created as a method of bringing people together, allowing non-kin groups to cohere *'horizontally'* but also of conditioning members to cohere *'vertically'* around ennobling principles or values, which enabled their collective minds to evolve to an elevated plane of cultural integration via agreed behaviours. In doing so they promoted the pursuit of peak experiences, through religious practice, as a method of further increasing both the horizontal and vertical coherence of the group. Thus it was our original impulse towards spiritual idealism which first developed coherent cultures; cultures which were effectively co-created by religious experiences and our highest level of consciousness.

In *The Varieties of Religious Experience* Harvard psychologist William James explored all aspects of religious belief and practice, concluding that the deepest truth revealed in his research was that most human-beings experience life as a '*divided self*', regularly pulled in opposite directions by conflicting thoughts, emotions and desires.[16] James was interested in the psychology of religion rather than theology per se, so didn't restrict his research to only activities which took place in the church. Believing that religious experiences were simply extraordinary human experiences, he also investigated the effects of other stimuli, such as nature and drugs, in producing spiritual feelings. James found that such feelings were common amongst both believers and non-believers in God, and that there were remarkable similarities between all accounts; in particular that they made people feel whole or at peace with themselves. James studied both the gradual and sudden development of elevated consciousness and was especially intrigued by the role played by awe, in sparking rapid spiritual transformation. Awe is a key emotion in transcendence and is experienced when an individual encounters a physical, emotional or conceptual phenomenon which is much greater than themself and which cannot be understood within their pre-existing schematic frameworks.[17]

Such encounters cause a dramatic reappraisal of reality by forcing the mind to accept the existence of alternative realities and producing paradoxical emotions within the individual, who simultaneously feels insignificant and powerless yet also connected to, or part of, the awesome phenomenon they have encountered. Through the ages, feelings of awe and transcendence have regularly been reported in accounts of religious revelation, or associated with transformational encounters with the power, vastness or beauty of nature. Irrespective of the stimulus, any experience which makes us feel insignificant automatically shrinks the ego, making us more passive and open, thereby increasing our potential for elevated consciousness and spiritual growth. However, scientific materialism has served to increase the secularization of many societies, so increasingly fewer humans have ever experienced genuine spiritual transformation.

Nevertheless, despite its despoliation of our planet most of us will have at least enjoyed a sense of elevation from being in the presence of nature. We may have felt similarly uplifted by a particular piece of music, a great artwork or even by another person and studies show that when we encounter anything we find inspirational, we actually experience changes in our neurophysiology with warm feelings rising in our chest along with a strong desire to help others.[18] These sensations may be linked to the release of the hormone oxytocin, which has been shown to create feelings of inner calm, love, trust and openness as well as a need to bond with other people and the desire to do good deeds. Whether the result of religious revelation, nature's beauty, a TED talk or Taylor Swift's latest track, anything which makes us want to increase both inner and outer coherence can only be a good thing. Through the ages such feelings have been strongly linked to the concept of soul; our higher, nobler sense of self which is sourced from the virtuous values often found in spiritual idealism. Once again, such a notion has been largely marginalized in the secular societies created by scientific materialism and in the maelstrom of moral relativism promoted by the post-modern mind.

As a consequence, and in spite of the evidence above, the concept of non-ordinary levels of consciousness which are accessible through methods such as meditation, possibly still sounds like mystical nonsense to the post-modern cynic who remains deeply immersed in scientific materialism and retains unerring faith in the power of reason. For anyone who has never experienced flow or peak experiences, the descriptions provided by those who have, perhaps still suggest delusion more than divinity. Sometimes we are so steeped in a culture that any challenge to its foundational premises creates a level of cognitive dissonance we find deeply uncomfortable, due to the difficulty we have in reconciling new ideas with our pre-existing mental models. In such circumstances we have two options. We can either bury our head in the sand and continue to confabulate comforting narratives which confirm that we are correct, or we can subject new ideas to scrutiny even if we can only do so within our current schematic frameworks. For those strongly wedded to scientific materialism, the benefits of higher consciousness have to make sense intellectually because they place so little value on whether they do so intuitively or spiritually. Can the concepts of elevating consciousness and cultivating coherence, for the purpose of global peace and personal happiness, be subjected to scientific scrutiny so that they even make sense to the secular cynic?

Science of Peace and Happiness

Science shows that inner coherence is the natural state of all living organisms so rather than looking outside for what we don't have, in order to make ourselves happy, we should instead look inside to remove the causes of our incoherence. Many different '*religions*' seem to agree with science, emphasising the need to let go of attachments or to remove the damaging detritus of everyday life, in order to find lasting peace. Peace is a feeling rather than a thought which, like happiness, is experienced primarily through our embodied right mind and emerges as a consequence of our inner and outer coherence. Critically scientific research does indeed confirm that outer-world attachments, particularly to material goods, are an illusory path to peace and happiness. Central to this discovery are what psychologists call the '*progress*' and '*adaptation*' principles.[19] In short, we receive a pleasurable dose of dopamine every time we take a small step towards a particular goal and another when we achieve it. In all cases the rewards are short-lived, so the pleasure we receive from the journey overall is far greater than the pleasure we get from finally reaching our goal, which is invariably an anti-climax compared to the enjoyment we have had along the way. Furthermore, under the adaptation principle we very quickly become used to the new '*thing*' we have acquired and discover that we grossly overestimated the depth and duration of the pleasure it would bring us. Our disappointment is particularly poignant when we have created an internal narrative in which our happiness is interwoven with having the Breitling or BMW or whatever else we were striving for. However, instead of learning from the let-down we have a strong tendency to simply set the bar higher next time and, labouring under the illusion that we now only need a Rolex or Porsche to make ourselves complete, begin striving once again. It is for these reasons that happiness is only very loosely correlated with wealth and why money, beyond its ability to ensure the essentials in life, is rarely the path to inner peace or personal happiness.[20]

However, economist Robert Frank did find that some purchases are better for our wellbeing than others, and that spending money on holidays with friends and family makes us feel much more whole and happy than buying expensive luxury items.[21] Frank's explanation drew an important distinction between conspicuous and inconspicuous consumption, concluding that the former was ultimately a futile exercise in expressing relative status and was therefore strongly susceptible to the adaptation principle. In such a game, players not only quickly get used to their own new item but each continually raises the bar for the other, negating the possibility of either enjoying long-lasting pleasure from the purchase of such goods. Frank found that more inconspicuous types of consumption, such as 'buying' extra time off work, often led to greater levels of happiness.

These findings were further confirmed by research which showed that subjects who spent money on social activities thought their cash had been better used and were happier overall with their purchases, than those who spent the same amount on material goods. Social activities and shared experiences bring us together with other people, while the way we use material goods, particularly luxury items, is often to separate ourselves from others by expressing status or superiority. Once again, this demonstrates that our left and right minds bring very different approaches to how we interact with the world. Extensive studies have also shown that the deeper the relationships an individual has, the happier he or she will be.[22] Those in long-term marriages are generally happier than those who aren't. People who have strong friendships tend to enjoy lower levels of stress and live longer than those who don't. Human activities most associated with happiness tend to be social, while those most associated with unhappiness tend to be solitary. Indeed in reviewing the findings of a Gallup World Poll on happiness, conducted in over 150 countries and with more than a million respondents, psychologist Daniel Kahneman concluded 'it is only a slight exaggeration to say that happiness is the experience of spending time with people you love and who love you'.[23] According to Robert D. Putnam of Harvard University, the single most common finding from half a century of research on the correlates of life satisfaction, is that happiness is best predicted by the breadth and depth of a person's social connections.[24] In his book *Bowling Alone* Putnam relays the tale of the inhabitants of Roseto, a close-knit community of Italian immigrants in Pennsylvania, which attracted the attention of US medical researchers in the 1950s because it mysteriously had a heart attack rate of less than half the national average, despite having higher than average risk factors. Over a 40-year period of in-depth study researchers concluded that their deep social interconnectedness was at the root of the Rosetans' rude health.

If we wish to become coherent, healthy, whole and happy, the learnings from science are twofold. First, letting go of attachments, particularly our powerful attachment to money and material wealth, is essential. Second, we are social animals and much of our mental, physical and spiritual wellbeing is derived from the relationships we have with others. We must all therefore be willing to subsume at least some of our individual needs or desires within the wider interests of our groups or societies. This is something people in the East have always intuitively understood but which is harder for those in the West to intellectually accept, reared as we are on the sham narrative of the self-determining individual. Yet the truth is that in becoming slaves to the ideals of scientific materialism, most of us have already relinquished our autonomy to fit in with modern society and, in doing so, are missing a massive opportunity to actualize our full potential both individually and collectively. By operating only at our lowest level of consciousness we have allowed our dominant culture, and its dualistic despotism, to dominate our unconscious and have thereby empowered that part of us which is prejudicially-divisive, hierarchically-striving, competitively-aggressive and materially-grasping, to drive our behaviour. Clearly this makes it difficult to build and maintain positive relationships because the ego-driven part of us acts as a barrier to social cohesion by regularly wanting to beat its opponent, express superior status or always be correct, while often refusing to consider the needs of the whole group, share wealth or show intellectual humility. To build healthy social relationships and thereby cultivate outer peace, we must first find inner peace but this can never be achieved if we are perpetually at war within ourselves, struggling for status, striving to have what society says we should have and ready to fight anyone who stands in our way of getting it.

When conflicts arise, as they invariably do in any dynamic system, this cognitive mode dictates that we must compete to win using all the tools we have available to prevail, including force if necessary. The most common causes of conflict are our attachments yet, while physical attachments can breed rivalry via emotions such as envy, it is actually our mental attachments – what we believe in – which are much more contentious and a far greater source of disharmony. Mental attachments will always cause some conflict because people will always disagree with each other, but in a dualistic culture in which intellectual modesty is often seen as a sign of weakness, the potential for fireworks is much greater. Each of us is using the same 200,000-year-old cognitive equipment as everyone else, yet the arrogance of our self-assuredness can often be breath-taking and many of us have become so transfixed by scientific materialism that we never operate beyond our lowest level of consciousness. We therefore cannot see that our dominant culture is fatally holed beneath the waterline or that many of its political, economic, social and spiritual support structures are fundamentally broken. Instead, we accept the narrowness of its vision and the shallowness of its values, busily occupying ourselves with trying to win the only game it allows us to play – competing with other human-beings – rather than helping them or uniting with them to change our culture for the benefit of everyone.

To do so, we must quieten the effects of the ego by letting go of our attachments and by becoming more aware of the pernicious influence of scientific materialism, in particular the degree to which it sustains left-mind dominance. We must each become more adept at balancing our brain hemispheres and no matter how influenced our mind is by preference or pre-disposition, we all *do* have the capacity to see every issue from the opposite point of view. Our mental attachments are naturally formed around our particular perspective on problems, which could be more liberal on some issues and more conservative on others. However, our overarching cultural dualism conditions us to believe that for our opinion to be right our opponent's opinion must be wrong, automatically leading to conflict. In a culture of integrative monism we instead understand that any perspective which is polar to ours isn't necessarily wrong, but that the holder may simply be approaching the issue from a different direction, looking at it through an alternative lens or holding contrary goals to ours. In any case, we all have the brainpower to place ourselves in the shoes of an adversary and choose to see an issue exactly as they see it, yet rarely do we do so, conditioned as we are to compete and critique rather than collaborate or compromise. Indeed we are usually quite adept at using our laser-like left mind to dissect the opinions of others, but rarely do we turn the microscope on our own beliefs and subject them to the same rigorous analysis. By introspecting the nature of our own attachments we can more readily release ourselves from them; genuinely considering issues through a 360-degree lens, reducing our incoherence, forming better judgements and becoming a more rounded individual. We may still end up disagreeing but the very act of perceiving a problem from another's perspective builds empathy and almost certainly improves the quality of our own thinking, adding nuance to our understanding, de-polarizing our opinions and encouraging us to find creative solutions to any issue.

We can all choose how we view the world and how we respond to it but only if we become more conscious of the influence our mental attachments have on us. The original meaning of the word responsible is response-able; we are all able to control our response to every situation

and must therefore take responsibility for our actions and their consequences. We can allow our habitual, ingrained attitudes to manifest in
prejudice and poor judgement or we can increase awareness of our own
cognitive flaws and cultural influences, proactively trying to overcome
them. We can consciously decide to cultivate coherence, peace, harmony,
tolerance and respect by bringing together the two brain hemispheres or
we can default to our unconscious pre-setting of division and competition.
At our lowest level of consciousness, even the liberal right mind can
become culturally conditioned to see the conservative left mind as an
opponent to be defeated, rather than as a complementary cognitive mode.
We see this manifest daily in the narrowness of the neo-liberal and neo-
conservative consensus, which defines capitalist economics as the only
game worth playing. Only at higher levels of consciousness can the much
broader focus of the right mind be fully brought to bear, enabling the third
and final phase of our right-left-right cognitive sequence to be optimized
by integrating *all* sources of knowledge, including those non-ordinary
sources inaccessible to the senses or intellect and incomprehensible within
the Newtonian-Cartesian framework.

So in summary, science concurs with spirit in concluding that the only
path to global peace and worldwide happiness is for sufficient individuals
to proactively cultivate inner and outer coherence. In doing so, those
people will find personal peace but could also cause cascading cultural
change across the whole human system, by taking a positive approach
to every single relationship they have. Letting go of material and mental
attachments allows us to suppress the influence of the ego on our everyday
actions, better enabling us to build strong relationships in the real world;
relationships which are ultimately the primary source of our happiness.
By quelling the effects of the ego, we overcome the need to always be
correct, competitive or in control and instead propagate tolerance, respect
and collaboration in their place. In doing so we elevate our focus from the
'*me-centric*' lens of our lowest level of consciousness to the '*us-centric*'
or even '*world-centric*' outlooks of higher levels, automatically
compelling us to seek coherence in the outer world and to signal that
co-operation is our overarching modus operandi. Critically this does not
force us to constantly compromise in discussions, debates or negotiations.
On the contrary, it enables us to support or refute positions using robust
reasoning and to convey opinions with honesty and passion. Our ability
and willingness to review all issues from a 360 perspective also
builds empathy, provides for more balanced judgements and reduces the

likelihood of any party resorting to obstinacy, defensiveness or anger. Paradoxically such superior cognition actually expends less mental energy than thinking at lower levels of consciousness, by subduing the effects of the energy-sapping ego and by negating the need for effortful confabulation. By letting go of our preconceived ideas, our desire for status, our focus on winning, our need to be right and so on, we automatically clear out the detritus which causes our incoherence and allow our naturally coherent inner-self to emerge; bringing a clear, calm lucidity to our cognition and enabling a better quality of thinking at lower levels of effort.

Moreover, a further benefit of elevated consciousness and the cultivation of coherence is that they resolve our ultimate paradox – how to become more conscious yet less self-conscious. Self-consciousness and incoherence are mutually reinforcing, each amplifying the other. The more incoherent our lives feel, the more we become self-conscious that something is missing but often without knowing what we need to make us whole and happy again. When we feel this way, our awareness of these anxieties can lead to behaviours such as hedonism or hyper-consumption, which may seem to fill the gap in the short-term but which actually exacerbate our unhappiness in the mid to long-term. This makes us feel even more incoherent yet still lacking the insight to ensure that the same, self-reinforcing cycle doesn't simply begin again. On the other hand, coherence actually serves to reduce our self-consciousness because by making us feel whole and happy, we feel far less need to stand back from our lives, to compare ourselves with others or to even consider how happy we are. Happiness and those feelings which sustain it, such as having a sense of purpose or the security we derive from stable relationships, aren't emotions we can actively pursue but are feelings which emerge as a result of the coherence in our lives. As such, they are like shadows which disappear as soon as we shine the light of self-consciousness on them – the more we chase them the more elusive they become. People who feel fully coherent don't tend to ponder their purpose in life, worry about their relationships or regularly review their own happiness because they are just so busy living life that such questions simply don't occur to them. It is those who experience a gnawing sense of their own incoherence who tend to be more self-conscious, sometimes even proactively planning ways to increase their own happiness, unaware that the very act of doing so may push their goal further from their grasp.

Thus, we can resolve our great consciousness paradox – the more conscious and coherent we become, the more the debilitating aspects of our self-consciousness retreat, reintegrated within our heightened sense of wholeness. And so, perhaps even the most committed supporter of scientific materialism may come to accept that consciousness is the key to a healthy human system and that the cultivation of both inner and outer coherence makes sense, even when subjected to the rigours of science and the logic of the left mind. If our happiness requires the release of attachments and is rooted in the relationships we develop, no-one could sensibly continue to believe that material consumption and adversarial competition are the best paths to personal wholeness, global harmony and a sustainable planetary ecosystem. Similarly, those who place their faith in any of the three monotheisms may begin to see the shortcomings of those spiritual systems, in particular the patriarchal attitudes which continue to suppress women and the dogmatic insistence of each, that theirs is the only true God. In fact, every single day people are choosing to leave behind the mechanistic and creationist worldviews, instead deciding to adopt an organic outlook and to act in a manner which is slowly cultivating the culture of integrative monism, even if few would recognize the term. However, far from forming a vanguard such individuals are only just catching onto a cultural trend which began before most of them were even born. Indeed, unbeknown to most 'members' they may now be very close to forming a global majority because the organic worldview has been growing steadily, and with increasing momentum, for at least the last 70 years.

The Organic Pioneers

The many social and political movements which radically shook up global society in the post-World War II period, particularly in the US during the 1960s, sowed the seeds of the cultural crisis we are now experiencing. By driving an agenda which was resolutely anti-war, pro-civil rights and ecologically-friendly, countless campaigns started to shift the cultural pendulum towards a new worldview which would eventually undermine and provide a viable alternative to modernism, but without invoking a lurch back to traditional, small-town creationism. The values and lifestyles which emerged are largely consistent with those of *The Cultural Creatives*, as described by Paul Ray and Sherry Ruth Anderson in their book of the same name. They identify a core value of cultural creatives as '*personal authenticity'*, in which an individual's attitudes and actions are consistent with what they genuinely believe, and describe how such coherence is derived from balancing intellectual learning with direct personal experience *'often using the perspective of whole systems and ecology'* – a distinctly whole-brained, organic outlook.[25] Ray and Anderson also detail how cultural creatives are deeply interested in their own inner world, consciousness and personal growth but, unlike the much-maligned *'New Agers'*, are also actively engaged in outer-world movements, with a powerful social conscience and a passion for politics, human rights, gender equality, environmentalism and social justice. By combining idealism with activism such individuals have been central to the growth of integrative monism and the organic worldview, consistently cultivating inner coherence via elevated consciousness and outer coherence via progressive social change. Equally illuminating is the degree to which they have undermined the foundations of scientific materialism and railed against our lowest level of consciousness by becoming:

> disenchanted with owning more stuff, materialism, greed, me-firstism, status display, glaring social inequalities of race and class, societies failure to care adequately for elders, women and children, and the hedonism and cynicism that pass for realism in modern society.[26]

Their adoption of an organic worldview is perfectly captured in their shared belief that:

> the world is too complex for linear analytic thinking now. To be smart in the global village means thinking with your stomach, thinking rhythmically, thinking organically, thinking in terms of yourself as an interwoven piece of nature.[27]

According to Ray and Anderson's extensive research, this group is large and getting larger – rising from 1 in 4 American adults in 2000 to 1 in 3 by 2008, with comparable numbers in Japan and Europe. Ray and Anderson also estimated that a further 10% of people were already transitioning towards an organic worldview so, if those growth rates have continued to the present day, we could already have reached the point where integrative monism is, in terms of population, the largest cultural perspective in the US, Europe, Japan and possibly many other countries or continents where research hasn't been conducted. What's more, Ray and Anderson credited cultural creatives with forming the core of an estimated $500 billion market for what they called *'Lifestyles of Health and Sustainability'* products across five key categories – sustainable economy, ecological lifestyles, healthy living, alternative healthcare and personal development – and to have been central to the growth of everything from wholefoods and holistic therapies to vocational vacations, yoga and hybrid cars. Such scale provides integrative monism with the potential to fundamentally reshape modern capitalism from the inside out, yet most cultural creatives are completely unaware of their collective commercial clout and are even astounded to learn just how great their numbers are.

How is it possible that such a body of people can be so large yet remain so relatively invisible? There are a number of reasons. Any culture needs the oxygen of publicity to spread its values and, in this regard, integrative monism has certainly struggled to gain momentum against scientific materialism which remains deeply embedded in all of our economic, political, social and media institutions. As a consequence, the views of cultural creatives have rarely been represented in the mainstream media nor have they yet acquired the influence to ensure that the organic world-view becomes sustainably embedded across our many societal structures. It therefore often remains the case that *'when they go to work they have to check their values at the door'*.[28] Furthermore, it is not in the nature of integrative monists to proclaim their worldview from the rooftops or to try to impose their perspective on others. They are, by definition, coherence seekers who value harmony in relationships and try to balance all standpoints into a holistic solution. Many are women – around two-thirds of core cultural creatives – but men continue to occupy the centre-ground of public discourse, often leading with a left mind which makes their attitudes more competitive and their opinions more adversarial. Finally, the many groups which make up the broad church of conscious-ness and social movements don't necessarily see themselves as being connected to each other. For example, civil rights supporters may not perceive environmentalists or anti-war protesters to be co-collaborators in a wider campaign promoting sustainable cultural coherence, indeed they may even see them as competitors for limited resources and airtime.

We therefore remain in a state of flux, poised at the edge of chaos. Amongst a large and growing group there is tacit agreement that all living organisms are essentially interconnected and that our experiences are therefore interrelated. However, there are few intellectual or institutional frameworks with which to co-ordinate and amplify this worldview, giving it common form, robust structure and a strong voice. While there are thou-sands of groups, communities, associations, networks and movements, all across the globe, which are aligned with the principles and perspectives of integrative monism, they need help to connect, intertwine and become mutually strengthening. This is particularly important when the organic worldview is up against two powerful and competitive alternatives, while simultaneously seeking to reshape, synthesise and reconcile their underlying principles and foundational premises. Elevated consciousness is an essential pre-condition but is, on its own, insufficient. We cannot simply think our way to a new future or passively hope that global peace emerges, because the forces which sustain our current culture are compelling and, if given free rein, will certainly shape a new world but not one in which harmony and happiness are pre-eminent.

If left unchecked, the continued dominance of scientific materialism – driven by an unfettered left mind and sustained by structures controlled by a cadre of elites – could easily lead to a more tyrannical form of global governance. This vision would continue to be characterized by militarism, free-market capitalism and levels of economic growth which are ultimately cancerous to our system and biosphere. An alternative vision, held by some religious fundamentalists, of a global society ordered solely in accordance with the scriptures of a single monotheism, is even more apocalyptic than the arch-modernist's dream. Opposing forces will always be a feature of our complex system but global peace requires a level of dynamic stability which can never be achieved within an overarching context of dualism, where either science or spirituality must come out on top. To grow together we must seek synthesis but the transformation required cannot be a negotiated settlement of the type the UN might broker between warring factions. The mechanistic worldview of scientific materialism and the creationist lens of the monotheisms can never ever be reconciled because they are both dominated by the left mind. Peace is therefore an impossible outcome with their approach and at their level of thinking. Only the synthesising qualities of the right mind, higher consciousness and a culture of integrative monism can reconcile our very human need for *both* science and spirit.

The self-creating properties inherent within our system demand on-going attempts to evolve to a higher level of complexity which, for human-beings and human societies, does mean ever-increasing levels of global integration. To develop healthy coherence we must successfully synthesise our innate impulses towards scientific materialism and spiritual idealism, because each is ultimately the result of the modus operandi of our two brain hemispheres – the former born of our left mind, the latter

of our right. Successful unification requires us to understand the fundamental human needs being satisfied by each impulse and to find creative
solutions which continue to meet those needs, but through their harmonious integration rather than by picking sides.

The leading 20th century sociologist Pitirim Sorokin observed that
the history of human culture played out in a dialectic between opposing
mentalities or worldviews, which he called *Sensate* and *Ideational*.[29] For
Sensate we can easily substitute 'materialistic' because it is the perspective
that the material world is the ultimate or only reality. We can also replace
Ideational with 'spiritual', for it is the worldview that true reality is
ultimately immaterial and exists beyond sensory perception. Sorokin
showed that global human history has periodically alternated between eras
dominated by either the materialistic (sensate) or spiritual (ideational)
point of view, and noted that transitions between the two were invariably
marked by the increased prevalence of war, conflicts and other crises.
Sorokin also observed that the evolution of global civilisation has occasionally been punctuated by eras he called *Idealistic*, which synthesised
the *Sensate* and *Ideational* mentalities. *Idealistic* eras were also called
'integrative' because they reconciled materialistic and spiritual perspectives, deeming that both the material and immaterial were real and
necessary for the flourishing of human culture and happiness. According
to Sorokin, in known history global civilisation has only ever undergone
two *Idealistic* or integrative periods – Classical Greece between 550BC
and 320BC and the Renaissance from 1200AD to 1500AD – and for the
past 500 years we have been within a materialistic era which Sorokin
called the *Age of Science*. He forecast the downfall of our *Sensate* culture,
'*now in its overripe stage*', but warned that the transition to an integrative
Idealistic era was not inevitable and we could just as easily flip directly
back to a spiritual *Ideational* era, as happened between the Greek Dark
Age (1200BC-900BC) and Archaic Greece (900BC-550BC) and again
from the Hellenistic-Roman era (320BC-400AD) to the Middle Ages
(400AD-1200AD). There can be little doubt that some modern-day
religious fundamentalists would dearly love to see a direct return to the
global dominance of immaterialism, bypassing the great opportunity we
have for synthesis. Nevertheless, a new Renaissance awaits us if we want
it – the potential elevation of our whole species to a higher plane of
collective wisdom, even if our rebirth can by no means be guaranteed.

How might we do more to bring it about? Well, in a nutshell we need
to wake up and take action. Adopting an organic worldview and increasing

personal consciousness are essential starting points and billions of people, possibly even a global majority, have already woken up to this perspective. However, it's not enough for integrative monists to practice yoga and diligently recycle their waste, while passively disapproving of the way our world is run. To leave our global system in the hands of those elites who have brought it to the brink of disaster, is tantamount to consigning our great-grandchildren to a life of misery or perhaps even no life at all. Much concern has understandably been expressed that we might destroy our planet and the biosphere which enables us to breathe, but this is overstating the danger and won't happen. Our biosphere is naturally self-regulating and will always eventually re-establish its own internal coherence. It is also infinitely more powerful than we are. If we damage it sufficiently, its rebalancing may well require the elimination of just one more of the millions of species which have already come and gone in evolutionary history; the one species which has done more harm to its fellow living organisms and their life-giving ecosystem than any other. While we can't live without planet Earth, planet Earth can certainly live without us. So, to avoid such an apocalyptic outcome, we must both elevate our consciousness *and* take action. Our future lies in our own hands and whatever we bring forth will be the emergent outcome of our collective thoughts and actions, the co-creation of our species and our environment. However, to bring forth a future in which peace and happiness prevail, we must first wake up and find our voice.

— 14 —

Counterbalancing Capitalism

THE ENERGY required to evolve our human system to a higher level of global integration can only come from elevated consciousness and the ordinary person becoming more active in demanding and driving fundamental changes to the way our world works. The reasons are twofold. First, most elites are too personally vested in the current system in which they have by definition succeeded, to be committed to the radical changes required if we are to avoid societal disintegration and environmental destruction. Second, those elites have the same flawed brains and are subject to the same cultural conditioning as everyone else, so have no more idea than the average person how to resolve the chaos we are experiencing. Consider the conflicts in the Middle East which created a humanitarian crisis around the Mediterranean, with millions of refugees risking their lives to seek shelter in Europe. The lack of a co-ordinated response from European and Arab nations showed a disregard for human life which was tantamount to murder by neglect. Similarly, the stand-off between the European Union and successive Greek governments over debt repayment led to punitive austerity measures which continue to cause misery to millions of ordinary Greek citizens. Many so-called experts have commented but few have articulated the case for prioritizing human considerations over economic matters. It would be rather ironic if Greece, the cradle of Western civilisation, were to feature prominently when the house of cards it helped to create finally falls, and make no mistake, the end of modern capitalism and its cultural architect – scientific materialism – has already begun. The degree to which their dominance is already undermined makes change entirely inevitable. The landscape may still look much the same on the surface but subterranean tremors are shaking their foundations and the tectonic plates are shifting. The cracks appearing in Greece and elsewhere are early warning signs of what is still to come. What we don't yet know is whether transformation will lead to global disintegration, with wars based on competing world-views resulting in the imposition of a more authoritarian style of governance with even more materialistic militarism. Or whether we can bring forth a global mind which unites the hemispheres, reconciles science with spirit and produces harmonious global integration resulting in world peace.

For the latter to occur, ordinary people will have to exert far greater influence on how the world we co-create unfolds. It is no longer a viable option to delegate decision-making to elites and to empower them to impose their views on the masses by means of economic or military might. Ordinary people operating with elevated consciousness in sufficient numbers are a pre-requisite, because only at a higher level of awareness can we realize our deep connection to our embodied selves, to each other, to all living organisms and to our whole planet. Such cognitive elevation can provide the essential human capital needed, to begin to counterbalance the pernicious effects of our narrow focus on capitalist economics. Absent higher collective consciousness it is simply impossible to see how enough people could become sufficiently agitated by the corruption in our current system, to mobilize themselves to modify the many political and social structures which protect and sustain it. For example, only 'people power' is able to elect new political leaders with mandates for policies which encourage economic co-operation and intercultural cohesion. Only consumer power can coerce companies into adopting growth goals and commercial strategies which are conducive to environmental sustainability and social responsibility. Only human empathy will insist upon the hand of friendship being extended to all individuals, irrespective of class, creed or colour, and on shared values being prioritised above economic value. It is only through civic engagement that people will find others who share their passion for debating and driving the kinds of social change they envision. It is only by exercising their democratic rights that ordinary people may insist upon an entirely new form of direct e-politics, which ensures that politicians hear their voices and accurately represent their views. It is only via social activism that such people will come together to reshape societies and rebuild the many communities which have been ravaged by modern capitalism and scientific materialism.

For all of this to happen, two conditions must be present over and above higher consciousness. First, as many people as possible must be involved in reshaping societal structures because it is only in large groups, representing a genuine cross-section of communities and classes, that we can be sure of hemispheric balance. Democracy is central to this but a type of democracy which goes way beyond the representative republicanism we typically have today, which invariably means devolving decision-making to elites. Second, all participants must adopt an attitude of episte-mological modesty because there is not an individual on the planet, nor has there ever been, with the intellectual ability to redesign such a complex system so that it produces guaranteed results. We aren't even capable of understanding ourselves, never mind genuinely comprehending the causes of experienced phenomena or accurately predicting future events. Even a grand master cannot predict how a game of chess will unfold or reduce an end-game back down into its constituent moves, and chess is an infinitely simpler system than global human society. Our supreme overconfidence in our own ability has several upsides but it also makes us rather delusional. Individually we're really not very smart animals but our ability to create a coherent global culture at least gives us the chance to be collectively clever. As Socrates suggested, the smartest thing we could do right now is recognize our own ignorance.

The Organic Approach

So we must approach the challenges ahead with heightened awareness, authentic democracy, active engagement and intellectual modesty. Adopting an organic worldview further informs us that we must abandon the idea of a world in which predictable outcomes can be ensured as the result of linear relationships. Live organisms cannot be repaired like machines but instead will heal themselves if exposed to environmental conditions which are conducive to their coherence. In *Collapse*, his study of how civilisations succeed or fail, anthropologist Jared Diamond identifies many sources of societal breakdown but concludes that the single cause over which humans have most control is whether or not they adapt their values to changing environmental conditions.[1] Just as a plant needs water and sunshine to be healthy, our global system needs the nourishment of a values-based approach because only by aligning ourselves with universal human values, do we stand a chance of bringing warring factions together and of creating the cultural conditions from which peace may emerge. The organic worldview is critical to cultivating such conditions because it perceives primary reality as the relationships between entities, rather than the entities themselves, and is organized around the principle of energy flowing to create new forms in which opposites are unified through oscillation and interaction. From this perspective, building new economic, political, social or spiritual structures which are solid and unchanging will never work, because our experiences are produced by the dynamic flow of data and made flexible by our free will, yet all the while driven by the underlying structural 'rules' from which experienced phenomena emerge. The mechanistic tools of the left mind are therefore accommodated but only as an enfolded part of the organic approach of the right mind, in which determinism *and* emergence, reductionism *and* holism, analysis *and* synthesis, competition *and* co-operation, intellect *and* intuition and so on, are all seen as complementary capabilities which, when used in appropriate balance, keep the whole system coherent and healthy. This understanding of how living systems actually work is completely at odds with how the social Darwinists of scientific materialism choose to see life; in terms of adversarial struggle in which one party must objectively win while the other must lose. This wrong-headed view of nature legitimized an approach to life, based on greed, exploitation and warfare, which has had a disastrous impact on humanity and our environment. However, this approach no longer has any basis in science and is therefore without possible justification because it fails to incorporate the contrary, yet integrative, principles via which living organisms self-organize.

Such is the complexity of our global system that the very best we can hope for is to develop local rules which are consistent with universal human values, and then hope that our desired outcomes emerge, all the while monitoring progress and retaining the flexibility to change the rules again if necessary. The concept of 'rules' perhaps needs to be revisited at this point because what we mean is not described by any conventional definition of the word. Recall in Darwin's *'tangled bank'* how the local rules were the small number of inter-related factors, such as the food-chain hierarchy and ratio of predators to prey, from which a pattern of order emerged as the result of each organism exercising their free will to oscillate between competitive and co-operative behaviours, in a mutual dance of co-existence. Our global human system is exponentially more complex than a small countryside ecosystem and no individual or group of any size has the cognitive capacity to write rules, in a conventional sense, which would be guaranteed to deliver desired global outcomes. The local rules, in this context, are the everyday structures of

COUNTERBALANCING CAPITALISM

ordinary life which make up civic society – all of the schools, associations, clubs, companies, colleges, churches, charities, guilds, groups, movements, institutions, organizations and establishments which are given life and sustained by the energy with which people engage with them. Edmund Burke called them '*little platoons*' and those which survive and prosper are those which are given greatest on-going endorsement, while those which struggle or die are those from which the life force of human energy is withdrawn.

Local rules, therefore, aren't created by any individual or even by politicians but form organically, as the result of where everyone in a community chooses to focus their attention and energy and how involved they become in challenging or changing 'how things work around here'. The natural growth of new rules necessitates the interweaving of new ideas with those already in existence, as well as the reshaping of societal structures to support and sustain new initiatives, but without significantly restricting the direction they take. When adopting the principle of epistemological modesty, no theory or model may be more fundamental than any other, so ideas may be simple, complicated, easy-to-accept, controversial, multi-layered or multi-valent but must be allowed to grow, change, shrink or die as per the energy-flow afforded to them by civic society. The transformation of complex systems must be process-led rather than content-led, recognizing that while the activities of machines are driven by their structure the exact reverse is the case with live systems, whose structure or form is shaped by the nature of the active energy flowing through them. While machines are manufactured using specific parts assembled to a fixed blueprint, living organisms require a higher degree of internal flexibility because it is only by ensuring information flow, fluctuation, feedback loops and a level of free will that we enable living organisms to adapt to changing environmental conditions. Our left mind, of course, hates such fluid uncertainty but nevertheless has a critical role to play. Within healthy living systems opposites must have space to oscillate, creating competition, contradiction and even mild conflict, but are ultimately unified in dynamic stability by the order restored through self-organization. In human systems it is ultimately our free will, exercised at the local level, which makes all the difference to what emerges at the global level because only our conscious choices can overcome the unconscious influence of culture on our actions. Free will exercised with an organic worldview, higher consciousness and intellectual modesty, then activated through genuine democracy and enthusiastic engagement in civic society are all pre-requisites for growing the global mind to a higher plane of integrated cognition.

So, having scoped out the necessary approach to the challenges ahead and having accepted that we can't define in advance what the local rules should be, how do we go about creating the environmental conditions which would be conducive to their development? Thankfully we don't need to begin with a blank sheet of paper, as our past can once again powerfully illuminate our path to a better future. Ironically one of the historical figures we can learn most from, about how to reshape modern capitalism, is its original architect and the founding father of economics, Adam Smith. We can learn from Smith because the capitalism of the 21st century, under the dangerously unrestrained direction of the left mind, has strayed a very long way from the form he envisioned back in the mid-1700s.

Cultivating Social Capital

Although he identified that healthy competition would help to regulate the market by keeping the self-interest of all players in check, Adam Smith nevertheless remained concerned that undesirable excesses would still emerge if humankind was given free and unfettered rein. Smith did not view economics as a purely financial system but as part of a much larger project in which civic society would play an essential role in moderating each individual's selfish impulses, to create a truly democratic market economy. Unfortunately, much of Smith's noble vision has now been lost in the modern-day *'dismal science'*, with its numbers obsession, price-modelling, multiplier effects and indifference curves, but to undo the damaging effects of the left mind we only need to review what Smith intended, to help us refocus on the bigger picture.

Civic society consists of all the structures of everyday local life – Burke's *'little platoons'* – plus larger institutions such as governments and corporations which are ultimately also sustained by ordinary people. Together, they form the complex web of interconnected networks in which we are all embedded and every day they act as the synapses which ensure the self-regulating and self-creating tendencies of our human system. They do so by setting the standards of behaviour, sharing the rules of reciprocity, nurturing the mutual trust and punishing the malfeasance, which are all essential for the smooth functioning of a market-based democracy. Social scientists call the sum of such structures *'social capital'* because, like human capital and economic capital, they are key resources in influencing how well things work in human societies.

Societies with strong social capital have dense social networks, a widely shared culture and high levels of trust, which all act as self-regulating forces because, as Adam Smith identified, personal reputation is a powerful human motivator. Smith understood that, as inherently social animals, we are driven by a desire to seek and be worthy of the approval of others, and that this universal human need incentivises the self-interested individual towards virtuous behaviour. According to Smith, our search for social approval appears in our mind as an '*impartial spectator*' which moderates our selfish impulses by enabling us to see ourselves as others see us, through placing ourselves in their shoes.[2] Today we would call this particular moral sentiment 'empathy' and, although we would be unlikely to find it mentioned in a modern economics textbook, Smith considered it to be fundamental to a healthy market economy. However, Smith argued that it would only emerge with full form and effect as a result of the many social networks – both economic *and* non-economic – which made up civic society.

Smith was first and foremost a moral philosopher so his overarching concern was for the betterment of society and, rather unusually for his time, he was deeply concerned about the welfare of all people including the poorest and most disadvantaged. Smith's great genius lay in understanding how humans are *actually* motivated and in his ability to identify societal structures which would simultaneously reward self-interest *and* benefit society as a whole. The free market moderated by competition was one such structure but Smith knew that competition, on its own, was insufficient to counterbalance the powerful influence on the individual of acquisitive avarice. He reasoned that inner virtues such as sympathy, duty, tolerance, fairness and self-control, also had to be cultivated from a young age and sustained throughout adulthood. He further believed that non-economic institutions such as family, school and church must play a vital role in nourishing such values. For Smith, all the organizations of civic society must act as social synapses through which feedback about non-virtuous behaviour, which would damage the reputation of an errant individual, should be given and duly acted upon to restore equilibrium. Smith recognized that if left unchecked, self-interest and its many undesirable manifestations could easily over-whelm society and result in behaviours which were destructive to the common good but also, in the long term, to the miscreants themselves.

He therefore built a civilising blueprint, which balanced our natural self-interest with the creation of structures through which social capital was strengthened by civic institutions, thus cultivating cultural conditions in which virtuous behaviour was beneficial to *both* individuals and society as a whole.

Smith intuitively understood the many flaws in human cognition and character, so he envisioned capitalism as a competitive economic model within a wider moral framework, which incentivised co-operation through mutual trust, reciprocity and fairness, all built upon a very personal desire to maintain a positive reputation. His conception of a healthy, coherent society was one in which the market would create wealth, while all other civic institutions would cultivate moderating virtues such as empathy, fellowship, generosity and altruism, for the common benefit of everyone. Thus economic capital, human capital, social capital and moral capital would all grow and be mutually reinforcing in a manner which was wholly democratic. In Smith's design:

> direct domination by political elites would be replaced by a network of institutions which promoted self-control among politically free citizens, while the rising level of material comfort would make it possible to expand sympathy and concern for others.[3]

Although the world he lived in was less complex than ours, Smith was nevertheless a master at balancing ideas which could integrate the economic structures of capitalism with the social and moral structures of civilisation, in a way which accommodated both the realism of human self-interest and the idealism of promulgating the greatest wealth, health and happiness for the whole of society. Contrary to critics of his system, at no time did Smith ever advocate unfettered economic freedom as a method of equitably distributing wealth via an *'invisible hand'*, indeed he remained deeply concerned that a relentless drive for profit would ultimately be destructive to social justice.[4] For him, capitalism would only work as he envisioned if individual self-interest was subsumed within a greater common good, underpinned by the moderating influence of non-economic civic institutions, more than by economic structures.

In many ways Smith's *Theory of Moral Sentiments* was therefore the 'bigger' book and should have been more influential than *The Wealth of Nations*, but while the latter still forms the bedrock of modern economics, the former has almost been forgotten. By now there's perhaps little need to elucidate what went wrong; suffice to say that the left mind of scientific materialism intervened. Not only did the Industrial Revolution shatter the structures and synapses which sustained social capital, the desire to convert all social sciences into 'proper' Newtonian sciences cleaved the material elements of economics from Smith's moral aspects, hiving off the latter to the fields of philosophy, divinity and the other humanities. Although some eminent economists, like Alfred Marshall, did continue Smith's legacy in calling for the quaintly Victorian '*economic chivalry*', the reunification of the material with the moral has mainly been absent from economic discourse and theory ever since.[5] Typically today, we don't see any connection between moral virtues and the incentive-driven mechanisms of the market because, since Marshall, economics has been increasingly built into a quantitative, technical science rather than anything to do with ethics or humanity. Over time, their capacity to drive fiscal growth became the sole benchmark against which all new ideas would be assessed, and financial prosperity became the primary measurement of the health of civic society. Other essential measurements of the 'benefits' of capitalism, including social, moral and human capital, all soon became subordinated to the only measurement deemed to matter – economic capital.

The Great Depression of the 1930s caused mass unemployment and sent a wave of economists scurrying to find a solution, amongst them a former Cambridge University student of Alfred Marshall, John Maynard Keynes. Keynes quickly became the shining light of modern economics by deducing that unemployment grows when commercial activity contracts during downturns in the business cycle, and by showing that government intervention, in the form of increased spending and other fiscal stimuli, could kick-start demand and pull an economy out of recession. Contrary to Adam Smith, Keynes placed politicians in a position where they could directly manipulate the market – an opportunity power-hungry people are never likely to pass up. Smith had seen only a restricted role for government and considered that politicians should largely leave the market alone, but Keynes placed them front and centre on what was increasingly seen as the most important of all social stages – the economy. Although Keynes had been a student of Alfred Marshall, the Victorian values of his teacher were at odds with the ethics of individual freedom and self-expression which were flowing throughout Edwardian England at that time. While Marshall had advocated economic chivalry and wanted to alleviate poverty so that all people could participate in the economy as a means of living more virtuous lives,[6] Keynes '*cared not a lick for*

A WORLD IN TWO MINDS

saving the souls of the poor' but *'located justice in the public manipulation of aggregate economic forces in the service of full employment'.*[7] While Smith and Marshall had understood the market as a complex, organic system, and as a subset of broader civic society connected through social networks and moderated by moral sentiments, Keynes brought the focus of classic science to the fore in seeing economics as an isolated entity which could be dissected, analysed and brought under the cold, impassionate control of the left mind. By the 1950s Milton Friedman and *the Chicago School* would challenge Keynesian principles, proposing that government involvement in remedial intervention be restricted to the stabilisation of money, but while Friedman resurrected Smith's *laissez-faire* attitudes all traces of his moral sentiments had disappeared. From Keynes onwards, the fight for macro-economic influence left behind the worldly philosophies of Smith and Marshall and became solely based around competing ideologies of governmental intervention – a truly dismal science indeed.

Ever since Keynes, we have effectively devolved management of our economies to government officials who have sought to manipulate markets in a manner consistent with conservative or liberal ideologies, yet with a shared, narrow focus and a common belief in the primacy of the individual over the common weal. This is still evident in the modern-day neo-conservative and neo-liberal consensus, although there are certainly some differences. Conservatives tend to prioritise personal freedom in the economic sphere, while demanding that their rights be protected in the social sphere through the imposition of laws which address their broad range of moral concerns. Liberals more often emphasise individual freedom in the social sphere, while demanding justice in the economic sphere to address their narrower range of moral concerns around care, liberty and fairness. The issue is not therefore that politicians are oblivious to moral matters or unaware of the need to balance individual freedom with social order. The issue is that, unlike Adam Smith, they usually have no idea how to do so. Like most of the economics 'experts' advising them, politicians tend to approach issues from a mechanistic perspective, believing too resolutely in linear determinism and focussing too narrowly on economic levers as the only solution to very complex social problems. Both the political left and right have consistently viewed economic incentives as the only method of modifying human behaviour and have re-distributed material wealth with varying effects, but always with unintended consequences in the social and moral spheres. The examples are endless. Urban planning which enables out-of-town retail development but also damages local business communities, welfare policies which protect children but also encourage young women to have babies out of wedlock, healthcare provision which provides a safety net for every individual but also diminishes personal responsibility for wellbeing and social behaviour. More broadly, global markets have brought prices down but also shifted power to nations with natural resources or cheaper workforces.

To be fair to modern-day politicians and economists they themselves are almost certainly a product of scientific materialism, which has provided their mechanistic worldview and the unsuitable set of linear levers with which they consistently try to solve societal issues. Nevertheless, attempting to repair a complex adaptive system with a Newtonian toolkit makes exactly as much sense as trying to nurture a plant using a spanner and, in many cases, the more governments have sought to bolster economic capital the more they have inadvertently weakened social, human and moral capital. Adam Smith had a brilliantly intuitive understanding of complex systems, centuries before the term was even coined, and his genius lay in recognizing that while the free market couldn't be controlled, its excesses could – indeed must – be moderated by the moralizing function of civic society. In Smith's vision the role of government in the free market was minimal and should be restricted to the enforcement of contract law and the administration of property rights. He did, however, consider that government officials had an important part to play in setting the highest moral standards, thereby acting as ethical exemplars for all other members of society.

It's difficult to know exactly what Smith would make of the deputy speaker of the UK's House of Lords snorting cocaine from a prostitute's breasts, but suffice to say that standards in public office may have slipped to suboptimal levels in the 21st century. In fact, so frequent are the scandals involving politicians that it is increasingly perceived by the general public that the entire political class is corrupt and anti-democratic, with unelected lawmakers holding too much sway and elected representatives actually working for big businesses and at the behest of the banks. Civic society no longer exerts any significant influence on markets, so we must now rely on shareholders to provide the essential moralizing function which moderates corporate excess. However, both banks and businesses are managed to maximise shareholder returns, creating a clear conflict of interest. Even in the unlikely event that shareholders are of a mind to complain, they may well find corporate shareholding to be dominated by abstract institutional investors rather than by real individuals who share their concerns. In fact, bank shareholders, whether individual or institutional, often provide a very small amount of total capital – for example, balance sheets of major UK banks show that shareholders provide just 4.9% of capital at Barclays, 5.1% at Lloyds and 5.8% at RBS. The remainder is provided by savers and others creditors, who have no power to elect directors or influence business practices.[8] Even in non-banks, it's difficult to find a FTSE 100 company where shareholders provide more than 50% of total capital and it's even rarer to find businesses where the most important corporate stakeholders of all – employees – have a say in appointing directors or hold a representative seat on the Board which might allow them to provide any sort of moralizing input.

It's worth stressing, of course, that not every banker or company director is inherently immoral but instead simply stating that the structures sustaining modern corporations and the marketplace do not always compensate for the lack of civic society, in providing much needed counterbalance to the drive for material growth. Companies themselves are complex adaptive systems, so while employees may well act morally and with positive intent, the effect of their collective actions, guided as they so often are by profit goals and a competitive will-to-win, can easily produce emergent outcomes which damage environments or negatively impact other stakeholders. In the absence of internal structures which incentivise stakeholder vigilance and enable democratic intervention, it is effectively left to company directors to self-regulate the morality of their decisions, yet executive remuneration packages often provide incentives which directly conflict with this responsibility. Furthermore, even if the public don't like their actions, or indeed if immoral behaviour strays into illegality, company directors are almost always protected by limited liability legislation. The problem, therefore, isn't with capitalism per se but with the manner in which the market is managed and, in particular, the way in which large corporations are owned, structured and run.

Adam Smith's model works because it shows an intrinsic understanding of how the human mind actually operates. We are slaves to self-interested passions which can easily overwhelm us and manifest in undesirable actions, unless moderated by self-control which is in short supply for some of us all of the time and for all of us some of the time. Smith identified our desire for the approval of others as a universal human need which, under the watchful eye of civic society, would induce self-regulating behaviour. The need for self-approval provides no such moderating effect. Furthermore, a genuinely free market operating on a level playing field is truly democratic because all members of society can participate in its self-creating and self-regulating dynamics, via tit-for-tat. However, our modern-day devolution of the market to political parties for their self-interested interference in the economy, under the strong influence of anti-democratic, self-regulating banks and businesses, is a very long way from Smith's vision of a democratic market economy. He wanted to replace the powerful mercantile institutions which held 18th century society under strict control, with a free market in which everyone could participate and which was unified by social capital and moderated by moral sentiments, converting self-interest into common wealth and lifting all individuals to higher levels of ethical behaviour. Smith warned that this could only work if society created a web of civic institutions which would direct individual self-interest towards the virtuous behaviours necessary for collective social order and the common good. In our liberal, modern age we wouldn't necessarily welcome the return of values such as '*prudence, vigilance, circumspection, temperance, constancy* or *firmness*' but according to his biographer Robert Skidelsky, John Maynard Keynes did confess that something of great worth had been lost in the abandonment of Smith's sentiments and Marshall's desire for economic chivalry.[9] Keynes regretted that the intellectuals of his Edwardian age so resolutely denigrated Victorian virtue, observing that the young '*who are brought up without it, will never get much out of life*' while believing his own generation '*had the best of both worlds*'.[10]

Perhaps Keynes did finally come to appreciate the essential role of moral capital in moderating the many dangers of economic capitalism. While we cannot return to the days of Adam Smith, to understand our morality, how we came to lose touch with it and how we might rediscover it, we must first go back once again to ancient Greece.

Growing Moral Capital

The Greek word *eudaimonia* is constructed from '*eu*' meaning good and '*daimon*' meaning spirit, and is usually translated to mean '*human flourishing*', '*wellbeing*' or simply '*happiness*'. Socrates was perhaps the first Western figure to suggest that happiness was achievable as the result of deliberate human effort, rather than a gift from the Gods, and he believed that the key to being in good spirits lay in the cultivation of the soul. Aristotle later considered *eudaimonia* to be the ultimate goal of life and saw a strong connection between living a good life and doing good in life. He thought that the cultivation of morality was the essential ingredient in both inner and outer worlds, and concluded that the pursuit of *eudaimonia* was therefore an '*activity of the soul in accordance with virtue*'. In his *Nicomachean Ethics* he further explained that the lifelong cultivation of virtue was valuable because it allowed us to live in accordance with our true nature, to improve our inherent character and to strive for the good of society, not just ourselves. According to Aristotle, *eudaimonia* would be achieved through virtuous acts because doing good deeds in the outer world would automatically nourish our inner world. Virtue should therefore be desired as a reward in itself, rather than for any short-term pleasures or material benefits it may bring. For the development of virtuous behaviour he advised following a '*golden mean*' between deficiencies and excesses, so the cultivation of courage, for example, would guard against extremes of cowardice or recklessness. Like many of his predecessors Aristotle understood the essential balance in nature and advocated moderation in all things, warning against extremes like avarice or indolence and observing that regular practice and self-discipline were required to resist the many temptations to stray from the virtuous path. *Eudaimonia* would be attained through habitually positive behaviour and the lifelong cultivation of the virtues which were essential to making a human life complete.

Aristotle was just one of many philosophers, throughout the ages, to have discerned a link between wholeness, happiness and the mutually-reinforcing relationship between behaving well in the outer world and being well in our inner world. Indeed Buddha himself taught that we should set our heart on doing good deeds because to do so would fill the heart with joy, and he gave us guidance in his Noble Eightfold Path which, like Aristotle, advocates the balanced moderation of a '*middle way*'. In fact, throughout history many spiritual systems have not only valued virtuous behaviour but have set out practical methods through which it could be inculcated in followers, via self-affirmation or parental and religious instruction. These methods have almost always come in the form of maxims, combined with procedures for continual practice to maintain discipline and reinforce good habits, because the ancients often had a better understanding of how the human brain actually works, than did those in later periods; knowledge which we have only rediscovered in relatively recent times. They may not have explicitly defined levels of consciousness but they clearly operated at and advocated our highest, spiritual level where our whole neurophysiological self is fully integrated with our sense of soul. Indeed, it was probably beyond their comprehension that it was even possible to shrink the human condition to our current shrivelled state.

As the ancients understood, our morality is rooted in feelings rather than thoughts; our intuitive sense of right or wrong bubbles up from deep in our unconscious via the right mind, for conscious appraisal by the self-controlling function of the left mind. Our instinctive, emotional impulses drive many of our actions so feelings of guilt, shame or embarrassment are an important part of our cognitive equipment, designed to keep us safe by alerting us to the need for self-regulation if our passions may lead to emotional, social or spiritual harm. Buddha, Aristotle, Adam Smith and others recognized that moral sentiments emerge in the form of feelings, and that tendencies towards either excessive or deficient actions can easily overwhelm the self-control of reason, knocking us off the moderate, moral path. They saw that the only way to control our passions was to condition the unconscious mind, through deliberate and disciplined drill work, to ensure that it automatically offers up the appropriate action in every situation rather than relying on the rationality of a lazy left mind. They also grasped that, as social animals, we instinctively understand the need to build healthy relationships and a coherent environment for the mutual benefit of everyone with whom we share our space. Feelings of fairness, love and empathy therefore also arise in order to guide us towards virtuous actions which will benefit both ourselves and others. Moral emotions, both positive and negative, are essential actors within our embodied cognitive system, which serve to amplify behaviours which promote health and well-being while dampening behaviours which cause harm or sickness, in both our inner or outer realms. In systems terms, therefore, moral behaviour can be considered to be any action which promotes coherence while immorality involves all actions which create incoherence.

When a society loses the social and moral capital it needs to moderate personal passions, unrestrained impulses easily and often manifest in excessive consumption or other aberrant actions because the rational left mind is simply incapable of over-riding the visceral desires which over-power it. So whether we want more food or new shoes or a bigger house, we tend to buy whatever we can afford. In the absence of equally powerful virtues, ingrained in the unconscious and maintained through strength of character, we are left at the mercy of our impulses, many of which are actually cultural mores rather than natural instincts. No-one really needs excessive calories or more clothes than they can wear but, when our moral compass is guided solely by reason, we often find ourselves weak in the face of temptation because the rational mind is simply no match for powerful emotions. Yet our rationality isn't made redundant. We often see ourselves as free-willed, self-contained and separate entities, so may reason that any decisions we make which only affect ourselves have no moral component, because we are sole arbiters of what is good for us. We may consider that our autonomy entitles us to engage in self-harmful activities should we choose to do so. We may further reason that others are equally autonomous, so if they are offended by our actions it is because they choose to respond in a way which hurts their own feelings, and they could just as easily select a different response. The emotional pain they experience is therefore their responsibility, not ours. When our morality is located in logic and governed by reason we easily become masters, in our own minds at least, of reversing nature's process so reason comes first and emotion second. Of course we can't *actually* reverse the cognitive sequence – emotion always comes first – but we can use reason to reassure ourselves that we are being perfectly moral. We do so by rationalizing a comforting narrative in which our behaviour is fully justified, without even being aware that the emotions driving us are actually negative feelings such as selfishness, greed, anger, jealousy or lust, which haven't been subjected to self-control or moral moderation.

The roots of our current societal incoherence are therefore inextricably intertwined with an underlying moral malaise, which fails to self-regulate and restore order within our human system. Under the influence of scientific materialism, and in the absence of sufficient moral moderation by civic institutions, self-interest ran amok and created individualistic societies, most of which still operate to the '*survival of the fittest*' mantra of social Darwinism. With this, the much welcome liberation of humankind from the suffocating stranglehold of the monotheisms, failed dramatically in its modernizing project. In making each individual their own God and in shifting their source of knowledge from collective faith to personal reason, the Enlightenment empowered the self-driven human to not only pursue their own fortune but to also determine the values with which they should do so – values based on logic rather than emotion. Morality therefore became vested in the individual rather than in civic society; society which was subsequently disintegrated by an Industrial Revolution which also served to dissociate humans from their own embodied emotions – the seat of their moral impulses – leaving them able to operate at only their lowest, psychological level of consciousness. Secularization gradually diminished the influence of the Church and, in the increasing absence of moral guidance from above, human reason became the sole arbiter of right and wrong for the individual in the modern world. Morality was thus transformed from feeling to thought, running directly counter to how the mind actually works. Morals became pluralistic and relativized, with no absolute imperatives, objective ethical standards or Platonic *Ideals* against which human behaviour could be judged.

However, this transformation made the social scientists of the late Enlightenment deeply uncomfortable, increasingly conditioned as they were by the maxims of Newtonian science and Cartesian reason. Their empirical observations continued to accurately assess that ethical behaviour was highly contextual so the subject of morality didn't easily fit into their new scientific framework, in which the abstract and general took precedence over the contextual and particular. Newtonian science works by identifying the smallest number of universal laws then reapplying them across the largest range of situations. Morality was far too messy a topic for this modern mind-set, so science had very little to say about it and it fell from favour as an essential subject for study. Nevertheless, with its locus now clearly in the head and with the triumph of reason over emotion firmly established, society would fundamentally alter how it provided moral instruction.

The philosopher Edmund Pincoffs argues that the effect was to shift the focus of ethical education away from the cultivation of intrinsic virtue and towards solving moral quandaries.[11] Instead of learning what sort of personal characteristics they should aspire to develop into adulthood, children began to be taught how to think about the ethical dilemmas they might face in everyday situations and this shift served to weaken morality and narrow its sphere of influence. If morality is only about problem solving, rather than deep personal virtue, it automatically becomes a shallower consideration and one which is processed exclusively in the head rather than in the heart, the gut or the soul. Moral issues which should be dealt with at the highest level of consciousness are therefore dealt with at only the lowest, psychological level, where our reason is incapable of controlling our most powerful passions. Moral decision-making also becomes a less frequent pastime, weakening intrinsic virtue through lack of habituation, because only occasionally do we perceive any moral dimension in the day-to-day issues we are dealing with.

Thus, while the ancient world saw personal virtue as a sort of inner garden worth cultivating over a whole lifetime, the modern world tends to see it as a toolkit marked 'morality'; to be taken down occasionally from a dust-covered shelf and replaced after use – the organic versus the mechanistic worldview writ large, yet not always obvious when we have all been born in the modern era. Ancient societies recognized the need to nurture inner virtue from a young age, in order to ensure that the emotional impulses reason was able to act upon were already well balanced, thereby conditioning the individual to tread a moderate path between excess and deficiency. In the absence of ingrained virtuous instincts or the self-discipline to control those which aren't, the modern mind is ill-prepared for moral cogitation. Moreover, and as a compensatory mechanism, modernism simply narrowed the scope of our moral considerations via an increasingly myopic education, so we no longer consider most issues to even have an ethical dimension to them.

At low levels of awareness we simply don't consider how everything in our human system is connected, so aren't conscious of the impact our decisions have on wider society. Yet, if choosing to buy our meat from an out-of-town supermarket means that the local butcher goes out of business, isn't that a moral decision? If we buy sportswear from a supplier which employs 'sweatshop' labour practices, even in another country, isn't that a moral decision? If we purchase coffee from a company which avoids paying corporation tax, or enjoy share dividends from a bank which helps wealthy individuals evade income tax, aren't these moral decisions? If we vote for a political party which imposes austerity on the poorest in society, pushing them further into poverty, isn't that a moral decision? The more we restrict our moral considerations to infrequent quandaries and the more our everyday decisions become devoid of moral concern, the more inevitable it becomes that our morality is weakened and less likely to cultivate intrinsic virtue or benefit society. Like an underused muscle, our morality will slowly atrophy and will no longer be an emotional reward in itself, as part of a life-long journey towards self-actualization, but will become a rare consideration in which risk and reward are subjectively rational.

In *After Virtue*, philosopher Alasdair MacIntyre suggests that the moral frameworks of Enlightenment philosophers were doomed to failure from the very beginning because, having abandoned the teleological structure provided by Aristotle's *eudaimonia,* the ethical discourse of the Enlightenment was reduced to nothing more than an incoherent list of meaningless words and definitions.[12] Shorn of overarching purpose, the behaviours emerging from such a framework would also inevitably be incoherent. MacIntyre further attributes failure to the act of reducing moral philosophy to mere opinion, when virtues should be based on an understanding of the *telos* (or purpose) rather than simply subjective. Finally, he attributes failure to ascribing moral agency to the individual without appreciating that, because morality is an integral part of society, interpretation of the *telos* must lie with the group, giving them moral authority as the ultimate arbiter of ethical behaviour.

French sociologist Emile Durkheim coined the term '*anomie*' to describe a society in which there are no shared values, norms of behaviour or agreed moral standards to be jointly upheld.[13] In anomic societies individuals are free to do exactly as they please, but the absence of a shared ethic can easily lead to the fragmentation of social identity, rejection of any self-regulating values, a breakdown of community bonds, increased anti-social behaviour and even to civic unrest. Without dampening feedback to quickly restore order, negative behaviour can easily amplify until it runs out of control. One of the best measures of anomie in society is the degree to which a community responds to curb anti-social behaviour or chooses to turn a blind eye to it. In 1982 social scientists James Wilson and George Kelling introduced their '*broken windows*' theory which has since been widely influential in shaping police policy in New York and elsewhere, and which succinctly demonstrates the effects of anomie.[14] Picture an empty building with a few broken windows. If they are left unrepaired, studies show an increased likelihood that more windows will soon be smashed and, if no remedial action is taken, the building may eventually be broken into, vandalised or even set on fire. However, if the broken windows are quickly replaced, the chances of further vandalism are reduced. A successful strategy is therefore to solve problems when they are small, because doing so signals that the community has standards and cares enough to uphold them. In the post-modern world we are conditioned to keep ourselves to ourselves, to mind our own business and to live and let live in the name of liberty. However, the evidence strongly suggests that moral standards being enforced actually encourages individual self-control and social harmony, while moral pluralism and complete personal freedom only lead to anomie.

The Effects of Anomie

When moral capital declines along with social and human capital, we become the atomistic, anomic societies we live in today. The role of the state invariably expands to try to fill the gaps created by societal disintegration and a whole host of functions, once performed by community groups, charities, volunteers or a rich network of social relationships, are left to the state to deliver. Private charity in the UK reached an all-time, per-capita high (in proportion to total wealth) during the Victorian era of Alfred Marshall, but since the moralizing function of society was effectively devolved to governments, banks and businesses post-Keynes, there can be little doubt that Western societies have become less caring.[15] Nowadays, citizens tend to pay taxes and view care of the poor, elderly or vulnerable as part of their return on investment, rather than the moral responsibility of individuals or communities. They may elect a slightly more or less benevolent political party but broadly accept that none of the major parties really care for anything other than power and cold, hard economics. While few of us would wish to return to Victorian times when young couples were humiliated before disapproving church congregations for indulging in '*ante-nuptial fornication*' and other such 'sins', shared moral standards and social approbation are essential to the regulation of human behaviour. While elevated personal consciousness can reconnect us to our nobler sense of self, it is, on its own, perhaps insufficient to ensure adequate self-regulation. In the modern age very few of us have been brought up with the daily practices needed to deeply ingrain virtue and self-discipline, so some degree of external influence is still required to keep us on the straight and narrow. Even for those individuals with deep morality written right through them it's still difficult to remain ethical in society, if surrounded by scoundrels or if their high moral standards mark them out as a soft touch. Civilisations need the moralizing effect of social pressure to self-regulate because, without it, the options are either increased governmental or religious control, or anarchy.

In nations with dense social networks and strong civic institutions, people can clearly see the connections from family to community, community to local government and local government to national government, but in atomistic societies, where no such connections are obvious, trust in government automatically diminishes. Fragmentation and factionalism are inevitable, as individuals split into groups and become suspicious of the intentions of others. Civic order, previously maintained organically via social and moral capital, is replaced by the mechanistic rule of law, which can only be upheld hierarchically through force and an increasingly intrusive state, further alienating government from the electorate. Community groups like Neighbourhood Watch are replaced by CCTV cameras and, having devolved a little more of the function of civic society to government, individuals become even less likely to interfere in others' affairs as it's no longer their role, but that of the police, to protect others' property or to ensure their safety. However, secular societies can't legislate for morality so as the written law – the black and white rules so beloved of the left mind – become the official arbiter of right and wrong, morality becomes even more marginalized and is replaced by less nuanced notions of legal and illegal. Ethical questions become questions of law and moral decisions are no longer guided by deep, emotional virtues but by cold, rational calculations of reward versus the risk of getting caught. In this type of society, the self-serving autonomy of each individual becomes progressively more sovereign and, as the same right is afforded to others, anomie begets anomie on a downward spiral of social and moral disintegration. This is particularly dangerous in the 21st century when so many nations are pursuing policies of economic austerity, resulting in the function of the state being rolled back, yet no compensatory measures are being taken to fill the gap created via refocussed ethical education or revitalised civic institutions which could rebuild much-needed moral and social capital. The inevitable outcome therefore isn't the automatic regrowth of Victorian-style virtue, volunteering or charity but the expansion of the void in which there is no safety net for the most vulnerable in society – the very essence of social Darwinism.

Despite this we often erroneously interpret the anomie surrounding us as being essential for our personal freedom so we may even fight to uphold it, thereby creating a real challenge for society which must strike a balance between individual autonomy and collectively agreed ethical standards. We aren't helped in this quest by the confused, contrary codes of many media outlets, which regularly expose individual indiscretions while failing to shine a light on political or corporate corruption, indeed occasionally even collaborating in its cover-up. Anomic societies aren't necessarily immoral but simply lack the agreed ethical standards against which all actions are judged. The afore-mentioned, cocaine-snorting member of the UK's House of Lords is a case in point. While his behaviour was condemned and his resignation called for by some media commentators, others railed against the invasion of privacy and contested that how he spends his free time is entirely a personal matter. When morality is assessed solely by subjective opinion there can be no antidote to anomie.

However, the question of coherence clarifies the validity of these contrary perspectives. Irrespective of the physical, emotional or spiritual damage done to the individual himself, such a high-profile, public figure acting in this manner is clearly damaging to his family, to the reputation of the House of Lords and to the wider UK political system, thus harming the health of these higher holons. With an organic worldview we can see more clearly how individual actions impact the coherence of both inner and outer worlds. Through this lens it is an immoral act to fill our body full of junk food, even if we harm no-one but ourselves, because we are damaging our own inner coherence and wellbeing. Furthermore, we rarely live isolated lives so our actions almost always impact others, such as the friend who is pained by our ill-health, the family member who feels obliged to care for us or even the taxpayer who must subsidise our hospital visits. Naturally such considerations can lead us into highly emotive territory and there aren't always easy answers. We should certainly resist all attempts to legislate for morality by governments, especially those under the influence of religion as evidenced by the many social injustices in non-secular nations around the world. Nevertheless, the great challenge for Western societies is to rebuild the moral and social capital required to overcome anomie as our default mode, while continuing to protect personal freedoms and guard against the grim gaze of traditional religion. Even if we accept, intellectually, that it is wrong to turn a blind eye to harmful actions, we are still without the visceral instincts and the civic structures required to regularly reinforce this ethos and to ensure ethical standards don't slip. Only higher personal consciousness, the re-cultivation of inner virtue and the rebuilding of civic society can create and consistently maintain such coherence.

Rebalancing Capitals

While minding our own business has become prevalent within anomic Western cultures, our inherent hypocrisy is exposed by the frequency with which our governments' interfere in other nations around the world. Such interventions may be cloaked as ethical crusades to depose tyrannical dictators but many people can see clearly that growing economic capital, rather than moral capital, is the ultimate goal of government strategy and the banks and businesses behind it. Crushing a country's infrastructure and shattering its society, thus 'liberating' its people to become as atomistic and anomic as us, is hardly an exercise in cultivating inner *or* outer coherence. Indeed, such is Western societal psychosis that we are even willing to treat our own in-groups in the same manner. Consider this. Money is not a natural resource but is man-made. It can never run out like oil because if we need more we only have to print it. Yet we are asked by elites to accept the morality of making ordinary people suffer punitive, government-imposed austerity measures in order to repay debt to banks; debt incurred in bailing out those same banks as the result of their own reckless actions and the failure of those same governments to adequately regulate them. We are expected to watch passively as citizens suffer degradation, hardship and humiliation because our economic system says their nation has too much debt. We should stand back as the proud country of Greece has its assets stripped by the very civilisation its ancestors effectively created, and do nothing but thank our lucky stars that the same thing isn't happening to us. No rhetoric about economic responsibility or fiscal stability can ever justify this level of immorality when we could, with the political will, simply print more money or write off Greece's national debt. The fact that this would only require around one-third of the bail-out money given to UK banks alone – and a tiny fraction of the total global cost – has surely set off alarm bells in the mind of anyone with a shred of morality left in them. If this is how the EU treats a member of its 'family' how would it treat its enemies? Does modern economic capitalism exist to serve human-beings or do we exist to serve capitalism, subservient to and at the mercy of a man-made system? How psychotic do elites have to be to think that this is either moral or reasonable? How comatose do ordinary people have to be to tolerate a system which is clearly cultivating neither inner nor outer coherence at any holonic level?

Every single day, more and more people are waking up to the realization that our global human system is politically corrupt and morally bankrupt, but as yet they have found no genuinely effective way to express solidarity, galvanise action or drive radical change. Economic capitalism can only be altered from the inside out and from the bottom up because those at the top have no incentive to change it and will resist, with military force if necessary, any attempts at external modification. We don't need a whole new economic system anyway – there's nothing inherently wrong with the free market per se – but there's a lot wrong with how it is currently structured and managed. It needs to be radically reshaped but even more crucially we need a coherent global culture to wrap around it. Such a culture must provide moral capital as an essential moderator of economic growth, must be fuelled by human capital operating at a higher level of consciousness and must be sustained by the social capital of millions of 'little platoons', each working towards the common goal of optimising inner and outer coherence at every holonic level. All three additional capitals – moral, human and social – must provide critical counterbalance to economic capitalism, indeed are perhaps even pre-requisites for producing the political will to fundamentally restructure our global economic system.

In future we must become much better at balancing the development of human, social, moral and economic capital, so that each moderates and mutually strengthens the other. Our prolonged obsession with only economic growth has dangerously destabilised our world – an imbalance which must be addressed if we are to recover the dynamic stability of a healthy organism. Our system is naturally self-regulating but unrestrained avarice and the myopic focus of the left mind have damagingly dissociated us from essential moderating influences, suppressing our global mind to its lowest level of consciousness. The effect has been to diminish human capital and to neglect the social networks and moral bulwarks necessary for dampening excesses and stopping our system from becoming incoherent. Replenishing human capital via higher consciousness is central to our healing because both social and moral capital will automatically grow as a result. A return to a spiritual level of consciousness will reconnect mind, body and soul, revitalising our desire to cultivate inner virtue and do good in the outer world. This will refocus us on the social relationships which are so essential to external coherence, which provide us with much-needed moral moderation and which are the main source of our personal happiness. Higher consciousness can also unleash the tsunami of creativity we need to rebuild civic society, by conceiving an array of new institutions, enterprises and associations – all with the shared goal of creating a climate in which econo-centric competition can take place within an overarching culture of socio-centric co-operation, restoring health and harmonious balance to our system. Although these conditions must be co-created by us all, there's simply no way of controlling or knowing in advance exactly what will emerge, as they will only take form from the energy flowing across the system; energy which must originate in the human brain. Only when enough people attain higher consciousness, then convert cognitive energy into physical energy by connecting and collaborating with others in social activism, will sufficient power cascade across the entire network to generate a significant and sustainable systemic shift.

The Soft Stuff

Critically, we don't have to reconstruct the village-based communities of Adam Smith's 18th century. Smart technology now makes each of us an active node in a global neural network, with the ability to transmit data to people way beyond those we know personally. Indeed, unlike the days of Smith and Burke, technology now enables us to build 'platoons' of any size and at every level of holon. Each day the worldwide web is growing larger and whenever we tweet, post, blog, chat, like or share, each of us is proactively, if imperceptibly, shaping the future of global human society which, as a living organism, is changing constantly. Where we focus our attention and what we choose to extract, use or share from the environmental data stream will ultimately influence the world we co-create. However, higher consciousness must perpetually permeate our thoughts and, more importantly, must guide our actions because smart technology on its own won't build the social capital required. New media can only facilitate the real-world relationships necessary for genuine empathy, social integration, ethical activism and human co-operation to flourish. Indeed new media is ambivalent to the content it carries, so can just as easily be used to further fragment our society by filling minds with banal distractions, enabling anonymous abuse, spreading falsehoods, setting groups against each other and increasing anomie.

A deliberate and determined democracy is therefore required; formed by engaged, "passionate citizens, all committed to individual and collective consciousness and actively creating ideas and institutions which interweave to "increase coherence, at every level of our system. Diversity of perspective is essential for this level of creativity, in which all participants must "approach problems with an open mind and intellectual modesty. Collaborating with those who don't think like us increases understanding, builds empathy, encourages tolerance and breaks down social and psychological barriers. Diverse groups also generate smarter ideas and make "better decisions because the strengths of some compensate for the "weakness of others, while the biases of one group counterbalance the "biases of another. Individually we're not so clever, the many flaws, "fallacies and foibles of our ancient brains are often exposed for all to see.

However, when we put our minds together we can genuinely change the world.

We are naturally self-creating, so our energy and ingenuity are automatically oriented towards seeking better solutions to the problems we face. However, the issues currently challenging humankind are so countless and complex that no individual can ever see the whole picture nor can a single '*silver bullet*' solution ever be found. Individuals therefore need only concern themselves with cultivating their own inner coherence and contributing towards the outer coherence of those holons of which they form part. Given that human happiness is heavily rooted in relationships and in the vital engagement we enjoy when contributing to something greater than ourselves, it makes perfect sense that our social activism should be aligned with our personal passions. That way, we can regularly find flow, enjoy peak experiences and strengthen our ability to suppress the ego – thereby sustaining higher levels of consciousness, employing elevated states in everyday functioning and benefitting from the better cognitive performance this brings. It therefore doesn't matter whether our personal passions lie in fighting inequality, eradicating poverty, educating children, recycling waste, campaigning for civil rights, releasing political prisoners, preventing global warming, supporting refugees, protecting wildlife or improving our local community, everyone can make a contribution. It is only from grassroots human energy that new forms will grow; forms which can become the sustainable structures needed to continually replenish resources of human, social and moral capital.

We are also naturally self-regulating so, perhaps rather controversially in the post-modern age, we actually need greater moral homogeneity rather than increased diversity, pluralism or relativism. In our drive for 'enlightened' economic freedom, we fragmented our moral frameworks and dismantled the civic scaffolding which sustained them, consigning the life-long cultivation of inner virtue to social history. Some religious fundamentalists would wish to re-impose medieval morality on modern society and this must be resisted, just as we must oppose attempts by governments to legislate on ethical issues. However, we must also accept that anomic societies aren't self-regulating and can only lead to authoritarianism or anarchy. Democracy must therefore yield a global consensus around morality, based on universal human values which, for example, enshrine the sanctity of life, ensure civil rights, guarantee gender equality and protect our planet. The happiness of all humans must become paramount and be placed above economic prosperity in our priorities, ensuring a *'balanced scorecard'* of measures, including social, moral, human and economic capital, against which the health and wellbeing of societies can be assessed. Coherence, both inner and outer, must be the ultimate goal of every human holon and the final arbiter of moral behaviour at every level of society.

In the final analysis, the cognitive revolution we require emphasises that healthy, dynamically-stable societies emerge out of the relationships between those in them, and, as David Brookes highlights in his best-seller *The Social Animal,* it's the *'soft stuff'* which makes the difference between successful synthesis and societal breakdown – *'the ultimate focus of political activity is the character of society'*.[16] He points out that any government can pump money into social issues but without the cultivation of virtues such as trust, confidence, responsibility and self-control, democracy won't flourish and an economy won't prosper:

> ...relationships are the seedbed of character. The reason life and politics are so hard is that relationships are the most important, but also the most difficult, things to understand.[17]

Ultimately, nurturing relationships – the very root of human happiness – requires the organic worldview and the societal pre-eminence of the right mind, if the divisive dangers of the left mind are to be brought under sufficient self-regulation in the global human system.

—15—

Fast-Tracking Our Future

T HERE CAN BE no single, '*silver bullet*' solution for addressing the wide array of issues in our vastly complex human system. The elevation of our collective mind to a higher plane, at which global peace, shared prosperity and environmental sustainability can prevail, will require the energy, ideas and activism of a great many people across every nation on Earth. However, there is one significant step which could potentially '*fast-track*' our species towards greater global integration and that is to make women more influential in how our world is run. Men may instinctively bristle at such a suggestion but let's be honest – any rational analysis of the state of human society in the 21st century would surely conclude that women certainly couldn't do any worse than men have done. Yet the proposal isn't simply to put more females in charge as a social experiment or borne from a sense of guilt that, after six millennia of sub-jugation, it should now be the girls' turn to set the rules – the case is rather more robust than that. The root source of the many conflicts highlighted throughout this book lies in the fact that the left mind has dominated human society for far too long and, while its strengths have brought us countless benefits, many of the unintended consequences have been to our significant detriment. As a species we have become dissociated from nature and from ourselves, from higher levels of consciousness and from our sense of soul. We have become detached from our own bodies, intuitions and emotions and from each other, subverting our true nature as social animals. We have lost touch with our essential spirituality and our ability to perceive the non-material connections between everything in our universe. We have become narrower, shallower, colder, more divided and more divisive, perceiving the world in polar opposites and seeing nature as material resources to be fought for, rather than the womb which sustains us all. In short, our species has become incoherent, fragmented and broken rather than whole, healthy and happy. Only the integrative orientation and synthesising capabilities of the right mind can heal us and it's a simple fact that women, overall, tend to be more right-mind dominant than men.[1] While it's not quite a silver bullet, we would be mad to ignore the opportunity this presents for humankind. It is worth re-emphasising that the right-mind dominance of women is in aggregate and on average. In other words, lots of females do have a preference for the cognitive mode of the left mind while plenty of men are right-mind dominant, and it remains absolutely true that we all use both sides of our brain all of the time. However, when taken in large groups the average distribution profile of men tends to skew left, while the overall orientation of women tends to be towards the right.

It should also be noted that many modern women have suffered, just as much as men, from the cognitive fragmentation and consciousness-suppression of our species, so simply promoting some women to senior business roles or electing more female politicians wouldn't necessarily make a difference. In our current culture, many of the women who have successfully climbed the corporate or political ladder have only done so by having '*bigger balls*' (aka left-mind attributes) than their male counterparts. Despite Angela '*Mutti*' Merkel's motherly image, the way the EU operates certainly suggests she may be more Margaret Thatcher than Mother Teresa. Genuine democracy, gender equality and widespread engagement are therefore essential, at every level of society from top to bottom, to ensure that the female voice permeates all of the social movements and civic institutions which will be required to spark and sustain change. This is particularly important given the many systemic barriers to full participation which women still face today – far more so than is the case for men. Women need to become more influential if global society is to heal itself but not because they are inherently smarter or more moral than men – there's no evidence that any such differences exist between the genders. However, there is plenty of proof that women are more likely to possess the cognitive characteristics humankind needs most, if we are to find peace in our future.

The Evolution of Gender Stereotypes

The past six thousand years haven't been kind to women. Up until that point – for over 95% of our entire existence – human society appears to have been relatively egalitarian and the female of our species was respected, perhaps even revered, for the birth-giving qualities she shared with Mother Nature. However, when Kurgan hordes used left-minded military muscle to conquer the pastoral plains of Europe and beyond, her subjugation by men became inevitable. For millennia to follow, men would become the product of a particularly powerful cultural upbringing, which still influences the unconscious male mind and shapes how we breed boys to this day. Men were trained for war and, as soldiers, were imbued with valuable attributes such as aggression, fearlessness and the ability to show no mercy. The training methods were repetitive drills and discipline, with fighting practice complemented by ritual humiliation and regular punishment. This both asserted hierarchical authority and inured soldiers to the effects of brutality, enabling them to both give and receive pain. Even when society wasn't at war, the psyche of the soldier didn't change; fighting for status and sexual partners, competing for resources and aggressively guarding his property and possessions.

We are now so familiar with the mythology of the male warrior archetype, we may assume the male of any species is naturally more aggressive than the female yet we only need to look to other creatures to see that this isn't necessarily the case. Lionesses, for example, perform almost all of the hunting duties on behalf of a lion pride and black widow spiders have famously been known to kill their mating partners. Maintaining dynamic balance in any complex ecosystem requires the periodic demonstration of both self-assertive and integrative behaviours, the former so animals aren't always taken advantage of, the latter so harmony can be maintained within the overall system. All creatures instinctively do both – sometimes dogs bark or bare their teeth, sometimes they submit by showing their bellies – and there is no difference between males and females in this behaviour. In any ecosystem, an animal which is only ever submissive or only ever aggressive won't survive for very long. We too still unconsciously understand this, sometimes strongly asserting our opinion but also sometimes just going with the flow to maintain group harmony. However, several millennia ago and almost certainly as the result of being social animals at the very top of the food chain, our ancient ancestors made a rather strange decision which would come to mould our minds in a radically different manner to how they had been shaped up to that time.

Our species chose to divide responsibility for self-assertive and integrative behaviours between the sexes, rather than continuing to keep both equally housed within every individual. While men became responsible for assertive attitudes and actions such as aggression, competition, protection, power, control and dominance, women became the integrators – listening, nurturing, caring, sharing, defusing and replenishing. While women were the creators and life-givers, men became the destroyers and life-takers. While men were trained to divide and conquer, women were conditioned to nourish and make whole again. As a result, rather than retaining a high degree of hemispheric balance within both sexes, our ancestors inadvertently sent us down a dual cognitive pathway which would dramatically reshape subsequent societies and eventually culminate in our current cultural crisis. The effect of our war-mongering was ultimately to cleave human-beings in two, along gender lines. By primarily adopting the dualistic, categorizing mode of the left mind, men would progressively become conditioned to see women as their opposite and inferior. However, in doing so they also began a journey which would curtail their own cognitive capabilities and consign their male descendants to being less than whole human-beings. Meanwhile, accidently allocated primacy of by far the more powerful of the two brain hemispheres, women would come to cultivate the skills of the right mind. However, the price they would pay for such a gift would be at least six millennia of male dominance and, with it, the social and cultural subjugation of all things feminine not least of all themselves.

It has been a very long and arduous road back to some semblance of equality. Only as recently as 1893 did New Zealand become the first nation to give women the right to vote and, even in the 21st century, suffrage remains far from universal with many restrictions still placed on women in some parts of the world; from driving bans to the jailing of rape victims for adultery. The three major monotheisms have done little to liberate our sisters and daughters, indeed the Vatican City and Saudi Arabia are two states where men have traditionally been allowed to vote but women have long been denied the same right. Globally, the reluctant retreat of patriarchy still has a long way to travel and can easily be reversed – the first thing the Taliban did when they retook parts of Afghanistan was to once again stop girls from going to school. In such conservative societies, women aren't afforded much control over their own lives or bodies and are often perceived as little more than chattel, whose function is to breed and whose virginity at marriage is a prized asset. Indeed, such is the cultural obsession with gender difference that many social codes of conduct, such as female genital mutilation or what women are allowed to wear, are simply tools of sexual oppression masquerading as moral codes which claim to cultivate virtues like modesty, chastity and fidelity. While these methods may indeed indoctrinate the unconscious female mind with such impulses, they undoubtedly do so through fear or pain and by denying victims full access to their own physical, emotional or spiritual existence, along with the happiness which feeling whole can bring. Despite their stated objectives they must therefore be deemed to be deeply immoral acts.

Even the relative liberalization of society has never been a guarantee of female emancipation. The women of ancient Athens, for example, were treated appallingly, even in comparison with their conservative Spartan counterparts.[2] No individual or society ever 'thinks' with only one hemisphere so there is always scope, even in liberal cultures, for the categorizing left mind to distinguish between those who should enjoy the full benefits of freedom and equality, and those who shouldn't. Although Western societies certainly evolved through the ages, the separation of the sexes and the clear delineation of gender roles didn't actually change very much for a very long time. Instead of becoming soldiers, self-assertive men simply became swashbuckling sailors, muscular manual workers, money-making businessmen or disease-fighting doctors, while women still played integrative roles as the landladies, homemakers, secretaries and nurses who supported them, providing tea and sympathy on tap.

However, the first few decades of the 20th century brought increasing demands for greater equality and, from the end of World War II in 1945, Western society started to see a more fundamental shift in gender function than at any time since the Kurgan waves first brought the advent of warrior societies. A whole range of philosophical, spiritual, cultural and political movements radically altered social attitudes towards civil, gender and minority rights, as well as common outlooks on subjects such as consciousness, labour, sexuality, war and ecology. Women soon realized that their roles need no longer be restricted to the housewives, receptionists and hostesses who provided comfort and a clean environment, while men performed the better-paid jobs upon which society placed the greatest value. Discovering that they were just as smart as boys liberated girls to train and compete for careers in a rapidly changing market, which was becoming less reliant on physical labour and increasingly knowledge-based. Not only were women better at adapting to the shifting social landscape they were also central to creating it, by playing influential roles in many of the counter-cultural movements which would progressively weaken scientific materialism and enable the organic worldview to gradually emerge.

There were two key reasons for this. First, as outsiders in the old culture women benefitted least from it and therefore had least to lose from its demise. In any clash of cultures, those who have the greatest vested interest in maintaining the status quo will tend to devote their energies to doing so, while people who benefit least are more likely to catch a new cultural wave in the hope that it might lead to something better. If enough people hop on board, the many streams of change may eventually find confluence with one another, forming a tidal wave which can sweep away the old guard and their incumbent culture. Second, the integrative roles women were assigned to during six thousand years of suppression, ironically imbued them with those qualities most required in the emerging culture. While men had been busy being warriors, women were learning how to negotiate, mediate and compromise in order to keep the peace. They had therefore become very good at cultivating collaborative environments by anticipating the needs of others, sharing feelings, listening as well as talking, empathising, demonstrating compassion, supporting each other and working together in teams. While men were out cutting, killing and destroying, women had been connecting, nurturing and co-operating, so when it became clear that relationships, communication and creativity were once again essential to our species, women were already several millennia ahead of men on the training programme. In such a context, the self-assertive swashbuckler is simply no match for a sympathetic synthesiser.

Becoming Whole Again

There can be little doubt that men have found it harder than women to adapt to changing social conditions over the past 70 years or so, in particular the increasingly blurred gender roles which had been clearly defined up until World War II. As women began to break free from the bondage of gender constraints, increasing their self-perception as whole human-beings and expanding their horizons accordingly, many men felt lost and under threat. Our dualistic left mind loves clarity so a simple social order, where men went out to work and women stayed at home, suited it perfectly. Although men were still dominant in many ways, it soon became clear that the old set of tools which had worked successfully for centuries, were no longer fit for purpose in a changing work environment. The military skills men had been steeped in – strutting, shouting and browbeating, showing stamina, strength and stoicism, demanding discipline, deference and loyalty – were strangely ineffective with this new type of troop. While some men embraced the challenge and found new ways of working, others simply got frustrated that females were encroaching on formerly all-male domains. Many became increasingly resentful that women were no longer reliant on them, especially when they felt just as dependent on women – emotionally, sexually and domestically – as ever before. Not only was their dominance of the workplace challenged but many men also found themselves increasingly ill-equipped, in terms of their cognitive capabilities, to cope with a dynamically-evolving social environment in which women were becoming ever more confident and increasingly determined to claim equality in all aspects of life.

Of course, some liberal, right-minded men were central to driving these changes and many more were happy to embrace the blending of formerly clear, delineated categorizations. However a lot of men, particularly those with a left-minded tendency to see things in black and white, felt confused, alienated and even under attack, retreating into themselves as a protective measure and collectively defining 'male' as anything which was definitively 'not female'. Naturally, as female freedom and the full participation of women continued to expand, the exclusive domains of such men shrank accordingly, in ever-decreasing circles, to the point where manual labour, contact sports, body building and beard growing are possibly the last few bastions of unequivocal male dominion. Yet this is simply another example of how the myopic lens of the left mind has narrowed the scope of men's experience and restricted their field of possibilities for what it means to be fully human. In this manner, mankind's oppression of women has also taken a great toll on the male of our species, and all men, no matter how open-minded, have been affected to some degree.

By restricting the male role to mainly contributing the self-assertive qualities required for systemic stability, our species relegated men to holding primacy of the left mind which is ultimately the weaker of the two hemispheres. Seeing the world primarily as pairs of polar opposites not only pinches our perception but also automatically creates negatives, so for masculine to be good feminine must be bad. Consequently, most men still shy away from doing anything which society deems to be distinctly feminine such as having long hair or wearing earrings, make-up or skirts. Indeed, many men still wouldn't choose much more subtle symbols of femininity such as the colour pink or certain types of car, movie or other categories of consumable goods. While some men might like to think that this is no longer the case, we're all restricted by cultural conditioning to some extent.

By great contrast, women are far more comfortable stepping over into traditionally-male domains and it has often been observed that girls mature earlier than boys and seem to be more rounded in the way they act throughout adulthood. For example, women have generally been more accepting of homosexuality in society and have been more welcoming of men into traditionally-female careers, such as nursing, than men have been ready to accept female scientists or engineers. Sexism is far more regularly reported in men's attitudes towards women than vice versa, and, while men don't often wear dresses, women are much happier to wear traditionally-male clothes such as trousers and shirts. The same goes for 'male' consumables and pastimes such as drinking beer or playing football. Over the years many hypotheses have been offered to explain the markedly different attitudes of each gender towards the other and, in particular, why women seem to be more integrative or whole than men. Theories include the observation that all humans are ultimately the product of the female womb, that the menstrual cycle enables women to more easily attune to the rhythmic essence of nature and that, because women tend to bring up children, they have greater empathy for masculinity than men do for femininity. Semioticians have even pointed out that the female sex organs are primarily circular and secondarily linear, while male genitals are primarily linear and secondarily circular. I'll leave you to ponder the significance of such ideas and suggest that the key difference lies, at least partly, in brain dominance.

Remember, the right mind is naturally holistic and oriented towards higher holons, while the left mind focusses on lower holons and is instinctively reductive. While our outer-world embedded right mind perceives a particular person as a unique living organism, our left mind automatically abstracts them to a decontextualized category within the schematic structures of our inner world. With its stronger connections to our limbic system, the interdependent right mind processes emotions more powerfully than our more independent left mind, which protects us by desensitizing us to feelings. While our right mind sees masculinity and femininity as two points on a continuum with a spectrum of gradients in between, our left mind sees male and female as two distinctly separate entities which are polar opposites – the single mixer tap versus two separate taps. While our left mind is therefore the source of our dualism, the monistic right mind appreciates opposites but perceives them as two parts of an integrated whole. In processing an individual, the right mind first perceives a human-being and only then recognizes sex, attaching less significance to gender differences than the left mind and feeling a greater degree of instinctive empathy than its counterpart. Conversely, the left mind processes gender first, then recognizes the whole human-being but still as a category of species rather than as a living organism or 'real' person. It then further categorizes, building solid walls between all perceived opposites – black versus white, gay versus straight, friend versus foe and so on – automatically homogenizing members of each category and exaggerating differences between groups. Of course, this phenomenon isn't specific to men or women. Anyone, male or female, with a cognitive preference for the right mind or who is naturally left-mind dominant, will experience each operating mode more acutely than their less pre-eminent thinking style. Lots of men feel deep empathy for others while plenty of women hold traditional attitudes towards the clear delineation of gender roles. No healthy human of either sex is capable of thinking with only one hemisphere and both genders are distributed across the whole spectrum of brain dominance. However, in aggregate and on average women do tend to be more right minded than men, which is a considerable contributing factor towards the empirically-observable evidence that women tend to be more empathetic, more inclusive, more caring, more tolerant, more balanced, more integrative and therefore more whole than men, in their attitudes and actions.

As the birth-giver of our species, this may be partly genetic but it has also been shaped by at least six thousand years of cultural conditioning. With its broader synaptic connectivity and more holistic orientation, the right mind effectively embraces, encapsulates and enfolds the narrower functional capability of the left mind, yet the same is not true in reverse. Recall from split-brain experiments that the right hemisphere works on behalf of the whole person, while the left hemisphere can only deal with the right half of the body for which it is directly responsible. While men may have won many battles by having bigger muscles, women ultimately won the gender war by taking primacy of by far the more powerful brain hemisphere. However, men need not panic because it is only the dualistic left mind which perceives any sort of adversarial competition between cognitive modes – the right mind sees no such contest. On the contrary, the synthesising right mind sees the left only as yang to its yin; a valuable colleague whose essential outputs must be integrated to optimise cognition. Unlike the left mind, it's not in the nature of the right mind to want to control, dominate or subjugate but only to cultivate a climate of collaboration and to co-operate for the common good. Fortunately for men, this also applies to the nature of right-mind dominant women. Despite aeons of repression, revenge simply isn't on their agenda.

Today, it's impossible to know definitively to what degree gender differences are intrinsic to each sex, the extent to which social conventions have slowly reshaped genetics or how much of our behaviour is simply the result of gender-stereotyping which can be reversed. What's much clearer is that our cultural conditioning begins the day we are born and that even though our brains do come with genetic pre-dispositions, they are also extremely malleable. While what we choose is to some degree influenced by how we are wired, our minds are also moulded by how we behave so when boys are taught, from a very young age, to play with mechanistic tools and trucks while girls are pointed towards relationship-based toys like dolls and teddy bears, it can really make a big difference in later life. Like the drills which make a good soldier or the disciplines designed to instil virtue, daily practice at anything shapes the unconscious mind so, by the time they reach adolescence, children will not only think in a certain way but will have developed core capabilities in the behavioural manifestations of those thoughts. Consequently, if boys are brought up as 'little soldiers' while girls are conditioned to build relationships and be caring, and if, in adulthood, it's boys who are disproportionately represented amongst political and corporate elites, it should really come as no surprise that assertive tendencies tend to outweigh integrative behaviours in modern society.

Breaking the Boy Code

Modern society remains very confused about whether or not we want boys to continue to conform to the ancient military ideal – square-jawed, aggressive, stoic and physically strong. After six thousand years of almost perpetual war-making, we are finding it both discomforting and difficult to shake off this deeply ingrained masculine archetype. As a consequence, many boys all over the world are still being steeped in a warrior ethos which could become increasingly redundant as the future we bring forth unfolds. Alternatively, it may become rather useful if the apocalyptic path we are currently on manifests in self-fulfilling prophecy. It is now so long-established that we can be forgiven for thinking that male aggression is completely natural but scientific evidence suggests that there is absolutely nothing inherent or inevitable about it. The trait is absent in the very few indigenous tribes which survived into modernity yet remained uninflu-enced by patriarchal control cultures, and all attempts to establish a universal, biological foundation for male aggression have repeatedly failed.[3] Studies also show that males are no more naturally prone to aggression than they are to other human impulses including empathy and nurturing. Indeed, even in Western societies boys are just as interested in younger infants as girls are, up until around the age of four when the cultural conditioning they have received since birth really seems to kick in. Research shows that by the time they go to school, boys are already more competitive than girls and, in the developing dualism of the male mind, for them to be winning someone else must be losing. Boys not only need someone to compete with but also an adversary they can blame if they are not succeeding, which, from adolescence through adulthood, can readily result in assertive, aggressive or even anti-social behaviour. The left mind automatically classifies in-groups from out-groups, so opponents could be kids from another school, rival sports fans or the immigrants they perceive have 'stolen' their jobs, but both boys and men are far more likely than girls or women to become involved in fist fights, street gangs or racist groups.[4] Indeed females can also constitute a competing out-group, with some men in all societies resenting women, not only for refusing to play traditional gender roles but also for beating men to social positions which they consider should be theirs by right. Such unhealthy attitudes in adult males have been shown to lead to domestic violence, sexism, gender objectification and sexual assault.

In her book *In a Different Voice,* American psychologist Carol Gilligan highlights the fundamental differences between boys and girls and tells a sweet anecdote about why they don't often play together. According to Gilligan, boys tend towards autonomy, justice and rights while girls are oriented towards community, care and relationships, so while boys like to follow rules, girls like to make connections and they don't play well together because these two 'voices' consistently clash. She tells the tale of a mixed-gender group playing a game of baseball, during which the little boy batting took his third strike and immediately burst into tears. While the girls all gathered round and wanted to give him another go, the boys stood unmoved saying rules were rules and the rules say three strikes and you're out. Gilligan observes that when girls see pain they want to help and heal, while boys view playing games as an initiation into the competitive male world of reason and logic. While boys will therefore hurt feelings to preserve the primacy of rules, girls will break rules to preserve the primacy of feelings.[5] Rules are, of course, rooted in the black and white world of the left mind which likes them because they are abstract, fixed and unfeeling. Relationships are much more fluid and fuzzy, so need the right mind for their navigation.

There can be little doubt that many of the problems in the world today are the result of a prevalent '*boy code*' which didn't teach boys – now our social, political and corporate elites – to share power or consider feelings, but instead taught them to fight to get to the top of the tree and, once there, to be as aggressive as possible in staying there. The prize for those who reach the pinnacle of any hierarchy is that they are allowed to reshape the rules which sustain that hierarchy; an opportunity the left mind will rarely pass up, to ensure that 'me and mine' continue to gain an advantage into the future. This cycle isn't gender-specific, of course, but simply how all dominant cultures enable their own self-perpetuation by building the social, political, economic or spiritual structures which define how their particular 'society' works, and which therefore skew future outcomes in favour of the status quo. Some women, certainly those who prefer the left mind, may well feel perfectly comfortable playing by the adversarial rules of the '*boy code*', and no doubt some right-minded females have even become adept at disguising their true nature to succeed in male-dominated worlds. However, it is relatively rare that women are afforded sufficient influence to set societal rules and the many structural barriers women face, in climbing to the top of political, corporate or civic organizations, are well-documented and need no elaboration here. If global society is to successfully shift beyond the narrow narrative of social Darwinism, perpetuated by the left mind and the on-going dominion of men, the voice of the right mind must be heard more loudly and women should be at the forefront of this peaceful revolution.

Indeed, women have already been central to the many innovations in education, healthcare, commerce, social enterprise, environmentalism, lifestyle and progressive politics which form the undercurrent of cultural change, bubbling beneath the surface of societies all over the world today. And they are not alone. Many males have also hitched their hopes for a better future to the integrative offerings of the organic worldview, but it's still true to say that men generally remain more wedded than women to the mechanistic lens, the fruits of scientific materialism and the behavioural manifestations of the left mind. Many men therefore continue to act as a barrier to positive change, even if their resistance remains unconscious and unintentional. Research shows that, on average, men are still more competitive and ego-driven than women, who find it easier than male colleagues to co-operate to achieve common goals.[6] Women also try to maintain equality in groups while men are more likely to strive for status, so while women will accept suggestions made by others, men more often see suggestions as an unwelcome attempt to exert authority. Women are therefore more likely than men to ask others for their ideas and opinions. Research also shows that women are less bothered about leading groups, are more inclined towards teamwork and are especially good at supporting each other, while men prefer to either be the boss or perform tasks on their own. Men are also less likely than women to ask for help when struggling, which can be debilitating in stressful situations where men become restricted to *'fight or flight'* responses, while women are more inclined to reach out to others – a strategy which not only calms stress but also increases the resources available to help find a solution. Some studies even suggest that the cultural conditioning boys receive from birth may lead to partial atrophy of the right mind, resulting in an inability to focus on more than one thing at a time and lending credence to the famous observation about each gender's ability to multi-task. For example, it's true that women can more easily listen to two simultaneous conversations, using both brain hemispheres to do so, while men tend to find this more difficult.

In all of the above examples, the behavioural biases of men act as a barrier to integration yet also hinder their own performance, unconsciously sustaining tendencies which are actually self-harming. Critically, they are all learned behaviours and can easily be replaced by different impulses if we can break the cycle of gender-stereotyping, especially in the earliest years of education. Ironically, this is one area of society where woman traditionally *have* had a significant influence and an opportunity to reshape the rules about how young children are brought up. Females tend to dominate both home-based child-rearing roles and the pre and primary school teaching jobs which educate children in their most formative years. Women must therefore share at least some of the responsibility for the perpetuation of gender-stereotyping in society and do more to reshape it going forward, so we are producing children with the balanced cognitive and behavioural skills required for the future. While it may still seem cute for mums and teachers to continue to raise boys as 'little soldiers', we are doing neither them nor girls, nor society in general, any favours in the long run.

Through the organic worldview, we come to see that the future isn't something which will automatically unfold regardless of our attitudes and actions in the present, nor is it the output of an objective outer world to which we will either successfully adapt or not. On the contrary, our future isn't yet written and could unfold in a number of ways, all of which will be co-created by every single human-being yet none of which are controllable by any of us. However, that isn't to say the future is entirely unpredictable. The future we bring forth will be simultaneously shaped by the interpenetration of all of our minds, by our consequent collective actions and by how well we subsequently adapt to the changes which emerge as a result of those actions. As Abraham Lincoln famously observed, '*the best way to predict your future is to create it*'. The biggest favour our species could do itself right now is to break from gender-stereotyping, particularly the prevalent 'boy code' of conduct, and to start to educate children of both sexes so they become balanced and rounded whole-brain thinkers.

Bringing Forth Our Future

As Daniel H Pink points out in *A Whole New Mind*, current trends suggest that the skills most required in the future will be those of the right mind – in his view design, storytelling, empathy, play, symphony (or synthesis) and the ability to derive meaning from life, beyond materialism and economic wealth. Pink envisions the future as a '*high concept, high touch*' environment in which the left-brain dominant, knowledge workers of the 20th century will be progressively superseded by right-minded creatives and empathizers, with the softer skills required to cope in a more networked and fluid global work environment.[7] Given our current position at the edge of chaos, there can certainly be little doubt that our future – however it unfolds – is going to look very different from our past or present. The historic transformation of our species via major periodic step-changes, has been well documented; from the very long Hunter-Gatherer era to the Agrarian, Industrial and Information Ages. At each step, technological innovation enabled human muscle-power to be replaced by machine-power and throughout the 21st century we'll continue to see our brain-work increasingly replicated by computers. Critically, the functions of the left mind will be more readily replaced than those of the right mind. Computers can already perform calculations and process rule-based, binary logic, much quicker and more accurately than any human, yet we are still a long way from developing a machine which can empathise with someone in pain. Any task which can be broken down into repeatable, sequential steps or any reductive process which follows a 'decision-tree' type model, is far more replicable by computer software than those which require the right mind's ability to synthesise data, create new connections or spot relationships between phenomena which are non-linear or non-local. In future it is therefore the skills of the right mind which will increasingly come to matter more in human cognition, than the capabilities of the left mind. We can continue to focus the education of our children on science, technology and mathematics, in order to create the doctors, engineers and accountants of the future, but moving forward we'll actually require these skills less and less. These professions will still be valuable of course, but as the diagnostic elements of a doctor's role, for example, are increasingly overtaken by technology-enabled, decision-tree based tools, their job will necessarily narrow. While we'll still need doctors to identify and treat non-routine illnesses, the market will simply need fewer of them. Nursing care, by comparison, cannot be so easily replicated as it requires a higher level of hands-on, relationship-based skills which only the right mind can deliver. As populations grow older, with improved medical care enabling people to live longer, the global demand for nurses can only increase.

So, just as human muscles were replaced by machines, much of our left-mind function will slowly be ceded to software and it is our right-minded capability which will therefore form the competitive playing field of our future. Only this cognitive mode can shift human society from the *Information Age* to the *Integrative Age*; from a narrow, knowledge-based economy of the left mind to a much broader, more balanced, ideas-based, multi-capitalism of the right mind. It is with beautifully brilliant irony that the past six thousand years, during which men have continually oppressed women, have much better prepared the female of our species for leading this transformation. We can choose to see this as amazing serendipity or as an evolutionary adaptation by our species, to both create new environmental conditions which are more conducive to human life and to better prepare itself for a successful transition to the new world in development. Women have been central to the emerging culture of integrative monism and to the many social movements which provide its powerful energy source, yet the organic worldview still doesn't fully flow through the mainstream of global society. While many men have supported these developments, much of the resistance has also come from men, in particular those who benefit most from scientific materialism and have the societal influence to defend the status quo. Moving forward, the future we bring forth will therefore depend as much on the reactions of men, as on the actions of women.

If boys continue to be subliminally raised as 'soldiers', no matter how subtle their conditioning becomes, they are going to find the future much harder and more frustrating than ever before. Strong muscles are inevitably an ever-devaluing currency in a world replete with machinery, and the ability to be stoically emotionless will also find decreasing utility in societies increasingly based on relationships. Manual work will be harder to come by and men will continually find that they are up against women for the best non-manual roles; adversaries who will often be better cognitively equipped than they are. For a while boys will continue to compete well for some jobs, for example in finance or IT, but as these roles are either off-shored to equally capable, lower priced, foreign workers or disappear altogether – replaced by smart software – the employment pool will slowly dry up for left-brain oriented operators. However, with the right attitude the societal shifts projected do offer men a great opportunity as well as presenting a threat. The traditional male role in which all emotions except anger and lust had to be suppressed and where 'feminine' values like empathy were considered unmanly, was just as restrictive to men in the past as the bleak landscape unreconstructed men will find themselves facing in the future. By denying themselves the chance to be whole human-beings, such men are subconsciously suppressing their natural instincts and unwittingly imposing incoherence, ill-health and unhappiness on their own being – a deeply immoral act. In doing so, they are also acting as obstacles to the full and fair participation of women in every aspect and at every level of society, thereby impeding the coherence and wellbeing of our entire human ecosystem.

Only by elevating consciousness beyond the dualistic gender paradigm and by embracing everything the right mind has to offer, will men be better able to reconnect with their own embodied intuitions, emotions and intrinsic spirituality. In doing so, they can become more aware of the essential interconnectedness of all living organisms and leave behind a world of unnecessary, ego-driven aggression and adversarial conflict, thereby opening themselves up to the possibilities presented by peaceful collaboration. Importantly, there will still be plenty of opportunities to exercise their competitive spirit but the new, values-based rules of the global game must be set by the right mind and their application moderated by a greater level of self-control. Competition will therefore take place within a wider framework of co-operation and men will have to learn to play the game with a greater degree of respect; for women and for each other. Over time, boys must be raised differently so they emerge as men who are already fit for purpose in a world in which the skills of the warrior are no longer relevant – a radically altered 'from birth' education which must ensure that society is creating whole children of both genders, rather than boys who are only equipped with half the skills they need. As Samuel Taylor Coleridge once noted *'the truth is, a great mind must be androgynous',* but individual minds cannot become balanced if nurtured in a culture which consistently cleaves separate gender roles and values one sex more than the other.

Moving forward, we have three options:

1) We can stick with scientific materialism and the short-term economic benefits it brings. Capitalism will remain unchanged and jobs requiring the logic of the left mind will gradually be off-shored or computerised, leaving a predominance of roles which need right-minded capabilities. Education will also remain unaltered, so boys will continue to be raised with a soldier's mind-set and imbued with a range of skills which have ever-diminishing utility in a changing world. However, those skills may still prove very useful as war is significantly more likely. Unfettered economic growth will continue to consume nature at an unsustainable rate, placing militaristic nations on a collision course as competition for dwindling resources increases. Economic inequalities will also continue to grow globally, causing increased tensions both within and between nation states. Whether in the form of civil revolution or international conflict, war is the inevitable outcome. Neither our grandsons nor granddaughters will benefit. Women will still struggle to gain equality in a world dominated by aggressively competitive men, who will continue to rise to the top of political, corporate and social institutions, even when less cognitively equipped than female candidates. Individual incoherence will therefore grow as men increasingly find themselves in positions for which they are intellectually ill-prepared, while women will be denied opportunities for which they have superior skills, instead having to settle for

less suitable alternatives. Societal incoherence will also increase as conflict between genders, social classes, ethnic groups or nations grows. Ultimately, this path can only lead to catastrophic consequences for humankind. In the end, we will either kill each other through nuclear warfare or the damage we do to our biosphere will cause the planet to eradicate our whole species. The only question is which will happen first.

2) We could return to a more 'traditional' society in which gender roles are once again more clearly defined; where women perform the integrative tasks and men do the 'real work', requiring superior assertive skills. It's difficult to imagine how this could ever be achieved without the authoritarian, patriarchal rule which still blights many nations around the world and is central to the on-going oppression of women in the 21st century. No doubt some women (and far more men) would happily return to living under such conditions but, for most people, the genie has been released from that particular bottle and isn't going back in anytime soon. It is, nevertheless, the direction of travel demanded by the fundamentalist elements of all three monotheisms, who believe that personal and societal coherence can be best achieved with a distinctly dualistic approach to gender. This logic can be rejected for several reasons. Most obviously, we have lived with clear gender divisions for the past six thousand years and rarely has it brought peace, wellbeing or happiness – witness our long history of wars and how it has brought our world to the edge of chaos today. Secondly, such patriarchal societies still exist and are the single biggest barrier to the genuine emancipation of women all over the world. There's also no evidence that either gender is happier in them, nor are they more prosperous; indeed there is much evidence to the contrary on both counts. Such societies cause incoherence in women by denying their human rights but they also create incoherent men, who find themselves restricted to living narrow, hollowed-out 'half-lives' without full access to the experience of being wholly human. Finally, while traditional societies may appear to have the ability to create collective coherence, with men and women working together (but apart) to create a complementary, harmonious whole, this is invariably an illusion. The left-mind dominance, cultural conditioning and physical superiority of men will inevitably lead to the subjugation of women, societal imbalance and collective incoherence.

3) We can adopt an organic worldview, elevate our individual consciousness and actively contribute towards a coherent culture of integrative

monism, thereby bringing forth a more peaceful world through the co-creation of a global mind operating on a higher plane of cognitive wisdom. Women have been essential to the many interweaving strands which make up this movement to date, but millions of men have also embraced its principles and now breathe its vision and embody its goals, every day in life. We only need to take a look inside some organizations in the creative industries, for example, to see better gender balance and harmonious teamwork in action. This is, of course, because many men also have a preference for the right mind and, irrespective of their brain biases, all men are capable of whole-mind thinking even if cultural conditioning from birth has weakened their right mind. Like physical muscles, cognitive capabilities can be rebuilt through exercise.

At the moment the future looks bleak for some young men, particularly those who lack the skills to adapt to a changing social environment in which the ability to leverage the right mind will increasingly mean the difference between success and failure. Society must better support both boys and girls by significantly improving the way it educates all children – moving away from the indoctrination of gender stereotypes and towards the balanced development of both brain hemispheres, giving every child the mental tools they need to become whole human-beings. Boys and men *can* adapt but to do so will require a number of attitudinal and behavioural adjustments. They'll have to leave their egos at the door and accept that girls and women are their equals who, in some areas at least, have better skills and more valuable insights which should be listened to. They'll have to learn to share power, embrace genuine democracy and, in some circumstances, be led by females. More than anything, they'll have to become aware of the limitations of the left mind and the pernicious implications of allowing it to dominate social discourse. In doing so, they can consciously increase self-control and suppress the more aggressive manifestations of their competitiveness. If left-minded men (and women) can embrace the possibilities presented by the future, rather than defending the gender divisions delivered by the status quo, they can open up a wide world of new opportunities. None are greater than the chance to experience how it feels to be whole and to fuel their own happiness by working for the betterment of society. By doing so, they can connect with others to create a global cascade of social activism which can reverse the damaging effects of economic inequality, social injustice, ecological destruction and military warfare, all over the world.

The optimal choice is surely self-evident but is one which women will find easier to make than men. Having benefitted from societal dominance for millennia, men have, on the face of it at least, more to lose from this essential cultural shift. Yet not only is it necessary for all of humankind, the potential benefits for men are also huge if only they can see the bigger picture. Of course, the co-creation of our future isn't ultimately about gender but about how each individual chooses to use their mind to help address the cognitive imbalance which has brought global human society to the edge of chaos. We all have two brain hemispheres and all contribute to the global mind, so we all have a role to play. However, our challenge is to restore dynamic equilibrium at a higher level of collective consciousness and while women don't provide a ready-made solution, six thousand years of cultural conditioning has at least given them the right-mind dominance which could help fast-track the transition of our whole human system. While increasing the influence of women on global society may not therefore constitute a silver bullet, it may be the best hope we've got for the future of our species.

What Happens Next?

Where the human race goes from here isn't written in the stars or pre-ordained by any sky-god. The future will emerge from our complex adaptive system as the cumulative result of the thoughts and actions of each and every one of us, including generations yet unborn. The destiny of our species is in our own hands but there is not a single person who can determine the exact path we should take or accurately predict which potential future will unfold before us. All that's certain is that if we are to survive and have any hope of finding peace, we cannot stay on our current trajectory. Some may find this truth deeply discomforting, others will find it truly inspiring but our complex reality is that we can and will co-create our collective future by simultaneously shaping and adapting to all of the environments in which we are embedded at every level of our multi-layered existence. At our most macro level the content of our global mind, the emergent output of the interpenetration of all of our individual minds, will ultimately determine the future of our species.

There's absolutely no point in waiting for politicians, bankers, corporate executives or media moguls to radically alter our current path because it won't happen – at least not as we would wish it to happen. Wedded to scientific materialism, if left unfettered these '*four horsemen*' will deliver a future which looks pretty much like our immediate past, with the continuation of rampant consumerism, environmental destruction, increased inequality, widespread poverty and global warfare. However, it would be a mistake to assume they are without vision. Their end-game is almost certainly a global super-state, with one centralized government in control of one worldwide market and a single money source, enabling a small, international banking cartel to continue to pull the strings of puppet elites. It is no co-incidence that the wealthiest nations, those which have benefitted most from modern capitalism, are also the most war-like. Since being founded in 1776 there are only 21 years in which the USA hasn't been involved in military conflict somewhere in the world,[8] and of the nearly 200 nations dotted around the globe, only 22 haven't at some point in history been invaded by British forces.[9] Despite rhetoric about the perils emanating from the Middle East, the US, UK and their major NATO allies, plus Russia, China and Israel present a far greater threat to our future than any other nations.

The major monotheisms won't drive positive change either. All three share an omnipotent, male God and an authoritarian approach to the interpretation and implementation of scripture. All three remain built around patriarchal organizational structures which exclude women from leadership roles and religion remains central to much of the violent extremism in the world, especially in the Middle East – the birthplace (and disputed territories) of Judaism, Christianity and Islam. The latter in particular, remains a major source of female oppression and while research shows little variation between mainstream Western and Islamic attitudes towards the principles of democracy, there are still major differences in attitudes towards gender. While 86% of Germans, for example, reject the proposal that '*men make better political leaders than women*', this view is endorsed by 91% of Egyptians.[10]

We therefore cannot wait for priests or politicians to reshape global society because they have neither the will nor the capability to do so, encumbered as they are with the same flawed minds as everyone else. Significant change will only happen if ordinary people wake up to how our world currently works and take action to alter it, yet there would be little point in storming the country estates of elites with pitchforks and blazing torches. They may be fortunate to have benefitted from scientific materialism but current elites are no more responsible for creating our global culture or capitalist system than we are. They're also not necessarily bad people (although some certainly are), just the beneficiaries and perpetuators of a system stacked heavily in favour of the left mind. However, this situation is changing and a global drift back towards the right mind has already been underway for the past 70 years. Sensing the sands shifting beneath their feet, those in power will continue to fight back and are undoubtedly dangerous adversaries with wealth, status, influence and a compliant media under their direction. The key unknown will be whether power ultimately lies with the people or with the elites; the former hold a huge advantage in terms of numbers but the latter, nevertheless, remain a potent force. If enough ordinary people want peace and a different kind of world, they will have to galvanise themselves to wrest control from those at the top but not in the form of a military coup which would simply replace leadership but do nothing to fundamentally change the current system. The same issues would inevitably just re-emerge further down the line, with new elites to be deposed. To achieve a sustainable shift in underlying dynamics, change must come from within the current system itself; sourced in the creativity of the human mind, fuelled by the energy of the human body and socialized through the universal love of the human spirit.

Higher consciousness, genuine democracy, decentralized power and civic engagement must be critical catalysts in a bottom-up revolution, which sees ordinary people unite to demand reform by changing political mandates, withdrawing labour, reducing consumption and by steadfastly refusing to be pawns of those in power or soldiers in wars waged solely for economic gain. For global co-operation to emerge, ordinary people must become more aware of their own biases, more conscious of each other, more interconnected and more suspicious of the messages promulgated by those in power. Through smart technology and social media every single person can, for the first time in human history, become a live node in a genuinely global network with the ability to debunk lies, share facts and promote transparency. Information can be disseminated instantly, ideas spread and replicated, corruption exposed and condemned. Moral actions which contribute to coherence must be amplified through social synapses and sustained through civic institutions, while behaviours which damage the health of the individual or ecosystem must be dampened by negative feedback. Systemic self-creation and self-regulation can thus be maintained in dynamic equilibrium, providing checks and balances which safeguard against unintended consequences and retain the flexibility to change course if required. Gender equality must be enabled as a priority to ensure our fastest route to hemispheric balance in the global mind and education must evolve to produce whole, mentally 'androgynous' children rather than sex-separated stereotypes. Skills in self-assertion and social integration can thus be equally allocated across both boys and girls, guarding against the more malevolent aspects of the left mind and ensuring the ultimate primacy of the holistic right mind.

Both men and women must play their part but the onus on each sex is not necessarily equal. Women must continue to do what their mothers and grandmothers have been doing for the last century. Keep pushing for equal rights and opportunities in every aspect of society and human existence. Keep reaching out, connecting, collaborating and supporting each other, while working with like-minded men wherever possible. Keep refusing to accept glass ceilings or any other systemic barriers to the fulfilment of female potential. Keep teaching your daughters and grand-daughters to do all of the above and keep reminding any woman, who isn't already actively involved, that it's never too late to start.

Men, in general, must do far more. They can continue to resist the development of our species by doggedly defending scientific materialism or they can work co-operatively to address the iniquitous aspects of our dominant culture. Through the latter, they can also liberate themselves from the myopia of the mechanistic worldview. The male left hemisphere undoubtedly remains the single biggest barrier to the successful evolution of humankind. Patriarchal attitudes and oppressive behaviours remain rife, the outputs of a left mind so sure of its own self-righteousness it cannot see the great damage it is doing. Men in religious cultures must shoulder the burden of guilt, perhaps more than those in secular societies, for the denial of fundamental human rights to girls and women – from access to education to ownership of their own bodies. Religious men must do more to subvert the oppressive, hierarchical nature of the monotheisms, either by changing them from within or by joining others to exert external pressure on them, in demanding equal status for all. Islamic men especially must do more to emancipate women, drive democracy and eradicate religious violence. More broadly, men, particularly those with a natural preference for the right mind, must become as proactive as women in championing connectivity, communication, collaboration, co-operation and creativity as core capabilities in the new world. They must also exert greater influence on their fellow males; to overcome the resistance of those fighting to sustain the dominance of scientific materialism and to provide reassurance and guidance to those who feel most threatened by gender equality and a more integrative culture. Like-minded men and women must find each other and bring form to their shared, progressive passions by creating organizations, associations, clubs, groups, societies, movements, enterprises or businesses; all inspired by integrative visions, goals, missions, manifestos or mantras and all fuelled by boundless human energy to drive positive change.

In addition, the colonial West must acknowledge and ameliorate the grievances of its many victims, both past and present – particularly those which still strongly persist in the Middle East and parts of Africa. To do so, the West must take responsibility for its crimes and should not be exonerated for its persistent war-mongering and smug self-righteousness. The West may be wealthy, and therefore successful in its own terms, but with its shameful record of colonial oppression, nature's despoliation, human atrocities, sham democracies, greed-based capitalism and faux gender-equality, the West has a lot less to be proud of than its supporters like to think. This should be reason enough for the greatest moral responsibility being placed on the West to lead and facilitate our shift to a more peaceful, balanced world, but there are other reasons why this makes pragmatic sense. First, change must grow organically from within the current system and Western nations are the originators, architects and main beneficiaries of scientific materialism. In becoming economically rich, they have also accumulated an unrivalled arsenal of weapons with which to defend their system and values, so any external attempts to create change will inevitably be met with force, leading to war. Peaceful adaptation can therefore only be achieved from systemic shifts within the West and these changes have already been happening for more than half a century. All Western nations now offer some form of democracy so, although their political systems will themselves need to be overhauled in future, they at least presently provide a vehicle via which ordinary people can exercise their democratic power through peaceful means. However, the most recent catastrophic conflicts in Iraq, Afghanistan, Libya, Yemen and Syria, have largely been caused by the very politicians we citizens in the West have elected, so it is incumbent upon all of us to appoint better, wiser representatives in future. Many current Western governments, in cahoots with the banks and big business, are more likely to shift global society towards a single super-state so it is essential that ordinary people in Western nations take action to stop this from happening. Finally, the change our world needs requires a combination of elevated consciousness and social activism at a level never before witnessed in human history. It is only in the materially-wealthy West that individuals have the spare time, energy and cognitive capacity to even consider such matters, never mind act upon them. It's hardly reasonable to expect people living in poverty and toiling daily to feed children or keep a roof over their heads, to be driving the elevation of the global human system to a new level. The onus must therefore be on the many middle-class citizens of Western nations to lead the way. That said, everyone can still play a part.

As a species we are poised at the edge of chaos and no-one knows with any certainty where we are heading. Our future isn't yet written because only we can write it and we will do so as the result of how we think and act. Each of us is but a single node in a vast global network, a tiny grain of sand in an infinite cosmos but, who knows, any one of us could be the grain which finally tips our whole human system into a new age.

References

PART ONE – SEEING

The Shifting Sands of the Human System

Chapter 1 – Our Self-Inflicted Sickness

1 http://unhcr.org/556725e69.html

2 http://economicsandpeace.org/wp-content/uploads/2015/06/2014-Global-Peace-Index-REPORT_0-1.pdf

3 https://www.populationinstitute.org/external/files/reports/The_Perfect_Storm_Scenario_for_2030.pdf

4 http://www.unicef-irc.org/publications/pdf/rc12-eng-web.pdf

5 http://www.businessinsider.com/map-divorce-rates-around-the-world-2014-5?IR=T

6 http://unsdsn.org/wp-content/uploads/2014/02/WorldHappinessReport2013_online.pdf

7 David G Blanchflower and Andrew J Oswald, 'Well-being over time in Britain and the USA', *Journal of Public Economics 88*, 2004 1359-1386

8 Carol Graham, *Happiness Around the World: The Paradox of Happy Peasants and Miserable Millionaires,* 2009

9 http://www.independent.co.uk/news/uk/this-britain/modern-britons-are-wealthier-but-less-happy-than-those-in-the-1950s-5336162.html

10 http://www.bbc.co.uk/news/uk-england-london-28881073

11 R Inglehart and H D Klingemann, 'Genes, Culture, Democracy and Happiness', *Culture and Subjective Well-being*, 2000, pp165-183

12 G Easterbrook, *The Progress Paradox: How Life Gets Better While People Feel Worse*, 2003, p170; and Richard Layard, *Happiness: Lessons from a New Science*, 2005, p34

13 John A Bargh, 'Our Unconscious Mind: Unconscious impulses and desires impel what we think and do in ways never dreamed of', *Scientific American*, 2014, pp30-37

14 Marcus W Feldman *et al*, 2002, https://web.stanford.edu/dept/news/pr/02/genetics18.html

15 Jerome Kagan and Nancy Snidman, *The Long Shadow of Temperament*, 2004

16 Walter Mischel, Yuichi Shoda and Monica L Rodriguez , 'Delay of Gratification in Children', *Science (New Series)*, 1989, Vol 244, No 4907

17 Helen Fisher, 'The Drive to Love: Neural Mechanism for Mate Selection', *The New Psychology of Love*, 2006

18 Jared Diamond, *Collapse: How Societies Choose to Fail or Succeed,* 2006

Chapter 2 – A War of Worldviews

1 Quoted by Stuart A Kauffman, *Reinventing the Sacred: A New View of Science, Reason, and Religion*, 2008, p10

2 Quoted by Fritjof Capra, *The Turning Point: Science, Society and the Rising Culture*, 1982, p66

3 *Ibid*, p66

4 *Ibid*, p70

5 https://stats.oecd.org/glossary/detail.asp?ID=1163

6 The magnetic compass was first invented in China as early as the Han dynasty of c 200BC and was used for military navigation by the Song dynasty in the 11thC. Paper-making was invented in China around 100BC. Gunpowder was invented in 9thC China, with the earliest formula for making gunpowder written in the 11th century Song dynasty.

7 http://www.pewforum.org/2012/12/18/global-religious-landscape-exec/

8 http://www.pewglobal.org/files/2014/03/Pew-Research-Center-Global-Attitudes-Project-Belief-in-God-Report-FINAL-March-13-2014.pdf

9 Quoted by Ivor Leclerc, *The Relevance of Whitehead*, 2002, p341

Chapter 3 – The Process of Life

1 Roger Lewin, *Complexity: Life at the Edge of Chaos*, 1992, p10-12

2 *Ibid*, p15

3 Stuart A Kauffman, *Reinventing the Sacred,* 2008, Ch 8

4 *Ibid*, pp105-109

5 Stuart Kauffman, *At Home in the Universe: The Search for Laws of Complexity*, 1995, pp78-80

6 Lewin, 1992, pp12-13

7 Charles Darwin, *On the Origin of Species*, 1859, p489

8 Kauffman, 1995, pp235-243

9 Hamid Dabashi, *The Arab Spring: The End of Postcolonialism*, 2012

10 Per Bak, Chao Tang and Kurt Weisenfeld, 'Self Organized Criticality', *Physical Review Letters*, 1987, Vol 59, No 4

11 Fritjof Capra, *The Web of Life: A New Synthesis of Mind and Matter*, 1996, Ch10

12 Stephen Jay Gould, *Wonderful Life: The Burgess Shale and the Nature of History,* 1989

13 Stephen Jay Gould, *Ever Since Darwin: Reflections in Natural History*, 1977, Ch16

14 Beverley Peterson Stearns and Stephen C Stearns, *Watching from the Edge of Extinction*, 1999, Preface

15 Stuart A Kauffman, *The Origins of Order: Self-Organization and Selection in Evolution,* 1993, p173

16 Kauffman, 1995, p86

17 Humberto R Maturana and Francisco J Varela, *Autopoiesis and Cognition: The Realization of the Living,* 1979, p49

18 Varela and Coutinho, 1991, cited in Fritjof Capra, 1996, p171

19 *Ibid*, p170

20 Lewin, 1992, Ch3

21 Quoted in *Ibid*, p138

22 Ervin Laszlo, *Quantum Shift in the Global Brain: How the New Scientific Reality Can Change Us and Our World,* 2008, Ch 2

23 http://www.internetworldstats.com/stats.htm

24 https://www.statista.com/statistics/330695/number-of-smartphone-users-worldwide/

25 http://www.uis.unesco.org/literacy/Documents/fs32-2015-literacy.pdf

26 Toynbee 1947, quoted by UNESCO, *Our Creative Diversity: Report of the World Commission of Culture and Development,* 1995

PART TWO – THINKING
The Modus Operandi of an Ancient Brain

Chapter 4 – The Power of Opposites

1 http://www.cmu.edu/homepage/health/2010/summer/the-last-frontier.shtml

2 Quoted by Tony Buzan, *Use Both Sides of your Brain,* 1991, p20

3 Ervin Laszlo, *Quantum Shift in the Global Brain*, 2008, p106

4 M Zimmermann, 'The Nervous System in the Context of Information Theory', *Human Physiology*, 1989, pp166-173

5 Daniel Kahneman, *Thinking Fast and Slow*, 2011, p43

6 Michael S Gazzaniga, 'The Split Brain in Man', *Scientific American,* 1967, Vol 217

7 Robert Ornstein, *The Right Mind: Making Sense of the Hemispheres*, 1997, p95

8 *Ibid*, p68

9 *Ibid*, p24

10 *Ibid*, p140

11 *Ibid*, pp101-105

12 Iain McGilchrist, *The Master and his Emissary; The Divided Brain and the Making of the Western World,* 2009, pp44-45

13 *Ibid*, pp22-33

14 *Ibid*, p50

15 *Ibid*, p50

16 Leonard Mlodinow, *Subliminal: The New Unconscious and What it Teaches Us,* 2012, pp62-64

17 Ornstein, 1997, p108

18 I Morrison, D Lloyd, G di Pellegrino & N Roberts, 'Vicarious responses to pain in anterior cingulate cortex: is empathy a multisensory issue?', *Cognitive, Affective and Behavioural Neuroscience*, 2004, Vol 4, pp270-278

19 McGilchrist, 2009, p55

20 *Ibid*, p46

21 Ned Herrmann, *The Whole Brain Business Book: Unlocking the Power of Whole Brain Thinking in Organizations and Individuals,* 1996, p35

22 *Ibid*, p72

23 *Ibid*, p 47

24 *Ibid*, p51

25 http://www.uphs.upenn.edu/news/news_releases/2013/12/verma/

26 http://www.bbc.co.uk/programmes/p0278p3p

Chapter 5 – Leaping to Conclusions

1 Plato, *Phaedrus,* 246a-254e

2 Daniel Kahneman, *Thinking Fast and Slow*, 2011, Part I

3 Drew Westen *et al*, 'Neural Bases of Motivated Reasoning', *Journal of Cognitive Neuroscience 18*, 2006

4 Shane Frederick, 'Cognitive Reflection and Decision Making', *Journal of Economic Perspectives 19,* 2005

5 V L Deglin and M Kinsbourne, 'Divergent Thinking Styles of the Hemispheres: How Syllogisms Are Solved during Transitory Hemisphere Suppression', *Brain and Cognition 31*, 1996

6 Shelley E Taylor and Jonathan D Brown, 'Illusion and Well-Being: A Social Psychological Perspective on Mental Health', *Psychological Bulletin 103*, 1988

7 Kahneman, 2011 pp98-99, plus Part II

8 Alexander Todorov *et al*, 'Inference of Competence from Faces Predict Election Outcomes' *Science 308*, 2005

9 Gary Klein, *Sources of Power: How People Make Decisions*, 1999, pp32-33

10 Leonard Mlodinow, *Subliminal,* 2012, p177

11 Kristina Durante *et al*, 'Changes in Women's Choice of Dress Across the Ovulatory Cycle', *Personality and Social Psychology Bulletin 34*, 2008

12 Dan Ariely, *Predictably Irrational: The Hidden Forces that Shape Our Decisions*, 2008, Ch 5

13 Shai Danziger, Jonathan Levav and Liora Avnaim-Pesso, 'Extraneous Factors in Judicial Decisions', *Proceedings of the National Academy of Sciences 108*, 2011

14 Kahneman, 2011, p225

15 Donald G Dutton and Arthur P Aron, 'Some Evidence for Heightened Sexual Attraction Under Conditions of High Anxiety', *Journal of Personality and Social Psychology 30*, 1974

16 Janine Willis and Alexander Todorov, 'First Impressions: Making Up Your Mind After a 100-Ms Exposure to a Face', *Psychological Science 17*, 2006

17 Malcolm Gladwell, *Blink: The Power of Thinking without Thinking,* 2005, p87

18 Timothy A Judge and Daniel M Cable, 'The Effect of Physical Height on Workplace Success and Income', *Journal of Applied Psychology 89*, 2004

19 William Apple *et al*, 'Effects of Speech Rate on Personal Attributions', *Journal of Personality and Social Psychology 37*, 1979

20 Mlodinow, 2012, p136

21 Michael W Krauss *et al*, 'Tactile Communication, Co-operation and Performance: An Ethological Study of the NBA', *Emotion 10*, 2010

22 India Morrison *et al*, 'The Skin as a Social Organ', *Experimental Brain Research,* 2009

23 Robin I M Dunbar, 'The Social Role of Touch in Humans and Primates: Behavioural Function and Neurobiological Mechanisms', *Neuroscience and Biobehavioural Reviews 34*, 2010

24 John A Bargh, Mark Chen and Lara Burrows, 'Automaticity of Social Behavior: Direct Effects of Trait Construct and Stereotype Activation on Action', *Journal of Personality and Social Psychology 71,* 1996

25 Thomas Mussweiler, 'Doing is for Thinking: Stereotype Activation by Stereotypic Movements', *Psychological Science 17*, 2006

26 Claude M Steel, 'Thin Ice: Stereotype Threat and Black College Students', *The Atlantic*, 1999

27 Margaret Shih, Todd L Pittinsky and Nalini Ambady, 'Stereotype Susceptibility: Identity Salience and Shifts in Quantitative Performance', *Psychological Science 10*, 1999

28 Anthony G Greenwald *et al*, 'Measuring Individual Differences in Implicit Cognition: The Implicit Association Test' *Journal of Personality and Social Psychology 74*, 1998

29 Brian A Nosek *et al*, 'National Differences in Gender-Science Stereotypes Predict National Sex Differences in Science and Math Achievement', *Proceedings of the National Academy of Sciences 106*, 2009

30 A K Kiefer and D Sekaquaptewa, 'Implicit Stereotypes and Women's Math Performance: How Implicit Gender-Math Stereotypes Influence Women's Susceptibility to Stereotype Threat', *Journal of Experimental Social Psychology 43*, 2007

31 Anthony G Greenwald *et al*, 'Measuring Individual Differences in Implicit Cognition: The Implicit Association Test', *Journal of Personality and Social Psychology 74*, 1998.

Chapter 6 – Confabulating Coherence

1 Walter Mischel and Ebbe B Ebbesen, 'Attention in Delay of Gratification', *Journal of Personality and Social Psychology 16*, 1970

2 Walter Mischel and Ozlem Ayduk, 'Willpower in a Cognitive-Affective Processing System: The Dynamics of Delay of Gratification' *Hand-Book of Self-Regulation: Research, Theory and Applications*, 2004

3 Angela L Duckworth and Martin E P Seligman, 'Self-Discipline Outdoes IQ in Predicting Academic Performance of Adolescents', *Psychological Science 16*, 2005

4 Henri Tajfel, *Human Groups and Social Categories: Studies in Social Psychology*, 1981

5 Henri Tajfel and A L Wilkes, 'Classification and Quantitative Judgement', *British Journal of Psychology 54*, 1963

6 http://www.theguardian.com/technology/2010/mar/14/my-bright-idea-robin-dunbar

7 Markus Brauer, 'Intergroup Perception in the Social Context: The Effects of Social Status and Group Membership on Perceived Out-Group Homogeneity', *Journal of Experimental Social Psychology 37*, 2001

8 K L Dion, 'Cohesiveness as a Determinant of Ingroup–Outgroup Bias', *Journal of Personality and Social Psychology 28*, 1973

9 Charles K Ferguson and Harold H Kelley, 'Significant Factors in Over-Evaluation of Own-Group's Product', *Journal of Abnormal and Social Psychology 69*, 1964

10 Henri Tajfel, 'Experiments in Intergroup Discrimination', *Scientific American 223*, 1970

11 Henri Tajfel *et al*, 'Social Categorization and Intergroup Behaviour', *European Journal of Social Psychology 1*, 1971

12 Henri Tajfel and John C Turner, 'The Social Identity Theory of Intergroup Behavior', *Psychology of Intergroup Relations,* 1986

13 Daniel Kahneman, *Thinking Fast and Slow*, 2011, p135

14 Michael S Gazzaniga and Joseph E Le Doux, *The Integrated Mind*, 1978, pp148-149

15 J I Yellott, 'Probability Learning with Non-Contingent Success', *Journal of Mathematical Psychology 6*, 1969

16 Richard E Nisbett and Timothy De Camp Wilson, 'Telling More Than We Can Know: Verbal Reports on Mental Processes', *Psychological Review 84*, 1977

17 Jonathan Haidt, 'The Emotional Dog and its Rational Tail: A Social Intuitionist Approach to Moral Judgement', *Psychological Review 108*, 2001

18 Leonard Mlodinow, *Subliminal,* 2012, pp201-14

19 Eric Luis Uhlmann and Geoffrey L Cohen, 'Constructed Criteria: Redefining Merit to Justify Discrimination', *Psychological Science 16*, 2005

20 College Board, 'Student Descriptive Questionnaire' *Princeton NJ Educational Testing Service,* 1976-77

21 Joseph T Hallinan, *Why We Make Mistakes: How We Look Without Seeing, Forget Things in Seconds and Are All Pretty Sure We Are Way Above Average*, 2010, p167

22 Keith E Stanovich, *What Intelligence Tests Miss: The Psychology of Rational Thought,* 2009, p109

23 K Patricia Cross, 'Not Can But Will College Teaching Be Improved', *New Directions for Higher Education 17,* 1977

24 Robert H Frank, *The Economic Naturalist: In Search of Explanations for Everyday Enigmas,* 2008, p129

25 Dunning and Kruger plus others, in Tori De Angelis, 'Why We Overestimate Our Competence', *American Psychological Association 34*, February 2003

26 Emily Pronin *et al*, 'The Bias Blind Spot: Perception of Bias in Self Versus Others', *Personality and Social Psychology Bulletin 28*, 2002

27 Terrance Odean, 'Do Investors Trade Too Much?' *The American Economic Review 89*, 1999

28 John C Bogle, *Common Sense on Mutual Funds: New Imperatives for the Intelligent Investor,* 1999, p213

29 Kahneman, 2011, p215

30 Brad M Barber and Terrance Odean, 'Trading is Hazardous to Your Wealth: The Common Stock Investment Performance of Individual Investors', *Journal of Finance 55*, 2000

31 Philip E Tetlock, *Expert Political Judgement: How Good Is It? How Can we Know?,* 2005.

32 Kahneman, 2011, pp222-227

33 Nassim Nicholas Taleb, *The Black Swan: The Impact of the Highly Improbable,* 2007, p69

34 Kahneman, 2011, p201

35 Richard E Nisbett and Timothy De Camp Wilson, 'Telling More Than We Can Know: Verbal Reports on Mental Processes', *Psychological Review 84*, 1977

36 Jonathan Baron and John C Hershey, 'Outcome Bias in Decision Evaluation', *Journal of Personality and Social Psychology 54*, 1988

37 Ulrike Malmendier and Geoffrey Tate, 'Who Makes Acquisitions?: CEO Over-confidence and the Market's Reaction', *National Bureau of Economic Research 10813*, 2004

38 Shelley E Taylor and Jonathon D Brown, 'Illusion and Well-Being: A Social Psychological Perspective on Mental Health', *American Psychological Association Bulletin 103*, 1988

39 Elaine Fox, Anna Ridgewell and Chris Ashwin, 'Looking On the Bright Side: Biased Attention and the Human Serotonin Transporter Gene', *Proceedings of the Royal Society B276*, 2008

40 Peter J D Carnevale and Alice M Isen, 'The Influence of Positive Affect and Visual Access on the Discovery of Integrative Solutions in Bilateral Negotiation', *Organization Behavior and Human Decision Processes 37,* 1986

41 Taylor and Brown, 1988,

42 *Ibid*

43 Kahneman, 2011, p212

Chapter 7 – Blending for Balance

1 http://www.theguardian.com/politics/2013/apr/08/margaret-thatcher-quotes

2 http://www.theguardian.com/politics/2014/oct/01/cameron-pledge-scrap-human-rights-act-civil-rights-groups

3 David Yanagizawa-Drott, 'Propaganda and Conflict: Evidence from the Rwandan Genocide', *Harvard University,* 2014; also Jean Hatzfeld, *Machete Season: The Killers in Rwanda Speak,* 2006

4 Jonathan Haidt, *The Righteous Mind: Why Good People are Divided by Politics and Religion,* 2012, Ch 7

5 *Ibid*, p158

6 *Ibid*, p204

7 *Ibid*, p213

8 Muzafar Sherif *et al*, 'The Robbers Cave Experiment: Intergroup Conflict and Co-operation, 1954, 1958, 1961

9 Haidt, 2012, p172

10 http://www.bbc.co.uk/news/world-25927595

Chapter 8 – Changing Structures

1 Nathan Novemsky and Daniel Kahneman, 'The Boundaries of Loss Aversion', *Journal of Marketing Research 42*, 2005, pp119-125

2 Paul Rozin and Edward B Royzman, 'Negativity Bias, Negativity Dominance, and Contagion', *Personality and Social Psychology Review 5*, 2001, pp296-316

3 Richard H Thaler and Cass R Sunstein, *Nudge: Improving Decisions About Health, Wealth and Happiness*, 2008

4 Daniel Kahneman, *Thinking Fast and Slow*, 2011, p 296

5 The concept of *The Prisoners' Dilemma* was first developed by RAND Corporation scientists Merrill M Flood and Melvin Dresher in the 1950s, and was later formalized and named by Albert W Tucker.

6 Robert Axelrod and William D Hamilton, 'The Evolution of Co-operation', *Science New Series Vol 211*, 1981, pp1390-1396

7 Robert Axelrod, 'Effective Choice in the Prisoners Dilemma', *Journal of Conflict Resolution 24*, pp3-25

8 Adam Smith, *Wealth of Nations*, 1776, Book 1, Ch 2

9 Adam Smith, *Theory of Moral Sentiments,* 1759, Part 1, Section 1, Ch 1

10 Smith, 1776, Book 5, Ch 1

11 https://www.pwc.com/gx/en/services/audit-assurance/publications/global-top-100-companies-2017.html

12 https://www.weforum.org/agenda/2017/03/worlds-biggest-economies-in-2017/

13 https://www.forbes.com/forbes-400/#66e8a00c7e2f

14 http://www.oxfam.org.uk/media-centre/press-releases/2017/01/eight-people-own-same-wealth-as-half-the-world

15 Richard K Wagner, *Handbook of Intelligence*, 2000, p382

16 David Brooks, *The Social Animal*, 2011, p198

17 Kahneman, 2011, p205

18 Carl G Jung, 'The Undiscovered Self' in *Collected Works of Carl Gustav Jung*, 1970, p 585-586

PART THREE – LEARNING
Origins and Oscillations of a Global Mind

Chapter 9 – Source of the Western Psyche

1 Iain McGilchrist, *The Master and his Emissary*, 2009, p242

2 Julian Jaynes, *The Origin of Consciousness in the Breakdown of the Bicameral Mind*, 1976, pp70-71

3 Jared Diamond, *Guns, Germs, and Steel: The Fates of Human Societies*, 1997

4 http://www.ancient-origins.net/ancient-places-europe/venus-figurines-european-paleolithic-era-001548

5 Diamond, 1997

6 Marija Gimbutas, *The Civilisation of the Goddess*, 1994

7 James Mellaart, *Catal Huyuk, A Neolithic Town in Anatolia*, 1967

8 Marija Gimbutas, *The Kurgan Culture and the Indo-Europeanization of Europe*, 1997

9 J P Mallory, *In Search of the Indo-Europeans*, 1989, p184

10 Jacquetta Hawkes, *Dawn of the Gods*, 1968

11 Michael Everson, 'Tenacity in Religion, Myth and Folklore', *Journal of Indo-European Studies 17*, 1989, pp277-295

12 Robert Drews, *The Coming of the Greeks: Indo-European Conquests in the Aegean and the Near East*, 1988

13 Howard Bloom, *Global Brain: The Evolution of Mass Mind*, 2000, p123

14 Herodotus, *The Histories,* translation by Aubrey de Selincourt, 1972

15 Aristotle, *On the Soul*, translation by J A Smith, 2016

16 Bloom, 2000 pp135-137

17 W G Forrest, *A History of Sparta*, 1968, pp30-33

18 Plutarch, *Lycurgus*, translation by Richard Talbert, 1988

19 Forrest, 1968, pp38-39

20 J M Moore, *Aristotle and Xenophon on Democracy and Oligarchy*, 1986, p97

21 Xenophon, *Spartan Society*, translation by Richard Talbert, 1988, p167

22 Bernard Randall, *Solon: The Lawmaker of Athens*, 2004

23 Aristotle, *The Athenian Constitution*, translation by Sir Frederic G Kenyon, 2009

24 Bloom, 2000, p142

25 *Ibid*, p174

26 Diogenes Laertius, *Lives of Eminent Philosophers*, translation by R D Hicks, 1925

27 Charles H Kahn, *Pythagoras and the Pythagoreans*, 2001

28 Bertrand Russell, *A History of Western Philosophy*, p37

29 Plato, *Dialogues*, translation by W H D Rouse, 2001

30 Richard Tarnas, *The Passion of the Western Mind: Understanding the Ideas That Have Shaped Our World View,* 1991, p7

31 *Ibid*, p8

32 Plato, *Thaeatetus*, 152e, translation by R Waterfield

33 Plato, *Republic*, 529d-530c, translation by H D P Lee

34 Iain McGilchrist, *The Master and his Emissary*, 2009, p285

35 Plato, *Republic*, 595-605, translation by H D P Lee

36 Plato, *Laws*, in Library of the Future, 1996, CD ROM

37 Tarnas, 1991, p56

38 *Ibid*, p57

39 *Ibid*, pp58-59

40 Heraclitus, *fr XLIX*, translation by Diels 126

41 Heraclitus, *fr L*, translation by Diels 12

Chapter 10 – Emergence of the Left Mind

1 Robin Lane Fox, *Alexander the Great*, 1973

2 Richard Tarnas, *The Passion of the Western Mind*, 1991, p108-115

3 *Ibid*, p113

4 *Ibid*, p224

5 Michael White, *Leonardo : the First Scientist*, 2000

6 Andrew Pettegree, *The Book in the Renaissance*, 2011

7 Tarnas, 1991, p231

8 Hartman Grisar, *Luther: His Life and Work*, 2012

91 Diarmaid MacCulloch, *The Reformation: A History*, 2005

10 Tarnas, 1991, p240

11 *Ibid*, p243

12 Max Weber, *The Protestant Ethic and the Spirit of Capitalism* (1905), translation by P Baehr and G C Wells, 2002

13 Quoted by Thomas Kuhn, *The Copernican Revolution*, 1957, p191

14 Isaac Newton, *Philosophiea Naturalis Principia Mathematica*, 1687

15 Quoted by Brian Lasater, *The Dream of the West Part II*, 2008, p543

16 Tarnas, 1991 pp272-275

17 Francis Bacon, *Novum Organum Scientarium*, 1620

18 Francis Bacon, *Meditationes Sacrae*, 1597

19 Rene Descartes, *Discourse on the Method*, 1637

20 Rene Descartes, *Principles of Philosophy*, 1644, chapter 203

21 Descartes, 1637, Part VI

22 *Ibid*, Part IV, p127

23 Peter Gilmour, *Philosophers of the Enlightenment*, 1990

24 Tarnas, 1991, p313

25 David Hume, *A Treatise of Human Nature*, 1738, Section III

26 Tarnas, 1991, p286

27 Ian Morris, *Why the West Rules ~ For Now*, 2010, p495

28 *Ibid*, p496

29 *Ibid*, p497

30 *Ibid*, p497

31 *Ibid*, p504

32 Frank Norris, *The Pit*, 1903, p57

Chapter 11 – Rise and Fall of Modernism

1 Isaiah Berlin, *The Roots of Romanticism*, 2000

2 Quoted by John Stuart Blackie, *The Wisdom of Goethe*, 1883, p151

3 Richard Tarnas, *The Passion of the Western Mind*, 1991, p373

4 https://plato.stanford.edu/entries/hegel-dialectics/

5 Tarnas, 1991, p380

6 Iain McGilchrist, *The Master and his Emissary*, 2009, p382

7 Quoted by Stephen Gaukroger, *The Emergence of a Scientific Culture: Science and the Shaping of Modernity*, 2006, p24

8 Tarnas, 1991, p383

9 Sigmund Freud, 'The Unconscious (1915)', *General Psychological Theory*, 1963, Part VI pp116-150

10 Carl Jung, 'The Structure of the Unconscious (1916)', *Collected Works of C G Jung*, 1966, Vol 7

11 Anthony Giddens, *Modernity and Self-Identity*, 1991 p27

12 McGilchrist, 2009, p391

13 Quoted by Daniel Pinchbeck, *Breaking Open the Head*, 2002, p100

14 Walter Benjamin, *Capitalism as Religion*, 1921, translation by Chad Kautzer

15 Louis A Sass, *Madness and Modernism*, 1994

16 *Ibid*, p12

17 McGilchrist, 2009, p396

18 *Ibid*, p404

19 *Ibid*, pp403-407

20 *Ibid*, p401

21 Fritjof Capra, *The Turning Point*, 1982, p420

22 *Ibid*, p42

23 Tarnas, 1991, p406

PART FOUR – GROWING
Pitfalls and Possibilities at the Edge of Chaos

Chapter 12 – Cultivating Coherence

1 Ervin Laszlo, *Quantum Shift in the Global Brain*, 2008, p119

2 *Ibid*, p120

3 Jonathan Haidt, *The Happiness Hypothesis*, 2006, p227

4 Fritjof Capra, *The Turning Point*, 1982, p71

5 *Ibid*, p72

6 *Ibid*, pp73-76

7 Laszlo, 2008, p104

8 *Ibid*, pp105-106

9 *Ibid*, p 105

10 *Ibid*, p106

11 http://www.stanislavgrof.com/wp-content/uploads/2015/02/A-Brief-History-of-Transpersonal-Psychology-Grof.pdf

12 Ken Wilbur, *The Spectrum of Consciousness,* 1977

13 A K Coomaraswamy, *Hinduism and Buddhism*, 1943, p33

14 Capra, 1982, pp415-416

Chapter 13 – Elevating Consciousness

1 Jaan Suurkula, 'Transcendental Meditation – neuro-physiological transformation by way of a unique fourth state of consciousness', published at website of *Swedish Physicians for Transcendental Meditation*, http://home.swipnet.se/tmdoctors/eng/tmunique.htm

2 Frederick Travis *et al*, 'Patterns of EEG coherence, power, and contingent negative variation characterize the integration of transcendental and waking states', *Biological Psychology*, 2002, Vol 61, No 3, pp293-319

3 Abraham Maslow, *Religions, Values and Peak Experiences*, 1964

4 Quoted by James Olson, *The Whole-Brain Path to Peace*, 2011, p276

5 Suurkula, 'Transcendental Meditation'

6 Amanda L Chan, *Mindfulness Meditation Benefits: 20 Reasons Why It's Good for your Mental and Physical Health*, 2013

7 Paramahansa Yogananda, *The Second Coming of Christ*, 2004, p55

8 Stanislav Grof, *Realms of the Human Unconscious: Observations from LSD Research*, 1976

9 Quoted by Fritjof Capra, *The Turning Point*, 1982, p411

10 W N Pahnke, 'Drugs and Mysticism', *International Journal of Parapsychology 8*, 1966, pp295-315

11 Huston Smith, *Cleansing the Doors of Perception*, 2000, p101

12 Mihaly Csikszentmihalyi, *Flow*, 1992

13 Jeanne Nakamura and Mihaly Csikszentmihalyi, 'The Concept of Flow', *Handbook of Positive Psychology*, 2001, pp89-105

14 Quoted by Jonathan Haidt, *The Happiness Hypothesis*, 2006, p224

15 Maslow, 1964

16 William James, *The Varieties of Religious Experience*, 1902

17 Dacher Keltner and Jonathan Haidt, 'Approaching awe, a moral, spiritual and aesthetic emotion', *Cognition and Emotion*, 2003, 17(2) pp297-314

18 Haidt, 2006, p197

19 *Ibid*, pp83-86

20 Philip Brickman, Dan Coates and Ronnie Janoff-Bulman, 'Lottery Winners and Accident Victims: Is Happiness Relative?', *Journal of Personality and Social Psychology*, 1978, Vol 36, No 8, pp917-927

21 Robert H Frank, *Luxury Fever: Weighing the Cost of Excess*, 2010

22 David Brooks, *The Social Animal*, 2011, p236

23 Daniel Kahneman, *Thinking Fast and Slow*, 2011 p395

24 Robert D Putnam, *Bowling Alone*, 2000, p333

25 Paul H Ray and Sherry Ruth Anderson, *The Cultural Creatives*, 2000, p8

26 *Ibid*, p17

27 Jean Houston quoted in 'Changing Our Minds', *Ideas*, CBC, 1984

28 http://culturalcreatives.org/cultural-creatives/

29 Pitirim Sorokin, *Social and Cultural Dynamics,* Vol 1-4 1937-41, abridged 1957

Chapter 14 – Counterbalancing Capitalism

1 Jared Diamond, *Collapse: How Societies Choose to Fail or Succeed*, 2005, p552

2 Adam Smith, *The Theory of Moral Sentiments*, 1759

3 Jerry Z Muller, *Adam Smith in His Time and Ours*, 1993, p8

4 Peter J Dougherty, *Who's Afraid of Adam Smith?*, 2002, p34

5 Alfred Marshall, *Social Possibilities of Economic Chivalry*, 1907

6 Gertrude Himmelfarb, *Poverty and Compassion*, 1991, pp301-303

7 Dougherty, 2002, p92

8 https://www.theguardian.com/commentisfree/2014/dec/11/break-stranglehold-shareholders-company-funding-key-decisions

9 Smith, 1759, Part VII, Section II, Ch III

10 Robert Skidelsky, *John Maynard Keynes: The Economist as Saviour 1920-1937*, 1992

11 Edmund L Pincoffs, *Quandaries and Virtues: Against Reductivism in Ethics*, 1986

12 Alasdair McIntyre, *After Virtue: A Study in Moral Theory*, 1981

13 Emile Durkeim, *Suicide*, 1897

14 https://www.theatlantic.com/magazine/archive/1982/03/broken-windows/304465/

15 Milton Friedman, *Capitalism and Freedom*, 1963

16 David Brooks, *The Social Animal*, 2011, p387

17 *Ibid*, p388

Chapter 15 – Fast-Tracking Our Future

1 Ned Herrmann, *The Whole Brain Business Book*, 1996, pp51-57

2 http://www.ancientathens.org/culture/women-athens

3 Philip Slater, *The Chrysalis Effect: The Metamorphosis of Global Culture*, 2009, p64

4 https://www.psychologytoday.com/blog/homo-aggressivus/201409/male-aggression

5 Carol Gilligan, *In a Different Voice*, 1982

6 Slater, 2009, pp56-57

7 Daniel H Pink, *A Whole New Mind: Why Right-Brainers Will Rule the Future,* 2005

8 http://www.globalresearch.ca/america-has-been-at-war-93-of-the-time-222-out-of-9-years-since-1776/5565946

9 http://www.telegraph.co.uk/history/9653497/British-have-invaded-nine-out-of-ten-countries-so-look-out-Luxembourg.html

10 Ronald Inglehart and Pippa Norris, *Rising Tide: Gender Equality and Cultural Change Around the World,* 2003

Index

United Kingdom 11, 14, 188-91
United Nations 11
unworlding 264
Upper Palaeolithic period 198
US Presidents (height) 121
us-centricity 288

Varela, Francisco 68, 69
Varieties of Religious Experience, The 305
varnas 49
Vedantism 296
Vedic gods 203
Venus figurines 198, 199
Victorian values 327, 331, 338
vital engagement 302, 303
Voltaire 235, 241
von Neumann, John 178

Wagner, Richard K 184
Watt, James 246
wealth distribution 12, 181, 183, 184
Wealth of Nations, The 326
Weber, Max 233, 260
Weinberg, Steven 35
Weisenfeld, Kurt 61
West, The 369, 370
Whitehead, Alfred North 51
wholeness 279, 280, 353, 354, 364
Whole New Mind, A 359
wide focus 86

Wilber, Ken 286, 289, 290
Williams, Robin 14
Willis and Todorov 121
Willis, Janine 121
Wilson and Kelling 337
Wilson, James 337
winner takes all 188, 189
Wittenberg Schlosskirche 231
women 346, 347, 349, 350
words 93
World Happiness Report 13
World Health Organisation 11, 15
World Trade Centres 9
World War II 70, 350
World Wars 259
world-centricity 289
worldviews 30, 31
worldwide web 77, 343
writing 76, 196

Xenophon 210

Yemen 11
yin and yang 24, 46, 89, 175, 275

Zarathustra 9
Zeus 203
zoom in/out 86
zoomorphic imagery 199
Zoroaster 212